Australia Reshaped
200 Years of Institutional T

*Australia Reshaped* is the capstone volume in the Reshaping Australian Institutions series, yet this book is structurally and qualitatively different from the others. Eight leading social scientists have written major essays on key aspects of Australian institutional life. Each chapter has the length and depth of a major contribution, acting as an overview of the field for both local readers and an international audience.

The essays encompass the scope of no less than 200 years of institutional transformation, and range from discussions of politics, economics and law to the unique nature of aboriginality, gender, political theory and leadership in Australia.

The contributors to the book are John Braithwaite, Geoffrey Brennan, Francis G. Castles, John S. Dryzek, Martin Krygier, Jonathan Pincus, Marian Sawer, Geoffrey Stokes and John Uhr.

**Geoffrey Brennan** is a Professor in the Research School of Social Sciences at the Australian National University.

**Francis G. Castles** is a Professor of Public Policy at the University of Edinburgh.

RESHAPING AUSTRALIAN INSTITUTIONS

Series editors: Geoffrey Brennan, Research School of Social Sciences, Australian National University, and Francis G. Castles, School of Social & Political Studies, University of Edinburgh.

Published in association with the Research School of Social Sciences, Australian National University.

This program of publications arises from the School's initiative in sponsoring a fundamental rethinking of Australia's key institutions before the centenary of Federation in 2001.

Published in this program will be the work of scholars from the Australian National University and elsewhere who are researching and writing on the institutions of the nation. The scope of the program includes the institutions of public governance, intergovernmental relations, Aboriginal Australia, gender, population, the environment, the economy, business, the labour market, the welfare state, the city, education, the media, criminal justice and the Constitution.

Brian Galligan *A Federal Republic*
   0 521 37354 9 hardback 0 521 37746 3 paperback
Patrick Troy (ed.) *Australian Cities*
   0 521 48197 X hardback 0 521 48437 5 paperback
Ian Marsh *Beyond the Two Party System*
   0 521 46223 1 hardback 0 521 46779 9 paperback
Elim Papadakis *Environmental Politics and Institutional Change*
   0 521 55407 1 hardback 0 521 55631 7 paperback
Chilla Bulbeck *Living Feminism*
   0 521 46042 5 hardback 0 521 46596 6 paperback
John Uhr *Deliberative Democracy in Australia*
   0 521 62458 4 hardback 0 521 62465 7 paperback
Mitchell Dean and Barry Hindess (eds) *Governing Australia*
   0 521 58357 8 hardback 0 521 58671 2 paperback
Nicolas Peterson and Will Sanders (eds) *Citizenship and Indigenous Australians*
   0 521 62195 X hardback 0 521 62736 2 paperback
Martin Painter *Collaborative Federalism*
   0 521 59071 X hardback
Julianne Schultz *Reviving the Fourth Estate*
   0 521 62042 2 hardback 0 521 62970 5 paperback
David Peetz *Unions in a Contrary World*
   0 521 63055 X hardback 0 521 63950 6 paperback
Moira Gatens and Alison Mackinnon (eds) *Gender and Institutions*
   0 521 63190 4 hardback 0 521 63576 4 paperback
Sue Richardson (ed.) *Reshaping the Labour Market: Regulation, Efficiency and Equality in Australia*
   0 521 65281 2 hardback 0 521 65424 6 paperback
Haig Patapan *Judging Democracy: The New Politics of the High Court of Australia*
   0 521 77345 8 hardback 0 521 77428 4 paperback
Tony Bennett and David Carter (eds) *Culture in Australia: Policies, Publics and Programs*
   0 521 80290 3 hardback 0 521 00403 9 paperback

# Australia Reshaped

*200 Years of Institutional Transformation*

*Edited by*
## Geoffrey Brennan
*Australian National University*

## Francis G. Castles
*University of Edinburgh*

PUBLISHED BY THE PRESS SYNDICATE OF THE UNIVERSITY OF CAMBRIDGE
The Pitt Building, Trumpington Street, Cambridge, United Kingdom

CAMBRIDGE UNIVERSITY PRESS
The Edinburgh Building, Cambridge CB2 2RU, UK
40 West 20th Street, New York, NY 10011-4211, USA
477 Williamstown Road, Port Melbourne, VIC 3207, Australia
Ruiz de Alarcón 13, 28014 Madrid, Spain
Dock House, The Waterfront, Cape Town 8001, South Africa

http://www.cambridge.org

© Cambridge University Press 2002

This book is in copyright. Subject to statutory exception
and to the provisions of relevant collective licensing agreements,
no reproduction of any part may take place without
the written permission of Cambridge University Press.

First published 2002

Printed in Australia by Brown Prior Anderson

*Typeface* Plantin (Adobe) 10/12 pt.   *System* QuarkXPress®   [PH]

*A catalogue record for this book is available from the British Library*

*National Library of Australia Cataloguing in Publication data*
Australia reshaped: 200 years of institutional
transformation.
Bibliography.
Includes index.
ISBN 0 521 81749 8.
ISBN 0 521 52075 4 (pbk).
1. Social institutions – Australia. I. Brennan, Geoffrey,
1944– . II. Castles, Francis G. (Francis Geoffrey), 1943– .
306.0994

ISBN 0 521 81749 8 hardback
ISBN 0 521 52075 4 paperback

# Contents

| | | |
|---|---|---|
| *Notes on Contributors* | | *page* ix |
| 1 | **Introduction**<br>Geoffrey Brennan and Francis G. Castles | 1 |
| 2 | **Australia's Institutions and Australia's Welfare**<br>Francis G. Castles | 25 |
| 3 | **Australia's Economic Institutions**<br>Geoffrey Brennan and Jonathan Pincus | 53 |
| 4 | **Globalization and Australian Institutions**<br>John Braithwaite | 86 |
| 5 | **Including Australia: A Democratic History**<br>John S. Dryzek | 114 |
| 6 | **Waltzing Matilda: Gender and Australian Political Institutions**<br>Marian Sawer | 148 |
| 7 | **Australian Democracy and Indigenous Self-Determination, 1901–2001**<br>Geoffrey Stokes | 181 |
| 8 | **The Grammar of Colonial Legality: Subjects, Objects, and the Australian Rule of Law**<br>Martin Krygier | 220 |
| 9 | **Political Leadership and Rhetoric**<br>John Uhr | 261 |
| *Index* | | 295 |

# Contributors

JOHN BRAITHWAITE is an Australian Research Council Federation Fellow and a Professor in the Law Program, Research School of Social Sciences, Australian National University. He co-ordinated the Reshaping Australian Institutions Project until 1996. He currently co-ordinates the Regulatory Institutions Network (RegNet). Recent works include *Global Business Regulation* (2000) with Peter Drahos and *Restorative Justice and Civil Society* (2001) edited with Heather Strang (CUP).

GEOFFREY BRENNAN is Professor of Economics in the Social and Political Theory Program, Research School of Social Sciences, Australian National University. He is author, with Nobel Laureate James Buchanan, of *The Power to Tax* (1980) and *The Reason of Rules* (1985), and with Loren Lomasky of *Democracy and Decision* (1993). His chief area of interest is rational actor political theory. He is an editor of *Economics and Philosophy* and from 2002 to 2004 President of the Public Choice Society. His most recent book is *Democratic Devices and Desires* (2000) with Alan Hamlin. He is currently working with Philip Pettit on *The Economy of Esteem* (OUP, forthcoming).

FRANCIS G. CASTLES is Professor of Social and Public Policy in the School of Social and Political Studies, University of Edinburgh, Scotland, having formerly held Chairs in Political Science and Public Policy at the Open University and the Australian National University. He was coordinator of the Reshaping Australian Institutions Project from 1996 to 2000. His main interests are in comparative public and social policy, focusing on the determinants of welfare state and public expenditure outcomes in OECD countries. His recent books include *The Great Experiment: Labour Parties and Public Policy Transformation in Australia and New Zealand* (co-editor, 1995), *Comparative Public Policy* (1998) and the *Welfare State Reader* (co-editor, 2000).

JOHN S. DRYZEK is Professor of Social and Political Theory in the Research School of Social Sciences, Australian National University. His most recent books, both co-authored, are *Post-Communist Democratization: Political Discourses Across Thirteen Countries* (CUP, 2002) and *Green States and Social Movements: Environmentalism in The United States, United Kingdom, Germany and Norway* (OUP, 2003)

MARTIN KRYGIER is Professor of Law at the University of New South Wales. He has edited and co-edited works including *Community and Legality: The Intellectual Legacy of Philip Selznick* (US, 2001), and *The Rule of Law After Communism* (UK, 1999). His work has been translated into numerous European languages. He delivered the 1997 Boyer lectures, *Between Fear and Hope Hybrid Thoughts on Public Values* (Sydney 1997).

JONATHAN PINCUS is the George Gollin Professor of Economics at the University of Adelaide. He is a Fellow of the Academy of Social Sciences in Australia and is co-editor of *Australian Economic Papers*. During 2002, he is a Visiting Researcher at the Productivity Commission. His most recent book is *Funding Higher Education: Performance and Diversity* (Canberra: DEETYA, 1997) (with Paul W. Miller).

MARIAN SAWER is Senior Fellow and Head of the Political Science Program, Research School of Social Sciences, Australian National University. Her books include *Waltzing Matilda: Feminism and Social Liberalism in Australia* (2002), *Elections: Full, Free and Fair* (2001), and *Speaking for the People: Representation in Australian Politics* (with Gianni Zappalà, 2001). She is currently leading the Democratic Audit of Australia.

GEOFFREY STOKES is Professor of Politics at Deakin University. He works in the areas of democratic theory, citizenship and Australian political thought. With April Carter, he has co-edited *Liberal Democracy and its Critics* (Polity, 1998) and *Democratic Theory Today* (Polity, 2002). He is editor of *The Politics of Identity in Australia* (CUP, 1997) and co-edited, with M. Leach and I. Ward, *The Rise and Fall of One Nation* (University of Queensland Press, 2000). He is also the author of *Popper: Philosophy, Politics and Scientific Method* (Polity, 1998).

JOHN UHR is Senior Fellow in the Political Science Program, Research School of Social Sciences, Australian National University, and author of *Deliberative Democracy in Australia: The Changing Place of Parliament* (CUP, 1998). He has written extensively on political ethics and is completing a book on democracy and ethical leadership.

# 1 Introduction

*Geoffrey Brennan and Francis G. Castles*

This book is the last in the Cambridge University Press series formally associated with the Reshaping Australian Institutions Project. The Project itself formally came to a close as an activity of the Research School of Social Sciences at the Australian National University at the end of 2001, after a decade of often intense activity. It is of course in the nature of the academic process that pieces of work originally planned under the ambit of the Project will continue to appear over the next five years or so. And, if the Project has been at all successful, it will continue to influence work done in the Australian social sciences for some considerable time. Any such influence will be reflected not only in explicit reference to work done within the Project but also in an increased attention to the specifically 'institutional' aspects of Australian social life.

This introduction is not the place to provide an account of the Project – even a brief one. Nor is this book to be seen as an attempt to offer some kind of 'final word' on Australian institutions. Nevertheless, it is interesting that this last volume in the series looks backwards rather than forwards. All of the chapters have a distinctly historical orientation. And in several cases, the narrative reach extends well beyond the life of Australia as a nation, back to the earliest days of European colonization. Moreover, it is possible to detect in several of the chapters a certain whiff of nostalgia – a sense of something of value lost.

There is certainly a consensus in this volume on the proposition that something significant has been happening in Australian institutional life over the last two decades or so – a kind of institutional repositioning, a move to a more 'competitive' institutional order increasingly like that of the United States and increasingly unlike the Australian egalitarianism of the past. Perhaps that shift is merely the logical working out of more abstract political institutional arrangements, as Castles' reading of Lijphart in Chapter 2 might seem to suggest. Perhaps it is the result of changed perceptions as to the 'best' economic policy regime among the policy-adviser 'elite'. Pusey argues this in his well-known account, *Economic Rationalism in Canberra* (1991), and as Brennan and Pincus in Chapter 3 concede in some measure. Or perhaps the decline of

Australian egalitarianism is best understood in the context of global competition for capital as Braithwaite in Chapter 4 argues. In any event, there seems to be widespread agreement that there has been a change, that the change is significant, and that it is to be identified as essentially an 'institutional' matter.

The historical orientation is interesting in another connection. When, in the initial phases of the Project, we settled on the term 'reshaping institutions', it was with the ambiguity in meaning firmly in mind. 'Reshaping' could refer to the normative ambition of the Project. We certainly wanted to accommodate the possibility that inquiry into Australian institutions might lead scholars to want to 'reshape' those institutions along particular lines. Much social analysis is motivated by a desire to improve the world we live in; and we wanted the Project to accommodate, at least in principle, the possibility of genuine policy bite. But 'reshaping' could also be understood as a purely descriptive term. 'Reshaping' is the sort of work that institutions might be seen to do. Institutions do not, on this reading, totally determine social outcomes: they merely shape them. Or *re*shape them, implying perhaps that in the absence of the particular institutions in place, outcomes would be different but not necessarily 'shapeless'.

One aspect of this 'shaping/reshaping' image is the idea of layers of institutional structure, the layers differing in terms both of abstraction/generality on the one hand, and temporal proximity on the other. Institutions are like pieces of social capital. They last. Even when one doesn't much like them, they can be hard to change and slow to respond. Ships and icebergs come to mind.

Such considerations encourage a long-term view of institutions. And perhaps a corresponding modesty about just how much reshaping of institutions can be done at any point, or about how long it might take for the full consequences of any current reshaping exercise to have full effect. In short, it seems appropriate as a critical part of the RAI Project to look back on the Australian experience and examine ways in which institutions have changed and evolved and what the consequences of those changes have been. In large measure, that is what the current volume seeks to do, choosing a range of institutional arrangements for detailed examination that seem to us either typical or especially significant or both. There is no attempt to be exhaustive. None of the chapters attempts to take a bird's-eye view of *all* the important institutions in Australia that have operated over the last two centuries. And it seems doubtful whether any such ambition would be achievable in the space available here. The topics chosen reflect the interests of the authors.

## Defining Institutions

The foregoing preliminary remarks presuppose some general understanding of what an 'institution' is. In fact, the term itself is a matter of some contention. Different disciplines in the social sciences have in mind slightly different phenomena, and lay emphasis on different mechanisms by which institutional effects might be wrought. So, although the rise in interest in institutional analysis has been a more or less common feature of the major social science disciplines over the last two decades, the precise objects of inquiry remain rather different. And confusingly so, because the same terms are used across disciplines with rather different meanings and connotations.

This has been an issue that the RAI Project has wrestled with from the outset. It has been particularly significant because one of the primary objects of the whole enterprise has been to stimulate interaction across disciplinary boundaries. But the use of the same terms to mean different things in different disciplines was hardly an advantage in cross-disciplinary communication. Several responses to this problem were possible. For the Project co-ordinators to have stipulated a particular understanding of terms from the outset was seen to run the risk of ruling certain disciplines out. The alternative was to gesture at what the co-ordinators took to be a fairly inclusive understanding, and to urge authors to clarify their uses of terminology on an individual basis. For the purposes of the current volume, we as editors have decided to attempt a broad stipulation of terminology – though with an eye to maximum generality.

In an earlier Cambridge University Press volume associated with the RAI Project, *The Theory of Institutional Design* (1996), Bob Goodin provided an excellent extended survey of this issue. From a description of developments in 'institutional' analysis across the main disciplinary groups (History, Sociology, Economics, Political Science, and Political Philosophy), he distils seven propositions which he suggests include the main themes of a 'new institutionalism' across the social sciences:

1. Individual agents and groups pursue their respective projects in a context that is collectively constrained; ...
2. Those constraints (include) ... institutions – organised patterns of socially constructed norms and roles and socially prescribed behaviors expected of occupants of those roles, which are created and recreated over time;
3. Constraining though they are, those constraints nonetheless are in various other respects advantageous to individuals and groups in the pursuit of their own more particular projects; ...
4. (partly because) the same contextual factors that constrain individual and group actions also shape the desires, preferences and motives of those agents;

5. These constraints characteristically have historical roots, as artefactual residuals of past actions and choices;
6. The constraints embody, preserve and impart differential power resources with respect to different individuals and groups;
(Though ultimately)
7. Individual and group action, contextually constrained and socially shaped though it may be, is the engine that drives social life (Goodin, 1996: 19–20).

As Goodin points out, different disciplines place different emphases on these various propositions. Some disciplines dispute some of them entirely. And the mechanisms whereby institutional constraints are presumed to exercise their influence on action also differ according to discipline. Economists, for example, with their conception of institutions as rules of the game, tend to focus on how changing such 'rules' alters the incentives for agents to act in different ways. Incentives here are understood as rewards and punishments, often understood in a rather narrow 'economic' sense. Economists are also inclined to emphasize individual agents as the core elements of social analysis: they are often sceptical about group agency. Historians often have a similar instinct. And even where they do not do their history through the prism of individual lives, they are often inclined to psychologize social processes in the pursuit of narrative interest. Sociologists and political scientists are more disposed to think in terms of group than of individual agent action and to think of structures and historical forces constraining individual freedom of action. Rather than offering accounts of institutional change in terms of changes in (often implicit) relative prices, as economists do, sociologists and political scientists are more inclined to think of institutions operating through desires, preferences and motives. These differences constitute a major divide within the social sciences.

A simple example may help to make this clearer. Consider a phenomenon that most social scientists would consider an 'institution' – democracy. The economist tends to focus on the incentives that individuals have to engage in political activity, and the way in which democratic procedures (competitive elections most notably) influence the behaviour of the main participants. So economists are struck by the fact that in large-scale electoral settings individuals seem to have a very small incentive to vote, because the chance that any individual might make a difference to the electoral outcome is very small. And they note that the desire on the part of candidates to be elected tends to give those candidates an incentive to attend to what the voters want. On this basis, economists seek to discover the circumstances under which that incentive is most effective.

By contrast, political scientists and sociologists are frequently more concerned with the values that the democratic process makes salient. One such value is the extent of explicit political representation for particular groups. And this democratic value can operate largely independently of the policy outcomes which different institutional configurations seem likely to generate. The historian *qua* historian is perhaps more likely to look for salient individuals in terms of whose life and action a compelling story about political conflicts and the operation of democracy can be told. The salient individuals in question might well be ordinary voter-citizens – drawn from the 'common people' – rather than prime ministers, admirals and generals. But if so, there will be an eye to a representative quality in the stories of those individuals and/or the events that are supposed to be illuminated.

These differences notwithstanding, Goodin is in our view entirely right to identify a considerable measure of overlap between the different disciplinary approaches. Even where there is a major difference of emphasis or downright disagreement, it is a major intellectual accomplishment to be clear as to where the differences lie, and as to what would constitute the kind of further argument (or evidence) that each of the disputants would regard as relevant. Every proper disagreement depends on prior agreement about *something*: otherwise, there is not a disagreement – merely a talking at cross-purposes. In that sense, the RAI Project, like other interdisciplinary exercises, has aimed precisely to secure a measure of clear 'disagreement' among disciplines.

And several specific points of agreement in the various approaches to institutional analysis are worth noting. First, institutional analysis occupies a middle ground between 'structure' and 'agency' and denies any false antithesis between the two. Whatever the precise nature of the agents chosen, their actions are neither totally determined (in general) nor totally contingent. Even if anything *could* happen, some things are much more likely to happen than others. And what is most likely to happen is framed by the 'institutional structure' within which it occurs. Second, though institutions can be influenced by explicit acts of collective choice, they are rather resilient things that have some life of their own. Institutions depend on existing practices, norms and habits (of behaviour, beliefs and ways of thinking about the world) that tend to be resistant to change. Third, an 'institution' is to be distinguished from an 'organization' – contrary to much common usage. If, in the spirit of Talcott Parsons, an institution is to be viewed as some amalgam of norms, practices, structures and organizations, an organization like a university or a large corporation can only be understood 'institutionally' when all the norms and habits and structures governing the actual relationships of players within the organization are filled in. Finally, there is agreement that the rules and norms that count are the ones that actually apply – not the ones that may be formally specified. What is formally specified may, to be sure, influence what actually applies – either because formal rules are backed by formal sanctions and rewards that have real effect, or because formal rules frame perceptions of what is to be done or what others are likely to do. But it is a mistake to think that institutions can just be legislated. Sometimes, often perhaps, there is more going on than the formal descriptions tell us.

## Normative Orientation

There is a separate issue that cuts somewhat across the disciplinary divide – though there are disciplinary orientations in play here as well. Social analysis is, as we have noted, often the servant of normative ambitions. We seek to understand how institutions work in order to make them work 'better'. Clearly, any such ambitions are dependent on a particular conception of betterness. And even where the normative ambition lies in the background, or where the scholar attempts to do strictly 'positive analysis', the analysis is necessarily focused on isolating particular effects or aspects that derive their 'interest' from an underlying normative scheme.

In the ensuing chapters, for example, although much of the concern is simply to describe the history of Australian institutions and related effects on policy, the values of the authors necessarily come into play. There is, just to take an obvious example, a shared judgement that Australian institutions have worked badly in the case of Aborigines, and that this is an area where institutional innovation is called for. John Dryzek's concern in Chapter 5 for effective democratic representation of the environment as an end in itself is doubtless more controversial.

At a more subtle level, the criteria of evaluation of the workings of institutions carry important normative implications. For example, it has become increasingly common over the last twenty years to evaluate institutions in terms of their capacity to generate economic growth – as measured in terms of GDP or GDP per capita. Economists will often do this unthinkingly as if that were the only relevant value or perhaps the only one that institutions can do anything about. But even in narrow economic terms, there are other possible 'games in town'. Some economists would want much more emphasis placed on the *distribution* of economic benefits. Non-economists might be sceptical as to whether GDP is a reasonable measure of well-being, and might want to consult a wider range of social indicators. Or indeed the criteria of evaluation may be such as not to admit fine calibration at all. Economists, sociologists and political scientists will tend to have differing views on these evaluative questions and differing inclinations as to how to approach them analytically.

It is worth emphasizing in this connection that the kinds of criteria appropriate for evaluating institutions at the most abstract level need not be the same as those that are operative under the institution in question. Institutional arrangements operate in part by articulating and promoting certain norms of behaviour. Such norms often develop an ethical edge. Violating them will bring upon the violator the disesteem of others, and possibly guilt depending on whether the violator has internalized the norm herself or not. But such institutionally specific norms are often not useful in evaluating the institutions themselves. It seems excessively self-referential to evaluate the norms of the medical profession solely by reference to those norms themselves. We would need something broader and more abstract to do the relevant evaluative work.

The norms that govern the work of academics and the structures of universities and professional bodies and disciplines can all be distinguished from broader questions about the criteria by which an increase in university enrolments or an expansion of the academic research system might be judged. Yet these latter more encompassing evaluative norms may themselves be institutionally 'shaped' – and certainly receive expression through institutions of one kind and another. For example, the evaluative context for certain types of medical experimentation is likely to be much influenced by the strength and organizational vitality of the Catholic Church and whether the Church is represented in relevant decision-making forums. In other words, the balance between rival normative considerations that is actually struck is significantly influenced by the institutions that operate at the most general level.

Different disciplines have their own evaluative traditions as well as their own conceptions of institutions. Economists tend to be broadly utilitarian, which gives their normative analysis an abstract, non-substantive quality. Political scientists are more likely to adopt a richer substantive evaluative scheme, often using what economists would regard as 'institutions' as immediate evaluative criteria for the values required. So, for example, political scientists and political theorists will often refer to 'democratic values' (such as 'inclusion' and 'participation' and 'critical energy', which are all in play in John Dryzek's Chapter 5). 'Inclusion' also plays a major normative role in the essays by Marian Sawer, Geoff Stokes and Martin Krygier (Chapters 6–8). And it seems absolutely clear that any evaluative scheme will have to decide on who is to be included. Even economistic evaluation will have to decide whose interests are to count. But economists are likely to take a more critical view of, say, 'political participation', regarding it less as an end in itself and more in terms of its benefits and costs across the board (and however exactly measured).

## What the Chapters Say

The chapters in the volume fall into three broad categories. First there are those that deal with the interplay between institutions and the external environment to produce particular policies or policy regimes. In this category lie the papers by Castles, Brennan and Pincus, and Braithwaite (Chapters 2–4). Castles aims to give an account of the broad policy consequences of Australia's institutional array. Brennan and Pincus attempt to explain the choice among policy regimes in the light of those perceived consequences. And Braithwaite looks at the same range of questions from the point of view of globalization, focusing specifically on the way in which Australia has responded to external forces over its 200-year history.

The second group of chapters deal in various ways with the theme of effective inclusion. Dryzek (Chapter 5) does so quite explicitly as a general test of Australia's democracy as 'a work-in-progress' (as he puts it). The chapter by Krygier (Chapter 8) can also be read through this 'inclusion' lens. His conceptual frame involves appeal to the distinction between 'objects' and 'subjects' of the law. He might no less have remarked of the 'rule of law' that it is a work-in-progress, to be seen not as an either/or state that nations have or have not yet achieved but as a multi-dimensioned institutional presence that nations exhibit to a greater or lesser degrees. The chapters by Sawer and Stokes (Chapters 6, 7) represent more detailed examinations of aspects of this 'inclusionary' project – Sawer dealing with the case of women, and Stokes with the case of Aborigines.

Chapter 9 by Uhr sits outside these two groups. His approach focuses on the role of rhetoric in defining and articulating 'leadership' in the Australian context. By directing attention to three cases of Australian prime ministers, his approach is at once more individuated and more historically specific than that of the other authors. It is more 'textually bound'. And at first sight less 'institutional'. But Uhr makes a good case for the claim that rhetoric is both a distinctive element of democratic regimes, where public accountability is central, and also a specifically rule-bound enterprise where the particular institutions of parliamentary debate and public address shape the kind of rhetoric that is acceptable. These facts make rhetoric itself a kind of institution and one that, in Uhr's view, plays a critical role in the Australian system.

In what follows, we offer a brief summary of each of the papers in the order in which they appear. We conclude our introduction by noting a few themes common to the majority of essays.

### Castles on Why Institutions Matter

Frank Castles' chapter opens the volume by going to a central question: do institutions have consequences? And if so what are they? Of course, institutional arrangements might be valued for their own sake. Direct democracy might be valued because citizens feel it gives them a more direct say in policy decisions; minimum wage laws might be valued because they express a concern for lower-wage workers. And these values might be essentially independent of the consequences of the arrangements. So the demonstration that minimum wage laws hurts lower-wage workers by making them unemployed, or that direct democracy actually reduces the effect of popular opinion on policy outcomes (both propositions that have received some support in relevant literatures) might on this account not be decisive – and may even be irrelevant. However, that seems unlikely. Consequences matter, even if they are not all that matters. And for the most part, institutions are valued because of the consequences they produce.

So what consequences do Australian political institutions have? Castles answers this question both in the macro-sense, looking at the broad features which Australia's political order shares with other Western democracies, and in the micro-sense, looking at the features which tend to distinguish Australia's political institutions. For both purposes, he relies on comparative analysis of a broad empirical kind. He illustrates his theme partly by presenting and interpreting the findings of a number of studies undertaken by others and partly by discussing the findings of his own research on the institutional development of the Australian welfare state.

The first study Castles looks at is the recent work of Adam Przewaski et al. on the relationship between democracy and development. This involves a statistical analysis of 141 countries, or 4730 'regime years' – with about one-third of these 'democratic' and the remainder 'authoritarian'. The object is to use sophisticated multiple regression techniques to uncover the relationship between democracy and per capita income – allowing for as many other factors as is possible. Although the focus of the study is the appropriate aid policies towards developing countries, there are other messages to be gleaned. The basic conclusion is that higher income per capita makes democracies more stable. So if one has reason to want democratic institutions, better to be rich! But another important conclusion is that democracy is conducive to higher per capita income, largely because the development path in democracies tends to be associated with lower rates of population growth. Authoritarian regimes can increase aggregate GDP by having higher levels of population: democratic regimes are constrained to achieve higher GDP by mechanisms that give a substantial share of the benefits to worker-citizens. In short, democracy is associated with higher GDP per head. That is good news for democrats. One can have democracy and higher wealth as well.

The second, more fine-grained, analysis derives from the work of Arend Lijphart. Lijphart attempts a broad classification of democratic institutional orders according to whether they are 'consensual' or 'majoritarian'. This distinction is essentially a two-dimensional one, involving a 'parties–executive' dimension and a 'federal–unitary' dimension, with Australia occupying the majoritarian or executive pole in the former dimension and the federal pole in the latter. This classification is the basis of an empirically derived pattern of policy outcomes. Across the sample of countries that Lijphart uses, he finds that, contrary to popular opinion, majoritarian governments are not better macro-managers than consensual ones, but that consensual governments do tend to have 'kinder, gentler' policies. 'Kindness' here expresses itself in a more generous welfare state, larger international aid and more extensive environmental protection. The implication is that institutions are causally connected to the policy regimes associated with them, and Lijphart (and Castles) conjecture what those causal factors might be. Within the Lijphart classification, it is easy enough to locate Australia: we are a hybrid case with strong majoritarianism on the parties–executive dimension but at the federal end of the unitary–federal dimension. Castles discusses the policy implications of this location: if we are true to type we ought to expect poor performance on the environmental front and low welfare spending. Both features are borne out by the facts. And on Castles' own analysis, federalism tends to magnify the welfare spending effect.

On the other hand, Castles' own work on the development of the Australian welfare state has always contended that Australia is a peculiar case in the sense that it has sought to achieve its welfare objectives not through public spending but through wage regulation. An implication is that shares of GDP spent on welfare are not reliable measures of the extent to which a government has pursued welfare goals. The point generalizes. Comparative work that relies on expenditure data may be misleading if countries vary significantly in the extent to which they rely on 'expenditure using' rather than 'expenditure saving' policy tools. Similar policy outcomes can be achieved via direct provision or subsidization of private provision or by regulation that compels private actors to act in specific ways. For example, a public social security system, or superannuation subsidies or compulsory savings schemes can have quite similar effects. But the public expenditure measures show them as very different. The Australian case of wage regulation as a redistributive device is one example. Our use of regulation to compel firms to insure their workers against industrial accidents with private insurance firms (as distinct from public social insurance schemes) is another such example. Australia's use of these public-revenue-saving policy instruments makes, in Castles' view, for a certain 'Australian exceptionalism'. Simply put, we have had a bigger welfare state than the public expenditure figures imply.

Equally, however, welfare gains by regulative means can also be *removed* without that fact being as evident as it would be if reflected in substantial public spending shifts. And Castles' claim is that they have been removed – largely by appeal to a policy rhetoric that ignored the primary distributional function that those measures played. Arguably, such removal was possible without a major clash of values because few ordinary citizens realized just what was at stake. The cost of achieving policy objectives relatively invisibly is that the relevant policies can be removed no less invisibly. Castles' final conjecture – that public-expenditure-intensive tools of the European style are unlikely to be implemented to substitute for the dismantling of the wage regulation system – seems right. And this leaves Castles, like other authors here, with a certain nostalgia for times past.

### *Brennan and Pincus on Economic Institutions*

Apart from later essays discussing Australia's institutional encounters with its indigenous population, the chapter by Brennan and Pincus is probably the least nostalgic in the volume. Its purpose is to identify the institutional dialectic through which Australia abandoned its traditional economic policy regime in favour of a new economic order based less on state regulation than on market competition. Their account of the dismantling of traditional and distinctive Australian economic institutions is the immediate counterpart to the move away from a regulated labour market and wages system chronicled by Castles in Chapter 2. For Brennan and Pincus, what made the Australian economy institutionally unusual at the time of Federation was its strong reliance on a system of tariff protection, behind whose walls national governments could tax and spend to further national economic development. These were the economic underpinnings of the Australian Settlement and Deakin's New Protection. Australia's economic story over the past one hundred years is of the consolidation of this regime in the first half of the century and of its dismantling in the final decades of the century.

For the most part, that dismantling occurred under the aegis of the Hawke–Keating Labor governments and of the Howard Liberal administration which succeeded them, although it was, arguably, Whitlam who set the ball rolling with a 25 per cent tariff cut in the mid-1970s. The components of the new economic policy regime as identified by Brennan and Pincus are familiar enough: financial deregulation, tariff reform, the use of competition policy both federally and in the states to effect microeconomic reform, labour market deregulation and a variety of new initiatives in industry policy. This refashioning of Australian economic institutions was not evolutionary and gradual, but came about through consciously articulated policies enacted through the political process. It was an episode or process of institutional reshaping on a major scale.

The lack of nostalgia in what Brennan and Pincus have to say comes directly from their conceptual take on the relationship between institutions and outcomes in the real world, which they see as taking the form of a feedback loop. Institutional structures constrain the functioning of the real economy, but the effectiveness and appropriateness of those institutions is eventually judged on the basis of perceptions of the satisfactoriness of the outcomes. The implication is obvious. Institutions may change very slowly, but, when they are transformed, it is unlikely to be under circumstances where they are widely seen as functioning effectively. That explains why Brennan and Pincus do not pine for Australia's economic past. A regime change occurred because Australia's old regime was perceived to have let Australia down!

Brennan and Pincus frame their discussion of the relationship between institutions and outcomes in explicit contrast to Michael Pusey's (1991) account of the economic rationalist takeover in Canberra. Pusey, they argue, sees the new economic regime simply as a consequence of changing intellectual fashions within the economics profession and that profession's elevation to positions of control within the Canberra bureaucracy. According to Brennan and Pincus, this is wrong on both factual grounds and conceptual ones. They point out that similar institutional developments have occurred elsewhere in the Western world and that Australian reforms were largely undertaken with bipartisan support. Further, Pusey's analysis suggests that major institutional change can occur with no reference to real economic forces, and that is a proposition that Brennan and Pincus decidedly reject. Possibly, in the end, as they concede, the contrast is overdrawn. Economists clearly did have an important role in the reshaping of Australian economic institutions in recent decades, but it seems eminently possible that is partly to be explained by their professional sensitivity to emergent problems in the functioning of the Australian economy. In such a view, economists themselves become part of the feedback loop by which outcomes eventually help to reshape institutions.

*Braithwaite on Globalization and the Global Perspective*

Braithwaite's paper advances two claims. The first is that Australia has developed a talent for good government but little talent at all for effective business practice. His second is that the development of Australia and its peculiar talents has been framed against shortages of specific factors of production – labour in the early years of the colony; capital more recently.

Introduction 13

Like other authors here, Braithwaite's instinct is to turn to history. The conviction seems to be that the prevailing structure of our institutions can only be explained historically. And that such explanation is important both in its own right and for understanding the constraints on what is likely to be feasible in the future. Institutions, like the *Titanic*, are difficult to realign. Sensible 're-shaping' involves both long lead times and a good sense of which particular levers in the institutional system are most effective in changing direction.

The factor-shortage aspect of Braithwaite's story explains the connection to 'globalization'. Braithwaite's conception of globalization is of a process of moving factors of production from areas of low demand to areas of high demand. Given that conception, Australia has, since the beginning of white colonization, been a 'global' player. Interestingly, alongside the long-term systematic import of labour and capital, there have been somewhat 'incidental' exports – of institutional innovations and institutional know-how and even of intellectual expertise (not least in Braithwaite's own area of criminology.

Braithwaite takes up the notion, familiar from the analysis of Hirst (1983, for example) and Neal (1991), that the demand for labour in the early years of the colony required a regime in which convict rights, both personal and property, were recognized (and in some cases invented). Settlers who were assigned convicts under the assignment system had an incentive to look after their convicts well. Good treatment was a means both of securing greater work effort from the convicts so assigned and of ensuring that other convicts would be assigned in future when the current crop had completed their sentences. Such good treatment included specifically creating economic incentives for hard work, which in turn required that convicts had tolerably secure rights to the private property thereby acquired. Clearly, the details of the rules for assignment are crucial here. If assignment of additional convicts was independent of the history of earlier assignments, then the incentive to 'look after' one's convicts would be moderated. Sticks could work as well as carrots in securing hard work, and would predictably be used more extensively unless such use had implications for future assignments.

Whatever the details, it is clear that at least some convicts in the early years did very well economically – and rather too well to satisfy the deterrence criteria that the British penal authorities demanded of the transportation system. It is also clear that labour shortages did not invoke similar treatment of Aborigines. Braithwaite's observations here are echoed in the chapters by Krygier, Dryzek and Stokes: the story of convict 'inclusion' stands alongside a no less telling story of

Aboriginal 'exclusion'. Labour shortage was not the only game in town, apparently.

The transition from labour-constrained to capital-constrained development is presumably part of what Braithwaite would identify as background for more recent changes in policy regime (of the kind addressed by Brennan and Pincus). What is not so clear from Braithwaite's account, however, is whether his two basic claims are related or independent. Is there an implication that the long tradition of cosseted manufacturing, protected explicitly with the aim of keeping wages high and promoting immigration (from desired locations) thereby, is (a significant part of) the reason why Australia is so bad at business? Was Australian business's failure to lobby effectively in US agricultural markets (a parable that Braithwaite uses to introduce his story) connected to our success in good government? After all, if a feature of good government is low returns to special interest lobbying, then Australia's 'good' institutions may be poor training for the arena of global politics where experience in the lobbying game is crucial. One implication does seem clear. If Australia is good at politics and not so good at business, then the public sector would be expected to play a rather larger role in optimal response to the new face of globalization than in other places where good business is better developed than good government. The trouble with that conclusion is that it seems likely to continue rather than eradicate what Braithwaite sees as one of our primary liabilities in the new global order.

### *Dryzek on Democratic Inclusions*

John Dryzek's chapter offers an assessment of 'Australia's democracy as a work-in-progress'. The dimension on which Dryzek measures democratic progress is 'inclusion' – and here not just formal inclusion, because 'formal political equality can coexist with continued exclusion or even oppression'. The concern is with 'effective and authentic inclusion'. Dryzek's definition of politics is broad. It encompasses specifically activities outside the state as well as inside; and indeed having a vibrant extra-state political sphere is an important goal for Dryzek. So a certain apparent paradox emerges at the outset: if formal inclusion within the state is at the expense of a vibrant extra-state presence, greater formal inclusion may not represent democratic progress in Dryzek's sense at all. This conclusion may seem more controversial than it is. At first, it might seem that Dryzek is arguing that in the long run it is good for some groups that they are excluded because that fuels the 'revolution' and leads to more authentic inclusion in the long run. And perhaps there is a touch of such thinking in his formulation. But almost everyone can concede that groups can be formally co-opted to the state establishment at a cost

Introduction

that the group would be well advised not to pay. Furthermore, to the extent that civil society depends on there being a critical mass of engagement, groups that are active within civil society support an environment that is beneficial to other groups. Accordingly, even if inclusion is in the interests of some particular group, it might not be in the interests of democratic inclusion overall.

Dryzek sets out the core of his analytic apparatus and then proceeds to assess the story of 'democratic progress' so defined – less as a historical project and more as an interpretation or 'representation' seen through the particular lens that he constructs. Thus he offers an account of the early inclusion of the bourgeoisie and the working class, and gradually of women and most reluctantly of indigenous peoples. In relation to women, his account should be read in conjunction with Sawer's chapter, and in relation to Aborigines in conjunction with the chapters by Krygier and Stokes.

Dryzek's chapter is, however, the only one that deals explicitly with the 'inclusion' of non-English-speaking immigrants. Here, the question of whether inclusion under the formal aegis of government policy was 'a good bargain for NESB people' comes to the fore. As Dryzek observes, 'multiculturalism' Australia-style was almost exclusively a top-down enterprise, with ethnic organizations playing virtually no direct role. Of course, if the structure of democratic electoral institutions is such that enrolling the NESB vote becomes of paramount importance, then one might think that electoral institutions were indeed doing the work that the project of democratic inclusion would want them to. But, without necessarily supporting an 'oppositional style' of ethnic politics, Dryzek acknowledges the force of the critique that government action in this arena has produced a quiescence within NESB groups, with leaders of ethnic groups distanced from and unrepresentative of their communities – the 'professional ethnics' syndrome. A certain ambivalence emerges here. Dryzek compares the Australian situation favourably with that in the United States where there are numerous instances of politically potent lobby groups exercising considerable influence over foreign policy in directions that are, in Dryzek's view, distinctly dubious. Dryzek's bottom line here seems to be a kind of resigned pragmatism.

More controversially, Dryzek extends the domain of democratic inclusiveness to cover the natural environment. Picking up on a long tradition of Australian writing in the area of 'green political theory' (much of it associated with the Research School of Social Sciences), he poses the question as to what would be institutionally required to recognize the intrinsic claims of the environment – claims that ought to be embodied in human institutions whatever the human agents at the time happen to think. He explores the history of environmental politics in Australia with this institutional test in mind. As he points out, where inclusion within the state was most extensive, it was at the expense of finding compromises with more mainstream instrumental concerns – of which Ecologically Sustainable Development was the clearest articulation. It is an interesting question as to whether the idea of 'democratic inclusion' for non-human subjects is not a contradiction in terms. After all, there is some measure of conflict over every act of inclusion. More effective representation of the interests of one group can be at the expense of the interests of groups already included. And analogously, inclusion of non-human subjects as ends in themselves will be at the expense of the interests of human subjects. One can imagine justifications for an institutional order that recognizes rights for non-human subjects that run in terms of the ultimate interests of (human) citizens. But a justificatory scheme that goes beyond this to include effects on the environment as being of intrinsic significance seems 'non-democratic' in some basic sense. Beyond a certain point, the notion of 'the people' in the standard democratic aphorisms (of government of, for, and by the people), critics might argue, becomes excessively strained.

### *Sawer on Women in Australian Institutions*

Marian Sawer's chapter focuses on the inclusion of women. Her general claim is that the 'social liberalist' orientation of Australian institutional designers at Federation – with its emphasis on equality of opportunity and 'fair-go' principles – provided the rhetorical resources for subsequent moves to establish equality for women, even though such equality lay beyond the imagination of those original institution-builders. Of course, Australian women had the vote early – the 'recognition' of them as political citizens in that sense was present at the outset. But policy intervention in the name of fairness (as evidenced in the Harvester decision) did not extend these principles to the issue of equal opportunities (or equal pay) for women. On the other hand, the old-age pension, introduced into Commonwealth legislation in 1909 following the recommendations of a Royal Commission, was provided to women at the same level as for men, and in 1910 at an earlier age (60 rather than 65). The common picture of the Australian welfare state as essentially a 'breadwinner' system focuses too much, in Sawer's view, on wage regulation, important though that may be. Including in one's focus important 'social liberal initiatives in education, maternity allowances and old-age pensions' rectifies the balance, because women were the 'primary beneficiaries' of these initiatives. The social liberal tradition provided not just the principles that could be mobilized for future female inclusion; as Sawer sees it, that tradition was explicitly gender-inclusive from the outset and in a tangible policy sense. Sawer also identifies in the Australian income tax, which has had individual rather than family income as the tax base from the outset, a recognition of the importance of economic independence for women.

Sawer emphasizes the significance of women's self-conscious institution-building within civil society. Some of these institutions, like the Australian Federation of Women Voters, had an explicitly political edge, and these are the ones on which Sawer tends to focus here. She provides an account of female participation as parliamentary representatives – and the contribution made in terms both of the style of politics and influence on the policy agenda (making sexual harassment a policy issue, for example). She describes the emergence of the 'femocrat' phenomenon in the Australian bureaucracy through the 1970s and 1980s (a matter that she has written on at greater length in Sawer, 1990b).

Perhaps the most novel part of Sawer's chapter addresses the 'gendered nature of the theory and practice of federalism'. Feminists have generally been inclined to identify threats to their rights as arising from sources other than the state. In that sense, they have been generally out of sympathy with that strand of 'classical liberal' political theory that emphasizes protection from abuse of state power as the primary object of institutional design. To the extent that federal structures specifically are justified primarily in such terms, they have tended to be centralist in orientation. A more extensive state, with less diffuse powers, has seemed to be more likely on balance to be friendly to women's interests and to a vigorous welfare state more generally. Devolution of social expenditures to state level, on Sawer's account, has been resolutely opposed by women's groups.

Sawer, like several other contributors to the volume, ends her chapter with a touch of nostalgia. She identifies the decline of 'social liberal' thinking in the face of an older form of 'classical liberal' thinking 'with their presumption of natural laws of economic competition and the dangers of state "interference" '. Although the 'fair go' makes an occasional appearance in political rhetoric, social liberalism as an organizing principle of Australian institutional and policy design seems to be seriously ailing in these early years of the new millennium.

*Stokes on Aboriginal Inclusion*

In Chapter 7, Geoffrey Stokes offers a history of Australian policy with respect to its own indigenous peoples based on three 'political logics'. These are: 'paternalist exclusion'; 'liberal inclusion'; and 'indigenous self-determination'. All three 'logics' are in play at any point, but the way in which they are manifested and the centre of gravity between them shifts through time.

'Paternalist exclusion' treats indigenous people as 'a problem' to be handled by policy administrators who regard themselves as technical experts. Aborigines are regarded as perpetual 'children' who have to be managed by those more capable. Although the rhetorical defence of this kind of policy regime invoked references to benevolence (hence the 'paternalist' reference), the reality of the policies was not always benign in intent and certainly more rarely benign in effect. In this sense, the gradual transition from paternalist exclusion to liberal inclusion – under which Aborigines came to be treated formally in ways equivalent to other citizens – can be seen to represent genuine progress. And Stokes certainly does see it in such terms. However, the recognition of the distinctive cultural identity of the Aboriginal peoples, and the possibility of using policy and political institutional arrangements as a vehicle for such recognition, invite a logic of 'Aboriginal self-determination' which becomes the third element in Stokes' trinity.

The discussion is oriented around the tension between these three competing logics; and is framed around two snapshot pictures – one of the period 1900–1910; and the other of the decade 1990–2000. Although the contrast indicates a significant shift away from exclusion towards inclusion, and a greater recognition of the claims of self-determination, Stokes is at pains to emphasize that the three logics remain in play. So for example, he notes that the Aboriginal and Torres Strait Islander Commission – an institution that involves a significant gesture towards the logic of self-determination – is subject to an unusually extensive array of accountability provisions. Apparently, the Commission cannot be trusted to manage its affairs without the special ('paternalist') scrutiny of a special array of 'checks and balances'. Of course, we live in an age of political 'accountability' more broadly – but Stokes identifies the special nature of accountability demands in the ATSIC case.

One interesting aspect of Stokes' conceptual framework is that it raises quite explicitly the question of the extent to which the 'self' which figures in the idea of Aboriginal *self*-determination is itself influenced by – perhaps is even a creation of – the institutions under which political recognition takes place. One substantial difference between 'Aboriginality' as at 1910 and as at 2000 is the declining role of explicitly racial reference. In 1910, Aboriginality was defined and operationalized by reference to the degree of 'Aboriginal blood'. In 2000, anyone is an Aborigine who so self-describes, whatever the genetic details. In 1910, defining Aboriginality was an issue for administrators and policy-makers; and it is clear that policy was understood in essentially racial terms. By 2000, the understanding had shifted somewhat; Aboriginality had become a much more *culturally* defined concept. Whether the common understanding of Aboriginality mapped at any point into the understanding that

Introduction

Aborigines had of *themselves* is an interesting question which would require anthropological resources that go beyond what Stokes offers in this chapter. Nevertheless, the role that institutions play in constituting identity is an important theme and one which the issue of indigenous politics makes salient.

### *Krygier on Convicts, Aborigines and the Rule of Law*

The issue of Australia's treatment of Aborigines is also a central theme in Martin Krygier's chapter on the rule of law. The central contrast that occupies his attention is the differing experiences of convicts and Aborigines under the British legal institutions imported with the convicts in 1788 – the contrast, that is, between 'the ultimately happy white' and the 'ultimately terrible black' stories. But Krygier's task is not just to retell those stories. It is also to diagnose the role that the concept of the rule of law played in the contrast. Krygier emphasizes that this diagnosis is a complex business; he refers to the 'paradoxical sway and effects of law' and 'the ambiguous bearing of the *rule* of law' (our emphasis). Part of his object here is to disclose something about the nature of the rule of law. If we can understand why it is that the law is a resource for one group, and fails (or seems to have failed) to be a resource for another, we can uncover something about the rule of law itself. For the rule of law does purport to *be* a resource for the people subject to it. The rule of law stands against the arbitrary exercise of power; it offers a concept of law as an instrument of the governed rather than of the governors.

In that sense the rule of law is a close cousin to notions like popular sovereignty: it is grounded in a normative scheme in which the institutions of government are rationalized and assessed in terms of the interests of the governed. So, in its idealized form, the rule of law provides the citizen with protection both from the arbitrary power of rule-enforcers and from the predatory actions of other citizens, and serves to facilitate the interactions of all so that the scope for mutual benefit is fully realized. To do this, Krygier emphasizes, requires more than merely having institutional rules of the right kind. That more is required is a message that post-communist transitions (on which Krygier has written elsewhere) have made loud and clear. What is important is what Krygier describes as a 'sociological' property – that law 'matters', it 'counts' in the way citizens act towards each other both in their private and public roles. The rule of law requires that people treat each other as proper 'subjects' of the law, as Krygier puts it, rather than as mere 'objects'. The rule of law demands an attitude of cool respect. How such an attitude might be institutionally supported is clearly an issue for any institutional interpretation of the rule of law – a challenge which Krygier acknowledges but does not pursue.

It is easy to say that the law did *not* count in the right way in the relation between whites and Aborigines. But the law need not have counted in that way in relation to convicts in the very earliest days of the penal colony. And yet it did – at least to a very significant degree. That fact is an accomplishment – or perhaps just a happy accident – that Krygier sees as proper cause for celebration. But Krygier rightly insists that the instinct to celebrate the good features of the past should be tempered with a clear acknowledgement of the bad features. And it hardly helps in understanding why the institutions that worked well did work well if one does not also examine the cases where they worked badly.

Krygier's account of the happy case – that of the convicts – follows broadly the outlines suggested by Neal and Hirst, and picked up by Braithwaite in his chapter in this volume. The Neal contribution comes from the wonderful story of the Kables – the First Fleet convict couple whose property rights were upheld in a Sydney magistrate's court in the earliest days of the colony and set the course for treatment of convicts in the colony as more or less full 'legal subjects'. The Hirst contribution, echoed by the Braithwaite chapter, runs in terms of the economic necessities of a penal colony that was, up to 1815 at least, more colony than penal institution. Convicts were the primary source of labour; they had to be well treated in order to elicit reasonable work effort from them, and in order to secure future allocations of convicts when one's current crop had served their sentences. Krygier is careful not to deny that some convicts were badly treated or to pretend that punishments for misdemeanours were not extremely harsh. But materially speaking, many convicts enjoyed better living standards than the average working-class Londoner and certainly better living standards than inhabitants of English prisons.

The failure of the rule of law to provide effective protection to Aborigines (despite explicit instructions from England that conciliatory methods towards the Aborigines were to be used) is traced by Krygier to two factors. First, there was the disregard of any Aboriginal claims to land use. Private property rights in land were determined and assigned to white settlers as if there were no standing conventions within the Aboriginal community concerning land use. Any action by Aborigines to violate legally constructed property titles (such as spearing cattle on tracts that natives had traditionally used for hunting) was punishable by force of law. And in that legal arena, if not in others, the authorities were content to contract the relevant enforcement to the property owners themselves. Conceivably, Aborigines may have had some legal recourse if they had been aware of the possibility of taking legal action. There would at least have been a forum in which argument by legal experts may have been forthcoming – including argument about legal standing if that had been denied. It is doubtful that this formal legal access would have achieved much at that period of history. Still, it is a mistake to second-guess the law. *Ex ante*, one might not have predicted much of a hearing for convicts either. In any event, no-one took the trouble to explain to the Aborigines how white-man's institutions worked or what they might do for the Aborigines. And so, more or less private enforcement of settlers' property rights against indigenous people was set in place.

Second, and more generally, the effective operation of the rule of law requires a certain kind of imagination – one that sees those under the rule as 'subjects' not 'objects'. That imagination was perhaps strained in the convict case, but a combination of economic necessity and a few salient successes gradually triumphed. The Aborigines were a different case. Krygier puts it this way:

> however one characterizes the motives of those who so degraded Aborigines, and they were doubtless various, there appears to have been all along a failure of moral imagination, that imagination which sees *all* persons as 'the kind of limit to our will, to our interests and desires, that we mark when we speak of respecting someone's rights, or treating them as ends rather than as means.

The issue for institutional analysis that emerges from this observation is not whether the rule of law can operate in the total absence of such a moral imagination. It clearly cannot. But there is an issue as to whether the rule of law might encourage the emergence of that moral imagination. And there is a further issue of whether morality on its own, without institutional reinforcement and support, can ever be enough.

### *Uhr on the Rhetoric of Leadership*

In an ambitious essay, John Uhr examines the connection between leadership, citizenship and rhetoric, refracted through the experience of three notable Australian prime ministers – Deakin, Menzies, and Keating. Uhr's ambition is to underline the significance of rhetoric both in the practice of leadership and in the framing of the ways in which leadership and citizenship are understood. The exemplars are well chosen here, because all three are notable for their rhetorical skills and styles – though the styles and the primary mediums through which their rhetorics were carried, differed considerably. These differences might make one wonder where exactly the 'institutional' aspect of rhetoric lies. Rhetoric's highly personal character might lead one to think that it should be categorized on the *other* side of any plausible 'institutional/other' divide. But as Uhr is at pains to emphasize, democratic institutions, and especially representative democratic institutions in the presence of strong parties, demand that those who occupy central positions of power rhetorically justify their actions and policies. Further, those rhetorical exercises are themselves institutionally framed – through *Hansard*, and Question Time, and (nowadays) television debates – and subject to institutionalized scrutiny by a free press and an ordered parliamentary opposition. So, our institutions explicitly demand rhetoric from our leaders and that fact tends to 'select for' leaders with rhetorical skills.

Moreover, the rhetoric itself is an activity pursued 'within rules', as an institutionalist analysis might put it. The rhetoric in question can be good or bad, telling or flat, appropriate to the distinctive political context or out of place. The rules in question may be very difficult to articulate, much like the rules of good musical performance. But that is not to deny their significance. It is, though, to suggest that the 'case-study' method is especially appropriate. Hence Uhr's choice of the trio of Deakin, Menzies and Keating.

Rhetoric is, however, crucially open-ended with respect to its content. And it is this open-endedness that forms the central normative theme in Uhr's treatment. Following Bryce's work *Modern Democracies*, Uhr distinguishes between rhetoric in the service of 'good government' on the one hand and in the service of mere political popularity on the other. The former is the mark of true 'leadership', normatively understood. The latter reveals the character of the populist demagogue. Bryce thought – and Uhr agrees – that Australian institutions permit considerable scope for the latter possibility, and indeed saw that possibility as the critical test for Australian political arrangements. Accordingly, how leaders shape the notion of leadership rhetorically, and how they articulate notions of responsible citizenship, turn out to be critical in the way popular government actually works. If the practice of notable exemplars serves to establish a rhetorical tradition in which the role of prime minister is understood – both popularly and to occupants of the office – in terms that support 'leadership' and denigrate demagoguery, then the powers of rhetoric are themselves rhetorically tamed. It is in beginning to uncover this rhetorical tradition about leadership that Uhr's contribution is so significant.

## Conclusion: Some Common Themes

It would be a mistake to try to offer in the final paragraphs of this introduction a set of judgements about where Australian institutions are at, or how they should be reshaped. For one thing, we have had a chance to state our views as contributors: to have a second crack as editors might seem self-indulgent. Further, as emphasized at the outset, we have not seen this particular book as representing any kind of 'final word', even in the temporal sense.

But there do seem to us to be some emerging points of consensus in the chapters that follow and it is perhaps worth underlining those.

First, it is generally agreed that the dismantling of the labour market regulatory regime over the last twenty years or so is a significant change in the Australian institutional array – and perhaps a more significant change than its executors allowed. Not all the contributors would necessarily consider the change to have been a 'bad thing'. But the rationale offered by primary supporters of the change – that of making labour markets more flexible – is not exactly the same as the grounds that critics offer. Critics are more inclined to focus on the redistributive role of wage regulation and the low probability of that role being taken up by other policy instruments that demand substantial public revenues.

Second, the issue of the appropriate treatment of Aborigines – and the failure of our institutions in the past to deal with this issue satisfactorily – is seen as being the major issue for the Australian democratic project. In some ways, perhaps, this issue has become so salient partly because more traditional aspects of 'social justice' – such as redistributive policies of the kind that wage regulation is seen to be – have played a smaller role. What is especially interesting in the case of Aboriginal concerns is the shift in the perception of the nature of the problem and the kind of solutions called for. The shift is away from perceiving the problem as one of *policy* towards conceiving of it as one of institutional reshaping or reform. The following chapters do not generate any clear specification of what the desirable institutional reforms should look like. But there is consensus that the strategy of 'liberal inclusion', to use Geoff Stokes' phrase, is not in itself enough.

Third, and perhaps a bit imaginatively, we see in these papers a common thread over a kind of popular/elite divide. John Uhr's Chapter 9 is most explicit about this in his reference to Bryce's anxieties about democratic populism, which Bryce saw as an especial risk in the Australian case. But it is a theme that arises in other chapters as well – whether in the reference by Brennan and Pincus to the significant role of 'expert committees', or in Dryzek's concerns about institutionalizing the 'intrinsic worth' of the environment, or in Braithwaite's judgement that 'governing' is a thing that Australia is good at. Government in the Australian context has typically been seen as an exercise in 'public management', requiring special expertise, rather than as a battle of rival interests demanding straightforward 'political' solution. What is at stake here is perhaps best understood in terms of an interests-versus-judgements conception of politics. Not all the contributors are entirely clear where they fall on this divide. But where one falls has serious implications for what institutions are perceived to be best and for how one views the institutions that we currently have.

The final 'common element' revolves around the dogs that do not bark. Common omissions are not necessarily judgements about relative importance. Omissions might no less reflect the nature and concerns of professional disciplines or the availability of relevant data or information. However, it is notable that in this book – as elsewhere in the RAI exercise – there is little discussion of 'civil society' as such, where civil society is that domain of activity that is neither economic nor political. Much discussion of institutions operates against the background of a bipolar distinction between the 'economy' and 'government' – between 'business' and 'politics' – between profits or votes, as the primary currency. There is, however, a domain of activities that fits neither of these categories – the domain of amateur sport, of choral groups, of book-clubs, of charitable organizations, of churches. These are part of the discussion 'at the edges' of John Dryzek's concerns, and therefore of Marian Sawer's and Geoff Stokes', but they come into play in that context primarily where they intersect with the 'political' and not in their own right.

But these too are 'institutions'. They operate under rules and norms. And their presence is nested within the broader frame of more abstract institutional arrangements. They represent a sphere, moreover, about which there has been increasing concern in some circles – most notably in the work of Robert Putnam and picked up in the increasing rhetorical appeal to 'social capital'. Against that background, it has been notable through the RAI Project just how difficult it has been to encourage work on this area of Australia's institutional life. Perhaps because it lies beyond the reach of direct influence (how could one influence amateur sport except by getting involved in its administration?), or perhaps because much of the data about it are thin or non-existent, scholars seem to have been reluctant to embark on studies of these institutions. They seem to be the forgotten element in the RAI story; and this is an omission that the current book does not remedy. Ten years of work and a few million dollars down the track it may seem feeble to say that this is an area where more work is needed. In fact, academics always reckon that 'more work is needed' on everything. But it is a source of some regret that the work in question is something that RAI has not even seeded.

# 2 Australia's Institutions and Australia's Welfare

*Francis G. Castles*

Although, as the introduction to this volume points out, key assumptions concerning the nature of institutions often differ across the social sciences, the common premise is that institutional differences are likely to be extremely important in shaping the nature of human conduct in contemporary societies. In essence, the argument is that similar institutions are likely to produce similar conduct and different institutions different conduct. Here, I attempt to exemplify this point in a more concrete way by showing that national differences in the forms of political institutions can lead to major differences in citizens' well-being and citizens' welfare. Cross-national comparison is the easiest way of demonstrating such effects, because, in political life, institutional differences usually coincide with the boundaries of nation-states. But if my method is comparative, my aim is to say something important about Australia. Australian institutions in some ways resemble and in other ways differ from those of other nations. Thus a demonstration that institutional differences matter strongly suggests that Australians need to be aware of how their institutions work and to be ready to change or modify those institutions where it becomes apparent that their consequences are out of kilter with citizen preferences.

I seek to establish my case by examining institutional differences and institutional outcomes at different levels of generality. At the most general level, I discuss evidence from recent research, which shows that democratic institutions are conducive to greater material well-being than authoritarian ones. Since Australian preferences for and adherence to democratic institutions are not in question, this research is most interesting from a foreign policy and humanitarian perspective, providing us with reasons for believing that some strategies of Third World economic and social development are more likely to be successful than others. I then go on to discuss evidence linking different kinds of democratic institutions with different kinds of policy outcomes. The questions addressed here are how majoritarian and decentralized institutional forms impact on policy effectiveness and whether these institutional forms contribute to or hinder the growth of welfare. Since Australia's constitutional settlement combines a majoritarian executive with decentralized federal government, answers to these questions will be relevant for our assessment of how well Australian institutions meet Australian policy needs. Finally, I examine an area – the control of wage levels through the conciliation and arbitration of industrial disputes – in which Australian institutional development over the past century has been highly distinctive. The impact of such arrangements on both welfare outcomes and economic performance has been a topic of active political debate ever since Federation, with judgements concerning the appropriateness of the past two decades of industrial relations reform dependent on our understanding of the effects of this most peculiar of Australian institutions.

## Do Democratic Institutions Make a Difference?

Apart, perhaps, from the capitalistic settings of its economy, the most basic institutional setting that Australia has in common with other advanced nations is that all authoritative allocations of value are made within a context of democratic rules. Indeed, Australia was a democratic pioneer. From the 1850s onwards, the Australian colonies were among the first to adopt the practices of representative and responsible government. Australia was also widely identified as the birthplace of the secret ballot, often referred to at the time as the 'Australian ballot'. At the turn of the century, Australia became the first country in the world in which a self-confessed party of the lower classes, the Labor Party, assumed office through the democratic ballot: in Queensland in 1899 and at a national level in 1904. Indeed, with a necessary caveat concerning the long delay in granting the vote to indigenous people, Australia can justly claim itself to be 'the first truly democratic state in the modern sense of fully representative government based on free, equal and universal suffrage' (Aitkin and Castles, 1989: 208). That landmark was passed in 1903, when women across Australia were for the first time entitled to vote in federal elections. Although Australia's zeal for democratic engineering has since abated, its status as a democratic nation has never been seriously challenged.

The question I now ask is what difference it makes whether a country has democratic institutions and, hence, whether Australia has reason to celebrate its past as a democratic pioneer and its continued embrace of democracy over 150 years. Part of the answer is, of course, axiomatic: contained in the very notion of what it is to be a democracy. Australia, in common with other democracies, is characterized by contested elections, alternation of governments, parties and interest groups that are free to organize, a judiciary that is independent, a free press and freedom from arbitrary arrest and imprisonment. Authoritarian governments, in contrast, lack at least one, and often more than just one, of these essential defining features of democratic rule. There is, therefore, every reason why we might prefer democratic to authoritarian rule on these grounds alone. However, that is not my main concern here. What interests me is an aspect of a less self-evidently answerable question, which has been extensively debated in the social sciences literature for much of the post-war period: whether the existence of democratic institutional arrangements makes a difference to the material well-being of those fortunate enough to live under them.

There have been two basic positions on this matter. The first – and much the most influential from the 1960s through to the fall of the Berlin Wall – is that, for all its virtues in terms of political liberties, democracy tends to undermine economic development. Because democratic rules give ordinary citizens a voice, it has been suggested that they make for an emphasis on consumption which crowds out the savings and investment required to underwrite economic growth (Huntington, 1968). Moreover, some commentators identify a similar process in the advanced democracies, with the uncontrolled growth of public expenditure simultaneously diminishing the capacity of the system to deliver on its economic goals and its welfare promises (see King, 1975; Brittan, 1977). Finally, it has been argued that the persistence of democratic rule over long periods is conducive to the formation of more and more complex networks of interest associations, whose rent-seeking activities gradually reduce the scope for productive investment and, hence, for economic growth (Olson, 1982).

Countering such views are more recent arguments suggesting that democratic rules lead to greater allocative efficiency. The economic historian Douglass North (1990: 109) notes that 'a modern democratic society with universal suffrage' maximizes the 'informational and institutional conditions' required to achieve efficient economic exchange. Other features of democratic rule seemingly propitious for economic activity are the protection given to private property and the opportunities afforded for free exchange of ideas and information. A classic demonstration of the role of democratic institutions in promoting the well-being of the community as a whole is the fact that history has not produced a single instance of a democracy that has experienced famine (Drèze and Sen, 1989). That is because 'a free press and an active political opposition constitute the best "early warning system" that a country threatened by famine can possess' (Sen, 1994: 34).

A recently published book provides interesting new evidence on these issues. *Democracy and Development: Political Institutions and Well-Being in the World, 1950–1990* is written by Adam Przeworski (the senior author), Mike Alvarez, José Antonio Cheibub and Fernando Limongi and was published by Cambridge University Press in 2000. It applies a sophisticated, econometric methodology, highly sensitive to the complex (recursive) nature of the phenomena under investigation, to data for 141 countries, 238 regimes and some 4730 'regime years', of which 1723 (36 per cent) were democratic and 3007 (64 per cent) authoritarian. The findings of this study are hugely important and merit reading even by those normally daunted by such statistical endeavours. In what can only be a brief summary of an extensive body of analysis, I will avoid all but the simplest numbers and merely note a number of conclusions, which either challenge conventional wisdom or underline major differences in the levels of material well-being of democratic and non-democratic nations.

Through much of the post-war period, the conventional wisdom in Western foreign policy thinking was that democratic institutions were likely to have perverse effects on Third World development. Democracy was to be preferred for the liberties it conferred, but was problematical in so far as it was seen to lead to weaker economic growth and to greater political instability. Moreover, the overwhelming consensus of academic opinion was that, with increasing affluence, the economic and social structures of non-democratic nations would become more favourable to democratic transition. In consequence, it was seen as sound – and, in the long run, ethical – foreign policy to give economic assistance to non-democratic regimes, so that they would generate the economic wealth and social infrastructure which would ultimately provide the basis for democratic viability.

The Przeworski book argues that this policy stance was wholly misconceived. Levels of per capita income have almost no effect on the probability of authoritarian nations making a transition to democracy. However, income levels are of major importance in determining whether democracies survive: poor democracies have a medium rate of attrition; democracies with middling income levels have a much reduced rate of attrition; and richer democracies seem invulnerable to political instability. It is this difference between dictatorships and democracies which accounts for the well-known identity between economic advancement and democracy. Rather than democracy being a product of economic development, as scholars since Lipset (1959) have believed, economic growth makes existing democracies more capable of weathering the difficulties they confront. On the one hand, this means that foreign aid to non-democratic countries can no longer be defended on the ground that it is ultimately propitious for the emergence of democratic institutions. On the other, it means that much the best focus for aid programs is on the democratic countries of the Third World. Or putting it in more concrete and contemporary Australian foreign policy terms: Megawati Sukarnoputri and any democratic successors she may have in Indonesia are far more deserving of Australia's support and assistance than ever was the Soeharto regime.

The conventional wisdom turns out to have been wrong in at least one further important respect. Przeworski and his colleagues present evidence that shows that growth rates of national product are no different under democratic and dictatorial regimes. In poor countries, poverty leaves no room for politics and the same set of economic fundamentals impedes development irrespective of regime. In richer countries, however, an identity of outcomes disguises major divergences in the pattern of economic development. In wealthier dictatorships, investment is higher and so too is the growth of the labour force. Wealthier democracies manifest superior growth in total factor productivity, generate substantially greater output per worker and pay much higher wages. The link between institutions and growth strategy seems clear. Wealthier dictatorships can invest by limiting consumption and 'can grow by using a lot of labour and paying it little' (Przeworski et al. 2000: 179). Democracies cannot be so exploitative. Because they cannot repress workers, they must pay higher wages and use labour more efficiently. In a sense, then, both of the arguments linking institutional forms to material well-being have a point. Dictatorship does help reduce consumption, and democracy does foster allocative efficiency; and, in respect of the growth of total income, these effects appear more or less to cancel each other out.

This is not true, however, in respect of the growth of per capita income, generally regarded as the best available indicator of national differences in levels of material well-being. Here, there are quite dramatic differences in favour of democracy, with average per capita incomes increasing 2.46 per cent per annum in democracies and only 2.00 per cent per annum in dictatorships (Ibid: 216). Per capita income is, of course, simply total income divided by population and, since it has already been established that regimes do not vary in their overall rates of income growth, this means that virtually all the difference between democracies and dictatorships ultimately derives from the population side of the equation. This is the truly novel and exciting finding of the Przeworski book. Well-being grows faster in democracies because the rate of population increase is lower under democratic than non-democratic regimes.

At all income levels, birth and death rates are lower in democracies, with the slower rate of population growth a function of the fact that the fertility effect considerably exceeds the mortality effect. The birthrate for democracies is 19.5 per thousand of the population; for non-democratic regimes, it is 36.2. The death rate for democracies is 9.4 per thousand; for dictatorships, it is 14.1 (Ibid: 227). These figures translate into huge differences in life expectation. 'Men live 66.2 years under democracy and 50.8 under dictatorship, women live 71.5 years under democracy and 54.2 years under dictatorship' (Ibid: 228). Even taking into account the very real differences in life expectation at different income levels, this still translates into a difference in favour of democracy of around four years of additional life expectancy in each income band. These differences impact most directly on the lives of women. The figures show that women participate in the labour market to almost the same degree under both types of regime, but that under dictatorships women 'bear many more children, see more of them die, and are themselves more likely to die' (Ibid: 265).

There can be no question whatsoever that these differences between democratic and non-democratic nations provide strong evidence for the proposition that democratic institutions do, indeed, matter. And that they matter not just in terms of the liberties they confer, but also in terms of material advantages for ordinary men and women. The research I have been reporting here is methodologically sophisticated, theoretically informed and empirically based. Before concluding that effects are institutional in origin, the researchers invariably test for structural and confounding impacts. There are good reasons to believe that the study will prove to be the considered defence of democracy of its generation, a social science 'classic' and a landmark of our state of knowledge concerning some of the most crucial economic and political questions of our times.

Clearly, findings as radical as these cannot be accepted on the basis of a single study, and the methodology employed will, in particular, require validation by the wider community of social sciences scholarship. However, if vindicated by further research, the implications are enormous. As we have seen, the findings challenge the foreign policy wisdom of a whole generation by giving us absolutely no reasons to prefer non-democratic to democratic outcomes and, hence, no reasons to give development aid to nations trampling on the democratic rights of their own citizens. They also give us genuine cause for optimism about the future of democratic development in the modern world. If the experience of the past four decades is any guide, increasing average world per capita income levels should guarantee the survival of more and more democracies, so that by 2030, according to the estimate of Przeworski and his colleagues, two-thirds of the world's population are likely be enjoying the material benefits that flow from democratic institutions. The same story is told by the latest United Nations *Human Development Report* (2001), which notes that progress in the last thirty years has been such that it now classifies more of the world as developed than underdeveloped and attributes that progress to the spread of democracy and human rights. More parochially, if Przeworski's conclusions are correct, the material advantages flowing from democratic institutions have been ones which Australians have enjoyed for many generations, giving us the strongest of reasons for celebrating the contribution to this country's economic and social life of its early democratic pioneers.

## Types of Democratic Institutions

To describe Australia as a democracy tells us something about the groundrules of Australian political life and something about the broad parameters of the Australian political process. Among other things, it tells us that elections occur at quite frequent intervals, that there is more than one party to choose from, and that there is some genuine prospect that parties will alternate in office. However, because democracy can accommodate a wide range of institutional variation, that description tells us little about specifics. Those who attended the constitutional conventions of the 1890s saw themselves as democrats to a man (and, of course, they were all men), but that did not make for easy agreement on the shape of the institutions required for the new nation. They had to make choices on a whole range of contentious issues, including the extent to which the ministry should be responsible to parliament, the powers of the federal government *vis-à-vis* the states, the appropriate degree of popular sovereignty, and future relationships with the mother country. For their solutions, they drew on a wide variety of constitutional models, with detailed analysis of, and borrowings from, Canada, Germany, Switzerland and the United States and, of course, from British and earlier colonial constitutional practice (Irving, 1999: 62–78).

The resulting constitution has been variously interpreted. The traditional view was that Australian democracy was, in most significant respects, akin to British parliamentarianism, with only some minor aberrations stemming from the federal contract (see Crisp, 1949). The commonplace notion of Australian government as following the Westminster practice conforms to this usage (for a recent iteration, see Constitutional Centenary Foundation, 1993). For the most part, academic commentary has moved away from such a position. Elaine Thompson (1980) has argued that Washington was as great an influence as Westminster and that the result may be seen as a 'Washminster' mutation. More recently, Campbell Sharman (1990) has suggested that pre-existing colonial practice combined with the American influence to create a 'compound republic' in some respects analogous to American practice, in which the dispersal of powers has been the main defence of liberty and guarantor of responsive government. Brian Galligan's important contribution to the Reshaping Australian Institutions series (Galligan, 1995) argues a similar case, suggesting that, with the enactment of the new constitution, Australia effectively ceased to be a 'parliamentary monarchy' and became 'a federal republic'. These latter views offer a perspective in which the continuity of British forms is now the real aberration of Australian constitutional design.

With diverse origins and some continuing disagreement on the nature of the resulting mix, an initial task in determining the possible welfare implications of the institutional choices made by the fathers of Federation and their successors is to provide a characterization of Australian democratic institutions in a comparative context wider than that constituted by the other English-speaking democracies. We do this by moving away from the particularities of Australian institutions as viewed through the eyes of Australian political scientists, and locating Australia on a conceptual map of democracy developed in the work of the Dutch political scientist, Arend Lijphart (1984; 1999a). His analysis starts from a distinction between what he calls 'majoritarian' and 'consensus' models of democracy, arguing that 'the majoritarian model concentrates political power in the hands of a bare majority ... whereas the consensus model tries to share, disperse and limit power in a variety of ways' (Lijphart, 1999a: 2). The differences between the models can be seen as resulting from the different answers democratic political communities give to the question: for whom does the government govern? What all democrats have in common is a belief that government *for* the people is incompatible with government on behalf of a minority. They may legitimately disagree, however, on whether the aim of popular sovereignty is to represent the will of the majority or to find a basis for consensus among as large a proportion of the people as humanly possible. Lijphart argues that the political arrangements required to realize these distinct conceptions of democratic rule are quite different in kind.

The mapping exercise proceeds by identifying ten major differences in the institutional form or political practice of contemporary democracies, which, supposedly, follow directly from the distinction between majoritarian and consensus government. Five concern what Lijphart calls the 'executive-parties' dimension of government and five what he calls the 'federal-unitary' dimension (Lijphart, 1999a: 3–4). The executive-parties dimension relates to the capacity of majority governments to get their own way *vis-à-vis* opposing parties. Majority rule is favoured where executive power is concentrated in a single-party cabinet; where the executive dominates the legislature; where there is a two-party system; generally as a consequence of a non-proportional electoral system; and where pluralism is the dominant mode of interest representation. Consensus government tends to be associated with power-sharing by a multiparty coalition, with a balance of power between executive and legislature, with the multiplicity of parties that generally results from PR electoral systems and with the continuous compromise and negotiation that are the stuff of corporatism.

The federal-unitary dimension relates to the capacity of governments to get their own way *vis-à-vis* other independent political actors. In fully majoritarian systems, once the executive arm of government has decided on a course of action, there are no further impediments to that decision becoming law. In consensual systems, there are sometimes additional hurdles that must be overcome before decisions can be enacted. The most important of these hurdles, according to Lijphart, are constituted by federalism, strong bicameralism, requirements for extraordinary majorities to effect constitutional change, judicial review, and central bank independence. There are two ways in which we may think about the impact of such institutional arrangements. They may be seen as delimiting the sphere in which governments may assert a legitimate claim to rule on behalf of the majority. They may, alternatively, be regarded as elevating the threshold of consensus required to make decisions of particular kinds.

Lijphart's initial hypothesis is that, in any given nation, institutional choices will tend to cluster at roughly the same point on a scale from extreme majoritarianism to extreme consensuality. This turns out to be simplistic, with no apparent connection between choices in respect of the executives-parties dimension and the federal-unitary dimension. In consequence, Lijphart's conceptual map of democracy identifies four distinct types of contemporary democratic system (Lijphart, 1999a: Figure 14.1). Two are polar types, with institutions largely at the majoritarian end of the spectrum or largely at the consensual end. The traditional Westminster model, combining a strong executive with unitary and centralized government, as practised in the United Kingdom – and in New Zealand until the introduction of proportional representation in 1996 – constitutes the polar model of majoritarian government. Countries like Switzerland, Austria and Germany, in which coalition government combines with territorial and institutional decentralization, exemplify consensual government. The remaining types are mixed. On the one hand, there is a group of nations, including Israel and all the Scandinavian countries, in which consensual practice on the executives-parties dimension occurs within the context of substantially unitary institutions. On the other, there is a small group of nations, including both Canada and the United States, which combine majoritarianism on the executive-parties dimension with strong decentralization on the federal-unitary dimension.

There are no ambiguities about Australia's location on Lijphart's conceptual map of democracy. He also sees the Australian constitution as a hybrid, combining a majoritarian executive with federal institutions. This location helps to put Australian debates on the nature of our constitutional arrangements into a proper perspective. For all the strenuous discussion at the constitutional conventions of the 1890s on how to combine what was best in the British parliamentary tradition with a constitutional division of powers along US lines, our system of government ended up being far more like the latter than the former, and this is the truth captured by descriptions of Australia as a 'compound' or 'federal' republic. Thus, when Australians describe their systems of government as conforming to the Westminster model, their reference point is to the executive-parties dimension of government alone. Even then, Australian practice is no longer as majoritarian as it once was, and certainly not as majoritarian as that of the United Kingdom or New Zealand prior to the introduction of MMP. The reason is a partial shift away from majoritarian practice as a consequence of the adoption of PR in Senate elections and the gradual emergence of multipartism in that House (see Lijphart, 1999b). When Liberal or Labor majorities in the House of Representatives have to bargain with the Democrats to get their way in the Senate, they are practising a version of consensus politics.

## The Consequences of Democratic Institutions

Lijphart's analysis shows that Australian political institutions are majoritarian on the executive-parties dimension and consensual on the federal-unitary dimension. The question I now ask is whether there is evidence that institutional characteristics like these have direct consequences for citizen welfare. Lijphart argues strongly that they do and, whether or not his analysis is accepted in its entirety, this conclusion is supported by a large and growing body of findings in the field of comparative public policy (for recent discussions of this theme, see Castles, 1998: 78–85; Swank, 2002). Here, I simply summarize Lijphart's own account and query some of his conclusions on the basis of my own research in this area.

### *Majoritarian Impacts*

Lijphart (1999a) seeks to test a number of hypotheses concerning the relationship between democratic institutions and public policy outcomes. One is the argument, almost as venerable as the study of modern democratic government, that majority government has the decisive advantage of providing effective government. The argument rests on the proposition that single-party rule is the only way of avoiding the fudged policy decisions that result from the need to broker compromises within multi-party coalitions. A further hypothesis is that consensus government, just because it seeks to obtain super majorities, will be constrained to offer policies which appeal to as many of the people as possible rather than to just a bare majority. Lijphart interprets this hypothesis as implying that consensus systems are more likely to lead to what he calls 'compassionate' policy and a 'kinder, gentler' sort of democracy, or what would more normally and less normatively be described as policies of a more redistributive and small-l liberal type.

The effectiveness argument is assessed by examining the degree of association between the position of countries on a composite scale measuring their location on the executive-parties dimension and those countries' levels of macro-economic performance (see Lijphart, 1999a: Table 15.1). Indicators of macro-economic performance include economic growth, inflation, unemployment, strike activity and budget deficits. His findings are negative, but, nonetheless, important. Contrary to the claim that majority government leads to effective policy performance, both inflation and unemployment levels were noticeably higher where majoritarianism was most pronounced, although neither relationship quite matches up to the standard criterion of statistical significance. Relationships with the remaining indicators were negligible, with majority governments experiencing slightly higher levels of economic growth, but also exhibiting slight tendencies to greater strike activity and larger budget deficits. These findings are based on simple models of economic performance and require further, more elaborate, testing. They are important because they demonstrate that the supposed virtues of majority government in effectiveness terms are far from being as self-evident as is often supposed.

The indicators Lijphart uses to test the proposition that consensus government produces more compassionate policies include measures of the development of the welfare state, of environmental performance, of the harshness of the criminal justice system, and of the generosity of foreign aid programs (Lijphart, 1999a: Table 16.2). In every instance, the findings are as hypothesized. Welfare expenditure is higher, energy efficiency is greater, capital punishment is less often utilized, and foreign aid programs are more generous in countries located towards the consensus end of the executives-party scale. Moreover, these relationships – although, for the most part, only modelled in simple bivariate terms – are all moderately to strongly statistically significant. Thus, the overall story, as Lijphart tells it, is not of a trade-off between policy effectiveness and what he calls kinder, gentler policies. Rather, it is of a world in which there is no evidence that majority government outperforms consensus government in effectiveness and much evidence that it underperforms in serving the needs of the wider community. Majoritarianism stands condemned by the policies it produces or, rather, by its institutionally conditioned proclivity to put the needs of the majority before the needs of the population as a whole.

Many Australians will wish to question how far this conclusion really applies in the Australian case. Indeed, I will later argue that such conclusions probably require some modification in light of the unusual character of labour market institutions in this country. However, looking only at the standard indicators of the extent and success of governmental performance that Lijphart offers, it does appear that his analysis has some bearing on contemporary Australian realities. Figures on post-war economic performance show that, until quite recently, Australia's rate of per capita economic growth has been well below the mean for countries of the Organization for Economic Co-operation and Development; and that our inflation rate has been marginally below, and our unemployment rate marginally above, the OECD mean (Castles, 1999: Table 3). Although Australia has generally performed rather better than the majority of OECD nations in terms of fiscal rectitude (OECD, 1998a), days lost in industrial disputes have exceeded the OECD mean. Overall, our economic performance record hardly makes good advertising copy for the policy effectiveness of majoritarian government.

On the other side of the equation, the OECD social expenditure database shows Australia lagging in many categories of welfare spending and close to the bottom of the distribution in terms of overall spending as a percentage of GDP (OECD, 1998b). In total public expenditure terms, only Japan, Switzerland and the United States spend less than Australia. Data from the World Bank (1999) also show that Australia is one of the worst performers among the advanced democratic countries in terms of energy efficiency. Figures from the same source indicate that Australian official spending on overseas development aid as a percentage of GDP was slightly below the advanced country norm. Australia's record on capital punishment is mixed. Queensland, in 1913, was a pioneer of the abolitionist cause, while Victoria, in the mid-1970s, was rather behind the majority of Western nations in renouncing use of the death penalty.

Only the briefest consideration is possible of the mechanisms underlying the relationships uncovered by Lijphart's findings. Almost certainly, the reason that majority government provides no clear effectiveness bonus is that the advantages it confers in terms of ease of decision-making tend to be offset by the propensity to arrive at decisions prematurely and without adequate consideration of their wider impact on the population as a whole. Lijphart does not provide a detailed discussion of the mechanisms by which consensus government leads to more compassionate policy outcomes beyond his argument that such institutions are conducive to a wider consideration of popular needs. There are, however, reasons to believe that the mechanisms may be rather more complex than he implies.

Research on the determinants of welfare spending and public expenditure more generally suggests that a crucial factor is the ideology of the party in office. My own work in this area (Castles, 1978; 1982) has been on the impact of parties of the right. It shows that such parties are best placed to contain the growth of public expenditure, where majoritarian electoral institutions serve as a deterrent to party fragmentation. Only where a party of the right can win a majority of parliamentary seats – and, in plurality systems, that may require far less than a majority of votes – can it hold the line against the advance of the welfare state. Research findings in other areas points to similar conclusions in respect of gender equality (Norris, 1987), overseas aid expenditure (Imbeau, 1988) and public spending on education (Castles, 1989). These findings suggest that the relationship between majoritarianism and compassionate government may be contingent on the way in which institutional arrangements enable particular bodies of opinion to surmount the critical thresholds required to influence the direction of public policy. It is political actors who make policy choices, but it is institutions that, in large part, determine which actors are in a position to make them.

*Federal Impacts*

Having demonstrated the importance of differences on the executives-parties dimension for both the quality and compassion of democracy, Lijphart repeats the analysis for the federal-unitary dimension. His findings here are much less spectacular and arguably, rather less convincing. Countries in which central government is hedged around with constitutional limitations appear to differ little from more unitary states in respect of the quality of democratic participation or in respect of kinder, gentler policy outcomes. His only statistically significant result relates to an aspect of the effectiveness of economic performance, with a strong and inverse relationship with inflation pointing to the greater monetary stability of nations with strong institutional safeguards against unfettered central authority. Lijphart does not regard this latter finding as particularly surprising, given that central bank independence is a key component of the federal-unitary dimension, and that this factor has been shown in many studies to be associated with favourable monetary policy outcomes (see Alesina, 1989; Grilli et al., 1991; De Long and Summers, 1992).

My own recent research in this area (Castles, 1999) suggests that it is not just monetary policy outcomes, but also economic growth, which seem to benefit from decentralized institutions. This research differs from Lijphart's in two significant respects. First, rather than being concerned exclusively with political institutions, I focus on the degree to which the tax collection system is decentralized. Second, rather than relying on simple models, I seek to incorporate measures of tax decentralization into fully elaborated econometric models accounting for a large degree of the cross-national variation in economic performance. Interestingly, my findings suggest that, once one takes account of the impact of tax decentralization on inflation, there is no evidence of an additional bank independence effect. A possible mechanism accounting for the link between tax decentralization and lower rates of inflation is suggested by Scharpf (1991), who argues that, where the proportion of taxation accruing to the central government is restricted by federal arrangements, it has proved far more difficult than in unitary nations to employ Keynesian demand-management techniques as a means of temporary stimulus. Since such techniques are seen by many economists as a potent source of inflation, it can be argued that federal arrangements have an in-built bias against inflation. A more generalised, but complementary, explanation, accounting for both the economic growth and inflation findings, is provided by theorists who suggest that economic efficiency will be enhanced under circumstances where political decentralization limits the 'fiscal appetites' of the state (Brennan and Buchanan, 1980: 181).

The fact that Lijphart only tests for simple relationships, together, perhaps, with a reluctance to entertain the idea that not all aspects of consensus government may be so favourable to compassionate policy outcomes, probably explains why he fails to comment on what the literature suggests is the single most significant impact of federalism: its effect in reducing spending on the welfare state. This finding is common to work in many research traditions, with federalism shown as moderating the effects of population ageing (Wilensky, 1975) and economic openness (Cameron, 1978) in accounting for the growth of social spending and as reinforcing the impact of the right (Castles and McKinlay, 1979) in retarding such growth. A recent study employing an index of constitutional veto points closely analogous to Lijphart's federalism-unitary scale suggests that the combined effect of institutional arrangements such as federalism, presidentialism, bicameralism, referendum procedures and single-member constituencies is strongly and negatively associated with spending on social security transfers, total spending on welfare and government revenue as a percentage of GDP (Huber et al. 1993). Research by Schmidt (1996: 175), using an alternative index of what he calls 'institutional constraints on central state government', produces similar findings, showing that, in addition to a negative relationship with the growth of big government, limitations on central state autonomy are also negatively associated with gender equality and expenditure on labour market programs.

The mechanisms that translate institutional constraints on central government into a lesser propensity for public spending follow more or less directly from differences in the rules by which federal and unitary politics are conducted. A major obstacle to new spending departures in federal systems is provisions for a particular division of powers between federal and state governments and the requirement of extraordinary majorities to alter those provisions. Obviously, there is nothing accidental about this: the founding fathers who built such stipulations into constitutional documents did so precisely because they wished to create institutions that were resistant to change in certain key respects. Another obstacle to spending initiatives in federal systems is the proliferation of political levers available to those who seek to frustrate the growth of the state. Federalism aids those who oppose the aggrandizement of central power, because it offers them so many institutional platforms – strong upper houses, state parliaments, processes of judicial review and referendum campaigns – from which to conduct their battles to preserve the status quo. In recent years, theorists of the 'new institutionalism' and public choice schools have generalized this argument as a proposition that institutional arrangements which proliferate the number of veto points or veto players in a political system serve to reduce its capacity for change (Tsebilis, 1995). Against this view, it is sometimes argued that the diversity of federal jurisdictions allows for social and other kinds of experimentation to occur in individual states prior to adoption more generally and at the federal level. This may well be so, but it is by no means clear that such a process of diffusion leads to more speedy adoption of reforms than occurs under unitary government, and it is certain that the possibility of individual states opting out from reform initiatives always leaves open the possibility of patchier, less universal adoption – a fatal flaw, when the object of the reform is to enhance supposedly equal rights of citizenship.

This body of evidence that federal institutions are inimical to policy departures that enhance the reach of the state has direct implications for our understanding of the welfare consequences flowing from Australia's hybrid constitution. We saw earlier that democratic institutions conferred major advantages both in terms of popular liberties and gains in material well-being. Democracy itself enhances the 'quality' of political participation and produces a gentler, kinder sort of political system. But, within the democratic context on which they were agreed, the Fathers of Federation opted for institutional arrangements of a particular type: ones that were majoritarian on the executives-parties dimension and federal on the federal-unitary dimension. If the analysis offered here is correct, both were choices that markedly reduced the prospects of the state being widely used to secure policy objectives of a compassionate nature. Clearly, this fits with the Australian experience of weak welfare state development and low public expenditure levels compared to most other Western nations. On the other hand, it also leaves us with a puzzle. Australian expenditures on the welfare state have never been large, but from the time of Federation through to the 1960s, Australian government was seen by a variety of outside observers and by many Australians as both activist and egalitarian in its objectives. It is to the institutional arrangements underlying this paradox of the pursuit of compassionate goals by ostensibly non-statist means that I now turn.

## Focusing on Australian Exceptionalism

I began this discussion by suggesting that the two basic institutional settings Australia had in common with other advanced nations were that political decision-making occurs within a democratic framework and that the economy is run along capitalist lines. In analysing the character of Australian democracy, I have attempted to show that the particular institutions that the fathers of Federation chose to implement their democratic intent have had a major influence on the outcomes of Australian democracy. My intention here is to demonstrate that the institutional rules that Australians developed early in the twentieth century to regulate the distributive conflicts and consequences of the capitalist form of production have similarly modified the character of Australian economic and social life.

Despite notions of uninhibited competition intrinsic to the design of capitalist economic institutions, there is nothing unusual about the emergence of institutional rules constraining the conduct of economic actors. Institutions are required to guarantee property rights and they are needed to prevent struggles over the distribution of rewards destroying the economic and social fabric. No capitalist economy can be allowed to function in a wholly unfettered manner, since, despite the system's undoubted potential for societal wealth maximization, consequences for substantial sections of the populace will often be adverse and, on occasions, quite disastrous (see Polanyi, 1944). Thus, over the course of the century, all advanced nations have developed sets of institutions which have sought to moderate the consequences of economic competition by regulating the permissible behaviour of capital and labour and by modifying the distribution of rewards deriving from the operation of the economic system (Richardson, 1999a). The claim for Australian or, rather, Australasian, exceptionalism – for, in this respect, Australian and New Zealand developments were quite similar – is that, in Australia, this process of institutional development took a quite different form from that of most other democratic nations.

It follows from our earlier analysis that, if Australian institutions in these vital areas of the functioning of the economy are different, so, too, will be outcomes for the wider society of which that economy is a part. Indeed, my argument is that the Australian paradox of state activism without state expenditure can only properly be addressed through an understanding of the unusual development of Australian economic institutions in the early years of the century that made the living standards of ordinary Australians a function of the systems of industry protection and wage regulation rather than of the generosity of state spending programs. I will also argue that, despite important dissimilarities in the direct role of the state in social provision, these institutions produced a system of social amelioration in Australia, which, for much of the century, was not obviously inferior to that of other advanced, capitalist democracies. I conclude this essay by suggesting that this now may be changing. The economic rationalist (or neo-liberal) agenda of Labor and Coalition governments in the 1980s and 1990s can be seen as an attempt to reshape those institutions which historically made the functioning of the Australian economy different from that of other nations. It is, at least, arguable that these changes leave Australians less well protected than they once were from some of the more unfortunate consequences of capitalist economic institutions.

## Regulating Capitalist Distribution

The minimum extent of intervention in the distributive mechanism of capitalism in advanced democratic societies has been the enactment of rules to govern the conduct of industrial disputes and the use of tax and transfer systems to provide the means of livelihood to those without access to income from employment. Bargaining rules are required both to provide some degree of security in the ownership of capital and to reduce the obvious potential for the exploitation of workers. Rules differ from country to country and are subject to change over time, but, in democratic nations, are likely to encapsulate some reasonably stable accommodation between the perceived rights of employers and employees. It is also difficult to imagine how the government of an affluent democracy could allow large sections of the population to starve on the streets. The use of government taxation or systems of social insurance to provide minimum payments in cash or in kind to those without any incomes is consequently universal in such societies. Old age, sickness and large families are the categories of need most widely accepted as qualifying for state assistance. Unemployment and inadequate wages are sources of need which are often more controversial, because of doubts that the resulting lack of income is wholly involuntary.

In some countries, regulation of the distributive side of the economy has gone well beyond this minimum. In Western Europe, in particular, relationships between capital, labour and the state have been comprehensively institutionalised through a set of arrangements often described as being 'corporatist' in nature (see Schmitter, 1974; Lehmbruch, 1977; Crouch, 1985). Institutionalization originally emerged through efforts at self-regulation by the major parties to industrial disputes: the peak organizations of business and trade unions. In the 1960s and 1970s, corporatist arrangements became more encompassing, bringing to the bargaining table a wider range of issues including wage differentials, working conditions, acceptable rates of profit and strategies of economic restructuring, as well as most legislative proposals relating to economic and social policy matters. The existence of such arrangements presumes that the parties to corporatist agreements are in some sense 'social partners', who, in a manner analogous to the assumptions inherent in the consensus model of democracy, have legitimate expectations that eventual outcomes will, in some considerable measure, incorporate the interests of their constituents.

The state's role as a provider not only of income, but also of services, has also been hugely extended. Since the early 1980s, it has become commonplace for Western European nations to spend 50 per cent or more of their GDP for public purposes. In such countries, the state provides not only minimum assistance to the poor, but also actively seeks to reduce social inequality. An important part of this strategy for equality has been to remove certain socially valued items of consumption, such as health care and education, from the influence of market forces. This extended role of the state has often been closely co-ordinated with developments in the sphere of economic management, with increases in the 'social wage' frequently serving as a legislative offset to concessions by the labour market players in the corporatist bargaining process.

The linkage between corporatist bargaining and the massive extension of the welfare state is a largely European phenomenon, which occurred as an institutionalized response to the distributional conflicts of the capitalist economy in the decades following the Great Depression and World War II (Katzenstein, 1985). What made the Australian response different was that it occurred much earlier and under quite different circumstances (see Castles, 1988). The New Protection emerged in the first years of the twentieth century, with much of the impetus deriving from the intense distributional struggles of the 1890s. The economies of the new nations of the Antipodes differed from those of Europe in being based on efficient agricultural production rather than on manufacturing. They also paid considerably higher wages, both in consequence of high levels of agricultural productivity and because of the relative scarcity of labour in the colonies. Political structures and the role of the state were also quite different. From the 1860s onwards, representative and responsible government based on manhood suffrage was the Australasian norm, while the state had a widely acknowledged legitimacy as the primary agent of national economic development. In much of Europe, democratic forces were only just beginning to challenge the prerogatives of oligarchic rule, while the economic role of the state was hedged around by beliefs in the sanctity of property or by the doctrine of laissez-faire.

In Australia and New Zealand, democracy and the strong bargaining power of labour conspired with state activism in the cause of national development to seek a way of tackling the distributional problems of capitalism considerably earlier than in Europe. Moreover, contrary to the later European experience, where the key issue was one of collaboration between 'social partners' in the labour market to promote efficient manufacturing in a competitive world market, the issue in Australia and New Zealand was one of transferring the surplus from the hugely profitable primary sector to the urban centres of a nascent manufacturing industry. The mechanisms chosen in both countries were industry protection and compulsory conciliation and arbitration of industrial disputes. The former channelled economic resources from the primary sector to support economic development in the towns, while the latter used the power of the state, in the form of courts of arbitration with compulsory powers of wage determination, to ensure that this flow of benefits went not only to urban employers, but also to their employees. Wage determination by the courts was a regulatory rather than a direct mode of state intervention. However, similarly to welfare state programs today, it was seen by its protagonists as a mechanism for making capitalism work more fairly. Alfred Deakin, not only a father of Federation but also the chief architect of the institutional settlement in the economic sphere, saw the 'old' protection provided by border tariffs alone as creating only a potential for fair wages. 'The "new" Protection', he argued, 'seeks to make them actual ... Having put the manufacturer into a position to pay good wages, it goes on to assure the public that he does pay them' (cited in Hancock, 1930: 64).

## Welfare Australian-Style

If the architect of the New Protection was Deakin, its presiding genius was Mr Justice Higgins, President of the Australian Commonwealth Court of Conciliation and Arbitration from 1907 to 1920. The connecting link between institutions originally designed to create industrial peace and the subsequent development of the welfare state in Australia was the use of an ostensibly social policy criterion for determining minimum wage levels. In his Harvester Judgement of 1907, Higgins argued that a 'fair and reasonable' wage for an unskilled labourer was to be one 'based on the normal needs of the average employee, regarded as a human being living in a civilised community' (Higgins, 1922: 3). Normal needs and actual costs were calculated from family budgets, on the assumption that the standard male wage should be sufficient to support a man, his wife and up to three children. Apart from necessities, the wage should also provide for such items as life insurance, friendly society benefits, travel to and from work, union fees, amusements and holidays, liquors and tobacco and saving. On this basis, a so-called 'basic' or 'living' wage was set at 7 shillings a day or 42 shillings a week. Other wage rates were determined by adding margins for skill to the basic wage, and, over time, the court established the custom of adjusting the basic component in relation to the changes in the cost of living. There have to be real doubts about whether the original 'basic' wage was really established according to social policy criteria or whether it really represented a rationalization of current labour market realities. However, what really mattered was the argument, which, in retrospect, served as the founding myth of the institution. Between 1922 and 1953, such adjustments became automatic and the 'living' wage became a symbol of what was properly due to the Australian workingman.

Over a period of many decades, the practice or myth of the 'living' wage deeply influenced the development of social policy in Australia, helping to shape what I have elsewhere called 'a wage-earners' welfare state' (Castles, 1985; 1994). The wage-earner focus was, of course, inherent in the institutional mechanism for delivering the means of fulfilling social needs. The 'living' wage promised men who had work that they and their families could, under most circumstances, maintain a decent life, one that conformed to the standards of the 'civilized community' in which they lived. Moreover, the principle that the employer was responsible for providing for the needs of his workers via the wage contract could be extended in a variety of ways. In the Engineers Case of 1920, Higgins accepted the proposition that, for workers receiving weekly wages, it was the employer's duty to provide for a number of paid sick days in any given year. Overseas commentators on the deficiencies of Australia's welfare state have been known to decry the very low level of expenditures on social security sickness benefits in this country (see Kangas, 1991), without noticing that all contracts of employment in Australia either provide for paid sick leave or provide a special loading where this right does not exist (Castles, 1992). In fact, the Engineers Case made Australia a pioneer in the area of compulsory sickness benefits rather than a laggard as is commonly supposed.

Institutional rules exclude as well as include. As we shall see, there are reasons for supposing that, for much of this century, the wage-earners' welfare state contributed to economic and social equality in Australia. However, for those outside the magic circle of wage-earners and their dependants, the picture was far less rosy. Because social expenditure programs have always been doubly residual – residual in being focused on the needs of the less well off and residual in being ancillary to the wages system — the Australian welfare state has ended up with a stronger emphasis on means testing than in any other Western nation. The historical presumption has been that income from employment produces the necessary means, and only when it fails is there a case for the state to step in with help. Where the reason why no employment income is available has been socially legitimated, as in the case of old age and disability, there has been no stigma in accepting the state assistance. Where the moral hazard is seemingly greater — where unemployment is seen to be in some sense voluntary or single parenthood is seen as a preferred option — the level of stigma has been greater. However, irrespective of stigma, the level of state assistance has always been relatively low, leaving welfare recipients considerably less well off than even those at the bottom of the wages pyramid.

There are two requirements for a system of the type we have briefly described to impact favourably on economic and social equality. The first requirement is that the protection afforded by the wage minimum extends to most members of the society. From Higgins' time through to the early 1970s, this was true in most respects. Virtually all able-bodied men between the ages of 15 and 64 were in the labour force and the vast majority of those in employment were covered by the awards system. In 1960, the male participation rate was just over 97 per cent; in the mid-1970s, it was still just over 90 per cent. Most women worked until marriage and then left the labour force to become dependent on male wage-earners. The proportion of the population above the age of 65 was extremely low at the turn of the century, when the first pensions legislation was enacted, and remained below 10 per cent throughout the 1960s and 1970s. Before the divorce law reform of the mid-1970s, the divorce rate was less than one per thousand of the population. With most marriages remaining intact, the presumption that women and children would be dependants of male breadwinners was a strong one. This left unemployment as the biggest chink in the armour of the wage-earners' welfare state, and from Higgins' time until the beginning of World War II, it was a big enough chink to call into question any claim that the wages system had created a sufficient basis for real economic equality. However, after the war, that changed. From 1945 onwards, there was an era of almost three decades in which the rate of unemployment scarcely ever exceeded 3 per cent and more generally remained in a band of 1–2 per cent of the working population. If ever there was a period in which a strategy of social amelioration built around the idea of lifting the bottom of the wages pyramid was likely to be a success, this was it.

The second requirement for such a system to work is that it is possible for the edicts of the courts to influence the overall distribution of incomes. This is a subject on which economists disagree, with the obvious supposition that increases in minimum wages will lead to a reduced dispersion of incomes sometimes contested on the grounds that market forces are likely to produce essentially similar outcomes (see Hughes, 1973). An early piece of evidence on the potential of the arbitration system to make a real difference was the fact that the Harvester minimum wage was some 27 per cent higher than prevailing unskilled rates at the time (Plowman, 1989: 29). In more recent times, a host of econometric studies have sought to compare the Australian dispersion of incomes with those in other advanced countries. A recent summary of these studies argues strongly that the bulk of the evidence points to a greater degree of wage compression in Australia than in other English-speaking nations (Borland and Woodbridge, 1999).

An important reason accounting for these differences is the impact of arbitration tribunal rulings in bringing about a progressive diminution of differentials between male and female earnings over the last three decades. Indeed, there is no simpler measure of the impact of Australia's regulative structure than the changing trajectory of women's wages. For more than six decades, the arbitration court's view that the remuneration of women should reflect their supposed dependence on male bread-winners produced rulings that kept women's pay rates well below those of men. Once the dependency assumption was abandoned, and the court decided that the appropriate rule was 'equal pay for equal work', women's pay rates jumped very markedly and wage differentials between men and women are now among the lowest in the Western world.

As the example of women's wages demonstrates, the institutional regulation of economic distribution can influence not only the overall level of inequality in a society, but also its incidence. In the 1960s, a popular commentator could describe Australia as 'a lucky country' in which 'not only are very rich and very poor people rare; the average income is not just a simple average; it is also close to the typical income' (Horne, 1964: 21). The findings of social research were less sanguine, discovering surprisingly high levels of poverty in supposedly egalitarian Australia. But the report on the condition of the Melbourne poor in 1966, which brought these findings to the attention of the nation, also noted 'the low incidence of poverty among families with non-aged male heads' and argued that this was a consequence of 'the fact that almost all adult males are able to secure employment incomes that are sufficient to keep their families out of poverty' (Henderson et al. 1970: 37). Evidence from an Australia-wide survey in 1973 suggested that Australian poverty levels were lower than those in Canada, the United Kingdom and the United States. The reason was 'that the high level and comprehensive coverage of minimum wage legislation in Australia as compared with either the United States or United Kingdom meant that Australia had a much smaller group of "working poor" ' (Henderson, 1978: 169). Whether or not the overall outcomes of welfare Australian-style were better or worse than in other nations, differences in strategies of social intervention and differences in the institutional arrangement designed to realize those strategies clearly produced quite different profiles of social disadvantage.

### The End of Equality?

My purpose has been to demonstrate that the rules that societies devise to regulate the conduct of their political and economic life have important implications for the well-being and welfare of those who live in those societies. Although seeking to highlight the importance of institutions in an Australian context, my approach throughout has been comparative. I have tried to show that, where Australia adopted institutions similar to those of other nations, it manifested outcomes similar to those nations; and that, where it opted for institutions similar to those in one group of countries, but different from those in another, it ended up with outcomes similar to those of the countries with which it had institutional similarities. Finally, in discussing the institutions Australia used to regulate the distributive mechanisms of its economy, I have argued that, where Australia opted for rules quite different from those of other nations, its patterns of outcomes were no less dissimilar.

I now conclude by providing an illustration of a point so far neglected. Because I have sought to underline the extent to which institutions shape our lives, I have paid no explicit attention to the manner in which we can reshape our institutions. But the traffic between institutions and political actors is anything but one-way. Institutions mould the conduct of political actors, but political actors often seek to modify institutions. Institutional choice does not stop dead at defining moments and historical settlements and, even before sufficient time has passed to make the retrospective judgement that the imposition of a given set of rules has constituted such a settlement, there are often individuals and groups seeking to undo it. They do so precisely because institutions usually have known consequences, meaning that, for those opposing such outcomes, the only option is to undermine rules predisposing to unwanted outcomes. We have noted the empirical evidence that suggests that federalism leads to small government and should not, therefore, be surprised that, for much of its history, the Australian Labor Party has been opposed to the federal division of powers (Galligan, 1995: 91–109). Similarly, given the declared redistributive aims of those favouring compulsory wage-setting by courts or tribunals of arbitration, the major campaigns mounted by business in the immediate aftermath of the Harvester

Judgement to overturn the legal basis for the New Protection are wholly comprehensible.

However long institutions last, they always remain vulnerable to the changing perceptions of those who function within their aegis. My illustration of the ever-present possibility of institutional reshaping spans almost a century of opposition to the consequences stemming from Australia's unique system of industrial regulation. Early attempts to strike down the enactments constituting the New Protection did, indeed, have a measure of success, but, as we have seen, they failed in their key objective of preventing compulsory arbitration from becoming the primary mechanism for regulating the distributive outcomes of Australian capitalism. Ultimately, that was because the institutional regulation of the less pleasant face of capitalism – whether through the wages system or via state intervention through the tax/transfer system – was a part of an historic shift towards egalitarian values brought about by the twentieth-century victory of democratic ideas. In more recent years, however, as the economic performance of the advanced democracies has declined, the linkages between democracy, equality and the efficient functioning of the economy have been subject to an increasing scrutiny. The credo of twentieth-century egalitarianism was premised on the question 'what price the efficiency of the economic system, if it cannot deliver reasonably egalitarian outcomes?' In the rhetoric of the economic rationalist school of thought that has dominated political debate since the early 1980s, that question has been turned on its head. Now the guiding question for those who are most active in reshaping our institutions is 'what price equality, if it cannot deliver reasonably efficient outcomes?'

All over the Western world, the answers to this latter question have given rise to serious criticism of long-established institutional mechanisms for controlling the distributive excesses of competitive capitalism. In Australia, this criticism was primarily directed at the functioning of the arbitration system. It came not only from the right – business groups, the H. R. Nicholls Society (named after one of Higgins' most prominent opponents) and the Liberal Party – but also from the Labor government of the early 1990s in 'Accord' with the organized labour movement. What united this disparate body of opinion was the view that Australia's centralized system of labour regulation reduced flexibility: in the eyes of the right, the flexibility to respond to the changing realities of a globalized economy by paying workers strictly according to their contribution to total productivity and, in the eyes of the trade unions, the flexibility to permit enterprises to pay wages in excess of award determinations. Labor's response was to begin a process of labour market decentralization that made the awards system, first and foremost, a safety-net device for protecting the low-paid, but which provided considerably greater leeway for stronger unions to negotiate productivity increases at the enterprise level. The industrial reforms of the post-1996 Liberal governments have continued the process of deregulation, further restricting the powers of federal arbitration tribunals, limiting the role of trade unions as bargaining agents and further shifting the locus of bargaining to the enterprise level (Hancock, 1999). In its heyday, the awards system protected around 80 per cent of Australian workers; that figure has now been reduced to around 50 per cent (Richardson, 1999a).

If, as we have argued here, institutions are a major factor determining the character of policy outcomes, it follows that institutional reshaping is likely to change the character of those outcomes. In our account of Australia's unique system for regulating the distributive consequences of a capitalist economy, we have sought to demonstrate that the existence of a system of compulsory arbitration, by compressing wage differentials, has served to reduce the extent of Australian income inequality and has been among the factors creating a welfare state rather unlike that of other Western democracies. An immediate implication of the reshaping of Australian labour market institutions that has occurred in recent years is that Australian wage differentials are now likely to increase quite markedly. The crucial questions, then, are how such a development will affect the structure of inequality in Australia and what will be the likely effects on Australia's existing system of welfare benefits.

One possibility – but a remote one in the present climate of opinion – is that the removal of social protection through the labour market will stimulate pressures to redesign Australian welfare institutions along more European (that is, consensual) lines. More probable scenarios are less optimistic from an egalitarian viewpoint. A real possibility is that the need to reduce the flight from low-paid work will actually create pressures for a reduction in the replacement rate of benefits going to the working age population (see Gregory et al., 1999). A further possibility, and one which fits nicely with the recent push to reframe the welfare system around the notions of 'mutual' or 'reciprocal' obligation, is that the compulsion to accept low-wage jobs will markedly increase (see Castles, 2001). Whatever happens, the effects of nearly two decades of reform of Australian labour market institutions look set to impact on citizens' welfare in dramatic ways for a long time to come.

## References

Aitkin, D., and Castles, F. G. 'Democracy Untrammelled: The Australian political experience since federation', in K. Hancock (ed.), *Australian Society* (Cambridge: Cambridge University Press, 1989) pp. 208–27.

Alesina, A. 'Politics and Business Cycles in Industrial Democracies', *Economic Policy*, vol. 8 (1989) pp. 55–98.

Borland, J., and Woodbridge, G. 'Wage Regulation, Low-wage Workers and Employment', in S. Richardson (ed.), *Reshaping the Labour Market: Regulation, Efficiency and Equality in Australia* (Cambridge: Cambridge University Press, 1999) pp. 86–121.

Brennan, G., and Buchanan, J. M. *The Power to Tax: Analytical Foundations of a Fiscal Constitution* (Cambridge: Cambridge University Press, 1980).

Brittan, S. *The Economic Consequences of Democracy* (London: Temple Smith, 1977).

Cameron, D. 'The Expansion of the Public Economy: A Comparative Analysis', *American Political Science Review*, vol. 72(4) (1978) pp. 1243–61.

Castles, F. G. *The Social Democratic Image of Society* (London: Routledge and Kegan Paul, 1978).

——. 'The Impact of Parties on Public Expenditure', in F. G. Castles (ed.), *The Impact of Parties* (London: Sage Publications, 1982) pp. 21–96.

——. *The Working Class and Welfare* (Sydney: Allen & Unwin, 1985).

——. *Australian Public Policy and Economic Vulnerability* (Sydney: Allen & Unwin, 1988).

——. 'Explaining Public Education Expenditure in OECD Nations', *European Journal of Political Research*, vol. 17 (1989) pp. 431–48.

——. 'On Sickness Days and Social Policy', *Australian and New Zealand Journal of Sociology*, vol. 28(1) (1992) pp. 29–44.

——. 'The Wage Earners' Welfare State Revisited: Refurbishing the Established Model of Australian Social Protection, 1983–1993', *Australian Journal of Social Issues*, vol. 29(2) (1994) pp. 120–45.

——. *Comparative Public Policy* (Cheltenham: Edward Elgar, 1998).

——. 'Decentralization and the Post-War Political Economy', *European Journal of Political Research*, vol. 36 (1999) pp. 27–53.

——. 'A Farewell to Australia's Welfare State', *International Journal of Health Services*, vol. 31(3) (2001) pp. 537–44.

Castles, F. G., and McKinlay, R. 'Does Politics Matter?: An Analysis of the Public Welfare Commitment in Advanced Democratic States', *European Journal of Political Research*, vol. 7 (1979) pp. 169–86.

Constitutional Centenary Foundation. 'Representing the Republic: The Role of Parliament in Australian Democracy', Discussion Paper, Melbourne (1993).

Crisp, L. F. *The Parliamentary Government of the Commonwealth of Australia* (London: Longman Green, 1949).

Crouch, C. 'Conditions for Trade Union Restraint', in L. N. Lindberg and C. S. Maier (eds), *The Politics of Inflation and Economic Stagnation* (Washington, DC: Brookings Institution, 1985) pp. 105–39.

De Long, J. B., and Summers, L. 'Macroeconomic Policy and Long Run Growth', *Federal Reserve Bank of Kansas City Economic Review*, fourth quarter (1992).

Drèze, J., and Sen, A. *Hunger and Public Action* (Oxford: Oxford University Press, 1989).

Galligan, B. *A Federal Republic* (Cambridge: Cambridge University Press, 1995).

Gregory, B., Klug, E., and Martin, Y. M. 'Labour Market Deregulation, Relative Wages and the Social Security System', in S. Richardson (ed.), *Reshaping the Labour Market: Regulation, Efficiency and Equality in Australia* (Cambridge: Cambridge University Press, 1999) pp. 200–22.

Grilli, V., Masciandaro, D., and Tabellini, G. 'Political and Monetary Institutions and Public Financial Policies in the Industrial Countries', *Economic Policy*, vol. 13 (1991) pp. 341–92.

Hancock, K. 'Labour Market Deregulation in Australia', in S. Richardson (ed.), *Reshaping the Labour Market: Regulation, Efficiency and Equality in Australia* (Cambridge: Cambridge University Press, 1999) pp. 38–85.

Hancock, W. K. *Australia* (London: Ernest Benn, 1930).

Henderson, R. F. 'Social Welfare Expenditure', in R. B. Scotton and H. Ferber, *Public Expenditures and Social Policy in Australia. Volume I: The Whitlam Years 1972–75* (Melbourne: Longman Cheshire, 1978) pp. 160–78.

Henderson, R. F., Harcourt, A., and Harper, R. J. A. *People in Poverty: A Melbourne Survey* (University of Melbourne: Institute of Applied Economic and Social Research, 1970).

Higgins, H. B. *A New Province for Law and Order* (London: Constable and Company, 1922).

Horne, D. *The Lucky Country: Australia in the Sixties* (Ringwood, Vic.: Penguin Books, 1964).

Huber, E., Ragin, C., and Stephens, J. D. 'Social Democracy, Christian Democracy, Constitutional Structure and the Welfare State', *American Journal of Sociology*, vol. 99(3) (1993) pp. 711–49.

Hughes, B. 'The Wages of the Strong and the Weak', in B. J. Chapman, J. E. Isaac and J. R. Niland (eds), *Australian Labour Economics: Readings* (Melbourne: Macmillan, [1973] 1984) pp. 144–67.

Huntington, S. P. *Political Order in Changing Societies* (New Haven: Yale University Press, 1968).

Imbeau, L. 'Aid and Ideology', *European Journal of Political Research*, vol. 16(1) (1988) pp. 3–28.

Irving, H. *To Constitute a Nation: A Cultural History of Australia's Constitution* (Cambridge: Cambridge University Press, 1999).

Kangas, O. *The Politics of Social Rights* (Stockholm: Swedish Institute for Social Research, 1991).

Katzenstein, P. *Small States in World Markets* (Ithaca: Cornell University Press, 1985).

King, A. 'Overload: Problems of Governing in the 1970s', *Political Studies*, vol. 23(2–3) (1975) pp. 283–96.

Lehmbruch, G. 'Liberal Corporatism and Party Government', *Comparative Political Studies*, vol. 10(1) (1977) pp. 91–126.

Lijphart, A. *Democracies: Patterns of Majoritarian and Consensus Government in Twenty-One Countries* (New Haven: Yale University Press, 1984).

——. *Patterns of Democracy: Government Forms and Performance in Thirty-Six Countries* (New Haven: Yale University Press, 1999a).

——. 'Australian Democracy. Modifying Majoritarianism?', *Australian Journal of Political Science*, vol. 34(3) (1999b) pp. 313–26.

Lipset, S. M. 'Some Social Requisites of Democracy', *American Political Science Review*, vol. 53(1) (1959) pp. 69–105.

Norris, P. *Politics and Sexual Equality* (Boulder, Co: Rienner, 1987).

North, D. *Institutions, Institutional Change and Economic Performance* (Cambridge: Cambridge University Press, 1990).

OECD. *Economic Outlook* (Paris, 1998a).

——. *Social Expenditure Data Base* (SOCX), CD-ROM (Paris, 1998b).

Olson, M. Jnr. *The Rise and Decline of Nations* (New Haven: Yale University Press, 1982).

Plowman, D. H. *Holding the Line: Compulsory Arbitration and National Employer Co-ordination in Australia* (Cambridge: Cambridge University Press, 1989).

Polanyi, K. *The Great Transformation* (New York: Rinehart and Company, 1944).

Przeworski, A., Alvarez, M., Cheibub, J. A., and Limongi, F. *Democracy and Development: Political Institutions and Material Well-Being in the World, 1950–1990* (Cambridge: Cambridge University Press, 2000).

Richardson, S. 'Regulation of the Labour Market', in S. Richardson (ed.), *Reshaping the Labour Market: Regulation, Efficiency and Equality in Australia* (Cambridge: Cambridge University Press, 1999a) pp. 1–37.

—— (ed.). *Reshaping the Labour Market: Regulation, Efficiency and Equality in Australia* (Cambridge: Cambridge University Press, 1999b).

Scharpf, F. W. *Crisis and Choice in European Social Democracy* (Ithaca: Cornell University Press, 1991).

Schmidt, M. G. 'When Parties Matter: A Review of the Possibilities and Limits of Partisan Influence on Public Policy', *European Journal of Political Research*, vol. 30 (1996) pp. 155–83.

Schmitter, P. C. 'Still the Century of Corporatism', *Review of Politics*, vol. 36(1) (1974) pp. 85–131.

Sen, A. 'Freedom and Needs', *The New Republic* (10–17 January 1994) pp. 31–7.

Sharman, C. 'Australia as a Compound Republic', *Politics*, vol. 25(1) (1990) pp. 1–5.

Swank, D. *Global Capital, Political Institutions, and Policy Change in Developed Welfare States* (Cambridge: Cambridge University Press, 2002).

Thompson, E. 'The "Washminster" Mutation', *Politics*, vol. 15(1) (1980) pp. 32–40.

Tsebilis, G. 'Decision-Making in Political Systems: Veto Players in Presidentialism, Parliamentarianism, Multicameralism and Multypartism', *British Journal of Political Science*, 25 (1995) pp. 289–325.

United Nations. *Human Development Report 2001* (New York, 2001).

Wilensky, H. L. *The Welfare State and Equality* (Berkeley: University of California Press, 1975).

World Bank. *1998 World Bank Atlas* (Washington, DC: International Bank for Reconstruction and Development, 1999).

# 3 Australia's Economic Institutions

*Geoffrey Brennan and Jonathan Pincus*

Our object in this chapter is to examine Australia's economic institutions and the changes in them that have occurred over the century since Federation. Our attention will focus especially on changes that have occurred over the last quarter-century or so, but we want to set that focus in a larger historical sweep. 'Examination' here is understood to include not just description: we want also to gesture at possible explanations of why what occurred did occur.

Historical explanation of this kind can lend the account a false sense of inevitability. After all, 'explanation' in the tradition that economists come from involves identifying certain, hypothesized causal factors. Equally, it involves abstracting from those countervailing forces which were present, but not decisive. Had those latter forces been stronger, the outcomes could conceivably have been quite different. But explanatory narratives rarely explore the counterfactuals, and ours will be no exception. We should just emphasize at the outset that, though the story we shall relate exhibits this 'causal' character, we accept that at each point in which human agency was involved, choices were made: choices as to what was important, as to whose interests took priority, as to what theoretical accounts of the consequences of particular actions were correct, and so on. Tracing the connection between those various choices and the institutions that were in place and the ensuing course of events – which is the exercise we set ourselves here – does not commit us to the view that the choices could not have been otherwise. We do not embrace any form of determinism – economic or otherwise.

### Will the Real Institutions Please Stand Up?

At the outset, we will need to make clear what we mean by Australia's 'economic institutions'. What economists mean by an 'institution' is itself distinctive – and even the use of the term by economists admits a range of phenomena, only some of which we will look at here.

'Institutional' analysis in the economics literature takes as its point of departure a distinction between economic outcomes and the more abstract structure of rules, practices and policies from which those outcomes emerge. A common analogy is with the rules of a sporting activity or parlour game. There is, for example, a clear distinction to be drawn between the play of a particular hand of bridge and the rules that govern that play. That distinction, between the 'institutional setting' of economic activity on the one hand and the activity itself on the other, is crucial in the economic analysis of institutions. The chief question at issue is how the rules of the game influence the nature of the play. One of the primary motivating factors in making this distinction is the conviction that normative judgement is better directed at the level of institutions than at the level of outcomes. Economic outcomes are to be explained, not applauded or deplored. They are to be explained in terms of the interaction among essentially rational, predominantly egoistic players, given the resource constraints that those agents face and – notably – the institutional structures within which such interactions take place. If one wants to influence the outcomes, changes in the rules are a more effective lever than attempts to change the outcomes directly.

It should be clear that the distinction between rules and outcomes could be applied at various levels of abstraction. For example, the choice of rules is itself governed by rules; in that sense, the choice of rules of the game can be regarded as the outcome of a more abstract process, which is itself also rule-governed. It is important to note this point, because economists often use the term 'institutions' to refer to rules at the most abstract level of the socio-political-economic game. Much of the literature on 'institutional analysis' has taken off from the work of Buchanan (1975) and Brennan and Buchanan (1985) and Olson (1982) and has revolved around a particular contrast between markets and democratic politics. These two institutional settings for decision-making, the one decentralized and the other directly 'collective', are often conceptualized in this literature as the fundamental 'institutional forms'. The relevant 'institution' in each case – market and political process – is thus defined in terms that are extremely broad, highly aggregated and relatively abstract.

In this spirit, we shall define a 'constitution' to be the rules that govern market and political processes at this most abstract level. The constitution so understood would include rules for the definition of property rights and specification of procedures whereby those property rights might be exchanged. It will also include the basic rules of democratic political process: how often elections are to be called; who is entitled to vote; the system whereby votes are aggregated to determine a victor; the system of checks and balances (if any); and so on. It would ideally also include a specification of the relative domains of the two decision-making forms – so, in particular, what areas of activity are assigned to markets and what to political process. This 'constitution', with the lower-case 'c', should be distinguished from upper-case 'Constitutional' legal documents, which may or may not include a specification of the basic rules of the socio-political-economic order. Understood in these terms, the distinctive features of the Australian 'constitution' lie mostly on the political side, not the economic. That is, we have compulsory voting, preferential voting, and an unusual bicameral structure, all combined with a strong party system – features which taken together make our prevailing political order interestingly different from others in the Western world. These distinctive features are of considerable interest in their own right and worthy of analysis in the style (now increasingly common elsewhere) which exploits the analytic techniques and conceptual apparatus of modern economics.[1] However, we shall not attempt that analysis here. Our focus is on the 'economic constitution' more narrowly conceived.

At the most abstract level of institutional structure, there is perhaps not a great deal that now distinguishes Australia's 'economic constitution' from that of Great Britain or Germany or Japan. All of these countries are predominantly 'market' societies in which the greater part of individuals' wants are satisfied through ordinary market exchange. But the regulatory and fiscal details –the particular rules as to what may or may not be sold or exchanged, and the terms under which such exchange takes place where it is permitted – can differ between countries markedly. Over reasonable stretches of time, these details can change within a given country; as can perceptions of the proper role of markets *vis-à-vis* governments, and the particular objectives of governments. Within a broadly market-driven system, governments can shape the outcomes that emerge by a variety of policy instruments, and in the light of a variety of objectives. Both the policy instruments used and the policy objectives sought can change over time, and can differ from place to place. That combination of instruments used and objectives sought constitute what we shall refer to here as a 'policy regime'. The 'policy regime', so understood, forms, along with the more abstract rules of market operation, the rules of the basic economic game. And it will be that policy regime – and changes in it – that will occupy our attention in this chapter.

**A Causal Map**

A picture may help here in communicating the structure of rules and outcomes and the relationships between them that we have in mind. In Figure 3.1, we depict the hierarchy of institutional arrangements, with the most abstract 'constitutional' elements at the top, running both directly, and indirectly through the intermediate 'policy regime', to the economic outcomes that emerge under that constitution at the lowest

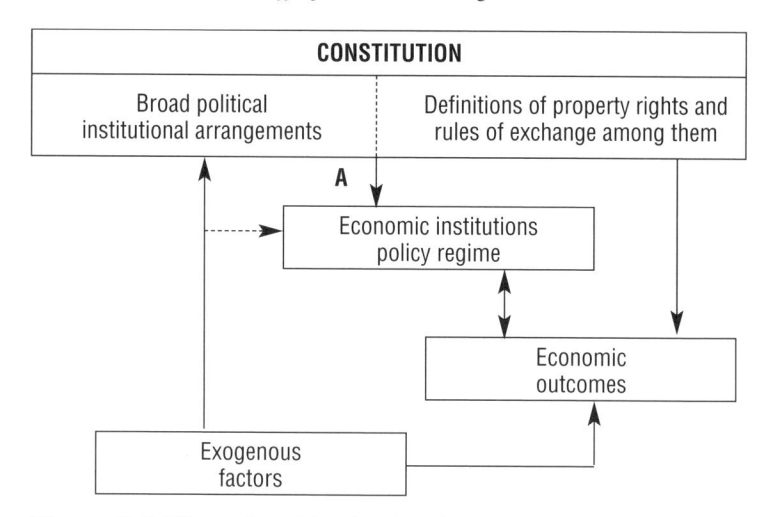

```
                    ┌─────────────────────────────────────────┐
                    │              CONSTITUTION               │
                    ├──────────────────┬──────────────────────┤
                    │  Broad political │ Definitions of property rights and │
                    │ institutional arrangements │ rules of exchange among them │
                    └──────────────────┴──────────────────────┘
```

**Figure 3.1** Hierarchy of institutional arrangements

level of abstraction. The arrows in the diagram indicate directions of influence.

Several features of the projected pattern of influences are worth underlining. One is the influence of non-institutional forces on economic outcomes – both directly, and indirectly via possible effects on the rules of political process and on policy 'choices'. The second feature is the feedback loops between economic outcomes and policy choices, which again occur both directly, and via an influence on the rules of political processes.

As indicated, our focus of attention in what follows is the middle box, labelled 'economic institutions/policy regime'. We shall say more in what follows about what precisely we take that box to contain. But we have in mind things like capital market regulations, labour market regulations (including wage regulation), tariff policy, and taxation policy in so far as it influences relative prices (and hence the terms on which various products are bought or sold). In principle, we should also include in the box the pattern of direct public spending decisions. After all, the state is an important economic actor in its own right, and direct public provision of education, health, defence, police protection, and so on, may all have a huge effect on economic outcomes.[2]

At this point, however, we set issues of content aside. Instead, we want to emphasize that, to the extent that our object includes that of *explaining* the elements in that box – and changes in them over the period under discussion – Figure 3.1 indicates the various possible aspects of causal influence that might be in play. Several general points are worth making in this connection. First, in the general economistic spirit, the causal structure is one of mutual interdependence: everything is related to everything else. And in principle, all causal influences are potentially operative. Still, some of these 'causal influences' are stronger than others. For example, by its nature the constitution of the economic-political order is fairly stable and reasonably robust to the influence of economic outcomes. The stronger causal links therefore run 'down' from the constitution – to 'economic institutions', and to economic outcomes directly by virtue of the general abstract rules of market processes. Again in the economistic spirit – though here in the economists' taste for parsimony – we shall abstract from those causal influences that seem weakest (and least relevant to the case at hand) and focus attention on those that are strongest. Accordingly, we shall abstract from the effects of various factors on the constitution itself.[3] Our object here is not to explain the constitution: we shall essentially take that as given.

## The Outcome–Institution Nexus: Two Examples

The feedback effects of economic outcomes on policy, by contrast, strike us as extremely important and will be a major focus of our explanatory account. Two simple examples will help make the point. Suppose that as a rough approximation, political institutions are designed so that political decision-making over 'economic institutions' reflects the broad public interest[4] – understood in terms of, say, the average level of economic well-being, supplemented with a particular concern to promote a tolerable distribution of that well-being across society. On that view, the prevailing economic institutions and policy regime will reflect prevailing views about how best to achieve that overall objective. The policy regime will also reflect perceptions as to what non-institutional forces are in play and how best to respond to them. For example, in the world league table of economic well-being (measured, say, in terms of GDP per head or some similar metric of average well-being) Australia is routinely depicted as having slipped from the very top in 1900 to somewhere about thirteenth a century later. It is natural to ask whether this change is a consequence of the particular policy regimes that have been in place or is attributable essentially to 'non-institutional' forces. If the former, there would be pressure to alter the policy regime. If the latter, then it may be a state of affairs that simply has to be endured; though there would still be an issue as to whether the policy regime was such as to allow outcomes to respond optimally to changed circumstances. One would expect, in short, that non-institutional forces would impact on the policy regime via their influence on economic outcomes, and via the feedback effect of economic outcomes on policy regime. Accordingly, within this particular framework, the perceived *consequences* of the economic institutional regime become part of the *explanation* of why that institutional regime exists. And it becomes automatic therefore to focus much of one's analytic attention on the consequences of particular economic institutions. In this way, the standard normatively grounded approach of policy analysis becomes an element in the *explanation* of why particular policies are in existence, or are likely to stay in existence.

There is a clear danger here of a confusion of normative with explanatory agendas. Normative analysis naturally focuses most attention on 'outcomes'. Here, we are not engaged in normative analysis as such. Nevertheless, on the basis of the (perhaps heroic) picture of political processes that we have painted, we can help ourselves to familiar propositions that are offered by the normative analysis of economic institutions and policy regimes.

Even within this broad heroic picture of public-interest politics, however, there is scope for a more nuanced institutional account. Suppose in particular, that there are rival views as to what the consequences of alternative policy regimes are. The rules of the political game may exercise a critical determinative role in affecting the weights given to rival views. In particular, we need to respond to Michael Pusey's (1991) charge that, in the last few decades, economists' views about the consequences of policies have had a predominant weight in determining government decisions – and thereby in determining the policy regime that is in place. Economists' views on many aspects of these matters are not uncontested. Those, like Pusey, with contrary views naturally complain.

Our interest here is not with the question as to whether the policy regime changes that Pusey and others lament are a 'good thing' or not. We are interested rather in whether Pusey's explanation of the changes is well grounded. In order to answer that question, it is worth underlining the assumptions about political processes that Pusey's analysis implies. The primary route by which the views of economists are seen to influence policy is via the process of 'policy advice', both through the bureaucracy and ministerial offices. Pusey's view of the way Australian democracy works, therefore, presupposes that those sources of advice are extremely influential – indeed, decisive – in the determination of policy outcomes. And correspondingly, more narrowly 'political factors', including electoral advantage, popular opinion, and so on, are of second-order relevance. In short, Pusey's claim reflects a broader judgement about the operation of Australia's political system that itself needs to be interrogated.

If Pusey's general account were accepted, explanations of regime change could appeal to a number of different lines:

- There might have been a change in the composition of the bureaucratic and advisory group, say, in terms of disciplinary background.

- There might have been a shift in the relative role of bureaucratic and advisory factors *vis-à-vis* electoral and 'political' factors.
- There might have been a change in the prevailing attitudes of economists concerning policy effects.
- There might have been a change in the external world, which in the economists' view called for corresponding changes in the appropriate policy regime.

These alternative lines are not mutually exclusive. But they do locate the basic cause of the regime change in a different place. The latter two focus primarily on the role of ideas. The third is interesting in that it is possible to detect a change in the predominant views within the economics profession along relevant lines over the period in question – and especially over the last fifty years, as the Keynesian predominance in Australian economics has eroded.[5] However, we should recognize that the mere fact that such changes occurred does not show that these were the determining factors in the regime change. In our view, and as we try to argue in the more detailed account that follows, there are other factors at work.

In any event, feedback effects of economic outcomes on policy regime are not limited to cases in which political processes work systematically to promote the public interest or in which promoting the public interest is the chief ambition. Suppose, instead, rather more in the spirit of public choice theory, that political processes are best understood as a scramble over interests, where the interests of both salient groups and of individuals are the significant motors of political action. On this view, policy determination is also linked to the consequences of policy, but here it is the consequences of alternative policies for the interests of the politically influential that drive the system. The policy regime – the economic institutional setting in place – will predictably reflect the 'political imperative' to serve the interests of the salient political groups. Some care must be taken in structuring the argument here, however. It would clearly be hopelessly circular to define political influence by reference to those groups and individuals who happened to benefit from the current policy regime. We obviously require some prior independent assessment of relative political influence. But where is that independent assessment to come from, if not from an inspection of policy outcomes? One could easily end up with a complex tautology that simply served as an elaborate description of policy outcomes without any real explanation at all. Many so-called 'private interest' accounts of policy outcomes exhibit this tautological character: they induce from the fact that particular policies have distributional *consequences*, a conclusion to the effect that those consequences *caused* the policy in question. Clearly, we would need an argument to support such a conclusion.

There is, however, one aspect of the private interest account that does seem to do genuine explanatory work, even if the base explanation of policy action itself is empty. The provision of 'special interest' support through the economic policy regime to some industry or group will often induce its own feedback effects on the level of political support for that policy. For example, protection for motor vehicle production tends to draw more economic activity into that industry – more workers, more capital, more capacity to fund lobbying activity, and more voters whose interests are in tune with the policy consequences. The general presumption that this observation supports is that, *ceteris paribus*, it is politically easier to *grant* a special interest tariff than it is to *abolish* it: special interest tariffs tend to breed their own political support.[6] On the same reasoning, the effect of changes in external economic forces on political muscle can serve to feed through patterns of voter interest and capacity of industries to lobby. A general decline in the fortunes of, say, the wool industry attributable entirely to changes in the world price of wool, can reduce that industry's political influence – alongside its declining economic significance. This in turn can lead to a reduction in policy support for the industry, arguably just at the time when 'it needs such support most'.

The special interest model of policy determination provides an example of another possible causal linkage – this time between the more abstract rules of the political game and the nature of the policy regime. Australia, like the United Kingdom and United States, but unlike many European countries, has an electoral system based on single-member, geographically based electorates (SM). The contrast is with a proportional representation (PR) system for the nation as a whole. The SM electoral arrangements have the effect that the spatial properties of policies have a special salience in those countries that have SM. The idea of a marginal electorate makes no sense in a PR system – special interest coalitions arise around aggregated interests, and often take the form of single-issue parties in PR systems, but the interests in question need have no particular spatial distribution. Therefore, coalitions of interests around certain issues – the environment or ethnicity or industries that have a wide distribution of producers thinly represented in any area but of some significance in the aggregate – will tend to be more extensively represented in PR systems than in SM systems. Within the single-member electoral system, by contrast, special interests need the right kind of geographic concentration in order to be maximally potent politically. Consequently, in the Australian system, geographically concentrated industries with a significant electoral presence in a small number of electoral districts are more likely to be granted tariff protection than industries that are more geographically dispersed – other things being equal.[7]

Australia's Economic Institutions

The introduction of modified PR in the Senate (from 1949 on), together with our small number of states, suggests that Australia would not be as prone to these geographically specific factors as the United States. To suggest that the introduction of PR contributed to the demise of tariff protection in the Australian case is perhaps to press the point too far. However, the argument nicely exemplifies how political institutions might feed into the determination of what we have termed 'economic institutions'.[8] It exemplifies, that is, the causal link marked A in Figure 3.1.

### What Exactly Is It that We Seek to Explain?

The object of investigation here is the 'economic policy regime' that has prevailed in Australia over the period 1901 to 2001 – and specifically to explain the changes in that policy regime. In this and the next section, we attempt to set out the salient features of that regime and the major changes. This part of the discussion is essentially historical description. But of course that description necessarily incorporates judgements about what was important and what not – judgements that may not be entirely uncontroversial. And the attempt to render the description in terms of a coherent account necessarily makes gestures at low-level explanation. In the later parts of this chapter we examine the broader explanatory issues and the inadequacy of a range of explanations that have had some currency in the Australian debate over these issues.

There is a story about Australia's 'economic institutions' that has achieved folkloric status among those who take an interest in such things. This story contrasts Australia at the opening of the twentieth century with Australia at century's end. Broadly, the picture in the first decade of the twentieth century is one of a highly regulated, highly 'protected' regime, building Deakin's New Protection via a layer of social welfare provisions and elaborate labour market and wage regulations. This picture is to be set against that of a substantially deregulated, privatized US-style economic regime, constructed mostly from the mid-1980s on. At 1901, the government is a large player in capital acquisition and investment; at 2001, it is a bit-player in capital markets, at least as a direct participant. At 1901, Australia has one of the largest government-spending-to-GDP shares in the developed world; at 2001, that share is one of the smaller. At Federation, market competition was regarded with suspicion at best; at the end of the century, competition was praised as essential and beneficent.

This story suggests two general questions: first, is the picture it presents true? And second, if true, what explains the spectacular changes? In answering this second question, it seems useful to give some attention to the consequences of these policy regime changes. However, as we have already emphasized, just which of the many consequences help explain the regime is itself a theory-laden issue.

Our discussion of these matters falls out as follows. First, we check the folklore against the facts, as best we can discern them. Subsequently, we discuss two features of the story with which any coherent explanation must be consistent. These features are: first, that the change in regime had a large measure of bipartisan support in Australia; and second, that this kind of policy regime change was common across a number of countries. In our account, we try to be attentive to any feedback loops from policy regime to economic outcome and back to policy regime. We also try to assess the effects of external non-institutional factors such as wars, technological developments and changes in world market conditions. As we have indicated, our own explanatory attempts are framed against a rival account that sees the changes as largely ideological, with the ideology in question essentially driven by economists, in their public servant and/or policy adviser roles.

With this as general background, we turn to the history itself. We shall divide our account here into four periods – from just before Federation to 1920; from 1920 to 1945; from 1945 to 1980; and then from 1980 to the present. We shall focus most attention on the first and last of these periods where the contrast is most marked, treating the intermediate periods rather cursorily as transitional phases.

*Australia: Federation to 1920*

Earlier, we noted broad similarities in basic economic 'constitutions' among a range of Western countries – specifically, extensive reliance on markets to provide most of what citizens consume – and we noted also the existence of specific differences in the policy regimes, in terms of the objectives sought and the means used. In the Australian case, especially after the granting of responsible government, colonial (mostly British) economic and political institutions were adapted to local conditions. Australia was then a land of recent Western settlement. Its policies were driven by a widely accepted objective of achieving a rate of economic development more rapid (it was believed) than could be provided without public assistance. Compared to the British case, Australian colonial governments were more willing to finance, construct and operate the major land transport enterprises and other public utilities; were more inclined to provide financial support to migration and primary education; and were more willing to reject the free-trade doctrines of the Manchester School. Innovative free banking, more Scottish than English, had assisted the rapid expansion of private economic activity over the 'colonial' period and by 1900, white Australia had achieved, through individual and collective action, a high standard of living and a high degree of equality. The broad economic and political 'constitution' – private property, and democratic political institutions – were generally conducive to economic development, though one can hardly overlook the significance of gold in contributing to Australia's pre-Federation development. Doubtless, Australia's relative prosperity under that institutional order discouraged significant interference with it at Federation. This is not to argue, however, that the prevailing colony-specific public policy regimes had significant positive effects on the level of economic prosperity.[9]

Commentators in 1901 regarded the 'fiscal question' – free-trade or protection – as the most significant economic issue left unresolved at Federation, and later scholars have agreed. Mancur Olson (1982) has argued that Australia took a crucial, retrograde step by adopting a protectionist regime shortly after Federation. The critical feature of Olson's 'institutional sclerosis' theory is that long-lived, stable democratic institutions permit or encourage the gradual accretion of growth-retarding coalitions of special interests. Olson believed that his theory explains the Australian protectionist regime well. In doing so, he is effectively claiming that the implementation of the new constitution in 1901 did not significantly disrupt existing pressure groups: Australia after Federation was just a continuation of the same old coalitions of interests that had dominated the separate colonies.

In the first years of Federation an important consideration was a political imperative upon the new Commonwealth government to provide revenues to the states of similar magnitude to those the states had achieved with their own, separate, custom duties and excises. Heavy reliance on direct taxation by the states or the Commonwealth was seen as unacceptable, both by the free-trade party and by moderate protectionists, on the grounds that alternative major revenue sources would release tariffs from their revenue-raising function and open the way to extremely protective, even prohibitive, tariff rates. Direct taxation was also likely to be more progressive, which was reason for the Labor Party to support it. And initially many Labor members of parliament were sceptical of the claim that the beneficial effects of tariff protection on wages were greater than the detrimental effects of the import tax on the cost of living of the workingman. However, by the time of the second Fisher government, when Labor achieved more than a fleeting control of government, it had committed itself to Deakin's New Protection, linking wage regulation with a regime of customs and excise taxes. The prevailing belief seems to have been that tariff protection could serve literally to 'protect' the Australian economy from international competition from low-wage countries. In fact, 'protection' served only to redistribute to the workers in industries that secured tariff protection, at the expense of workers in other industries. However, the whole package of protection and wage regulation *could* serve to redistribute from landowners to workers and – via publicly funded old-age pensions – from higher-income to lower-income families. Its capacity to do this successfully depended, however, on a further measure of 'protection' – against the entry of low-wage, high-productivity immigrants – through the White Australia policy.

It is worth noting here that the mixture of policies chosen was relatively economical in its use of taxation revenues.[10] To assist the full range of industries helped by the tariff through subsidies (as was done for iron and steel) would have required a much higher level of aggregate taxation. Equally, to increase wages by direct subsidies, rather than by regulation, would have required very significant public revenues. Some elements of the policy package, like passage assistance or pensions or public works, did consume public funds; but these were elements for which there was then no plausible regulatory alternative. (It has been argued in the US case that passage of the constitutional amendment permitting the federal income tax paved the way for tariff reductions. A similar argument could be entertained about the longer-term effects on tariff protection of the Commonwealth's control of income tax after 1942.)[11]

Revenue scarcity at Federation can be attributed in significant measure to two further elements of the policy regime: significant public spending on economic development; and extensive public ownership and operation of public utilities. Effectively, the government's role as borrower encouraged a more extensive role as economic planner. Butlin et al. (1982) has estimated that, in the 1920s before depression struck, public capital formation had reached over half the economy's total, with public enterprises accounting for around half of the public component. About 15 per cent of the workforce was then employed in the public sector, a portion much higher than in other countries with similar living standards. With large parts of the public revenue committed to capital investment, it is hardly to be wondered at if governments avoided revenue-intensive means of pursuing welfare and other objectives.

But the public sector involvement in capital development carried further implications. In an economy that was mostly private, with the public sector a large borrower, the only rules available to guide public investment were those of business. Private lenders, especially foreigners, were concerned with the capacity of governments to repay. Accordingly, large public investments were generally first promoted as eventually being able to 'cover' costs from receipts. That stringent standard was later relaxed and investments were 'credited', as it were, with financial advantages that would flow to other parts of government (like extra taxes or land sales or rents), so that the public sector was considered as one vast enterprise (a whole-of-government approach). Ultimately, the justifications for public investments included the value of the spillovers to the *private* sector, instituting a whole-of-economy approach.[12] In this way, the idea grew that market-like outcomes could be achieved by non-market means.

One incidental feature of this 'calculative confidence' seems to have been a deep mistrust of private competition as a mechanism to achieve socially desirable outcomes – including high living standards and rapid economic development (and rapid population growth).[13] Instead, competition was typically regarded as a transitional stage leading to the creation of monopolies by private action or by nationalization, or as properly confined to arenas where it would do no great harm. Non-competitive behaviour by private business was permitted, even encouraged, under non-Labor governments, while Labor accepted monopolies as inevitable and simply wanted them to be *state* monopolies.[14]

As serious questions began to arise in the management of the protectionist regime, a demand arose for public administrative and planning bodies. If import competition, for example, was to be restricted so as to provide maximal advantage to Australian worker-consumers, then zero or low rates of tariff protection would be required for products not made in Australia, or not likely to be made except at prohibitive rates of duty. But who could tell which products these were? Where import protection was to be provided, what was the correct level? Although the legislature itself made tariff and other tax decisions, politicians wanted informed advice: the planning mentality could not admit explicit determination of such matters on the basis of mere political clout. The first effort in this direction was the (Quick) Royal Commission on the tariff, 1905–8. That Commission collected much information and though it did not lead to precise tariff recommendations, it did come up with a general formulation that the tariff should bridge the gap between the costs of efficient Australian producers and those of appropriate foreign producers – whatever these were. The long-term solution was the creation of the Tariff Board in 1921 to make such (impossible) determinations.

The protective tariff was gradually extended in range beyond the coverage already established by 1901, and beyond the industries born during the interruption of imports caused by the Great War, to include horticultural and agricultural exportables.[15] Thus was born the principle of Protection All Round, a logically impossible notion that disguised the fact that there were always losers – in this case, the factors of production used intensively in Australian exporting industries. The extreme point in this process was reached in the 1950s. During that decade, most imports were regulated by quantitative restrictions; banks compulsorily acquired foreign exchange, on behalf of the Reserve Bank, at rates that left the regulated market hopelessly uncleared; and most agricultural markets were riddled with state interventions (Campbell, 1973).

Similarly, there were Royal Commissions and continuing statutory bodies on the wages side. These latter bodies – wages boards and industrial courts – were empowered to make rulings that, in contrast with those of the Tariff Board, had the effect of law. In other respects, however, they were similar – called on, as they often were, to make judgements that later generations of economists would come to regard as simply impossible.

## 1920–1945

When we turn to the final abandonment of the protectionist regime, one important element is the set of tensions generated within the protection policy regime itself, and between that regime and the external circumstances of the nation. By the decade of the 1920s already some of those tensions were beginning to show. There were Labor elements that decried the tariff as being on balance disadvantageous to the working classes, and more radical labourites who saw the tariffs as assisting big business and/or promoting private enterprise. Page, in the early 1920s, had to persuade his Country Party colleagues to refrain from a wholesale attack on tariffs, in favour of a more 'moderate' approach that looked to bounties on agricultural inputs and machinery, the introduction of various (price-raising) 'agricultural marketing schemes', and the promotion of publicly funded agricultural research. Bruce, the National Party leader, ultimately lost government over a proposal for the Commonwealth to abandon the field of industrial relations.

In the late 1920s, a group composed mostly of economists reported to government (mostly) favourably on 'the Australian case for protection'. The basic finding was that the tariff had been successful in stimulating immigration without causing an appreciable diminution of the living standards of workers. However, the inquiry reported, the development strategy had about reached its economic limits. As to primary industry, the results of closer settlement schemes were excessive production of certain products and, consequently, appeals for government assistance in their marketing (that is, for schemes to inflate artificially the prices paid by Australian consumers in order to finance the subsidization or dumping of surpluses in foreign markets). Regarding secondary industry, the Tariff Board in the late 1920s, after less than a decade of operation, worried that the protective system had a tendency to excess. Wages boards had increased pay rates on account of profitability, which was itself boosted by tariff rises granted on account of the cost disadvantages of Australian industry caused by high wages; and so on. Both the Tariff

Board and tariff inquiry also warned of the dangerous inculcation of what now would be called 'rent-seeking' mentalities.[16] That the tariff strategy had reached its own limits; that further increases and extension of import protection would not contribute much if at all to overall development, or to growth in employment, population and production – these conclusions, if accepted, suggested either that the goal of boosting development had to be moderated, even abandoned, or that other developmental means had to be found.

### *1945–1980*

In the immediate post-war period, the major Australian political parties professed to share goals of rapid population growth and economic development.[17] Although the parties differed over the preferred *means* of post-war reconstruction, with Labor unsuccessfully seeking access to stronger federal levers of economic control, both sides of politics wanted to use tariff protection as a chief instrument of development. There were, however, new complications – the fear of external public debt; and, more importantly, the needs of stabilization policy and a desire to maintain fixed exchange rates. During the Great Depression, when world commodity, credit and labour markets had collapsed, the burden of external public debt had dominated the Australian policy outlook. In consequence, after World War II, the pattern of public investment was shifted to the more commercial and profitable (such as a duopolistic airline)[18] or to the social. The emphasis moved from increasing population and the size of the workforce, to improving the *quality* of the workforce, now in need of more than a primary education. In consequence of the Great Depression and armed with the confidence that Keynesian economics had all the relevant answers, governments had added to the goal of economic development another overarching economic objective, that of macro-economic stability. From 1945 on, it was increasingly argued that the achievement of macro-economic stability, by enabling the economy to operate closer to capacity over the business cycle, would represent the primary contribution to secular economic development. Macro-policy tended to displace economic development goals and the instruments of Keynesian macro-control sometimes rendered nugatory the means used to stimulate economic development.[19] Keynesian theory stressed mechanisms of control that did not rely on the incentive and market-equilibrating functions of the price system, but operated directly on incomes and spending, via economic commands. However, the period immediately after World War II saw a worldwide 'dollar shortage', as the demands of reconstruction and suburbanization outstripped supplies. In Australia during the 1950s, quantitative import controls were used as a supplementary means of non-price rationing of foreign exchange. In the process, the tariff was temporarily displaced as the chief agency of protection, a change important to our story.

A further relevant piece of the general economic background through this period concerns the long post-war boom of the 1950s and 1960s. This boom was experienced internationally – in Europe, in Japan and elsewhere, and strongly in the UnitedStates. At this point, the United States itself was engaged in reducing its own tariffs and vigorously encouraging others to free up their internal and external goods and finance markets. The Australian manifestation of this boom cannot be – and, as far as we can discern, was not – primarily attributed to the continuation of the protectionist strategy. In fact, per capita GDP growth rates in Australia were seen to lag behind those of comparable countries. And this fact, increasingly widely, began to be attributed precisely to Australia's protectionist regime. With this change in perceptions came the beginning of the process of tariff reform, and with it the dismantling of the whole protectionist package.

**A Change of Regime**

Under the Hawke and Keating Labor governments, 1983 to 1996, wide-ranging micro-economic reforms were enacted or begun. These reforms were generally supported by the Liberals in opposition federally, were driven by some State governments, Liberal and Labor, and were certainly not reversed by the Howard federal government. In at least some cases, Howard's Liberals pushed them further. In brief, the last two decades of the twentieth century witnessed a broad shift in policy regime, towards putting much greater reliance on market competition as a mechanism to achieve policy aims. In the ensuing discussion we will briefly outline the changes made, and then discuss some aspects of the change in greater detail.

In finance, the exchange rate was floated; it became legal for ordinary Australians to own gold bullion and foreign bank accounts. Subsidiaries and subsequently branches of foreign banks were permitted to operate in Australia; regulatory requirements on banks and non-bank financial enterprises were substantially lifted

In international trade, the Australian tariff and other forms of industry assistance were gradually reduced and then effectively eliminated, except in a small number of instances. The Tariff Board became, via a sequence of rhetorically significant moves, first the Industries Assistance Commission (free to shift focus from tariffs to broader issues), and then the Industry Commission; and then the Productivity Commission (with a broader remit and merged with a number of other bodies).

In the mid-1990s, a 'national competition policy' was agreed between the Commonwealth and the States designed to achieve competitive neutrality between publicly and privately owned enterprises and to institute new forms of regulation of natural monopolies. A number of what had traditionally been regarded as primary government functions were increasingly 'contracted out' to private firms.

Competition within the private sector was also strengthened. Labor established the Australian Competition and Consumer Commission (based on the Trade Practices Commission and the Prices Surveillance Authority), with greatly expanded powers over private as well as public enterprises.[20]

A number of features of the change towards a more competitive policy regime are worth noting. First, the change encompassed a broad range of industries and economic activities – goods as well as services, internationally traded as well as domestic, publicly owned as well as private. Second, it involved changes in a great variety of laws and regulations – again, public as well as private. Third, partly because of constitutional requirements, the changes involved simultaneous action by the Commonwealth and all of the State governments (and also local governments as creatures of the states). Although there was some criticism and opposition from within and without the major political parties, the change in policy regime clearly had bipartisan support, with the lead taken at the federal level by Labor governments, and in the states by Liberal or National or Coalition governments. The important role played by a series of committees of inquiry, usually headed by prominent businessmen or others outside the ranks of public officials, was a further noteworthy feature of the changes. And finally, there was the prominence within the new regime of a long list of independent statutory bodies, of which the Australian Competition and Consumer Commission is one example – although certainly a most significant one.

As was recognised at Federation when the original package of tariffs, immigration control and wage regulation was constructed, a satisfactory policy regime is an amalgam of mutually supporting elements, each one of which contributes to the coherence of the overall scheme. This fact is no less relevant when a policy regime is dismantled. Conducting that dismantling – and reconstruction – exercise piecemeal can lead to internal contradictions and to important objectives or mechanisms being overlooked. And the coherence test here is not just a matter of the economic and social *effects* of the policy regime: it is also a matter of the rhetorical defences for that regime that need to be politically constructed and the intellectual ambience within which the regime operates. In the current case, there was, in particular, a significant intellectual shift away from a conception of competition as destructive towards the idea that competition, for the most part and with appropriate safeguards, embodies a discipline on the operation of both business and politics that is essentially benign. Accordingly, it is interesting to examine in somewhat greater detail the sequence of the policy changes and the provenance of them.

### Financial Deregulation

During the middle years of the Fraser government, the Campbell inquiry was instituted to report on ways of improving the functioning of the monetary system.[21] The committee had reported in 1981 before the Fraser government fell in 1983, but Fraser had engaged in only very limited financial deregulation. However, the incoming Hawke government, with Paul Keating as treasurer, implemented most of the Campbell recommendations. These included: deregulation of foreign exchange and the floating of the dollar; removal of ceilings on deposit and on loan rates; permission for entry of new banks, including foreign-owned; changing to interest rates as the primary targets of monetary policy control; new forms of prudential regulation; and the treatment of company profits tax as a withholding element of the personal income tax rather than a revenue-raising instrument in its own right.

In many accounts of financial deregulation, the theme of necessity appears: the claim is that there was simply no alternative. Gruen and Grattan (1993: 140) offer a subtle version of this line, suggesting that the previous regulations had inadvertently reduced the efficacy of monetary policy because those regulations had drastically diminished the share of financial assets under the control of commercial banks. On this reading, there had been no change at all in policy objectives – macro–economic control remained the goal, but the means had to change. Other more general policy objectives (and equity goals specifically) did not seem to have been met, or were no longer being met, by the prevailing financial regulations: the efficacy of regulation had been undermined by technological change and globalization in banking and finance, and by the increasing capacity of financial institutions to evade regulatory strictures. Furthermore, a conservative financial system was increasingly seen incapable of allocating scarce capital in the manner needed to maintain Australian competitiveness and comparative living standards. Nonetheless, the victory for deregulation was not assured – at least, not immediately. Within the bureaucracy, Secretary of the Treasury, John Stone, vehemently opposed relaxation of exchange regulation and control. (Interestingly, he later praised the floating of the Australian dollar in late 1983 as the most significant change in economic policy since the end of World War II: see Kelly, 1994: 144.) The long delay between the announcement by the Fraser government of an inquiry into the financial system and the appointment of the members was indicative of the opposition of Prime Minister Fraser and Deputy Prime Minister Anthony to financial, and especially exchange rate, deregulation. That government's delay in acting on the Campbell Committee's recommendations is further evidence of that reluctance. Financial deregulation was opposed by the Labor Party platform upon which Hawke was elected, and Labor in opposition had rejected the Campbell recommendations. It is therefore difficult to explain Labor's about-face on this issue as deriving from perceived political necessity. It seems more likely that the Labor Treasurer Keating was personally persuaded by the arguments in favour of reform – and perhaps influenced by the enthusiasm issuing from the Reserve Bank. Interestingly, the 1983 decision to float the dollar did not go to the Labor caucus. Later endorsement by the Liberal parliamentary leadership of a set of policies more consistent with a free enterprise ideology than had been Liberal practice could be interpreted within the usual spatial competition model of a two-party democracy. As Labor moved towards a policy regime with greater scope for market competition, the Liberals were forced to follow suit (as, eventually, were their Coalition partners).

There had been no serious attempts in advance to model the consequences of the float or of financial deregulation more generally. However, it seems clear that what followed was not generally expected. There was considerable volatility in the exchange rate, a surprising persistence of apparently inefficient banking practices and high margins, and huge losses from bank loans made during the asset price boom. A number of inquiries in the later 1980s and early 1990s investigated criticisms of banks' margins, interest rates and returns. However, for the most part, the criticisms were not found to be well-grounded. (See the Martin reports of 1984 and 1991; Prices Surveillance Authority in 1992 and 1995; State Royal Commissions, especially as reported in Edwards and Valentine, 1998).

Many commentators have remarked on the connection between the two seemingly contradictory elements of the Hawke–Keating economic agenda: deregulation of financial markets so as to make them more competitive; and re-regulation of the labour markets, via the Accord. According to Kelly (1994: 77), Treasurer Keating expected that floating the exchange rate would not only open the Australian economy to an anti-inflation discipline but also would destroy the parochial and conservative mentality of Australian business. Those in business who welcomed the financial (and subsequent micro-economic) changes tended not to be supporters of the Coalition. Hawke and Keating apparently believed in the efficacy of markets in general, but thought that the labour market was a 'special case'. Part of the special quality in question doubtless lies in the connections between the labour market, the union movement and the Labor Party's funding base. (Equally, one might conjecture, some of the enthusiasm within the Liberal Party for labour market deregulation owes its origins to the same set of associations.)

*Tariff Reform*

A Liberal politician, Bert Kelly, had vigorously opposed tariffs through the 1960s, but his was then almost a lone voice among politicians and his views were notable for their eccentricity. Gradually, however, the policy emphasis shifted away from the extension of protection, towards doubts about its preservation, and finally to ways to simplify and reduce the Australian tariff. Although Labor governments led the way, this was a largely bipartisan movement, eventually including even the National Party (whose support for tariffs, given the rural interest base of that party, was always somewhat surprising). The first major break was a 25 per cent tariff cut under Whitlam. Subsequently, although the Fraser government endorsed the idea of reducing and simplifying tariffs in theory, its practice was to cut some tariff rates and increase others (in already highly protected industries), so that the average rose a little above the post-Whitlam level, and the range increased. Fraser was, in this and allied matters, at odds with a large and growing 'dry' faction within the Liberals; and with the op-ed writers of the *Australian Financial Review* and *The Australian* newspaper. The Hawke Labor government in May 1988 and March 1991 embarked on gradual reductions in most tariff rates to 5 per cent by the year 2000, measures warmly supported by the Liberals in opposition (who nevertheless criticised some 'corporatist' elements in securing the changes). Finally, having ridiculed Dr Hewson's plank of zero tariffs during the election campaign, a re-elected Keating in 1993 effectively enacted that policy. Apart from the troublesome sectors of textiles, footwear and clothing, and passenger motor vehicles, this result was achieved under the Howard government in the last years of the century.

In discussing the regulation of markets for goods and non-labour services generally, we have stressed the role permitted or expected of foreign competition. The small size of total Australian production and the small number of Australian firms of 'efficient' scale have long been used as the bases for scepticism about the extent of rivalry among Australian producers, and thus the efficacy of purely domestic competition to achieve the theoretical efficiency benefits of private markets. As the Hawke and Keating governments saw it, the threat of foreign competition was supposed to encourage more efficiency and innovation in the banking sector. Interestingly, however, they and subsequent Coalition governments have supported the 'four pillars' policy of prohibiting mergers among the major Australian banks and finance companies. Apparently unregulated foreign competition is deemed insufficient to discipline domestic 'giants'.

*Competition Policy*

What then of domestic competition itself? As mentioned earlier, parts of the first Commonwealth effort to regulate Australian competition, the Australian Industries Preservation Act, were declared invalid; and in any case, the Act was primarily designed to restrict competition, not encourage it. Constitutional and other barriers prevented any effective legislation until the Trade Practices Act of 1965. The responsible minister, Garfield Barwick, professed to have found himself of the view that the maintenance of competition was, in the broad, indispensable to economic growth. According to the Attorney-General, the Act was designed to preserve competition to the extent required by the public interest. It prohibited collusive tendering and bidding, and required that firms notify, in secret, agreements in constraint of trade; notification of over 13,000 was duly provided, of which few were examined.[22] In 1971, like its 1906 forerunner, Barwick's attempt was substantially declared invalid and the Coalition government initiated an inquiry into its possible amendment. Under the 1974 Act, introduced by Lionel Murphy, more emphasis was put on protecting the consuming public, and a public interest test was inserted for the authorization of restrictive agreements. Price-fixing and retail price maintenance were prohibited; and a test for mergers was devised that turned on market dominance. The Fraser government amended the Act in 1977 in order to relax some of its more stringent sections. Then followed a long series of inquiries of various kinds, and associated amendments. Although there is still some controversy about the appropriateness of the legislation and its supporting bodies, a more or less satisfactory general competitive framework was achieved. Private monopolies, statutory corporations and activities protected by state Acts, however, remained in place.

Meanwhile, reforming state governments, pressed by the demands for capital from public enterprises, were showing themselves willing to cooperate with the Commonwealth (Painter, 1998). Almost all Commonwealth trading and producing enterprises had been corporatized or partly or wholly privatized under the Hawke and Keating Labor governments; various State governments were taking similar actions. Subsequently, the Howard Liberals sold one-third of Telstra and almost completely deregulated the telecommunications market. Further significant microeconomic reform required the co-operation of the States, with respect to their public enterprises and their regulatory powers. In this reform process, State governments were prominent, independent of party identity (though only South Australia had a Labor government). Ultimately, extensive micro-economic reform was achieved by 1996 through a series of agreements both among the states and between the States and the Commonwealth. These agreements covered road transport, rail freight transport, electricity grids and mutual recognition of regulatory standards. An incidental feature of this process of engaging the states in micro-economic reform seems to have been a significant upgrading of the State bureaucracies. For much of the century, certainly since the expansion of the Commonwealth bureaucracy after World War II, the main expertise and authority in intergovernmental relations had lain with the Commonwealth (at least at the bureaucratic level). That situation appears to be changing: the central Commonwealth departments no longer seem to have a monopoly on professional expertise. The *Competition Policy Reform Act 1995* introduced a framework, the National Competition Policy, to extend competition to all public enterprises, largely implementing the proposals of the Hilmer Report of 1993 (see Painter, 1998). These proposals included regulation of 'access' to the facilities of pipelines, and other 'natural monopolies'.

### Labour Market Regulation

Regulation of industrial relations was, it will be recalled, an integral component of Deakin's New Protection. The story in relation to 'deregulation' in this area is more complicated and less linear. The Hawke government deregulated the financial markets while utilizing a form of corporatist regulation, the Accord, in the labour market. However, subsequently the Keating Labor governments' moves towards free international trade sparked claims that, without labour market deregulation, Australian industries would be at a competitive disadvantage. Labor's first response was to attempt to create larger unions, with the expectation that they, like their peak body, the Australian Council of Trade Unions, would take greater account of the wider, even the national, economic interest; or would be easier to control by the ACTU or government. However, to a large extent these amalgamations proved to be just a way-station towards the re-creation of industry and enterprise unions (rather than multi-industry craft unions), engaged in 'enterprise bargaining'. Labor eventually introduced some significant flexibility into the system, which Howard and Peter Reith much increased. Earlier, Greiner, who as premier of New South Wales had been most vocal on the need for a more collaborative federalism, offered to yield industrial relations powers entirely to the Commonwealth; Victoria's Kennett did so.

## Industry and Related Policy

Following the Mortimer inquiry, budget assistance to industry was boosted under Labor as part of their strategy of tariff reductions. More recently, the Howard government has focused on promotion of investment, exports, innovation, competitiveness and resource sustainability. However, the Howard government did give some modest support to research and development, areas usually regarded as exhibiting 'market failures'. In the public sector, the Coalition implemented the recommendations of the National Commission of Audit, extracting what were called 'efficiency dividends'. The picture in relation to 'human capital' went somewhat against this trend. Public support for 'private' schooling had been in place since the 1960s and the private sector enjoyed rapid growth at the secondary level, especially through the 1980s and 1990s. However, effective control over syllabuses continued to be exercised by the state, partly directly as a condition of funding and partly through the requirements for university entrance under a state-controlled tertiary education sector. The gradual expansion of the tertiary education sector that had occurred since World War II reached a crescendo through the 1980s and 1990s as the system moved from 'elite' to a 'mass' higher education. During the 1980s the number of universities was doubled and Labor, having abolished university fees in 1972 under Whitlam, effectively reintroduced them under the Higher Education Contribution Scheme as a means to help fund the expansion of the system. Price competition within the higher education sector continues to be sharply curtailed where it is not expressly forbidden. Interestingly, although the government's role in private capital allocation has declined spectacularly over the century, its role in human capital provision remains overwhelming. In this aspect, the contrast between 1910 and 2000 may not be as marked as it might appear. Arguably, human capital has replaced physical capital as the most significant element in economic development. Although the state role in physical capital markets has diminished markedly, its role in education at the increasingly important tertiary level remains overwhelmingly predominant.

## Towards Explanation

In explaining the change of policy regime outlined in the preceding section, two intersecting forces were foreshadowed – internal contradictions arising within a policy regime, and pressure of external forces. Both operated in the Australian case – at least, as we ourselves see it and as we see the architects of the changes themselves to have seen it. However, the perceptions are important here. And institutions are significant in influencing whose perceptions get to count. A particular theme in much recent commentary on these matters has been the role of 'experts', and especially economists, in the determination of Australia's policy regime. That is an issue to which we will also attend in the discussion that follows. Earlier, we reported how in the 1920s the 'experts', taking the form both of the Tariff Board and an independent economic inquiry, had thrown doubt on further extension of the tariff. War and import controls had pushed tariffs off centre stage in Australia until the late 1950s. But when the tariff schedule started to become, once again, the chief vehicle of protection against import competition, expert opinion on the tariff had become fairly uniformly negative. For example under the 1957 UK Trade Agreement, UK producers were to be given 'full opportunity of reasonable competition on the basis of relative costs of economic and efficient production'. However, in its 1958–59 report, the Tariff Board declined to offer any detailed interpretation of these words. Indeed, the Board confessed itself ultimately unable to justify large differences in tariff rates (many of which were struck during the emergency of the 1930s) – or possibly any differences at all. The validity of the underlying strategy, of setting made-to-measure tariffs, was again thrown into considerable doubt – though in very different economic circumstances from those that had prevailed in the 1920s.

In the early 1950s, Australian export policy was caught between the desire for price stability through international commodity agreements and the attraction of a more liberal trade regime. The outlook for primary exports was clouded because the British government had declined to extend beyond the 1950s those bulk purchase arrangements remaining from World War II. In any event, the value to Australia of preferential access to British markets had fallen; and the United States, with its huge food stockpiles, did not play by the rules of the General Agreement on Tariffs and Trade. Subsequently, Britain declared its intention to join the European Economic Community and abandon Commonwealth preferences. Moreover, Japan, which had already become a significant market for Australian products, sought admission to GATT in 1952 and joined in 1955. New bilateral trade treaties with Britain and Japan in 1957 spelled the end of the Ottawa Agreements of 1932 and began movement towards relatively normal trading relationships between Japan and Australia. Within a decade, Japan had become Australia's largest trading partner. Australia was little involved in the rounds of tariff cuts under GATT auspices. However, during the GATT review of 1954–55 it achieved a relaxation of the GATT rules on tariff 'bindings', and thereby calmed the worst fears of Australian import-competing industries that any new trade agreement with Japan would unleash fearsome import competition, especially in textiles, footwear and clothing. Eventually, in

1963, and much later than other contracting parties to GATT, Australia finally relinquished its right to discriminate against Japanese imports (which it had done since the 'trade diversion' episode of the 1930s). By this point, a new mining boom and import replacement had relieved anxieties about the balance of trade. Indeed, there was some pressure for an appreciation of the Australian currency.

The displacement of the United Kingdom by Japan as Australia's primary trading partner extended the life of a trade regime focused on bilateral and other restrictive trade agreements. Under Protection All Round, significant recompense for manufacturing tariffs and other burdens of the protective regime had been offered to some primary producers, including subsidized delivery of many rural services and privileged access to British markets. Access to the booming Japanese market, therefore, permitted the continued affiliation of the Country Party to the protectionist regime and the continued access to special interest support that the protectionist regime embodied. However, the world trade framework that had given Japan access to developed country markets attracted other Asian Tigers. The country that had formerly been a threat to Australian import-competing manufactures now itself faced competition. And as the world price of those manufactures fell, the economic burden of attempts to maintain Australian import competition rose.

Continuous and large reductions in transport and travel costs reinforced the economic message. The saving made by shopping offshore could offset the cost of the airfare to Asia. The spectacle of a federal minister, caught smuggling a television set through Customs, eloquently communicated the problem to the general public. Exports of services, like education and tourism, were facilitated by the falling airfares.

The role played by economists in this entire story can easily be overemphasized. As we see it, theirs was a supporting part, not a leading one. They gave comfort to tariff sceptics among politicians and leader writers. They provided estimates that showed that the rates of *effective* protection differed greatly from the nominal tariff rates set by the legislators and, in a few instances, were well over 100 per cent. They showed that only a small percentage of jobs were in highly protected industries, and that labour turnover in those industries was high. They ignored or dismissed 'the Australian case' for protection as a means of economic development. They asserted, without much proof, that protection was a major reason why Australian material living standards had not risen as fast as those in some other rich countries. Certainly much was made of the fall in Australia's ranking in the Organization for Economic Co-operation and Development, and later within a broader set of countries in which set the Asian Tigers figured conspicuously. Keating's famous quip about Australians becoming the 'white-trash' of Asia nicely encapsulated the general anxiety. One agent of influence over this period was Fred Gruen, economist, farmer, and close adviser of successive Labor governments. Gruen's own account (in Gruen and Grattan, 1993) of Labor's sharp tariff reductions omits any reference to his own role, crediting rather the favourable exchange rate, the gradualist approach taken, the use of adjustment assistance and export and other incentives. Although this omission could be explained by modesty, we are inclined to take Gruen's account at face value. The message, rather than the messengers, was the decisive factor.

**Two Salient Aspects**

Two features of the Australian experience are worth underlining. The first is that the shift in overall policy regime is in a direction that is shared with most Western countries – especially the English-speaking ones, but to some extent more broadly. The precise timing and the magnitude of the changes may have differed a little between locations. New Zealand, for example, is notable for having moved earlier, and further, and faster than Australia and from an even more protectionist, anti-competitive starting point. And the distance moved and the rapidity of the change in New Zealand are arguably attributable to constitutional factors – not least the fact that New Zealand has a unicameral legislature. The rhetorical accompaniment of the changes also differed between locations. Thatcher's British variant and Reagan's American one were both marked by a kind of ideological defence that the Hawke–Keating policy realignment never appealed to, even though the character of the changes was comparable.

If this 'universality' claim is accepted, then it seems clear that any merely local explanation of the changes is inadequate. One might seek to explain details of the changes and in particular any distinctive features by reference to factors specific to Australia; but the main causal forces will have to satisfy a broad 'international' test. Of course, the recognition that the *changes* were virtually universal does not deny that Australia remains rather different from other countries – most notably, the European ones. If Australia had sought to move in other directions, there would have been no shortage of alternative models to choose from. But that would have been to go against a trend that was operative even in the European countries that Australia might have tried to imitate. Using the language of Hall and Soskice's (2001) 'comparative capitalisms' analysis, there can be little doubt that in the array of possible 'capitalism models', Australia has located itself closer to the UK and US 'ideal type' than to the Japanese or German. We might conceivably have done otherwise. But we would have done so at a time when the Japanese and German institutional arrays were themselves shifting in a somewhat 'liberal' direction.

The second (related) feature is that generally since the mid-1980s the relevant changes had broad bipartisan support, at least at the level of the leadership of the major parties, and especially when in government. For example, the Campbell Committee, which ushered in major capital market deregulation, was established by the (Liberal) Fraser government. But the committee's recommendations were implemented by the (Labor) Hawke–Keating government. Equally, although it was the Fraser government that introduced indexation of personal income tax, the original policy impetus came from the Whitlam (Labor) government, in establishing the Mathews Committee of Enquiry on the issue. The apparently influential Hilmer Report on competition policy was an initiative of the then Labor government – and again was the output of a putatively independent committee. Much of its thrust was implemented by subsequent Liberal governments and by supportive Liberal governments at the State level. In all these cases, and significant numbers of others, the recommendations for such broad changes in the policy regime originated not in political party platforms but in dedicated 'committees of inquiry'. It is our impression that Australia has had a more extended reliance on such independent committees of inquiry (and earlier, Royal Commissions) as the initiators of broad policy regime changes than have other comparable countries. It seems to us notable that so much of what we identify as our 'economic institutional framework' owes its origins to committees of inquiry that were putatively non-partisan politically and operated independently from ordinary political process. Of course, any such committee's recommendations have to be broadly endorsed by the government of the day if they are to be implemented. And the selection of participants and the nuances in terms of reference provide scope for the current government to colour the recommendations. Nevertheless, the process does involve some loss of control by the government of the day – even if the 'independence' is only partial. The introduction of the goods and services tax by the Liberals in the last years of the century is striking because it is an exception to this rule. But even this case is instructive. Although the introduction of the GST was in the upshot a politically contested matter, the introduction of a reformulated broad-based indirect tax system had been at one time or another an agenda item for various 'inquiry' exercises since the Asprey Committee's report to the Whitlam government in 1975.

Of course, the extensive use of independent committees lends some support to the claim that economists have played a significant role in framing the basic policy regime. And support too for the conjecture that a primary element in explaining significant changes in that regime has been changes in the prevailing views of the economics profession. However, more extravagant claims to the effect that those prevailing views are to be thought of as ideologically extreme and/or are driven by extremely eccentric views of what the public interest entails are difficult to sustain. On the whole, with (perhaps significant but essentially second-order) differences between parties, the changes in Australia's economic institutions seem to have enjoyed bipartisan consensus. Furthermore, if economists have 'captured' the policy debate, they have done so not only in Australia, but also across the Western world, and in a manner fully consistent with prevailing democratic arrangements.

There are nevertheless two rather different accounts of how changes of this kind come about, and where the 'consistency' with democratic institutions bites. One such account locates democratic constraints at the level of prevailing public opinion – and public opinion specifically on questions of *policy*. An economistic version of this view is that something like the median voter theorem in public choice theory prevails in the domain of broad economic policy. On this account, the shift in policy reflects shifts in the preferred positions of an appropriate subset of the voting population.

An alternative account relies on policy decisions being taken elsewhere than in arenas where there is party political influence. We have already mentioned this possibility in relation to the roles of bureaucracy and of 'expert' committees. This account would seem to involve the implication that competitive elections are fought on grounds other than policy choices – perhaps on rival rhetorical positions, which have little purchase on policy regimes, or perhaps on the basis of the personality characteristics of leaders. This view would accommodate the possibility that policy decisions might be made that differ markedly from prevailing views among the citizenry as to what is appropriate. But this is only possible while the citizenry do not regard policy considerations as sufficient grounds for changing the way they cast their votes. We consider such a picture of democratic processes to be implausible. One does not have to argue that policy is the only thing that drives voting behaviour (as many public choice models do) to argue that policy choices are electorally relevant. Or would become electorally relevant if any party or candidate offered policies that were too far out of line with prevailing public opinion.

In summary, these two 'facts' – the international similarities in the directions of movement, and the apparent bipartisan support for the direction of change – act as disciplines on any plausible first-round explanation of Australia's economic institutions and the changes in them. No candidate for explanation of the changes that is inconsistent with these facts seems worth consideration. If there are in operation forces that have changed views about what policies are desirable, those forces cannot be purely local. They must reflect larger global movement. And in each political community that movement must be broadly spread across the voting population.

None of this denies the importance of economic ideas or of changes in them. The shift in policy regime away from protection and regulation and towards greater reliance on market competition certainly matches a shift in the views of economists about both the advantages of market-like arrangements and the limits of non-market alternatives. But it is doubtful whether economists' views played more than a peripheral role.

Certainly, there are forces other than the policy views of economists at work. In particular, the issue as economists have seen it is one of optimal response to certain exogenous factors – some of them specific to Australia and others of them merely Australian manifestations of worldwide trends. The most significant of these external factors are:

- the long-term secular decline in the world price of most of the commodities in which Australia has traditionally held a comparative advantage and on which Australian relative wealth in 1901 was based
- the increase in the relative significance of human to physical capital
- the reduced transportation costs in product markets
- increased competitiveness in world markets for almost all goods and services
- increased mobility in labour markets (both domestically and internationally) and greater competitiveness in international capital markets.

In our view, the change in Australia's 'economic institutions' – understood as the basic policy regime in which markets operate – is to be explained as what both major political parties, and certainly most informed commentators, have regarded as the optimal response to those external changes. Particular aspects of the broader political institutional framework (strong political parties, single-member electoral districts, the role of 'expert committees') have played some role in the nature, timing and extent of that response. But the idea that governments or their advisers are masters of the country's destiny in economic affairs reflects a 'fallacy of control'. That idea was a fallacy even in 1901. And the unfolding of the century has simply made its status as a fallacy more conspicuous.

### Notes

1 For some preliminary attempts along such lines, see Brennan and Hamlin (1993), and Brennan and Mitchell (1999).
2 Or alternatively, it might have rather little effect, depending on what goods individuals would have purchased in the absence of government provision. See Brennan and Pincus (1983).
3 For this reason we have shown the causal influences there as dotted lines.

4 The supposition is somewhat heroic, but it is one that has a vigorous life in much policy analysis and has a better claim to empirical reality than much of the economic theory of politics has been inclined to concede. See, for example, Brennan and Hamlin (2000) for argument to this effect.
5 This erosion arguably took longer and was accepted more reluctantly in Australia than elsewhere. The tradition of the best Australian graduate students going to Cambridge, which lived on as a tradition long after Cambridge had ceased to be the predominant intellectual force in economics that it had been, is one part of this story. The rise of US influence, significantly mediated through the NSW Department of Agriculture and the tendency of agricultural economists increasingly to train in the United States, is another part. See Groenewegen and McFarlane (1990).
6 It is worth noting that the proposition does not necessarily generalize across policy instruments. Some kinds of industry 'support' (such as regulation that limits entry and creates quasi-monopoly rents) serve to *reduce* the number of workers (and hence voters) in the industry. On the other hand, the effects on industry profits and the corresponding capacity to make lobbying expenditures and campaign contributions are as for other forms of special interest policy.
7 McGillivray (1997), contrasting what industries obtained higher protection in the 1970s in Canada and the United States, argued that in majoritarian systems with low party discipline, tariff protection will favour large, electorally dispersed industries.
8 Garnaut (1994) suggested that the demise of tariff protection was assisted by the formation of peak national bodies to 'represent' industry and unions, in a 'corporatist' manner.
9 See Siriwardana (1991), on the difficulty of measuring the effects of Victorian tariffs.
10 Along these lines, there is a longer and more complex story to tell about the choices made by government, from among the various available policy instruments, especially between those that raise or make little call on public revenue, and those that use it intensively. See Smith (1993) for an overview of tax history.
11 Advocates of low tariffs in the United States firmly supported the first imposition of the federal income tax in the 1890s; the tax was declared unconstitutional, and it reimposition required an amendment of the constitution. Hansen (1990) emphasized the importance of customs tax revenue in the determination of US tariffs from 1829 to 1940 (as well as the distributional aspects central to the interest group explanation).
12 The value of spillovers was exaggerated and the indicators used were often conceptually flawed (e.g. the private benefits were estimated by the expected increase in private output). See the discussion in Part 4 of Butlin, Barnard and Pincus (1982) and the dispute between Frost (2000) and Boot (1998). Also, see the discussion of the Development and Migration Commission in Roe (1995) and Greenwood (1955).
13 A classic expression, of the dangers of 'cut-throat competition' and the possible advantages (to customers and to workers) of agreements in constraint of trade, is to be found in the 1912–13 High Court judgment in the (coal) Vend case. 'Cut-throat competition is not now regarded by a large portion of mankind as necessarily beneficial to the public … the intention of the parties was to put the Newcastle coal trade on a satisfactory basis, which

Australia's Economic Institutions    83

would enable them to pay adequate wages to their men and sell their coal at a price remunerative to themselves': cited in Fitzhardinge (1964: 270). There is a remarkable parallel with the rationale, given in July 2001 by Professor Allan Fels, for the authorization by the ACCC of collective agreements between sugar growers and sugar crushers.

14  The Australian Industries Preservation Act attempted to prevent the takeover of Australian enterprises by foreigners, especially non-British ones.

15  In keeping with our explanatory scheme, we note that many countries, but not all, increased their levels of import protection and other interferences with international trade, substantially before the onset of the Great Depression, and dramatically in the late 1920s and early 1930s.

16  By 1931, the Tariff Board was complaining about the 'tariff habit': the tendency of some manufacturers to turn to the customs tariff for assistance without first making reasonable efforts to increase their production by other means available to them. Similar sentiments were expressed by the 1929 Tariff Inquiry: 'The most disquieting effect of the tariff has been the stimulus it has given to demand for government assistance of all kinds, with the consequent demoralizing effect upon self-reliant efficiency throughout all forms of production.' See Hall (1958: 90); Brigden (1929: 6).

17  In population policy, both parties first abandoned emphasis on British stock, and later the White Australia policy itself.

18  State rail investments continued to be protected against private trucks, using public roads, into the 1960s.

19  This is splendidly illustrated by the 25 per cent, across-the-board tariff cut under the Whitlam administration – which was purportedly to increase market supplies in an economy facing rapid inflation. However, Whitlam had supplementary motivations. He believed that the system of tariff protection had poured funds into the coffers of the non-Labor parties; and that a more efficient allocation of economic resources, which the cut in tariffs was expected to cause, would expand the tax base to fund his government's spending plans.

20  A useful check-list is Industry Commission (1997).

21  The Campbell Committee comprised four businessmen and one official each from the Treasury and the Reserve Bank. Before the Hawke government acted, it commissioned its own review of the recommendations, called the Martin review (*Report of the Review Group*, Australian Government Publishing Service, 1984). Kelly describes the battle within the Labor government and its advisers over the strategy of financial deregulation. In their survey of financial inquiries, Edwards and Valentine (1998) attribute changes in regulation partly to endogenous factors (like the evasion of controls by banks setting up non-banking institutions) and 'autonomous factors, reflecting the evolution of economic thinking and changes in fashion' (p. 297). However, in their and others' accounts, it is difficult to disentangle the one from the other. In particular, what Edwards and Valentine describe as the 'general agreement that in many cases financial regulation was not achieving its objectives' (p. 299; similar claims have been made by many other commentators) is surely to be attributed to the interaction of endogenous factors and economic investigations, theoretical and practical.

22  Brunt (2000: xii) claimed that an advantage of the original Trade Practices Act was 'the invention of that unique, multi-disciplinary, quasi-judicial body, posed between the courts and the (Trade Practices) Commission, the (Trade Practices) Tribunal'.

## References

Australia. (Asprey) *Taxation Review Committee* (Canberra: Australian Government Publishing Service, 1975).
Australia. (Campbell) *Committee of Inquiry into the Australian Financial System: Final Report* (Canberra: Australian Government Publishing Service, 1981).
Australia. (Martin) Parliamentary Inquiry into the Australian Banking Industry, House of Representatives Standing Committee on Finance and Public Administration, *A Pocket Full of Change: Banking and Deregulation* (Canberra: Australian Government Publishing Service, 1991).
Australia. (Hilmer) Independent Committee of Inquiry into Competition Policy in Australia, *National Competition Policy* (Canberra: Australian Government Publishing Service, 1993).
Australia. (Mortimer) Review of Business Programs, *Going for Growth*, <www.isr.gov.au/events/Mortimer/>, 1997.
Boot, H. M. 'Government and the Colonial Economies', *Australian Economic History Review*, vol. 38 (1998) pp. 74–101.
Brennan, G., and Buchanan, J. *The Reason of Rules* (New York: Cambridge University Press, 1985).
Brennan, G., and Hamlin, A. 'Rationalising Parliamentary Systems', *Australian Journal of Political Science*, vol. 28 (1993) pp. 443–57.
*Democratic Devices and Desires* (Cambridge: Cambridge University Press, 2000).
Brennan, G., and Mitchell, N. 'The Logic of Spatial Politics', *Australian Journal of Political Science*, vol. 34 (1999) pp. 379–90.
Brennan, G., and Pincus, J. J. 'Government Expenditure Growth and Resource Allocation: The Nebulous Connection', *Oxford Economic Papers* (November 1983) pp. 351–65.
Brigden, J. B., et al. *The Australian Tariff*, 2nd edn (Melbourne: Melbourne University Press in association with Macmillan, 1929).
Brunt, M. 'Preface', in R Steinwall (ed.), *25 Years of Australian Competition Law*, (Sydney: Butterworths 2000).
Buchanan, James M. *The Limits of Liberty* (Chicago: University of Chicago Press, 1975).
Butlin, N. G., 'Colonial Socialism in Australia, 1860–1900', in H. G. J. Aitkin (ed.), *The State and Economic Growth* (New York: SSRC, 1959).
Butlin, N. G., Barnard, A., and Pincus, J. J. *Government and Capitalism: Public and Private Choice in Twentieth Century Australia* (Sydney: Allen & Unwin, 1982).
Butlin, S. J. *The Australian Monetary System, 1851 to 1914* (Sydney: Sydney University Press, 1986).
Campbell, K. O. *Agricultural Marketing and Prices* (Melbourne: Cheshire, 1973).
Edwards, V., and Valentine, T. 'From Napier to Wallis: Six Decades of Financial Inquiries', *Economic Record*, vol. 74 (September 1998) pp. 297–312.
Finn, P. *Law and Government in Colonial Australia* (Melbourne: Oxford University Press, 1987).
Fitzhardinge, L. *William Morris Hughes: A Political Biography* (Sydney: Angus & Robertson, [1964] 1979).
Frost, L. 'Government and the Colonial Economies: An Alternative View', *Australian Economic History Review*, vol. 40(1) (March 2000) pp. 71–85.
Garnaut, R. 'Trade and Tariffs and Australian Business', in R. G. Stewart (ed.), *Government and Business Relations in Australia* (St Leonards, NSW: Allen & Unwin, 1994).

Goodwin, C. D. W. *Economic Enquiry in Australia* (Durham, NC: Duke University Press, 1966).
Greenwood, G. *Australia: A Social and Political History* (Sydney: Angus & Robertson, 1955).
Groenewegen, P., and McFarlane, B. *A History of Australian Economic Thought* (Melbourne: Routledge, 1990).
Gruen, F., and Grattan, M. *Managing Government: Labor's Achievements and Failures* (Melbourne: Longman Cheshire, 1993).
Hall, G. J. 'The Australian Tariff, 1922–1956', M.Com. Thesis, University of Melbourne, 1958.
Hall, P. A., and Soskice, D. *Varieties of Capitalism* (Oxford: Oxford University Press, 2001).
Hansen, J. M. 'Taxation and the Political Economy of the Tariff', *International Organization* (Autumn 1990) pp. 527–51.
Independent Committee of Inquiry into Competition Policy in Australia. *National Competition Policy* (Canberra: Australian Government Publishing Service, 1993).
Industry Commission. *Microeconomic Reforms in Australia: A Compendium From the 1970s to 1997* (Canberra: Commonwealth of Australia, 1997).
Kelly, P. *The End of Certainty. Power, Politics and Business in Australia* (St Leonards, NSW: Allen & Unwin, 1994).
McGillivray, F. 'Party Discipline as a Determinant of the Endogenous Formation of Tariffs', *American Journal of Political Science*, vol. 41(2) (April 1997) pp. 584–608.
Olson, M. *The Rise and Decline of Nations: Economic Growth, Stagflation, and Social Rigidities* (New Haven, Conn.: Yale University Press, 1982).
Painter, M. *Collaborative Federalism: Economic Reform in Australia in the 1990s* (Cambridge: Cambridge University Press, 1998).
Pincus, J. J. 'Liberalism and Australian Economic and Industrial Development', chapter 16 of J. R. Nethercote (ed.), *Liberalism and the Australian Federation* (Annandale, NSW: Federation Press, 2001).
Pusey, M. *Economic Rationalism in Canberra: A Nation-Building State Changes Its Mind* (Cambridge: Cambridge University Press, 1991).
Quiggin, J. *Great Expectations: Microeconomic Reform and Australia* (Sydney: Allen & Unwin, 1996).
Roe, M. *Australia, Britain, and Migration, 1915–1940: A Study of Desperate Hopes* (Cambridge: Cambridge University Press, 1995).
Siriwardana, A. M. 'The Impact of Tariff Protection in the Colony of Victoria in the Late Nineteenth Century: A General Equilibrium Analysis', *Australian Economic History Review*, vol. 31(2) (1991) pp. 45–65.
Smith, J. P. *Taxing Popularity* (Canberra: Federalism Research Centre, ANU, 1993).
Stewart, J. 'Trade and Industry Policies', in S. Prasser, J. R. Nethercote and J. Warhurst (eds), *The Menzies Era: A Reappraisal of Government, Politics and Policy* (Maryborough, Vic.: Hale & Iremonger, 1995).

# 4   Globalization and Australian Institutions

*John Braithwaite*

**Parables of a Clever and Stupid Country**

Australian culture today is significantly shaped by US television and by the marketing of late modern identities by US corporations. Indeed, even Prime Minister John Howard's foreign policy – his indiscreetly articulated dream that we might be Uncle Sam's regional deputy sheriff during the Timor crisis – seems to have a touch of Hollywood.

At the same time, it is true that in global politics Australia boxes out of its weight division. In United Nations institutions, the Organization for Economic Co-operation and Development, indeed in most intergovernmental organizations Australia has been more influential and respected than our political and economic significance would suggest. This is not true of international business organizations. In Geneva, New York or Paris intergovernmental agencies are riddled with Australians in influential positions. But down the road from the OECD at the International Chamber of Commerce, Australian business organizations are not important contributors to the debates that matter.[1] Similarly, in the lobbies of Geneva and New York, it is not the Australian business leaders who are shaping agendas among the business movers and shakers.

A revealing case study of Australia's global significance or insignificance is the creative and masterful leadership of Australian bureaucrats in establishing the Cairns Group during the Uruguay round of the GATT (Capling, 2001). The creation of this group did change the game. In previous GATT rounds the only real players had been the United States, Europe and Japan. Once the Cairns Group declared 'no agriculture, no round', they forced the United States to take them seriously. The United States said back to them: 'no intellectual property, no round'. The upshot seemed win-win, a triumph of Australian bureaucratic entrepreneurship within global institutions: agriculture and intellectual property both became big new disciplines of the World Trade Organization. Unfortunately, however, while Australia complied assiduously with its new intellectual property obligations, the United States chose not to comply with the new agricultural disciplines. The cost of this dual loss to the

Australian economy was enormous, given that Australia is a significant net exporter of agricultural products and a significant net importer of intellectual property rights: rural Australia was thrown into steeper decline, the health system was further crippled by being forced to pay years of extra monopoly profits to Northern pharmaceutical patent holders. Worse, through its seemingly clever support of TRIPs (the Trade Related Intellectual Property agreement of the Uruguay round) as an influential member of the Friends of Intellectual Property Group in Geneva, Australia played its part in making AIDS drugs unaffordable for developing nations, with catastrophic consequences across the globe and especially in Africa.

The Cairns Group fiasco is a parable of Australia's strengths and tragic weaknesses within global institutions. Australian trade bureaucrats were able to see the wood for the trees, making themselves a real force through the vehicle of the Cairns Group. But at the end of the day, Australia's interests were not served because the decisive end-run lobbying was done by US business groups. In the intellectual property field they actually managed to persuade Australia to exceed its TRIPs obligations, for example extending pharmaceutical patents beyond the twenty years mandated by TRIPs, and in the case of agriculture they persuaded Washington to increase agricultural subsidies instead of reducing them. It is a parable of comparative Australian governmental ingenuity, but of ultimate submission to the greater comparative strength of business interests in Northern nations.

Telecommunications is another such contemporary parable. The PMG/Telecom ran one of the most efficient public telecommunications systems in the world, in the face of comparatively difficult logistic challenges – a huge continent thinly populated with telephone subscribers. Part of this success was the Australian governmental innovation of the statutory authority to run a business enterprise relatively independent of political interference. One might have thought that, once privatized, Telstra would be well placed to become a formidable global player. Instead, the private sector management of Telstra has been abysmal; a publicly generated comparative advantage has been squandered when it became a private opportunity. I am not suggesting that the privatization was a mistake, simply that our public telecommunications operated at above the international average of public provision, but that as a private provider it has performed comparatively poorly. Indeed in the telecommunications market generally, Australia is no Finland. No Nokia knocks.

Among developed nations, Italy, a source of many of our immigrants, is our mirror image. Italy with its incompetent, unstable, corrupt public administration has creative private entrepreneurship that has given us many familiar brand names, from typewriters to fashion. Australia, with its innovative public sector management and stodgy business management, registers its greatest claim for international notoriety in the field of corporate crime. So my third parable is the life of Alan Bond, beloved winner of the America's Cup. Bond was an English immigrant convict of sorts, convicted as a young Perth signwriter for a professional burglary business he was running on the side (Barry, 1990). He secured controlling interests in businesses that matter in Australia – beer and television – and thereby became a confidant of premiers and prime ministers. The scale of the losses his shareholders and creditors suffered, a ten-figure sum, may not have been exceeded by any corporate criminal in the history of the world so far.

There was genuine competence and flair in Bond's criminality and in his sporting accomplishments. Like Christopher Skase he was a master of laundering funds around the world financial system. But no-one would allege that he improved the quality of our beer or television.

Australia is a nation whose accomplishments in good government, in sport, in the arts and in intellectual endeavour have far exceeded our accomplishments in business management, as the Karpin Report (Industry Task Force on Leadership, 1995) somewhat timidly documented. Why are we as wealthy as we are, then, it might be asked? The things we are good at do add greatly to our wealth. Australian filmmakers compete with Hollywood successfully, our novelists compete for Booker prizes. Our biomedical scientists produce incredible breakthroughs which, while they are mainly exploited by Northern corporations, occasionally create wealth through Australian companies creating Australian jobs. We even have generated some wealth by putting on Olympic Games and Grand Slam tennis tournaments. Australian workers are not only competent at sport; they are literate, and wise, and are avid readers of newspapers compared to people of other lands. This helps make up for the economic deficit of the poor ways their talents are managed. It makes us an attractive regional office location for well-managed multinationals from the North. In fields where workers are fairly autonomous from managers, notably agriculture and winemaking, Australian efficiency has been extraordinary throughout our history. Mining is another area of high productivity where workers are relatively scattered into autonomous work groups beyond the gaze of management control. And of course Australia has natural comparative advantages in agriculture and minerals extraction. So in spite of Australian business incompetence we are not poor, though we are getting comparatively poorer as the prices decline for our agricultural and mining outputs.

Comparatively good government is also an economic plus for Australia. One of the positives for business investment in Australia is that in general you do not need to bribe a government official to get things done.

Australian business regulation has its flaws, but by and large it is recognized in my field as among the most sophisticated in the world, mostly managing to avoid the excesses of adversarial legalism we see in the United States and the extremes of business capture and corruption that characterize most states. The institutions of micro-economic reform discussed in the previous chapter have been internationally influential. Not only have they been modelled in significant ways by other states, but the Industries Assistance Commission model – robust expert economic diagnosis of the effects of industry protection, tabled as a draft report and subject to deliberative critique and revision through open public hearings – has been copied by the Trade Policy Review Process at the World Trade Organization (Braithwaite and Drahos, 2000: Chapter 10).

The argument of this chapter is that we can enrich our understanding of this contrast between Australian governmental innovation and business sluggishness by putting Australia in global perspective. Globalization, conceived here simply as the 'intensification of economic, political, social and cultural relations across borders' (Holm and Sorensen, 1995: 1), is not something new. While there clearly are some arenas, like entertainment and brand names, in which the effects of globalization have accelerated since World War II, I am not interested in tired debates about the relative importance of the global and the national across time. What I will discuss is how the distinctive nature of Australia requires us to include a consideration of global factors from 1788. These include: global movements of labour to sites of labour shortage like Australia; and the ways in which global movements of capital were shaped by a triple investment in corporate scale, scope and management that Australia failed to make because of protectionism, early failures of competition policy and because for a long time we did well by investing in extractive industries that did not require the triple investment. Australia's problem, I will argue, became corporate dependency on state hand-outs, as reflected in an unwillingness of Australian capitalists to take private responsibility for research and development or for human capital formation. Welfare dependency of the poor in an Australian welfare state that became modest by international standards was not a deadweight on Australian competitiveness. The sorry effect of the corporate finger pointing at coddling of the poor, instead of corporate coddling as the root of our problems, left Australia both a more unequal and a less entrepreneurial society.

## A Government Colony in a World of Corporate Colonies

Three of the four largest nations in the world today – Indonesia, the United States and India – were ruled by private corporations in the seventeenth and eighteenth centuries. The British East India Company wanted to form the government of the fourth, China, in the way it governed the Indian sub-continent, but the Chinese Mandarins combined with the competing claims of other Western powers to form an opposition too formidable. The Dutch East India Company formed the government of what we today call Indonesia. Most of the important early North American colonies were governed by companies like the Virginia Company, the Massachusetts Bay Company, the Dutch West Indies Company and later the Royal African Company (with New York), and the Hudson's Bay Company. Others, like Pennsylvania, were formed by individual businessmen leading a religious minority group. The Virginia Company was quite insignificant and short-lived commercially, but it did settle the first English colony in America, and wrote a constitution for Virginia that provided for the first representative legislature in America (Davis, 1961: 168). Thus, it was private corporate governance that first tilled the soil of democracy in Virginia, which in turn later grew a Jefferson and a Madison.

Similarly, the Massachusetts Bay Company developed a democratic constitution of Massachusetts with checks and balances and a separation of legislative and judicial powers. This constitution, along with that of Virginia, became a model for other colonies aspiring to governance by elected representatives constrained by a rule of law. 'The constitution of the colonial trading company was therefore perpetuated to a large extent in the State and Federal constitutions of the United States' (Davis, 1961: 201). In America, governmental institutions 'largely derived from corporations' (Ibid: 205) had a democratic vitality that was lacking elsewhere because they took root in American soil clear of feudal institutions. In the 1980s a new wave of colonization of the state by the corporation commenced: corporatization within government. The monolithic state bureaucracies were divided into separately managed corporatized operating units (Hood et al., 1999: Chapter 9). While Australia experienced this latter colonization of the state by the corporation, there were no important corporate players in its early history. It is this as much as the fact that Australia was a convict colony that made Australia distinctive. For example, Australia developed a large public sector that for most of its history compensated for the low private investment in human capital formation and research and development (R&D) with comparatively strong public investment. Since Keith Hancock's (1930) *Australia*, a theme in Australian historiography has been that this is a society that looks to and values things being done well by governmental institutions.

My hypothesis is that to understand the institutional trajectory of former colonies it is important to understand how their institutional foundations were laid. Was the colony built on pre-existing feudal foundations that would hold back democratic experiments? Was the initial constitution that of a business corporation? Was it formed as a white settler colony (like Canada, the United States, Australia, New Zealand) or as a colony with a population mainly consisting of indigenous inhabitants with transient white colonial masters returning to the metropole after a period managing the colonial business? Or was it a hybrid like South Africa, characterized by competition between two large white settler communities (the British South Africa Company and the Dutch East India Company) both smaller in number than indigenous populations? To understand why an institutional framework like Apartheid arose in South Africa, but not in Australia, we might need to understand these hybrid South African institutional foundations. To understand why economic growth in Australia is driven by governmental investment in R&D, not private investment, we might need to understand the profound governmentalism of our own history. In the next section, I seek to develop an insight into Australian institutions by focusing on the global currents swirling at the nation's foundations. Then I move on to argue that in the twentieth century, it was global movements of capital that supplanted global movements of people as the greatest force reshaping Australian institutions.

## Global Population Movements and the Global Penal Debate

England in the late eighteenth and early nineteenth centuries was suffering a crime wave (Braithwaite, 1989: 111–13). The growth of professionalized police services from Peel's innovation in 1829 was a later institutional response to this crisis, as were the Sunday School and a variety of other measures in civil society. But the initial response was a contest waged between two competing policy ideas – transportation and the penitentiary. Jeremy Bentham (1802) was the most prominent critic of transportation and advocate of the penitentiary. Indeed, Bentham put more effort into this debate than any other with which he engaged. At first, transportation was in the ascendancy. It was seen as a way of purifying England by casting out its dangerous classes. And in one fell swoop, the dregs of the army could also be exiled, sent to the other side of the world to guard the convicts. So when the revolution ended transportation to America, England embarked upon a much more ambitious program of transportation in order to conquer the continent of Australia for the empire. Investors were not interested at first in the transportation of convicts, so this would have to be a government colony rather than a private corporate colony, though later Wakefield's South Australian and New Zealand companies would be responsible for the colonization of those places, with many of the immigrants coming from elsewhere in Australia.

Transportation was part of a larger picture of global movements of colonial labour power, other pieces of which were the slave trade and indentured labour. I seek to show here that Australia became a governmental colony because of a particular kind of labour surplus England wished to exclude. Because of its labour shortage, Australia became an innovator in institutions that would include them. After 1820 two and a quarter million convicts were transported to destinations that included Australia, Siberia, Singapore, New Caledonia, French Guiana, Gibraltar, the Nicobar Islands, Brazil, Sumatra, the Andaman Islands, Bermuda, Penang, Malacca and Mauritius (Nicholas and Shergold, 1988). There would have been more had Britain not thrown its weight around to prevent other states following the path to colonial development that Britain itself had pursued. For example, it resisted attempts by Austria, Italy and Germany to establish penal colonies in the Pacific. France was too powerful for Britain to resist, though Britain did manage to persuade it that a French penal colony in Western Australia would be ill-advised. The state of Hamburg actually signed a contract to ship convicts to the Australian Agricultural Company, but the British Secretary of State, Lord Glenelg, put a stop to it with the convicts waiting on the ship.

While this transportation after 1820 accounts for the highest volumes, there was also considerable English transportation of convicts to North America in both the seventeenth and eighteenth centuries and some to Africa (Shaw, 1966: 32–4). There was also some Swedish transportation to New Sweden (Delaware) during the seventeenth century and a momentary Dutch flirtation with transportation to Surinam (Spierenburg, 1995: 68). During these centuries and throughout the sixteenth and some of the fifteenth century as well, Spain, France, Austria, most Italian states and other Mediterranean principalities banished prisoners to galley slavery, but again in numbers that were modest compared to nineteenth-century transportation.

Transcontinental shifts of convict labour, especially by Britain and Russia, were of a piece with millions of indentured Melanesians, Chinese and Indians and millions of African slaves moved to spaces where labour was scarce as part of empire-building strategies. As penality became an instrument of imperial expansion, it was transformed in paradoxical ways. It showed us how well restorative justice might work with slum dwellers from the largest metropole. Macquarie's Sydney reinvented what we now describe as restorative justice and Macquarie even used the language of restoration (Braithwaite, 2001). The colony invented the ticket-of-leave, which was modelled in England and became parole (Finnane, 1997: 162). The administration also established an institution for juvenile offenders and stopped executions in public for the same reasons that these things occurred in England decades later.[2] In its

English-driven reaction against the restorative justice of the ticket-of-leave, the Australian convict administration produced Edmund Du Cane (1885), who became the driving administrative force and theoretician of the severe centralized Benthamite state penitentiaries in Britain. Du Cane was both the author and pre-eminent implementer of the principle of lesser eligibility. At the Norfolk Island penal settlement, Alexander Maconochie was given the opportunity to implement his new synthesis of progressive movement from confinement to reintegration into the community. This approach was the dominant influence on the US reforms in the aftermath of the 1870 National Congress of Penitentiary and Reformatory Discipline[3] and the Irish system of Sir Walter Crofton (Rotman, 1995: 173), and it was central to understanding how Keynesian welfare state probation-prison-parole institutions evolved everywhere (Barry, 1958).

Agriculture soon came to flourish after the Australian penal colony was established. As a result there was a shortage of labour to develop the land. The colony needed more and more convicts. Landholders wanted convicts once they arrived to be released to them on assignment almost immediately. They also wanted to keep the convicts once allocated and to have them work hard. Landholders therefore had an incentive to treat their workers well and to offer side-payments for special effort. As a result, convicts enjoyed a standard of living comparable to that which free workers might expect in that era. Once convicts had the skills to work properties, governors wanted to give them land to open up new frontiers. While recalcitrant convicts would often end up on a noose or flogged to death, convicts willing to work were given opportunities to be integrated into respectable society and to achieve economic success that they never would have been afforded in England. From the First Fleet, Governor Phillip accorded convicts the protections of a rule of law never before afforded to English criminals. Australian convicts had a right to hold property and could sue to protect that right; they could sell part of their labour; they were given status to appear as witnesses in court cases; and they were entitled to write petitions to a Governor who mostly took them seriously. English prisoners did not enjoy these rights. Convicts could and did press charges against their masters for ill-treatment in ways that are impossible in contemporary Australian prisons (Hirst, 1983: 109–11). Perhaps most remarkably, convicts assigned to work for landowners could obtain a writ of *habeas corpus* to protect them from being locked up without trial. Without a court order a convict could not even be put in irons for any reason other than prevention of escape. In a famous case in 1827 Justice Stephen upheld a writ of *habeas corpus* from some convicts who had been locked up for five or six weeks for stealing cattle without being sent to court. The judge ordered the prisoners to be released, finding that 'the rights of prisoners were as sacred in the eye of the law as those of free men' (Ibid: 118). A courageous judgement; yet Chief Justice Forbes backed Justice Stephen when Stephen was subjected to some political pressure over it. It was not an isolated instance. A year after the English courts ruled that questions about previous offences could not be asked during criminal trials, Judge Willis refused to allow the NSW Attorney-General to ask a witness 'what were you sent out for?' (Ibid: 119). Neal (1991: 25) concludes that the courts acted as a *de facto* parliament:

The American and French revolutions gave political actors in New South Wales recent models for political change. Neither the ideology of universal rights nor the strategy of armed revolution was adopted in New South Wales. The presence of Jacobins, Irish rebels and political leaders who were well versed in those ideas and strategies meant that the strategies actually adopted were not adopted in ignorance of other possibilities. (Instead) protagonists relied on their British birthrights and deployed the language of the rule of law to secure them and to forge new social and political order out of the penal colony at Botany Bay.

In Chapter 8 Martin Krygier examines this theme of Australia's early development as a society where the rule of law counted for something. After the abortive Irish Rebellion of 1804, there was no convict uprising. A single settler employing a number (sometimes dozens) of convicts hundreds of miles from the reach of state authority would seem to have reason to fear such uprising. Yet the Australian bourgeoisie lived less in fear of a rebellion of their dangerous classes than the European bourgeoisie did or American plantation owners in relation to possible slave uprisings. Such confidence was possible, I will argue, because the convicts had hope, a stake in the future,[4] and some prospect of fair procedure to deal with the injustices of the present. And landholders knew that convicts had that hope, that stake, that prospect of legal redress. The literature of the social psychology of procedural justice shows that even in the context of a harsh criminal justice system, adverse outcomes combined with a perception of fairness of procedures can deliver high compliance with the law (Lynd and Tyler, 1988; Tyler, 1990). One reason for this is that when one shares an identity as a citizen of a just legal order, there is a willingness to comply with that order (Tyler and Dawes, 1993). To realign the identities of convicts to those of law-abiding citizens, convicts need to be persuaded that they are now in reach of a society where the rule of law is something that offers them practical protection and is therefore worthy of being honoured. Brutality is more bearable when its end can be imagined and seen and when its excesses can be challenged by fair procedure. Neither Australian Aborigines nor American slaves could imagine its end in the same way the white

Australian convicts could. Defiance of a legal order springs more from the combination of adversity with perceived injustice (Sherman, 1993).

The convicts worked shorter hours, were better housed, better clothed, and had better access to medical care (Nicholas, 1988: 187–94) than free English workers (but see the questioning of this conclusion for Moreton Bay by Evans and Thorpe, 1992). Because Victorian morality regarded convicts as less deserving of such things than free workers, some backlash was perhaps inevitable. It came at the hands of Edmund Du Cane in the form of the principle of 'lesser eligibility': penitentiaries sufficiently tough that convicts got nothing that law-abiding poor were denied. By the late nineteenth century the victory of the penitentiary as an institution over transportation was almost total, though French transportation continued until 1938. The early-nineteenth-century writings of Bentham in England and de Tocqueville in France in defence of the penitentiary, particularly of its American variants, were seen as vindicated.

I have argued in more detail elsewhere that labour shortages were the fundamental reason why convicts were extended a level of procedural justice and reintegration into legitimate society not seen in institutions of criminal law that preceded or superseded it (Braithwaite, 2001). French fact-finding missions from the earliest days were amazed by the results. Péron reported for the members of one 1802 mission:

Never perhaps has a more worthy object of study been presented to a statesman or philosopher ... There, brought together, are those terrible ruffians who were for so long the terror of the government of their country: thrust from the bosom of European society ... The majority, having atoned for their crimes by a hard bondage, have rejoined the ranks of the citizens. Obliged to concern themselves with the maintenance of law and order to safeguard the property they have acquired, having become nearly at the same time husbands and fathers, they are bound to their present state by the most powerful and beloved ties. The same revolution, brought about by the same means, has taken place in the women; and miserable prostitutes, gradually restored to more proper principles of conduct, are today bright and hard-working mothers of families (quoted in Forster, 1996: 11).

Interest in transportation as an institution globalized. In the long run, however, that interest could not be historically sustained: colonial powers simply ran out of suitable *'terra nullius'* to occupy.

The next big compositional fact of the Australian population after the convicts, however, was equally driven by the global dynamic of shifting people from regions of labour surplus to regions of labour shortage, and it was even more important in its impact on the nature of contemporary Australia. Before we move on to consider Australian and global institutions of transnational free migration, we will consider Australia's role as

```
Australian convict society              US slave society
Procedural  ──▶ Reintegration           Procedural   ──▶ Exclusion
Justice     ◀──                         Justice      ◀── Stigmatization
      ↘      ↙                                ↘       ↙
     Lower crime                             Higher crime
```

**Figure 4.1** Differences between Australian convict society and US slave society

a colonist of its Aboriginal people and of people of the Pacific. And before we leave the institutions of the convict colonies, we must not miss pointing out that transportation seems to have been remarkably effective in moving England and Ireland's dangerous classes and their children away from lives of crime. This seems particularly so of the destination of most of the most serious offenders, Tasmania. Keith Hancock (1930: 40–1), Manning Clark (1968: 10) and Henry Reynolds (1969) have all commented on how law-abiding Tasmanians became, even though in the late nineteenth century it was still the case that most of the population was descended from convicts. In 1875 Tasmania still had an imprisonment rate higher than anywhere in the world today: by the beginning of the twentieth century it had an imprisonment rate lower than any nation in the world today (Braithwaite, 2001). In the thirty-two years to 1916 only one Tasmanian was convicted of homicide, and there were also hardly any convictions during those years for other serious offences such as robbery and rape (Mukherjee et al., 1989: 440–5). This experience is of enduring relevance to a reconsideration of the failure of institutions of criminal justice and of regulation more broadly during the twentieth century and is being drawn upon in the new debates around abandoning punitive justice in favour of reintegrative or restorative justice. Braithwaite (2001) has summarized the relevant differences between Australian convict society and American slave society as in Figure 4.1.

## Aboriginal Exclusion

Tasmania, the site of the greatest triumphs of the reintegrative institutions of convict society, was also the site of a dispossession and murder of Aboriginal people that was so total as to justify describing it as genocide. No full-blood Aboriginal Tasmanians survived the century. Given the labour shortages, why was Aboriginal labour not called upon to assist? Why were black African slaves and Melanesian indentured labourers valued on the world labour market, but not Aboriginal Australians? Partly it was because, like North American First Nations, Aboriginal Australians were a domestic enemy to be expunged from the land as opposed to a pacified people to be imported to work. Also it probably was partly because they were seen as a Stone Age people, not more hated than the Chinese, but seen as incapable of fitting into a complex division of labour in the same way the Chinese could. English capital exporters understood investing in British workers across the globe, but might have baulked at funding investments based on the uncertain ingredient of harnessing Aboriginal human capital (see generally Denoon, 1983).

While we cannot be confident about the reasons, we can be certain that in the century when convicts were being reintegrated, Aborigines were being exterminated and almost totally excluded from labour market opportunities in the dominant society. It was only in the remote northern and western extremities of the continent that Aborigines ever secured large numbers of jobs in the pastoral industry. The cultural estrangement from the European labour market was so total, except in those pockets, that one wonders why people are so puzzled when Aboriginal people today find it difficult to seize the still limited opportunities for jobs open to them.

The enduring accomplishment of the institutions of convict society is that they equipped the unemployable dregs of British society as one of the best workforces in the world, arguably the best rural workforce. That literate rural working class met at places like the tree of knowledge in Barcaldine to form the Australian Labor Party, and trade unions successfully lobbied for the institutions of the wage-earners' welfare state (Castles, 1985; 1994) – a welfare state that gave Australia its distinctive institutional shape for most of the second century after the arrival of the First Fleet. For all its male egalitarian progressiveness, however, its philosophy of the employability of all white males was never extended to Aboriginal males. The notion of a fair go for people whom respectable society would regard as dangerous and unfit for free labour, epitomized in the legend of Ned Kelly, would become a resource for much later egalitarian movements for Aborigines and women, but at the height of its power the inclusionary community of the fair go excluded as many as it included. None more so than Aboriginal Australians. The gifts of land that made emancipists respectable were thefts of land that destroyed Aboriginal cultures, depriving Aboriginal people of the font of their self-respect. The very distinctive property institutions that included the one group excluded the other. The Australian story is a story of the dignity of the land as the crucial resource in human capital formation (Fitzpatrick, 1941). Peter Read (1997; 2000) is on to something important in his discussion of the distinctive affinities of European as well as Aboriginal Australians with the land, just as Read was also on to something in seeing the compounding of the loss of dignity from loss of country with the indignity of loss of children, the stolen generations.

So the history of Australia is a history of a unique kind of rule of law – a procedural law and property law (the post-feudal innovation of the Torrens system), that created extreme forms of inclusion and exclusion.

## Colonial Australia

It is worth more than a footnote in the pursuit of the Australian identity to understand Australia as a colonist in the Pacific. We have already observed that Australia's own institutional experience as a colony was not of governance by a colonial trading company. Nevertheless, there was more of an element of that in Australia's experience as a colonizer. Companies like Burns Philp (Buckley and Klugman, 1983) and the Colonial Sugar Refining Company (Lowndes, 1956) were among Australia's few early successful corporations. It was CSR which sought Indian indentured labourers for Fiji to work its sugar plantations, sowing also the seeds of twentieth-century racial coups in that country. Burns Philp was one kind of *raison d'être* of Papua New Guinea as a colony. A plantation and trading company economy was the rationale for German New Guinea that Australia inherited after World War I. It was an economically flawed rationale. Germany was plucking too little too late from the presumed fruits of imperialism's tree. Australia coming in after them to pick up the pieces made no economic sense.

While expatriate racism in New Guinea was rife, the bigger story of Australian colonialism in New Guinea was of trying to protect the cultures of the other big southern island from destruction by European invasion. The high point of this aspiration was Gough Whitlam's grant of independence in 1975 and the subsequent Australian underwriting of half the Papua New Guinea budget for decades through foreign aid. As Dryzek argues in Chapter 5, democratization is a work-in-progress; in the twentieth century Australia became a missionary in the region for a more inclusionary vision of democracy than it had grasped during its own development. Australia as colonist wanted to do better than Australia as colony in institutionalizing the autonomy and integrity of indigenous peoples. For New Guinea, there was never the dream of a white settler society, no conception of *terra nullius*, and there was always the aspiration that the labour power fuelling a future Melanesian nation-state would be Melanesian. Throughout its region, Australia has been an advocate of democracy and autonomy based on economic development. When the inevitable tensions have arisen between national unity and local autonomy, it has mostly (though not consistently, as Timor illustrates) been a constructive broker of peace, from Bougainville to Fiji and the Solomons. Part of the story here is that its colonial companies, Burns Philp and CSR, were never great forces in the land. They were not brilliantly managed and slowly declined. The extractive corporates who were active in Melanesia – CRA and BHP among them – were much more formidable. But they were also causes of political and environmental disasters in Bougainville and Ok Tedi. So Australian support for indigenous autonomy mostly trumped support for corporate colonialism. The Pacific as a result has been persistently one of the most democratic zones of the post-colonial world.

**State Experiments in Australia**

William Pember Reeves' two-volume work, *State Experiments in Australia and New Zealand*, published in 1902, documents the extraordinary innovation that occurred in the Antipodes in the late nineteenth and early twentieth centuries. This was an era of exceptionally high immigration between Australia and New Zealand, facilitating the trans-Tasman movement of institutional ideas. Often Australia was the second nation in the world to launch a democratic innovation, as with compulsory voting (after Belgium) and votes for women (after New Zealand), and often New Zealand was the state that was first (see Sawer, 2001). But Australia developed the most important forms of preferential voting; it was first with the secret (or 'Australian') ballot, and saw the first Labor government in Queensland in 1899. Democratic socialist experimentation perhaps attained its zenith under T. J. Ryan's Queensland government. Ryan died in 1921 at forty-five years of age before he attained his destiny of being a great experimenting Labor prime minister. Ryan was a frustrated advocate of effective antitrust laws, though he did break the sugar monopoly of CSR. He successfully introduced compulsory workers' compensation insurance, a progressive tax on the unimproved value of land, and withholding taxes on dividends, among other reforms (Murphy, 1975). Some of the experiments were genuine disasters, like state-owned cattle properties and butcher shops to guarantee cheap meat for workers' families. But in fairness such failures were typically abandoned when they became inefficient vehicles for jobs for the local party faithful.

Without any doubt, the most consequential experimental reshaping of Australian institutions was state and federal conciliation and arbitration of labour relations. Its principal architect, Justice Henry Higgins, was a disciple of experimentation: 'the greatest gains that humanity has made for itself have been the result of bold experimentation, with correction of mistakes' (Higgins, 1922: 167). Higgins' vision of industrial relations was of relational justice, restoration of harmony and basic social justice in a way that resonates with Governor Macquarie's project of restoring emancipated convicts to a co-operative place alongside exclusivists, and with contemporary New Zealand and Australian experiments in restorative or relational justice (Burnside and Baker, 1994). For Higgins (1922: 60-1), 'The arbitration system is devised to provide a substitute for strikes and stoppages, to secure the reign of justice against violence, of right against might – to subdue Prussianism in industrial matters.' Co-operative conciliation rather than mandated arbitration was designed to be the main game. It may be that procedural and relational aspects of the model continue to be relevant to the contemporary realities of global markets even if the substantive inflexibility of a rule-bound regime was not. Perhaps the real problem with the regime was that it failed to make the transition from command and control to responsive regulation that other regulatory regimes did make (Ayres and Braithwaite, 1992).

Experimentalism oriented to social justice is the more general point about the formative period of Australian history at the time of Federation. There was the refinement of older experiments like the Torrens land system, old-age pensions, workers compensation, professional electoral office administration of continuously maintained electoral rolls, and many more. It is telling, though, that Reeves' last case study (1902: II, 325) is 'The Exclusion of Aliens and Undesirables': 'Alone among the chief divisions of the Empire the Commonwealth and New Zealand are not split up by any race-fissures. None of their cities are babels of tongues – none of their streets are filled with dark faces.' For Reeves, the important experiments in government that had delivered this were the exclusion laws of the nineteenth century, particularly directed against the Chinese, but also the return of Kanaka indentured labourers to Melanesia. His vision still weighs on Australian political institutions, as John Howard's remarkable 'turn-away-the-ships-and-bomb-the-Afghans' election victory of 2001 showed. For Reeves, 'At first sight the case for a kindly practice of laissez-faire seems very strong' because 'it is an unwelcome task to interfere with the transit of civilised human beings from one friendly land to another' (Reeves, 1902: 358–9). But Reeves saw the great future project of Australian social justice as the elimination of unemployment, that is, state involvement in fostering demand for work and substituting labour market opportunities where demand would not arise in the market. He did not think this project could be realized if immigration could not be regulated according to the capacities of such programs. Exclusionary institutions of immigration therefore had an inclusionary side. We need to see the dialectic of inclusion and exclusion as central to the greatest injustices of the wage-earners' welfare state, but we need to see it with some nuance (see generally Holton, 1998).

## From Global Labour Dynamics to Global Capital Dynamics

My argument has been that transnational movements of labour to locales of shortage explain the distinctive fair-go institutions of convict society. This foundation combined with the continuation of labour shortages explains the wage-earners' welfare state described by Castles in Chapter 2. This meant well-organized labour enjoying a strong bargaining position because chronic labour shortage made returns to investment in labour very high, extracting attractive conditions to draw new workers to the continent. As Castles' chapter demonstrates, distinctive welfare institutions, most notably conciliation and arbitration courts, ossified egalitarianism for workers. Later, after the 1972 equal pay decision, it institutionalised a high degree of structural equality for women. Sawer in Chapter 6 conceives of Australia becoming socially liberal, committed to themes of equal opportunity and the ethical state that ultimately redounded to the advancement of women. Ultimately, from Whitlam to Keating, it also came to endorse the very multiculturalism that was feared in the heyday of the wage-earners' welfare state.

The same conditions of labour shortage explained high levels of immigration subsidized by the Australian state. Workers' organizations were wary of the immigrants, however. Would they undermine the solidarity of the wage-earners' welfare state, refuse to join unions, break strikes, undercut wages? Working-class Australia translated this wariness into a continuum of prejudice; Asians were most likely to threaten cheap labour, followed by Continental European immigrants, with Anglo-Irish immigrants seen as least likely to do so. So we can conceive the White Australia policy as an institution of population born of the insecurities of a 'workers' paradise' planted on a globe with many different supply options from labour-surplus states. Just as with the inclusion of convicts and the exclusion of Aborigines, race was the fundamental marker of inclusion. From Henry Lawson to Pauline Hanson, racism remains the greatest taint on Australian solidarity and egalitarianism.

At some point during the twentieth century that is hard to specify, capital shortage became the more critical problem for Australia than labour shortage. When the once limitless supply of English capital dried up, we became keen to acquire Asian business migrants with money to invest. In these new conditions, the wage-earners' welfare state came to be seen as a liability for attracting global capital. Once the White Australia policy was dismantled, attracting workers was less of a problem than limiting their flow. Boat people and human traffickers today are seen as a threat to rationing population growth to capital- and skill-rich immigrants. The detention centre is the institution of their exclusion, just as the gallows and Norfolk Island were for the convicts, and reserves for Aborigines. Hulks rotting in the water are perhaps the coffins in common for excluding convicts and boat people through death. The phases of Australian history, more than that of other lands, are marked by their peculiar institutions of exclusion, juxtaposed throughout with the warm inclusiveness of mateship. Centripetal forces of transnational migration out of surplus states sucked in to the centrifugal inclusiveness of an Australian solidarity with definite boundaries policed by men with chains and dogs.

As Castles explains in Chapter 2, the wage-earners' welfare state collapses in conditions of capital rather than labour shortage.[5] Labour markets are deregulated, particularly in the 1990s. Workers compete for capital instead of capital competing for workers. Protectionism is unsustainable, as Pincus and Brennan explain in Chapter 3. The institutions of competition policy acquire the centrality once enjoyed by the institutions of labour market regulation. Allan Fels, the Chairman of the Australian Competition and Consumer Commission, is now regularly described in the financial press as the most powerful bureaucrat in the nation, usurping the institutional significance once enjoyed by the successors of Justice Higgins as president of the Arbitration Commission and those who presided over the Tariff Board. Continuous reinvention of microeconomic reform is needed to compete for global capital.

## The Demise of Egalitarian Australia

The work of Deborah Mitchell (1995) among others has suggested that labour market deregulation over the past decade has probably undermined the structural gender equality that had been delivered by centralized wage-fixing constrained by equal pay decisions. The inclusion–exclusion parameters of the male mateship that had its origins in convictism, on the frontier, and among the rural working class were culturally sexist but the institutions it spawned ultimately became structurally egalitarian with respect to gender. The neo-liberalism of the new century is more culturally but less structurally egalitarian with respect to sex. This is particularly so for Asian women, increasing numbers of whom are ensnared in networks of sex slavery managed by people traffickers into the Australian sex market. Often this is based on debt bondage – teenage girls are sold into sex work to pay off family debts. For Australian-born women, it is drug bondage rather than debt bondage which is the primary factor that provides the grip on sex workers. The heroin markets that have delivered this problem are global.

Globalization has also had a profound impact on the distributive effects of the institutions of taxation in Australia. In the first half of the twentieth century only the wealthy paid income tax. It was beyond the regulatory capability of governments to chase shearers around the country and get them to pay income tax. So governments did not try. Today it is beyond the regulatory capability of governments to chase the assets of wealthy people around the world, so they are more interested in the appearance of trying to do so than in succeeding. In the course of the twentieth century income tax has seen a complete reversal of its distributive effects – from being an instrument of redistribution from rich to poor to being a tool of redistribution from the poor to the rich. This is one of the most fundamental reasons why Australia has ceased being an economically egalitarian society.

The story of how this happened is a global one. An important stage was the phenomenon of the early 1970s where nations that clung to a radically redistributive income tax system like Sweden were ridiculed by media barons when super-rich citizens like Bjorn Borg and the members of Abba threatened to leave for tax reasons. The realization that the wealthy were both more geographically mobile than in the past and more able to shift their assets around the world generated constant downwards pressure on top marginal tax rates everywhere in the world for the next three decades. The egalitarian Australia of Menzies when a top marginal income tax rate of 85 per cent prevailed would never return. The same thing happened with corporate tax rates and even more so with corporate tax expenditures that replaced the Keynesian welfare state with a corporate welfare state. Increasingly, economic elites would say to each other and to prime ministers privately, but never publicly, that allowing wealthy corporations to get away with not even meeting these declining obligations was in the national interest. If we got tough on corporate tax non-compliance, investment and employment would flee to other shores. So we reached a situation in the late 1990s where a majority of the corporations which were the responsibility of the Large Business and International Business Line of the Australian Taxation Office were paying no company tax. This exaggerates how bad things are, because many large corporates will control some entities that pay no tax and others that pay some. But there are significant numbers of multinational corporations that pay no company tax across all their entities for highly profitable Australian operations. Equally, there are hundreds of extremely wealthy individual Australians with tens of millions of dollars in assets who pay no tax. OECD leadership in attacking the tax havens that are an important part of this global problem collapsed with the election of George W. Bush, though concern about the financing of terrorism is causing some rethinking. Tax havens are just one of a number of 'fiscal termites' (Tanzi, 2000) that global forces are causing to eat away at the integrity of the Australian taxation system.

Of course as the revenue side of the budget comes under increasing pressure from competition for capital and other global threats like e-commerce, redistributive capabilities on the expenditure side of the budget are also threatened. Corporate welfare is handed out not only by the Commonwealth but also by state governments competing for capital through tax breaks, grants, cheap electricity and the like; the result is that the poor cross-subsidize the rich through their electricity bills, their land taxes, and so on. Traditional Keynesian welfare for the poor is not only driven out by the budgetary demands of corporate welfare; the poor actually make direct contributions to corporate welfare. The rural poor, who previously enjoyed cross-subsidies on expenditures like their telephone bills, now contribute to cheap telephone rates for large corporate subscribers. A major reason for Hansonism and the curious anti-globalization alliance of the rural and regional right with the urban left is to be found in the emerging realities of the corporate welfare state.

## Globalization and the New Regulatory State

Not only is the Keynesian welfare state largely a phenomenon of the past, so is the nightwatchman state of classical liberal theory (Nozick, 1974). We live today in what scholars in my field increasingly refer to as a new regulatory state (Majone, 1994; Loughlin and Scott, 1997; Parker, 1999; Braithwaite, 2000). This means a state where most police are private police, where many prisons are private prisons, regulated by the state. Not privatization and deregulation – the Hayekian policy package – but privatization and regulatory growth. When we privatize telecommunications, we create Austel, a new regulatory authority. Privatization moved to the heartland of the Keynesian state with the privatization of the Commonwealth Employment Service. The Keating government could not implement that privatization without creating the Employment Services Regulatory Authority; when the Howard government pushed on without the regulatory agency, considerable chaos and fraud ensued, as it did when the British government privatized rail without credible investment in regulatory co-ordination. For Sawer (Chapter 6) Australian social liberalism from quite early on was characterized by commitments to state regulation. This regulation ultimately saw interventions such as affirmative action for women and anti-discrimination laws that secured rights for gay men and lesbian women as its social justice agenda extended its reach to the excluded (see Gatens and Mackinnon, 1998).

To use the metaphor of Osborne and Gaebler (1992), we live in a world where the state might be doing less rowing, but it is doing more steering. University teachers, slumped over their oars, know this from personal experience. The metaphor actually does not go far enough in capturing the changes that have occurred in the nature of governance. Foucault's (1991) governmentality lectures get us closer to an understanding of the way government is no longer a unified set of state instrumentalities. The sovereign is not dead, the state is not powerless (Weiss, 1998), but the state is only one of many sources of power. Moreover, the state is an object as well as subject of regulation. It is regulated by the International Monetary Fund, Moody's, the Security Council, the International Organization for Standardization, the World Trade Organization, among other institutions. We live in a world where many centres of institutional power both steer and row. And each steers its own rowing while mindful of the steering and rowing undertaken by other private and public institutions.

Many of the standards of the new regulatory state are global. For years some of Australia's air safety standards have been written by the Boeing Corporation in Seattle, or if not by it, then by the US Federal Aviation Administration in Washington. Our ship safety laws have been written by the International Maritime Organization in London. Our motor vehicle safety standards come from Working Party 29 of the Economic Commission for Europe. Our food standards are established by the Codex Alimentarius Commission in Rome. Many of our pharmaceuticals standards have been set by a joint collaboration of the Japanese, European and US industries and their regulators, called the International Conference on Harmonization. Our telecommunications standards have been substantially set in Geneva by the International Telecommunication Union. The chair (and often the vice-chair) of most of the expert committees that effectively set those standards in Geneva are Americans. The Motorola Corporation has been particularly effective in setting telecommunications standards through its chairmanship of those committees. As a consequence, Motorola patents have been written into many of the ITU standards that we all must follow.

### The Late Arrival of Managerial Capitalism in Australia

Australia the colony was born as a government colony. Over time, it grew institutions designed to empower a regulatory state to ensure a fair go. In this polity that Sawer describes as socially liberal, excellence in government was always more valued than excellence in business. Efficient primary production and extractive industries meant that the Australian economy did quite well without the benefit of the early development of indigenous multinational corporations. Australia had a radically different pattern of growth from the United States. There the effect of enforcement of the Sherman Act by American courts was not exactly as intended by the progressive era social movement against the railroad, oil, steel and tobacco trusts. Alfred Chandler Jr noted that 'after 1899 lawyers were advising their corporate clients to abandon all agreements or alliances carried out through cartels or trade associations and to consolidate into single, legally defined enterprises' (Chandler, 1977: 333–4). US antitrust laws thus actually encouraged mergers instead of inhibiting them because they 'tolerated that path to monopoly power while they more effectively outlawed the alternative pathway via cartels and restrictive practices' (Hannah, 1991: 8). The Americans found that there were organizational efficiencies in managerially centralized, big corporations that made what Chandler called a 'three-pronged investment': first, 'an investment in production facilities large enough to exploit a technology's potential economies of scale or scope'; second, 'an investment in a national and international marketing and distribution network, so that the volume of sales might keep pace with the new volume of production'; and third, 'to benefit fully from these two kinds of investment the entrepreneurs also had to invest in management' (Chandler, 1990: 8). None of these elements of the three-pronged investment occurred in Australian corporate capitalism. The Australian investment until the 1960s and beyond, as Pincus and Brennan show in Chapter 3, was in lobbying for protection, and this was the investment that the state rewarded.

According to a revealing study in the Chandler tradition by Tony Freyer (1992), the turn-of-century merger wave fostered by the Sherman Act thrust US long-term organization for economic efficiency ahead of Britain's for the next half century, until Britain acquired its *Monopolies Act 1948* and *Restrictive Trade Practices Act 1956*. One might have applied the same analysis to the Australian comparison, if not more so. Until the 1960s the British economy continued to be dominated by family companies which did not fully mobilize Chandler's three-pronged investment. Non-existent antitrust enforcement in Britain for the first half of the twentieth century also left new small business entrepreneurs more at the mercy of the restrictive business practices of old money than in the United States. British commitment to freedom of contract was an inferior industrial policy to both the visible hand of American law-makers' rule of reason and the administrative guidance of the German Cartel Courts. For the era of managerial capitalism, liberal deregulation of state monopolies formerly granted to Indies companies, guilds and other corporations was not enough. A special kind of regulation for deregulation of restrictive business practices was needed which tolerated bigness.

Ultimately, this American model of competitive mega-corporate capitalism globalized under four influences:

- extension of the model throughout Europe after World War II under the leadership of the German anti-cartel authority, the Bundeskartelamt, a creation of the American occupation

- cycles of Mergers and Acquisition (M&A) mania, to which Australia was not immune, catalysed in part by M&A missionaries from American law firms
- extension of the model to the dynamic Asian economies in the 1980s and 90s, partly under pressure from bilateral trade negotiations with the United States and Europe (who demanded breaking the restrictive practices of Korean *chaebol*, for example)
- extension of the model to some developing countries with technical assistance from UNCTAD.

While Australia was among the latest developed economies to see mega-corporate capitalism, ultimately we came to live in a society where more of the significant things done in the world were done by corporations rather than individuals acting on their own behalf or by the state. Australian managerial reluctance to make Chandler's three-pronged investment meant that when Australian corporations did become larger they did so by controlling a monopoly, like BHP with steel, or an oligopoly, like the Murdochs, Packers and Fairfaxes with the media; or by demanding tariff protection like our largely failed industrial firms; or via tax expenditures such as the tax deductions for research and development demanded by our largely failing information technology industry and other post-industrial corporations. So our corporates were flaccid and they rarely established multinational brands of major significance. It was not so much the residue of the wage-earners' welfare state that shackled the Australian economy but the failure of coddled corporates to make Chandler's three-pronged investment a century ago and to invest in the R&D needed for success in the information economy of the past two decades. Rather, they sat back expecting the state to pay for national R&D. Instead of a three-pronged investment, the Australian corporate investment was one-pronged – in lobbying for the Australian state to solve their problems. Instead of funding institutions of national development like universities, Australian corporations expected universities to fund them, to divert resources from the pursuit of basic science to the serving of their applied needs. OECD statistics revealing Australia almost at the bottom of OECD rankings on private R&D investment actually understate how parlous the situation is. Much of the Australian corporate R&D that is in these numbers is phoney, representing aggressive tax planning schemes in R&D rather than the real thing.

The very decades in which Australia was such a leader in governmental experimentation, the last decade of the nineteenth and the early decades of the twentieth century, were the decades when US experimentation in corporate organization started the process of corporate capitalism in which Australia is such a laggard. Paradoxically, in these new global conditions, being a laggard in corporate capitalism was part of the push that moved us from being a leader to a laggard with respect to the welfare state.

**Whither the Fair Go?**

As Dryzek shows in Chapter 5, over time Australian democracy has become more inclusionary of previously excluded groups – in turn, non-propertied men, women, Continental European immigrants, Asian immigrants, Aborigines, gay and lesbian people, the institutionalized aged, the disabled, and even children to some degree. An exception to this trajectory is convicts (and imprisoned asylum-seekers), who are subject to greater exclusion in greater numbers than in decades past and who are granted less procedural justice than our original convicts. Today our stories of the appropriate ways of dealing with crime are from Hollywood rather than being informed by the more instructive lessons of our own history.

The previously excluded groups are more politically included in a society that is less economically equal. When Australia and New Zealand were among the wealthiest few societies in the world a century ago, they were also among the most equal and the most innovative few. A century of protectionism, a continuing failure to invest in corporate management and in the scale and scope of its sway, left Australia comparatively poorer, less able to afford a decent welfare state. As our focus shifted from competing for labour to competing for capital, global competition drove high Australian wages back to the pack. Global competition also drove down taxes on corporations and the rich, further eroding our capability to replace the wage-earners' welfare state with a more conventional one.

While the demise of Australian egalitarianism is best understood in the context of global competition for capital, this does not mean it is inevitable that we must surrender our egalitarian aspirations. The traditional economic analysis is that generous welfare states lose investment and jobs because the strong welfare net pushes up taxes. Leibfried and Rieger (1995) reverse this argument. States with a weak safety net find it politically and industrially impossible to restructure and lay off workers in response to rapid economic and technological change. States where retrenched workers will be protected by adequate social security and labour market retraining programs can adapt to global pressures earlier and with fewer strikes; they can find the political will to eliminate protection of inefficient industries which are a drain on national wealth. Strong social welfare is a precondition for a political capacity to cut corporate welfare. In this analysis, a strong welfare state, understood as compliance with safety-net labour standards, is an advantage in global competition, not a liability. When strong welfare states pay for services like public health, this saves employers from footing the bill, actually making investment more attractive. There is now a considerable accumulation of research evidence showing that it is simply not true that foreign direct investment is shifting to the nations with the lowest labour standards. Instead, direct investment is continuing to circulate among OECD states with comparatively high labour standards (Tripartite Working Party on Labour Standards, 1996: 41; United Nations Conference on Trade and Development, 1996).

There are some prospects that harmful tax competition between states can be limited by international agreement. Australia, as a nation that commands respect in intergovernmental forums, can show some leadership in this domain. Competitiveness in post-industrial economies will depend on diffusion of new ideas and know-how. Perhaps none of the nations in the Asia-Pacific region, probably not even Japan, are net exporters of intellectual property rights. If Australia saw its interests clearly it would not be a Deputy Sheriff to the United States on the information economy. We would seek to muster regional leadership so that international bodies such as the Council on TRIPs at the World Trade Organization were used to set a ceiling on the ratchetting up of intellectual property monopolies that redistribute wealth from poor to rich countries. We would show leadership in organizations like UNESCO to combat the digital divide globally. We would conclude that we had more to learn from diffusion-oriented Japanese models of patent office administration than from British and US models. In this kind of work, our natural regional partners would be the emerging powerbrokers of Asia, China and India. Like us, they have significant new economy exports while having little prospect of ever becoming net exporters. Our shared interest is in helping the region develop by quicker diffusion of new technologies through some partial deregulation of intellectual property rights.

Part of the astute Australian diagnosis in setting up the Cairns Group was that there are a set of rich countries like Australia, New Zealand and Canada that have more in common with poor countries, in terms of agricultural liberalization (just as in intellectual property deregulation), than they have in common with the United States and Europe. Australia has the international credibility to show more determined international leadership in Geneva and New York. Happily, leadership in world trade debates for a fair go for India and Africa will mostly help Australia. Australian non-government organizations have been major advocates of a more inclusive and egalitarian citizenship of world society at least since Jessie Street, founder of the United Associations of Women and convenor of the 1943 Women's Charter conference. In Dryzek's conception of democracy as a work-in-progress, the next challenge for Australian institutions is to reach for more inclusive international citizenship. That means no more decisions in Geneva to sentence millions of AIDS victims in Africa to death by expanding patent monopolies on pharmaceuticals without any Africans being in the room. Australia was in the room when these key decisions were made. While we voted against the poor in that case, there is no structural imperative of globalization that we must abandon a fair go for the poor in future.

One way forward is for us all – intellectuals, political parties, trade unions, non-government organizations, the state – to seek to persuade Australian business to invest in a new kind of triple bottom line for itself and for the nation that involves a new sense of responsibility for the nation's future. This will require a new imagination for how to invest in its people and promote a social justice that can underwrite restructuring for competitiveness. The corporate sector might also begin to see an interest in desisting from conniving in the collapse of the Australian tax system so that the state might also resume its once internationally competitive role in funding human capital formation.

### Notes

1  I have interviewed hundreds of leaders of these organizations. See Braithwaite and Drahos (2000).
2  Governor Bourke ordered that executions be carried out in private after a convict named Jenkins made a famous traditional speech from the drop:
    Well, good bye my lads, I have not time to say much to you; I acknowledge I shot the Doctor, but it was not for gain, it was for the sake of my fellow prisoners because he was a tyrant, and I have one thing to recommend you as a friend, if any of you take to the bush, shoot every tyrant you come across, and there are several now in the yard who ought to be served so [Ward, 1966: 139].
3  Some of the Declaration of Principles of the American Prison Association was taken word for word from Maconochie's writing.
4  '[E]ach governor, at least until the end of Macquarie's term of office, was diligent in engendering belief in ... providing convicts and emancipists with "a something to lose"' (Nichol, 1986: 13).
5  More precisely, the early colonists confronted a high ratio of land to both capital and labour. But it was easier to import capital from England than labour.

### References

Ayres, I., and Braithwaite, J. *Responsive Regulation: Transcending the Deregulation Debate* (New York: Oxford University Press, 1992).
Barry, J. V. *Alexander Maconochie of Norfolk Island: A Study of a Pioneer in Penal Reform* (Melbourne: Oxford University Press, 1958).
Barry, P. *The Rise and Fall of Alan Bond* (Sydney: Bantam Books, 1990).
Bentham, J. *Panopticon Versus New South Wales* (1802).
Braithwaite, J. *Crime, Shame and Reintegration* (Cambridge: Cambridge University Press, 1989).
——. 'The New Regulatory State and the Transformation of Criminology', *British Journal of Criminology*, 40(2) (2000) pp. 222–38.

──. 'Crime in a Convict Republic', *Modern Law Review*, 64 (2001) pp.11–50.
Braithwaite, J., and Drahos, P. *Global Business Regulation* (Cambridge: Cambridge University Press, 2000).
Buckley, K., and Klugman, K. *The Australian Presence in the Pacific: Burns Philp, 1914–1946* (Sydney: George Allen & Unwin, 1983).
Burnside, J., and Baker, N. (eds). *Relational Justice: Repairing the Breach* (Winchester: Waterside Press, 1994).
Capling, A. *Australia and the Global Trade System: From Havana to Seattle* (Cambridge: Cambridge University Press, 2001).
Castles, F. *The Working Class and Welfare* (Sydney: Allen & Unwin, 1985).
──. 'The Wage Earners' Welfare State Revisited: Refurbishing the Established Model of Australian Social Protection, 1983–1993', *Australian Journal of Social Issues*, vol. 29 (1994) pp. 120–45.
Chandler, A. D. Jr. *The Visible Hand: The Managerial Revolution in American Business* (Cambridge, Mass.: Belknap Press, 1977).
──. *Scale and Scope: The Dynamics of Industrial Capitalism* (Cambridge, Mass.: Belknap Press, 1990).
Clark, C. M. H. *A History of Australia, Vol II: New South Wales and Van Diemen's Land, 1822–1838* (Melbourne: Melbourne University Press, 1968).
Davis, J. P. *Corporations: A Study of the Origin and Development of Great Business Combinations and their Relation to the Authority of the State* (New York: Capricorn Books, 1961).
Denoon, D. *Settler Capitalism* (Oxford: Clarendon Press, 1983).
Du Cane, E. F. *The Punishment and Prevention of Crime* (London: Macmillan, 1885).
Evans, R., and Thorpe, W. 'Power, Punishment and Penal Labour: Convict Workers and Moreton Bay', *Australian Historical Studies* (1992) pp. 90–111.
Finnane, M. *Punishment in Australian Society* (Melbourne: Oxford University Press, 1997).
Fitzpatrick, B. *The British Empire in Australia: An Economic History, 1834–1949* (Melbourne: Melbourne University Press, 1941).
Forster, C. *France and Botany Bay: The Lure of a Penal Colony* (Melbourne: Melbourne University Press, 1996).
Foucault, M. 'Governmentality', in G. Burchall, C. Gordon and P. Miller (eds), *The Foucault Effect: Studies in Governmentality* (London: Harvester Wheatsheaf, 1991).
Freyer, T. *Regulating Big Business Antitrust in Great Britain and America, 1880–1990* (Cambridge: Cambridge University Press, 1992).
Gatens, M., and Mackinnon, A. (eds). *Gender and Institutions: Welfare, Work and Citizenship* (Cambridge: Cambridge University Press, 1998).
Hancock, W. K. *Australia* (London: Ernest Benn, 1930).
Hannah, L. 'Mergers, Cartels and Concentration: Legal Factors in the US and European Experience', in Giles H. Burgess, Jr, *Antitrust and Regulation* (Aldershot: Edward Elgar, 1991).
Higgins, H. B. *A New Province for Law and Order* (London: Constable and Company, 1922).
Hirst, J. B. *Convict Society and Its Enemies: A History of Early New South Wales* (Sydney: George Allen & Unwin, 1983).

Holm, H.-H., and Sorensen, G. 'Introduction: What Has Changed?', in Hans-Henrik Holm and Georg Sorensen (eds), *Whose World Order: Uneven Globalization and the End of the Cold War* (Boulder, Co: Westview Press, 1995).

Holton, R. J. *Globalization and the Nation-State* (New York: St Martin's Press, 1998).

Hood, C., Scott, C., James, O., Jones, G., and Travers, T. *Regulation Inside Government: Waste Watchers, Quality Policy and Sleazebusters* (Oxford: Oxford University Press, 1999).

Industry Task Force on Leadership. *Enterprising Nation: Renewing Australia's Managers to Meet the Challenges of the Asia-Pacific Century* (Canberra: Australian Government Publishing Service, 1995).

Leibfried, S., and Rieger, E. *Conflicts over Germany's Competitiveness ('Standort Deutschland'): Exiting from the Global Economy?* Occasional Paper, Centre for German and European Studies (Berkeley: University of California, 1995).

Loughlin, M., and Scott, C. 'The Regulatory State', in P. Dunlevy, I. Holliday and G. Peele (eds), *Developments in British Politics 5* (London: Macmillan, 1997).

Lowndes, A. G. *South Pacific Enterprise: The Colonial Sugar Refining Company Limited* (Sydney: Angus and Robertson, 1956).

Lynd, E. Allan, and Tyler, Tom R. *The Social Psychology of Procedural Justice* (New York: Plenum Press, 1988).

Majone, G. 'The Rise of the Regulatory State in Europe', *West European Politics*, vol. 17, (1994) pp. 77–101.

Mitchell, D. 'Women's Incomes', in A. Edwards and S. Magarey (eds), *Women in Restructuring Australia* (Canberra: Academy of Social Sciences, 1995).

Mukherjee, S. K., Scandia, A., Dagger, D., and Matthews, W. *Source Book of Australian Criminal and Social Statistics* (Canberra: Australian Institute of Criminology, [1989] 1994).

Murphy, D. J. *T. J. Ryan: A Political Biography* (St Lucia: University of Queensland Press, 1975).

Neal, D. *The Rule of Law in a Penal Colony: Law and Power in Early New South Wales* (Cambridge: Cambridge University Press, 1991).

Nichol, W. 'Ideology and the Convict System in New South Wales, 1788–1820', *Historical Studies*, vol. 22 (1986) pp. 1–20.

Nicholas, S. (ed.). *Convict Workers: Reinterpreting Australia's Past* (Cambridge: Cambridge University Press, 1988).

Nicholas, S., and Shergold, P. R. 'Transportation as Global Migration', in S. Nicholas (ed.), *Convict Workers: Reinterpreting Australia's Past* (Cambridge: Cambridge University Press, 1988) pp. 28–42.

Nozick, R. *Anarchy, State and Utopia* (Oxford: Blackwell, 1974).

Osborne, D., and Gaebler, T. *Reinventing Government* (New York: Addison-Wesley, 1992).

Parker, C. *Just Lawyers* (Oxford: Oxford University Press, 1999).

Read, P. *Returning to Nothing* (Cambridge: Cambridge University Press, 1997).

——. *Belonging: Australians, Place and Aboriginal Ownership* (Cambridge: Cambridge University Press, 2000)

Reeves, W. P. *State Experiments in Australia*, 2 vols (London: Grant Richards, 1902).
Reynolds, H. 'That Hated Stain: The Aftermath of Transportation in Tasmania', *Historical Studies*, vol. 14 (1969) pp. 19–31.
Rotman, E. 'The Failure of Reform: United States, 1865–1965', in Norval Morris and David J. Rothman (eds), *The Oxford History of the Prison: The Practice of Punishment in Western Society* (New York: Oxford University Press, 1995).
Sawer, M. 'Peacemakers for the World?', in M. Sawer (ed.), *People's Choice: Australia's Democratic Experiments* (Sydney: Federation Press, 2001) pp. 1–27.
Shaw, A. G. L. *Convicts and the Colonies* (London: Faber and Faber, 1966).
Sherman, L. W. 'Defiance, Deterrence and Irrelevance: A Theory of the Criminal Sanction', *Journal of Research in Crime and Delinquency*, vol. 30 (1993) pp. 445–73.
Spierenburg, P. 'The Body and the State: Early Modern Europe' in N. Morris and D. J. Rothman (eds), *The Oxford History of the Prison: The Practice of Punishment in Western Society* (New York: Oxford University Press, 1995).
Tanzi, V. *Globalization, Technological Developments, and the Work of Fiscal Termites*, IMF Working Paper WP/00/11811 (Washington, DC: International Monetary Fund, 2000).
Tripartite Working Party on Labour Standards. *Report on Labour Standards in the Asia-Pacific Region* (Canberra: Australian Government Publishing Service, 1996).
Tyler, T. *Why People Obey the Law* (New Haven, Conn.: Yale University Press, 1990).
Tyler, T., and Dawes, R. 'Fairness in Groups: Comparing the Self-Interest and Social Identity Perspectives' in B. A. Mellers and J. Baron (eds), *Psychological Perspectives on Justice: Theory and Applications* (Cambridge: Cambridge University Press, 1993).
United Nations Conference on Trade and Development. *World Investment Report 1996: Investment, Trade and International Policy Arrangements* (New York and Geneva: United Nations, 1996).
Ward, R. *The Australian Legend* (Melbourne: Oxford University Press, 1966).
Weiss, L. *The Myth of the Powerless State: Governing the Economy in a Global Era* (Cambridge: Polity Press, 1998).

# 5 Including Australia: A Democratic History

*John S. Dryzek*

We can reconstruct the democratic history of any society in terms of the progressive inclusion of groups or categories of people in the political system. At a basic level, that inclusion proceeds in terms of the achievement of full citizenship rights. But citizenship tells only part of the story: in practice, formal political equality can coexist with continued exclusion or even oppression, as feminists and advocates for indigenous peoples, gays and lesbians, the underclass, recent immigrants, and the disabled, among others, remind us. Thus my concern here is with effective and authentic inclusion that involves a substantive rather than symbolic say in the production of collective outcomes (of which public policies are an important subset) and participation in political institutions. I wish to undertake a brief survey of Australian history with a view to assessing the character and quality of this inclusive aspect of Australia's political institutions. My intent is not to judge these qualities by some absolute standard. This I believe can only be done in terms of a crude test for what constitutes democracy, which Australia was perhaps the first country in the world to pass (given its role in pioneering near-universal adult suffrage[1] and secret voting, still sometimes referred to in the United States as the Australian Ballot). Rather, I want to assess Australia's democracy as a work-in-progress. In these terms, a positive assessment would be based on a record of continued inclusions and the capacity to effect further inclusions. A negative assessment would reflect any expulsions that have occurred, any persistent exclusions, and any incapacity to contemplate further inclusions. I will show that there are both positive and negative aspects to the report card, as well as a few surprises.

Inclusion in the state is only part of the story. I will argue that, for Australia as for elsewhere, inclusion in the polity beyond the state may be equally important, indeed in some circumstances preferable, and not necessarily a recipe for powerlessness for the group in question. Accordingly, though counter-intuitively, an exclusive state can in some special cases be beneficial from the point of view of democracy. It is important to note that the public sphere and civil society can constitute important sites for (democratic) political activity. Indeed, the public sphere when it takes an oppositional form can be thought of as a kind of counter-institution, which in the long run can lead to the reconstruction of more conventional institutions and so change the character of the state itself. Of course, this means attending to what exactly we mean by those contested concepts, the state, the public sphere, and civil society. In a moment I will say what I mean by these three concepts. The contested concept of democracy itself is still harder to pin down – my preference is to talk about democratization rather than democracy *per se*. This emphasis is consistent with my focus on the dynamics of inclusion and exclusion, and the idea that democracy is always a work-in-progress.

My historical reconstruction will proceed through reference to a specific set of categories of people (and one nonhuman category), rather than to the whole range of groups and categories that could justifiably claim treatment in these terms. The groups and categories are the bourgeoisie, the working class (whose inclusion in the state Australia pioneered), women, indigenous peoples, non-English-speaking immigrants, and nonhuman nature (the story of which must be told in part through reference to its human advocates). My justification for this selection is that either the categories in question have figured large in Australian political development, or their interests can be connected in revealing ways to the established or emerging core imperatives of the Australian state (and in some cases both). Readers may ask why I do not discuss (for example) emancipist ex-convicts, the aged, the young, those now caught on the wrong side of the digital divide, gays, Catholics, lesbians, rural residents, the unemployed, and so forth. One has to stop somewhere (I would welcome parallel analyses for these and other categories).

Any assessment of the effectiveness of inclusion in the state and the democratic well-being of the public sphere and polity as a whole makes sense only in comparative cross-national terms. It is easy but not helpful to identify shortcomings in relation to democratic ideals, much harder to assess their real significance in comparative terms. While a full-scale comparative analysis is beyond my scope, in each section I will try to point out some terms in which Australia does more or less well than elsewhere in terms of facilitating or blocking democratization. (By way of summary comparison with countries where I have carried out empirical research on related issues, I believe Australia currently has a more inclusive state than the United Kingdom, the United States, Germany, and New Zealand, but less inclusive than Norway. Its public sphere is in better shape than Norway and New Zealand, worse shape than Germany, probably in similar shape to that in the UK and the United States.)

My intent here is a bit different from that of the historian. What I seek to develop is an interpretation of history based on a particular theoretical framework (initially developed in Dryzek, 1996b). Rather than engage in any original historical inquiry of my own, I will make use of the existing efforts of the best authors I can find dealing with the political experience of the group or category in question as it relates to questions of inclusion. As we will see, Australia has generally done better than average when it comes to inclusion within the state, though there are important exceptions to this rule. The corollary is, however, that patterns of inclusion in the state precluded effective inclusion in the public sphere. Australia long had a depleted public sphere, which in turn impeded democratic development. This deficiency began to be rectified in the 1960s, but since then social movements have often been easily absorbed into the state – and the bargain has not always been a good one, sometimes from the point of view of the defining interest of the group, or sometimes for democracy itself. In this light, exclusions (verging on expulsions) from the state seen in the 1990s and beyond could paradoxically benefit Australian democracy by revitalizing oppositional public spheres. However, those expelled have done little to contribute along these lines, devoting their energies instead to re-entry into the state.

The broad-brush approach I take means that historical nuance will be lost along the way. When I point to periods of quiescence, there are always a few counter-examples that cheerleaders for particular categories and movements can seize upon to say that there always was a struggle. While I will try to note these counter-instances, judgements about degree can still prevail.

### Some Basic Concepts

Before proceeding any further, it is necessary to nail down some core concepts.

*The state* is in the first instance the set of individuals or organizations with the authority to make decisions that are legally binding for a society within a given territory. US-based political scientists have long noted that the state so defined has permeable boundaries and internal conflicts, thus making it more sensible to speak of 'the political system' rather than 'the state' – for this reason, 'the state' was banished from the vocabulary of US political science, until its partial comeback in the 1980s.

The idea of *state imperatives* would at first sight seem to run against this recognition of the permeable and differentiated character of the state. But such imperatives are necessary to my historical reconstruction. A state imperative may be defined as any function that structures of government must perform for the sake of their own longevity and stability, thus responding to exogenous parameters and existing independent of the preferences or desires of government officials. At present, the list of established imperatives is that states must keep internal order, compete externally, raise revenues, prevent disinvestment and capital flight thus securing economic growth, and legitimate the political economy in the eyes of the citizenry. Later I will contemplate possible additions to this list. These imperatives are not static. Historically, they were changed by the terms under which the bourgeoisie and then the working class were included. Later I will show how environmentalism at least could change the character of the core.

We can define the core of the state in terms of organization to pursue these basic functions. In the language of Lindblom (1982), this is the 'imprisoned' zone of policy-making (though Lindblom is concerned only with the economic imperative). It covers the essential areas of state activity that establish the need for the state in the first place. Major matters of foreign policy, security, taxation, economic policy, the welfare state, criminal justice, industry, agricultural, natural resources and environmental policy belong in the core. However, when the monetary stakes become high, other policy areas can enter the core, via their encroachment on economic concerns. (For greater detail on these issues, see Dryzek, 2000: 83–5.) Of course, governments carry out all kinds of activities that are not located in this core. These residual activities can be defined as the periphery of the state.

*Inclusion in the state* for individuals or categories of people can come via acceptance as an interest or lobby group; involvement in policy-making through negotiations with public officials; affiliation with an established political party or constituting a party of one's own to contest elections and seek office; the taking up of government appointments by group leaders; or having advancement of the political standing of the group itself a conscious goal of government policy.

The *public sphere* is any arena of political association and communicative interaction oriented to the activities of the state, but not included in the state; it is the politicized aspect of civil society. Public spheres so defined can be plural; so (say) a green public sphere is not coterminous with a feminist public sphere. Some definitions of the public sphere would weaken the concept's analytical purchase by allowing that state actors (parliament, minor public agencies, parliamentary parties) can participate in opinion formation in the public sphere. I am especially concerned here with oppositional public spheres that do not easily accommodate state actors in their roles as state actors (though state actors can participate in other roles; at issue is an oppositional discourse that does not blend seamlessly into policy-making).

*Democratization* occurs whenever there is an advance on any one of three dimensions of democracy, so long as it is not bought at the expense of retreat on either of the other two dimensions. The three dimensions are franchise, the number of empowered participants in any political setting; scope, the domains of life under democratic control; and authenticity, the extent to which popular control is substantive rather than symbolic, engaged by competent and informed citizens (see Dryzek, 1996a: 4–9, for more detail). These criteria can be applied to the state alone, to the public sphere alone and, most importantly, to the polity as a whole.

With these definitions in hand, there are two criteria that can be applied to any group offered a choice between the state and continued emphasis on the public sphere where most groups begin their life. (As we shall see, one of the groups I cover – people of non-English-speaking background – never constituted a public sphere in these terms, beginning political life only when fostered by the state.) First, can the group's defining interest be attached to an established or emerging state imperative? If the answer is no, then inclusion can only be conditional, as the group's influence will be confined to the periphery of the state. The group will always lose when it encounters the core, and so face frustration and co-option if and when such an encounter occurs.[2] Whether or not this location in the periphery is acceptable depends on the substantive ends sought by the group – they may be fully achievable within the periphery, though I will show that this is not the case for any of the groups I cover. If the answer is 'partly', then a dual strategy, perhaps even bifurcation of the movement into moderate and radical wings, is appropriate. The second criterion would ask whether full commitment to inclusion in the state would leave behind a thoroughly depleted public sphere. If it does, then a major source of democratic vitality is lost, so from the point of view of democracy inclusion may be a bad idea – because it may bring democratization as just defined to a halt, rendering further democratization of the state itself less likely. I will demonstrate that, while not always the case, this is a perennial problem in Australian democratic history. This second criterion might seem to ask a group to put the public good of democratic vitality above its own defining interest. However, an inactive public sphere constitutes one less reason for the group's interests to be taken seriously in the state (this recognition underpins the advocacy of 'dual' strategies in state and civil society by writers such as Wainwright, 1994).

Life in the public sphere does not mean political irrelevance. Influence over collective outcomes can still be exercised, most powerfully by changing the terms of discourse in ways that can lead directly to cultural change (one major achievement of feminism), and come to pervade the understandings of policy-makers, thus affecting the content of public policy.

In the rest of this chapter I will apply these concepts to Australia's political experience.

## The Bourgeoisie

It might at first seem odd to begin an examination of democratic inclusions with the bourgeoisie, accustomed as we are to a close working relationship between government and business, what Lindblom (1977: 170–88) calls 'the privileged position of business' in public policy-making. But it was not always so. As Habermas (1989) points out, the early bourgeoisie in European countries constituted an oppositional public sphere, denied entry to the state controlled by monarchy, theocracy, and aristocracy. The early modern state was generally authoritarian and exclusive. Its imperatives were to keep order internally, fend off external enemies in a hostile world, and raise the revenues necessary to finance these first two activities (Skocpol, 1979). With time and the development of capitalism, it became apparent that raising revenues need not be a matter of forcible extraction from a fixed-size pie, but rather of taking a share of the growing pie that capitalism could produce. Thus the defining material interest of the bourgeoisie in profit maximization, capital accumulation and economic growth became consistent with the state's revenue imperative, so the bourgeoisie could be included in the state and immediately enter the core. Over time this relationship has only strengthened, such that today the most important imperative of all states is to keep actual and potential investors happy, to prevent disinvestment and capital flight (Lindblom, 1982; Dryzek, 1996a). The oppositional bourgeois public sphere is now but a distant memory in all countries, though bourgeois institutions such as universities and newspapers still give sustenance to public spheres, oppositional or otherwise. The right-wing think tanks that proliferated in the 1980s are public sphere institutions too. Their oppositional aspect comes with radical market liberalism, which may favour the market, but not necessarily the bourgeoisie (which often seeks protection from real market forces).

Australia was of course different: it never had an absolutist state or aristocracy to struggle against, though in the 1850s proposals were advanced by William Wentworth and others to create an aristocracy to populate upper houses of parliament, in imitation of the House of Lords. Ridiculed as a 'bunyip aristocracy', such proposals got nowhere (Macintyre, 1999: 93). Australia did however have colonial administrations, whose interests were not the same as the emerging bourgeoisie. For example, in 1842 the Legislative Council of New South Wales passed an Act abolishing tariffs for trade with Van Diemen's Land and New Zealand. This Act was vetoed by the Colonial Office on the grounds that it was not for colonies to choose to apply non-uniform conditions of trade of the sort that differential tariffs would connote (Reeves, 1902: 145).

The first elections to the Legislative Council of New South Wales (while it still encompassed the whole eastern side of Australia) were held in 1843. However, colonial governors appointed from London were still not initially answerable to the council, and retained veto power over legislation (see Blainey, 1995: 113–15). The council itself was not initially controlled by the bourgeoisie. All that was to change in short order, as self-government arrived in the colonies in the late 1850s, and elected governments soon came to be dominated by the bourgeoisie.

In the middle of the nineteenth century there was a class struggle between the emerging urban bourgeoisie and the squatters who monopolized agricultural land in the colonies. In the 1840s and 1850s the squatters controlled the legislative assemblies of New South Wales, Victoria, Queensland and South Australia under a restricted franchise. But the squattocracy was a poor reflection of a European landed aristocracy, and could do little to resist expansion of the franchise which put an end to this political domination. By 1859 all the colonies except Western Australia and Tasmania had near-universal adult male suffrage. In practice successful politicians still all came from the wealthier classes, partly because members of parliament were not paid (and property qualifications remained for voting for upper houses, actually persisting in South Australia until 1973). Thus self-government and universal suffrage at first meant full inclusion only of the bourgeoisie, not more general popular inclusion.

In the 1860s the legislative councils of all four states passed Selection Acts that opened crown land to 'selectors' and so ended the squatters' monopoly; though in practice squatters managed to secure control of the best land while many selectors constituted a class of rural poor that was reviled by squatters and bourgeoisie alike (Macintyre, 1999: 98–9). Still, the Selection Acts signalled a key political defeat for the squatters, and the beginning of what Manning Clark (1969: 132–56) calls the 'golden age of the bourgeoisie' in Australia, lasting until the 1890s. Thus if Australia did have a bourgeois public sphere in opposition to the state(s), it was extremely short-lived, and gave way almost immediately to bourgeois entry into, and domination of, the state. Such domination was facilitated by the reduction in the power of governors appointed from London and rise in the power of elected governments.

Applying the two basic criteria for assessing inclusion in the state, it is first of all clear that in instrumental terms the bourgeoisie benefited from their inclusion because their defining interest in profit maximization could be attached to the economic imperative. Public policies both facilitated the inward flow of finance and created an active state role in promoting economic development. As Macintyre (1985: 24–50) points out, the bourgeoisie in power may have trumpeted the laissez-faire theories of

Adam Smith and John Stuart Mill, but in practice enacted statist policies. Federation of the colonies, achieved in 1901, was vigorously promoted by employers in the 1890s on economic grounds. Employers sought freedom of contract and an end to tariffs between the different colonies (Clark, 1969: 167), though they divided over the issue of free trade versus protectionism in relation to the rest of the world. Overall, there was a clear coincidence between the defining interest of the bourgeoisie in profit and capital accumulation and the economic developmentalist imperative of the state in Australia that began in the 1860s and continues to this day.

In terms of the second criterion for assessing the democratic merits of inclusion, the terms of the bourgeoisie's inclusion itself helped to create another vital public sphere: that constituted by the organized and politicized working class. Thus from the point of view of democracy of the polity as a whole, as well as the state in particular, the bourgeoisie's inclusion was beneficial. However, as we will now see, the working-class public sphere too proved to be of very short duration in Australia.

### The Working Class

The migration of the bourgeoisie from the oppositional public sphere to the core of the state was in most countries followed much later by that of the organized working class, whose very existence was arguably a direct consequence of that earlier migration. For as capitalism, now promoted and supported by governments, flourished in the nineteenth century, it produced a working class that began to mobilize politically. At first the working class's political organizations – trade unions and socialist parties – were excluded from the state. Property qualifications for voting in most countries ensured that socialist parties could not win elections, and some of these parties adopted a revolutionary stance in relation to the state. Whether revolutionary or reformist, the political representatives of the working class constituted a public sphere in opposition to, and excluded by, the liberal capitalist state. This public sphere had its own meeting places (union halls, Methodist chapels in England and Wales) and publications, even international networks (the First and Second Internationals). But with time the capitalist state's oppression of the workers – portrayed in such graphic terms by Karl Marx – softened. This softening took two forms: the development of welfare state arrangements that insulated workers from the worst effects of capitalism's boom–bust cycles, and the acceptance of social democrat parties into parliament and – much later – government. The latter was made possible by extension of the franchise to virtually all adult males (though this extension proved not to be a sufficient condition for social democratic party success).

Contrary to the hopes of revolutionary socialists and the fears of liberals and conservatives, the oppositional public sphere of the working class culminated in inclusion in the state rather than revolutionary overthrow of the state.

This inclusion was in many cases a long time coming, incomplete until the middle of the twentieth century. By this time most European liberal democracies had seen social democratic parties take at least some share of governing power, and the development of reasonably comprehensive welfare states.[3] Inclusion of the working class could occur because its defining material interest in redistribution and income security could be aligned with a changing state imperative. In the face of the threat to political stability that the working class offered, it became clear that domestic order could be secured most straightforwardly through welfare state arrangements and labour market regulation rather than coercion; and thus was born what came to be called the legitimation imperative of states (O'Connor, 1973; Habermas, 1975). Legitimation here means securing support for the basic parameters of the political economy from those with the capacity to disrupt it – in this case, the working class.

Again Australia was different. Just as for the bourgeoisie a few years earlier, inclusion of the working class in the state came early and rapidly. When it comes to basic citizenship for the working class, the Australian colonies were the first places in the world to have near-universal adult male suffrage. This was achieved by 1859 in all the colonies except Tasmania and Western Australia, which had to wait until 1901 and 1907 respectively. Of course, the right to vote does not necessarily mean that inclusion as I defined it earlier has occurred, let alone inclusion that reaches to the core of the state. Indeed, near-universal adult male suffrage at first benefited the better-organized bourgeoisie more than the working class. The late nineteenth century saw a labour movement take shape in Australia, but until the 1890s strikes were only ever about wages, working conditions and dismissals (Clark, 1969: 165) – though broader political issues had been raised, famously, at Eureka Stockade in 1854. Organizations such as Friendly Societies and Mechanics' Institutes with an orientation to public affairs did exist prior to 1890. But only in the 1890s did a labour movement with broad political concerns take form, such that it is possible to speak of a working-class public sphere. The impetus for this was the class polarization that followed defeat of the Maritime Strike in 1890, in which governmental coercion backed by liberal politicians proved decisive (Macintyre, 1999: 125). The formation of Labour Electoral Leagues at first in New South Wales in 1891 signalled the arrival of a working-class public sphere, which confronted what was briefly an actively exclusive state that suppressed workers and their organizations (Clark, 1969: 166). But 'From the beginning, Labour's aim was to capture rather than destroy the institutions of the bourgeois state' (Ibid: 169). Given the extent of the male franchise in Australia, electoral success came very quickly; Labor formed a government in Queensland in 1899, federally in 1904.

As Castles (1988) points out, Australia's economy by the 1890s featured commercialized agriculture that paid high wages due to high productivity, a shortage of labour, together with a state whose developmentalist role was accepted. This combination of circumstances put labour in a very strong bargaining position. Thus having its well-being the direct target of governmental concern – one aspect of inclusion – occurred early too. Welfare state arrangements that took most European countries until the middle of the twentieth century to consolidate were achieved in Australia at the very beginning of that century. Unlike their European counterparts wedded to nineteenth-century ideas about the limits of the state, Australian liberals (such as Deakin) recognized the threat to social stability posed by uncontrolled laissez-faire economics, in which respect Australian liberals resembled British Tories rather than liberals (Macintyre, 1985: 141).

The lifetime of the organized working class as an oppositional public sphere excluded by the state was very brief indeed. Conflicts that took up to a century to play themselves out in Northern Europe were compressed into scarcely more than a decade in Australia, resolved by the inclusion of the leadership of the organized working class in a redistributive and interventionist state. Australia therefore never had anything like, for example, the large communist union federations found in Italy and France in the second half of the twentieth century. Compulsory government arbitration of wage disputes played a key role, foundational to what Castles (1985) calls Australia's 'wage-earners' welfare state'. Protection against imports was granted only to manufacturers who provided adequate wages and conditions of work as defined by the Commonwealth Arbitration Court.

Inclusion in the Australian state proved to be a good bargain for the organized working class. Its material interests were aligned quickly and easily with the legitimation imperative, and the results in terms of public policies and socio-economic outcomes were impressive. There was perhaps a price to be paid in terms of foreclosure of the possibilities of more radical social change that might have benefited the working class (only 'perhaps' because no such change occurred elsewhere until mid-twentieth-century Scandinavia). As Macintyre (1999: 128) laments, its 'precocious success stunted the Australian labour movement. The achievement of office while still in its infancy turned the Labor Party into a pragmatic, majoritarian electoral organisation.' Nevertheless, the system of compulsory arbitration did produce income security as well as a very egalitarian distribution of earnings by international standards. Of course, those not part of the wage-earning *organized* working class – the unemployed, single parents, the disabled, the old – did not do quite so well out of these arrangements, though means-tested benefits did eventually flow in their direction (see Castles, 1985). What these categories of people share is not just a lack of any capacity to destabilize the political economy, but also a social isolation that makes it very hard for them to contribute to any effective public sphere.[4]

Thus from the point of view of democracy, the inclusion of the organized working class in the wage-earners' welfare state was a mixed blessing. It made the state more democratic – but at the expense of a deradicalized and structurally co-opted labour movement, and, perhaps more seriously, emptying the public sphere of any oppositional content that is the normal source of democratic renewal. Remnant working-class public sphere activity could be found only in the Communist Party from the 1920s to the 1950s which, given its Leninism, was hardly a beacon of democracy. An oppositional public sphere also flickered into life with the green bans organized by the Builders Labourers' Federation in Sydney in the early 1970s (Burgmann and Burgmann, 1998). Until new social movements began to raise their heads in the late 1960s, there is little to report in the way of Australian democratic development. Thus there were no local memories to inform these new movements, only contemporaneous overseas examples. In some European countries (such as France and possibly Britain) the full inclusion of the organized working class in the state had not been achieved by the 1960s; in others (such as the Scandinavian countries) inclusion was at most only two or three decades old. Thus the working-class public sphere that preceded this inclusion was a recent local memory. If Australia did have a democratic deficit in the late twentieth century, herein perhaps lies the key.

Unfortunately the history of the organized working class's entry into the state does not end with 'and they all lived happily ever after'. With time, the Australian Labor Party looked less and less like a workers' party. Today its parliamentarians are mainly professional politicians, few of whom were ever manual workers. More seriously, the economic rationalism adopted by the federal government and some state governments beginning in the mid-1980s and embraced, even instigated, by ALP governments, thoroughly undermined the wage-earners' welfare state. In a contest between the economic and legitimation imperatives, economics prevailed. Castles (2000) sees the 2000 McClure Report (Department of Family and Community Services, 2000) as the final nail in the coffin. McClure proposed reinstating a discretionary welfare regime in which supplicants have to prove that they deserve support. There are clear echoes here of the Poor Laws that preceded the rise of the modern welfare state, when the poor had to appear before Boards of Guardians (in Britain) to demonstrate that their poverty was not a result of bad character, and that they would work if they could. By the end of the century the proportion of workers covered by awards had fallen from a high of 80 per cent to 50 per cent, unemployment and income insecurity had increased, and the distribution of earnings and incomes was more unequal.

Until Labor was defeated at the 1996 federal election, the Australian Council of Trade Unions had entered into a series of Accords with the government. These quasi-corporatist arrangements arguably softened the impact of economic restructuring attending government's pursuit of marketization and free trade. Perhaps union leaders had forgotten what an oppositional politics rooted in the public sphere could look like, given that almost a century had passed since they had acted like this. Their participation in the Accords, even as their membership declined and their members' conditions of employment deteriorated further, confirmed a loss of the will, if not the capacity, to destabilize the political economy. Even if the legitimacy imperative still operated, the economic imperative now pointed firmly against the immediate material interests of the organized working class. Pleasing investors and international financial markets had to mean exposing workers to the market and its associated instabilities. It could be pointed out in defence of the ACTU's Accord strategy that unions in the United Kingdom and New Zealand who had no such option were simply crushed in the interests of economic restructuring (in New Zealand, ironically at the hands of at first a Labour government).

It is not just workers' material interests that are at issue here, but also the health of the working-class public sphere, whose potential revitalization the Accords precluded (though again, no such revitalization occurred in the United Kingdom or New Zealand, testifying to the reach of the actively exclusive state of market liberalism). In this light, the anti-union attitude of the Howard Liberal–National government (shared by the Kennett government in Victoria, among others) has perhaps inadvertently helped to re-create the preconditions for a working-class public sphere – though at the time of writing, this potential is far from realization, despite the odd piece of excitement such as the reaction against the attempt by government, employers, and the National Farmers' Federation to destroy the Maritime Union of Australia in 1998. The attitude of the unions since 1996 illustrates the fact that groups used to life in the state do not readily take to the public sphere if they are expelled, instead putting their energies into re-entry.

Changes in Australia's class structure also impede the revival of a working-class public sphere. Many paid employees are more clearly members of a middle class than a working class. Members of the 'new' middle class have career paths that run through the public sector, be it in government departments or universities. Although such people may form a major recruiting base for new social movements (of which more later), they are not easily aligned with any working-class-based public sphere in opposition to a state that provides them with relatively pleasant employment conditions (in comparison with the factory floor or shearing shed). On a very different dimension of class politics, those with low income and no prospects of paid employment, whose relationship to government comes mainly in the form of welfare dependency, constitute an underclass whose conditions of life are not conducive to any kind of public association and action.

## Women

Women's suffrage came relatively early to Australia, in South Australia in 1894, for federal elections in 1902, and finally in Victoria in 1909. Just like the contemporaneous working-class public sphere and the earlier bourgeois one, the duration of the women's suffrage movement as an oppositional sphere (complete with its own associations and journals such as the well-named *Woman's Sphere*) was extraordinarily brief by international standards. Like these other two spheres it was a victim of its own success, though unlike the case for the (male) working class, success took the form only of a formal citizenship demand – suffrage – and not entry into the state, let alone the core of the state. Suffrage itself was seen as instrumental to a number of policy goals: 'temperance, laws against gambling, control of prostitution, an increase in the age of consent, prevention of domestic violence' (Macintyre, 1999: 134). However, sections of the movement also sought more equal social and economic opportunities for women, and more equal laws relating to marriage and property, not just cures for the masculine evils besetting family life. Votes for women did not signify any more substantial political inclusion, such as the presence of women's organizations in policy-making, or even the presence of women as individual members of parliament.

The women's public sphere at the end of the nineteenth century encompassed women active in labour movement politics and 'educated women of social standing and influence in liberal political circles' (Grimshaw, 1988: 73). But by far the most important organization was the Woman's Christian Temperance Union, founded in 1882 (assisted by members of the corresponding American organization). In its attack on male drunkenness and associated domestic irresponsibility, this dominant temperance wing of the women's movement stood shoulder to shoulder, if by coincidence rather than design, with the bourgeoisie's interest in disciplined and responsible employees (though the temperance movement had connections with radical organizations and was not itself bourgeois). The evangelical Protestants who were the core of the WCTU's activists (Grimshaw, 1988: 71) supported an ethic which, as Max Weber was soon to note, was uniquely suited to capitalist development. Thus it was not hard to align this defining interest of the women's temperance movement with the state's economic accumulation imperative.

The women's movement of first-wave feminism in fact practised a kind of self-limiting radicalism that stopped at suffrage. Consistent with its model of the responsible male accompanied by an ideal 'colonial helpmate' (to borrow a term from Grimshaw, 1988: 77), it offered little opposition to the foundational principle of the wage-earners' welfare state announced by Henry Bournes Higgins, president of the Commonwealth Arbitration Court, in 1907. The basic principle was that male wages should be set at a level capable of supporting a family, while women's wages were pegged at a level sufficient only for the needs of a single person. Some women were active in Labor politics from the 1890s onwards on behalf of better employment chances for women, but the Labor hierarchy was generally unsympathetic (and sometimes hostile).

The achievement of suffrage was not followed by any attempt to get significant numbers of women elected to parliament, still less the formation of a women's political party. 'The central goal (suffrage) having been won, the movement splintered' (Grimshaw, 1988: 78), its profile reduced. Lake (1999) disagrees with the conventional wisdom that there is little to report between 1909 and 1969, pointing to struggles that took place (outside the major parties) for childcare, equal pay, temperance, maternity allowances, and the rights of Aboriginal women to keep their children. Thus the intervening period is not devoid of interest, just much less striking than what came earlier and later.

In the late 1960s the incipient women's liberation movement, inspired by events in other countries (particularly the United States) began to question systematic disadvantages to women. These included political representation (even in 1979 there were no women in the federal House of Representatives); lack of employment opportunity and protection against sexual harassment; unequal pay; access to childcare, contraception and abortion; and media exploitation of women. In the 1970s the women's movement rapidly institutionalized (the Women's Electoral Lobby was founded in 1972, receiving government funding from 1983 until 1999), and equally rapidly entered the state. Australia pioneered the role of 'femocrats' in government, dealing with women's issues (Bulbeck, 2000: 82–3; Kaplan, 1996) in institutions such as the federal Women's Affairs Section (1974). Advances in representation in parliaments came more slowly, though by 2000, 23 per cent of Australian parliamentarians were women, up from 2 per cent in 1972 (Sawer, 2001: 172). These developments did perhaps deplete, if not completely impoverish, the women's public sphere. Sawer (2001: 177) describes EMILY'S LIST, founded in 1996, as an 'alternative public sphere', though geared as it was to getting feminist women elected to parliament, in fact it had a very close connection to electoral politics and so inclusion in the state. More clearly oppositional public spheres may be found in connection with more radical organizations and (mostly short-lived) collectives. But even radical feminists found that their rape crisis centres, women's shelters, and so forth, could secure themselves via applications for government funding, though 'most detested having to do this' (Grimshaw, 1988: 84). As the century drew to a close, feminisms became more diverse, qualified by adjectives such as radical, socialist, difference, power and victim, and displaying a seeming generational split, as well as increasingly apparent variation in women's experience in different classes, races and sexual orientations. This diversity indicated that there was much of concern to women that was not being incorporated into the state so easily as liberal feminism in the 1970s and 1980s, which itself was facing harder times in the teeth of economic rationalism. These debates featured plenty of soul-searching and some lamentation concerning what had become of the movement. But from the point of view of democratic vitality in the public sphere, all this was no bad thing.

In the terms that I have developed, the inclusion of women and their concerns via liberal feminism into the core of the state in the 1970s and beyond is no mystery. The patriarchal family can be thought of as a remnant feudal structure (see Fraad et al., 1994), whose lingering presence impedes the effective deployment of labour in the capitalist economy. Many of the policy advances achieved by women in the 1970s and 1980s had the effect of enabling their more effective participation in the workplace; all to the good, from the point of view of the state's economic imperatives, and more labour market participants meant a larger tax base. So, for example, childcare was funded by government once it was shown to be good for the economy, not just good for women. More feminist demands for changed gender relations including (for example) politics based on an ethic of care rather than competition were not so easily assimilated.

Though the story of the past thirty years of feminist and women's concerns is complex, one way of interpreting it is in terms of a dual strategy. Part of the movement entered the state and found some success in instrumental terms – also in democratizing the state, through the greater presence of women and their concerns in the corridors of power, be it the femocracy or parliaments. Paradoxically, some of the femocrats came not from the liberal Women's Electoral Lobby, but from the women's liberation movement, establishing feminist enclaves within the state. The more radical aspects of the movement resisted such incorporation, constituting a lively public sphere (if one that seemed to be experiencing a crisis of confidence by the 1990s). The picture here is complicated by the degree to which femocrats in government helped to secure funding for collectives that provided services to women. Resistance continued to make sense in terms of the absence of any plausible connection between radical feminism and any state imperative; political stability and so legitimation were never seriously threatened. Thus entrance into the state by femocrats and groups such as the Women's Electoral Lobby did not, at least over the time scale of thirty years (1970–2000), empty the feminist public sphere.

### Indigenous Peoples

Public policy towards Australia's indigenous peoples began with conquest and displacement and changed to segregation on reserves in the late nineteenth century. In the 1930s assimilation began to be promoted, in part through the removal of laws directed specifically at Aborigines, though such laws persisted in Queensland into the 1970s (Rowse, 2000: 88–9). Discriminatory references to Aborigines were removed from the Australian constitution in a 1967 referendum. In the 1930s Aboriginal activists themselves argued that Aborigines could aspire to capacities that would qualify them for Australian citizenship (Ibid: 87–8), a far cry from later demands for the recognition of indigenous identity. In the 1970s assimilation gave way to 'self-determination' or 'self-management' (Burgmann, 1993: 27), given a boost by all the organizations created in the wake of the federal *Aboriginal Councils and Associations Act 1976*.

Indigenous peoples were long the target of active exclusion from the mainstream of Australian social and political life, though their right to vote was confirmed by federal legislation in 1962, and by Queensland legislation in 1965. But as with other groups, formal citizenship rights do not necessarily connote full inclusion in the state or polity more generally. Since the 1960s the road to reconciliation with the non-indigenous population has been a rocky one. The establishment of institutions such as the Aboriginal and Torres Strait Islander Commission in 1989 appears to connote more meaningful inclusion, though ATSIC in practice has often been highly critical of government policies, and so exists in a quasi-oppositional orientation to the state. The more conventional but less prominent government department is the federal Department of Reconciliation and Aboriginal and Torres Strait Islander Affairs (until 2001 this was the Office of Indigenous Policy within the Department of Prime Minister and Cabinet). ATSIC both recognizes advancement of the social, economic and political standing of Aborigines and Torres Strait

Islanders as a target of public policy, and provides an alternative means of representation for people who are otherwise a very small minority in most electoral districts, and for whom conventional parliamentary representation cannot therefore work very well. As Stokes points out in Chapter 7, ATSIC has also been intended as a means for Aboriginal self-government, as well as a conduit for inclusion, though in practice paternalistic and liberal elements outweigh its democratic aspects. ATSIC and its role have often been at the centre of controversy, not least within the Indigenous community itself.

There remains a large issue of what inclusion in the state, whether or not it is via institutions such as ATSIC, can and should mean for Australia's Indigenous peoples. For the Australian state is constructed along Western lines, alien to indigenous political tradition. Rowse (2001: 103–4) points to ethnographic studies in Central and Northern Australia that demonstrate suspicion of large political units, support for hierarchy based on birth or ritual prominence rather than (say) voting, preference for consensus over adversarial politics, and for delegates rather than representatives with any leeway in formulating their own positions in larger forums. These characteristics perhaps constitute an additional reason for indigenous politics to emphasize the public sphere rather than the state, for in the public sphere there are fewer constraints on the kinds of social and political interaction that can occur. As Rowse (2001: 112–13) notes, these features do not necessarily apply to urban Indigenous communities. Still, when it comes to the kinds of claims upon the political system, Stokes points out in Chapter 7 that not all are easily assimilated to standard Western notions of what inclusion and citizenship mean, especially in connection with claims based upon attachment to the land that do not fit well with liberal ideas about property and its ownership. With the public sphere in mind, it is noteworthy that some unofficial land councils have been constituted – with an orientation to pressing for governmental response, but maintaining political distance from the state.

Aboriginal inclusion in the politics of the liberal state, then, has been partial, contested, sometimes resisted by more radical activists (Burgmann, 1993: 24–76), and often ambiguous in institutional terms. Even those leaders who have taken up governmental positions have often remained critics of government policy. It is hard to describe this complex situation even in 'dual' terms. That is, it is not clearly the case that some Aboriginal activists have chosen the state while others have chosen a critical distance in the public sphere; indeed, various individuals operate on several levels at once. What has all this achieved in terms of public policies? Again there is no easy answer: there have been both advances and setbacks, the latter not least in connection with issues of native title

Including Australia 131

in the late 1990s. But if Australian democracy is a work-in-progress, all this ferment provides plenty of material for the reconstruction of the political system in ways that involve innovative conceptions of what citizenship can mean – for Aboriginal and Torres Strait Islanders, and perhaps for everyone else too (Rowse, 2000).

One way of cutting into this complexity would be to ask whether or not Indigenous interests can be connected to any established or emerging core state imperatives. When it comes to issues of native title, Aboriginal interests in land rights and access to their land are often seen by pastoralists, miners and other landed interests as potential threats to the economic security of property tenure, which in turn is central to Australia's economic well-being.[5] If so, there is a conflict with the economic imperative of the state. As Burgmann (1993: 60) puts it, 'decommodifying the land' means that it will not necessarily be put to use that is productive in conventional economic terms. However, economic imperatives clearly benefit from the removal of racial discrimination, which is an impediment to the free operation of the market (especially the labour market). Yet this complementarity only goes so far as supporting the standard set of liberal rights for everyone. When it comes to Indigenous Peoples, there is an important body of concerns that cannot easily be expressed in the language of individualism, of liberalism, even of rights. At issue is what Rowse (2000: 86) calls 'a set of communal, not merely individual, capacities and rights'. (The policy of assimilation had involved destroying communities for the sake of individual rights.) This kind of 'indigenous collectivism' (Ibid: 96) was finally recognized in the 1992 *Mabo* decision, which accepted the validity of a kind of land tenure vested in the community, not in the property rights of identifiable individuals.

More important when it comes to advancing Indigenous interests is the connection that can be made to the legitimation imperative. In an interdependent world, the Australian political economy requires legitimation not just in the eyes of its own population, but also in the eyes of the world: and that legitimation depends on the extent to which effective reconciliation with Indigenous peoples is seen to occur. In this respect Australia currently seems to be getting more scrutiny than countries such as the United States and Canada, whose treatment of their indigenous peoples was historically little better. Perhaps the difference is that in these other countries the legal status of indigenous peoples and their land rights was resolved much sooner (if generally on an unfair basis).

Indigenous interests do, then, coincide with the legitimation imperative, even as they clash with the economic imperative. This situation perhaps helps to explain the complexity and ambiguity in Indigenous accommodation with, and opposition to, the Australian state. Whatever the explanation, the politics of Indigenous issues features perhaps the liveliest public sphere in contemporary Australia – if anything, livelier than in comparable countries such as the United States and Canada.

### Non-English-Speaking Immigrants

In the case of women, we saw that the effective inclusion of the organized working class in the wage-earners' welfare state at the beginning of the twentieth century was accompanied by an exclusion in that women's wages were pegged at a level adequate to support a single person, not a family. At the same time, the inclusion of women as voting citizens and the working class as a participant in government was explicitly tied to a White Australia policy. One of the motives for Federation, as held by Deakin for the liberals for example, was to keep Australia white and render it strong enough to resist Asia and Asians (Macintyre, 1999: 141–2). Labor for its part 'adopted White Australia as its primary objective' (Ibid: 143) at its first federal conference in 1905. Writing in 1930, W. K. Hancock (1930: 77) observed that 'The policy of White Australia is the indispensable condition of every other Australian policy.' This policy had its beginnings in the Anti-Chinese Acts of 1881, and was really only abandoned in the 1960s – though by that time the definition of 'white' had been expanded a bit beyond the original North European conception.

On the broadest of definitions, those of non-English-speaking birth or origin now constitute up to 25 per cent of the population (Jupp, 1991: 43). This is a result of post-1945 immigration into what was a fairly homogeneous society, often described as 'Anglo-Celtic' – though that term would make no sense outside Australia, especially in places where Anglos and Celts are at each other's throats. Until the late 1970s immigration was mostly from Europe (though what counted as Europe was itself a matter of contention); thereafter there was a large Asian component. Unsurprisingly, new immigrants did not step immediately into the corridors of power of the state. We therefore need to take a look at whether and to what effect such a large category of people was eventually included in the state and the polity more generally.

Despite the diversity of their national origins, people of non-English-speaking background (NESB) have at least two common interests. The first is in non-discrimination when it comes to social and economic opportunity, which in a capitalist society is easily attached to the economic imperative. The second is in the very idea of Australia as a multicultural society. From the late 1940s to the early 1970s, public policy promoted assimilation or integration into the dominant culture. The terms of discourse on this issue began to change in the early 1970s, beginning in the

Whitlam Labor government, with Immigration Minister Al Grassby playing a leading role. Multiculturalism was adopted as policy by Malcolm Fraser's Liberal–National coalition government in the late 1970s in the wake of the landmark Galbally Report (Galbally et al., 1978).

Castles, Cope, Kalantzis and Morrissey (1988: 57) argue that the Fraser government's promotion of multiculturalism was 'a key strategy in a conservative restructuring of the welfare state whose main purpose was the destruction of Whitlam-style social democracy'. That is, programs to improve economic mobility by removing prejudice and increasing understanding of different cultural backgrounds would substitute for more expensive broad-ranging social policy expenditures. Castles et al. also believe that 'The Galbally programme ... was designed not to meet a mass demand, but to achieve a limited political goal: the incorporation into conservative politics of the ethnic middle class' (p. 66).

Whatever the motives, multiculturalism was introduced to Australia in top-down fashion, be it in the speeches of Grassby or the policies of the Fraser government. Leaders of ethnic organizations played only subordinate parts in an agenda determined by the government of the day. Was this direct entry into association with government a good bargain for NESB people and their representatives?

Again we can answer this question with regard to established state imperatives, three of which turn out to be at issue here. Large-scale non-British immigration was justified after World War II in terms of linked economic and security imperatives. In the face of possible threats from Asia, Australia had to increase the size of its economy and potential for military preparedness. However, this did not translate into influence in policy-making on the part of immigrant leaders. If immigrants were organized, it tended to be into trade unions, preoccupied with class-based issues.

The policy turn to multiculturalism made possible two connections to core state imperatives. The first was economic. Assertions have been made since at least the Hawke Labor government's 1989 *National Agenda for a Multicultural Australia* (Office of Multicultural Affairs, 1989) that multiculturalism benefits the economy both externally and internally. Externally, companies seeking to trade with other countries can benefit to the degree they employ people from the culture in question. Internally, companies have access to more employees and more business from NESB customers to the degree they are sensitive to linguistic and cultural variety. In the Howard government's 1999 *New Agenda for Multicultural Australia*, 'productive diversity' is specified as one of the four foundations for multiculturalism (for the basic argument, see National Multicultural Advisory Council, 1999: 63–6).[6] These assertions suggest a link to the economic imperative (though the magnitude of their economic impact is hard to measure), or at least a recognition of the need to frame equal opportunity arguments in economic terms. The second link is to legitimation. If indeed multicultural programs are a partial substitute for more expensive welfare state expenditures, then they are a low-cost means of achieving the legitimation function that is one main task of the welfare state.

These linkages, however tentative, help to explain why a more contentious ethnic pluralism is an unlikely prospect in Australia. Along these lines, Jayasuriya (1990: 57) calls for a movement from 'cultural pluralism' to 'democratic pluralism', by which he means 'a shift away from the *expressive* to the *instrumental* dimension of ethnicity'. Instead of speaking in terms of NESB, this shift would mean 'invoking the concept of minority status' for groups that are 'oppressed and discriminated against' (Ibid.). In other words, the transition would be towards the American model of multiculturalism, where rewards accrue to those who can make a successful claim to victimhood. (Jayasuriya invokes a Canadian comparison, but what he proposes strikes me as much more like the United States.)

Setting aside any misgivings about the attractiveness of such a model, and also the right-wing reaction it would probably provoke, the contentiousness it would have to involve is hard to envision. For it would have to involve NESB leaders turning their backs on the state that has both fostered their leadership and indicated that the defining interests of their communities can indeed be linked to core state imperatives. The expense that Jayasuriya's 'democratic pluralism' would necessarily impose upon the state means that any link of multiculturalism to the legitimation imperative would be severed, because multicultural programs would no longer be a cheaper substitute for broad-gauge social expenditure.

NESB groups do, then, differ from all the other groups and categories addressed in this chapter in their lack of experience in an oppositional sphere – however short-lived this experience may have been for the bourgeoisie. Such oppositional spheres can exist elsewhere among immigrants and their descendants – for example, in Britain among those of non-white background, who occasionally take to the streets. More conventional state-related forms of organization – political parties and interest groups – are also conceivable. In Israel, for example, Russian immigrants have their own political party. In the United States, ethnic groups are often well-organized as lobby groups (for example, Florida-based Cubans).

Bottom-up ethnic organizations do exist in Australia, but they do not generally take political form. Associations such as Ethnic Communities' Councils and the Australian Greek Welfare Association have long been encouraged and accepted by the political establishment, including the major parties. However, organizations with an orientation to public policy are generally sponsored and funded by government, with no membership base needed as a source of funds. This is especially true of pan-ethnic umbrella groups.[7] The most prominent such organization is the Federation of Ethnic Communities' Councils of Australia, created as a peak body in 1979. Brown (1997) calls this situation 'ethnic corporatism', under which organizations act as arms of government rather than as independent pressure groups. The effects are not exactly salutary from the point of view of democratization, because leaders of these groups have little incentive to be responsive to the grassroots, and any influence on policy they do exercise is unconstrained by the need for such responsiveness. Their critics call them 'professional ethnics', enmeshed in patronage networks and unrepresentative of their communities (Zappalà, 2001: 151). Attribution of political accommodation and quiescence to the way ethnic groups are organized into government is a long-running theme in the literature on Australian ethnic politics (e.g. Jakubowicz, 1984: 22).

Aside from these state-sponsored associations, the other major venue for organized ethnic politics is the Australian Labor Party. Especially in Melbourne and Sydney, areas with a high proportion of NESB people are dominated by the ALP when it comes to both local politics and representation in state and federal parliaments. This concentration does not translate into NESB members of parliament, because seats in such areas are safe and so tend to be reserved for party high-fliers who are usually from an Anglo-Celtic background. The ethnic presences within the ALP tend to play out in terms of numbers games and faction politics. Its critics point to 'ethnic branch stacking', as people from NESB are recruited by party factions to influence candidate selection. As Zappalà (1998) points out, this is actually a form of clientelism that pervades Mediterranean and some Asian cultures. Patrons are expected to perform favours for their clients, especially by intervening on their behalf with government officials. Clients in turn promise their support to the patron. Clientelism and a civil society conducive to democracy are generally treated as mutually exclusive (see, for example, Putnam's (1993) study of Italy). But as Zappalà argues, clientelism is actually a way of drawing on the solidarity of NESB communities to integrate them into the political system, as well as strengthening the hand of community leaders in relation to other actors.[8] Irrespective of the democratic merits of clientelism, its presence in the ALP shows that NESB communities have contributed to the reshaping of Australian institutions. Thus it falsifies the claim by Davidson (2000: 53) that immigrants' forced acceptance of Australian institutions has meant 'the silencing of the voices of a quarter of the Australian population about such matters'.[9]

Ethnic politics in Australia does not, then, feature much in the way of active political association, still less any public sphere at a distance from government – and this perhaps explains why, clientelism aside, it has had little impact on the structure of Australian institutions. A glance at the kind of ethnic politics on offer in (say) the United States might suggest that this relative quiescence is no bad thing. In comparison with the United States, Australia has three striking features. The first is that US multiculturalism is tied up with claims to being a victim. Given the benefits attached to being designated a victim in American society and politics, ranging from a social cachet to government programs, there is something of a competitive bidding process in this regard (especially notable within American universities in recent years). The second is that in Australia, foreign policy is not held hostage to the interests of a concentrated ethnic minority (such as Cubans in Miami, or pro-Israeli Jews around New York). Third, and relatedly, immigrants in Australia generally leave behind old ethnic conflicts, rather than perpetuate them at a distance (obviously there are exceptions to this rule, notably among Serb and Croat communities, though even here the conflict is muted in comparison to its ferocity in the former Yugoslavia). These three differences mean that multiculturalism is less socially pathological in Australia than in the United States – but it also means that ethnic politics is a much more low-key affair.

Zappalà (2001: 159–60) concludes his analysis of NESB representation in Australian politics with a call for a reinvigoration of NESB associational life, partly in recognition of the fact that relying on state-associated organization is unpromising if no state imperative is at issue. However, I have argued that links can indeed be made to both economic and legitimation imperatives, such that Zappalà's call is likely to go unanswered. Even if these links are tenuous, it requires a huge effort on the part of group leaders to turn their backs on the state once they have been included. Historical examples are almost non-existent. Occasionally a group gets expelled from the state, as in the case of trade unions under the Thatcher government in Britain, or – much more gently – under the Kennett government in Victoria in the 1990s, and the federal Howard government in the late 1990s. But even then, the response has been less the construction of an oppositional public sphere, and more a desperate scramble for ways to re-enter the state (such as the unions in Britain selling their souls to New Labour).

One could perhaps imagine such expulsion were the far right to make greater inroads into Australian government and dismantle multiculturalism (so far, the established ethnic organizations have been remarkably quiet in responding to the far right as represented by the One Nation Party, quieter than the mainstream parties). Controversies pertaining to the detention of asylum-seekers meet with little interest from NESB communities, which are far more engaged by family reunion issues. Important though such issues may be, it is hard to imagine a public sphere constructed around them.

Zappalà (2001: 159) himself thinks that a livelier NESB public sphere could come into being not through expulsion or the traumatization that one could envisage if the far right ever entered government, but through the opposite: positive and benign government action, along the lines of the 'associative democracy' proposed by Cohen and Rogers (1992). The problem with this strategy is that it is hard to imagine a state agency taking the initiative in fostering groups that would take any kind of oppositional stance – in this case or in any other. The Whitlam government in the early 1970s was unique in attempting such initiatives (but look what became of it). More usually, when state agencies foster groups, they want them to be compliant and state-associated – exactly the problem with existing ethnic associations. Cohen and Rogers postulate a kind of state that cannot be sustained in contemporary liberal capitalist societies, so there is no point in relying upon it. (For a discussion of how the Norwegian state's well-meaning interventionist approach to civil society ends up impoverishing the public sphere, see Dryzek et al., 2001.)

For better or worse, then, no oppositional public sphere has ever accompanied ethnic politics in Australia, and I have explained why its emergence is unlikely, irrespective of the extent of future immigration and ethnic mixing. Despite the deficit this absence implies in the contribution of ethnic politics to Australian democracy and democratization, there is no denying that ethnic politics has led to a more democratic, because more inclusive, Australian state. But what we see today is probably as good as it gets.

## The Natural Environment

At first sight it might seem odd to include a nonhuman category in this catalogue of democratic inclusions. After all, if students of politics can agree on anything at all it is surely that politics in general, and democracy in particular, are attributes only of systems constituted by people (though primate ethology has described political behaviour and interaction in some of our close relatives). Yet green political theorists (especially those based in Australia) have begun to think about ways in which nature might be granted the status of a political subject (Dryzek, 1995; Plumwood, 1995; Eckersley, 1999; Goodin, 1996). Such thinking is an extension of ecocentric perception of intrinsic value in nature, irrespective of human interests. Such 'deep green' thinking actually begins in Australia with the work of Routley and Routley (1973) (later Sylvan and Plumwood) on *The Fight for the Forests* – and such ecophilosophy informs the green movement at venues such as the annual Ecopolitics Conferences (beginning in 1986 in Brisbane). The political implications are manifest in the call by Christoff (2000: 211–12) for an 'ecological redefinition of citizenship' in Australia that entails 'the extension of representation and responsibility to other species, future generations, and non-territorial humans and ecosystems'. In common with the United States and Canada, but unlike almost all of Europe, Australia possesses large ecosystems relatively unmodified by human agricultural, sylvicultural, and industrial activity. (It cannot be styled pristine nature because it has long been modified by Australia's indigenous peoples, and of course some of Australia's ecosystems have been heavily modified by agriculture.) This characteristic has major implications for the kind of green politics that occurs.

What might the political inclusion of nonhuman nature entail? At one level, the question can be framed in purely institutional terms: we can evaluate institutions in terms of how well they can receive signals pertaining to the well-being or otherwise of nonhuman nature. So, for example, large bureaucracies or corporations managing resources according to general principles devised without reference to local ecological circumstances are easily condemned in this light. Few institutions have been designed with such receptivity in mind, but that does not prevent an evaluation of them in terms of this capacity. Perhaps more straightforwardly, and more commensurably with the preceding sections of this chapter, the story can be told through reference to the human advocates of nonhuman nature. One measure of the successful inclusion of such advocates would be the emergence of institutions with the capacity to receive signals from nonhuman nature.

Let me begin with the more straightforward history of the advocates. The stereotypical view is that European settlers saw in the Australian environment only something to be subdued in their interests. This view has recently been challenged by Bonyhady (2000) and Hutton and Connors (1999), who can point to particular individuals and associations who from the early nineteenth century on saw much worth preserving in the Australian environment (even though they would not have used the word 'environment'). But until the 1970s such voices were generally few in number and power compared to the dominant developmentalist ethos. Moreover, if they sought protection it was only for the sake of human interests, be it in resource conservation, recreation, or scenery. (One possible rare exception to this rule occurs in 1909 with lobbying by ornithologists to protect native bird species that produced a ban on bird exports.)

Australia's first national environmental organisation was the Australian Conservation Foundation, founded in 1965. But the ACF at first was hardly an ecocentric advocacy group. Initially it was financed by large corporations and government, and put a premium on scientific respectability. In June 1973 Moss Cass, environment minister in the Whitlam Labor government, threatened to cut its government funding unless the ACF became *more* radical in its advocacy (Hutton and Connors, 1999: 135). The year 1973 did see something of a changing of the guard in the ACF, but ecocentric advocacy received a much larger boost with the founding in 1976 of the Tasmanian Wilderness Society, which later adopted a national focus and was re-named The Wilderness Society. Its first director, Kevin Kiernan, proclaimed an ecocentric emphasis: 'We have to try to sell not the wilderness experience – that is, wilderness as a recreational resource – but the right of wilderness to exist ... an emphasis on the philosophical and the eternal – that is, wilderness for its own' (quoted in Ibid: 161).

The 1970s and 1980s saw a number of high-profile wilderness defence campaigns that defined the environmental issue in Australian politics. These included actions against the drowning of Lake Pedder in Tasmania (1970–72), sand mining on Fraser Island (1971–76), clearfelling of native forests (early 1970s onwards), the Gordon-below-Franklin dam (1982–83), development in the Queensland wet tropics (1983 onwards), uranium mining in Kakadu and elsewhere (mid-1970s onwards). The results ranged from spectacular preservation success (the Franklin dam) to compromise (the restriction of uranium mining to three sites) to persistent unresolved struggle (woodchipping of native forests).

Between 1983 and 1990 green groups became more professional and heavily involved in electoral politics; indeed, instrumental in securing federal election victories for the Labor Party. Once again, it appears that an oppositional public sphere maintains only a fleeting existence before giving way to inclusion in the state. Hutton and Connors (1999: 167) argue that the major groups (ACF, World Wide Fund for Nature – WWF, Greenpeace, TWS) nevertheless retained their critical edge, though it is hard to know by what standards. Still, this same era saw a three-way division. Some believed such engagement with the political mainstream was most productive. Others sought to establish a separate green party (eventually established at the national level – still excluding Western Australia – in 1992 after green candidates had already been successful at the state level in Tasmania and won federal Senate seats in Western Australia). Then there were those on the fringe, who disdained electoral politics of any sort. If Australian environmental problems constitute a tractable set solvable in the terms established by existing institutions of government (as Papadakis, 1996, believes) then the first of these groups has the better argument. But a persistent strand of environmentalism doubts that such piecemeal reformism is sufficient.

Inclusion of the movement in the state reached a high point with the Ecologically Sustainable Development process sponsored by the federal Labor government in 1990–92 (see Christoff, 1995). Consistent with the consensual style of Prime Minister Bob Hawke, the process involved a series of working groups defined by economic sector (agriculture, energy, fisheries, forestry, manufacturing, mining, tourism, transport), each with representatives from industry, environmental organizations, unions, and Commonwealth and state governments. The environmentalist banner was carried by the ACF and WWF. TWS chose not to participate, and Greenpeace withdrew in mid-process, though the ACF continued to consult with groups outside the process. The exercise eventually came to nothing as the working group reports were mangled and diluted by the Commonwealth–state committees that subsequently reworked and agglomerated them into a national ESD Strategy that was rejected by both ACF and industry working group members. A new prime minister, Keating, proved hostile to environmentalism. Though the ESD story is a complex one, it shows that environmental concerns could not prevail once they encroached upon the core activities of the state, especially those associated with the economic imperative. This was especially evident in a period when deregulatory economic rationalism was accepted as necessary to meet the economic imperative (Christoff, 1995: 73). Indeed, public officials enforcing this imperative showed themselves far less able to accommodate environmental concerns than were the industry representatives on the ESD working groups.

Now, there are ways for environmental concerns to be assimilated to economic imperatives, notably in the form of 'ecological modernization' that has made inroads in European countries such as the Netherlands and Germany. The basic idea of ecological modernization is that environmental and economic values can be mutually reinforcing (see Hajer, 1995; Christoff, 1996). In this light, pollution indicates inefficient resource use; a clean environment provides high-quality inputs for production and a healthy, happy workforce; there is money to be made from green products and processes. There are two reasons why as yet ecological modernization provides no solution to the inclusion of the interests of nonhuman nature as a political subject in Australia. First, since the mid-1990s Australia has been busy establishing its 'old economy' credentials, most prominently by seeking special treatment as a heavy fossil fuel user at the Kyoto negotiations on climate change in 1997, though this stance is a contingent feature of government policy, not any kind of necessity. Second, ecological modernization is in the first instance mostly about retooling the economy; the interests of nonhuman nature can enter only via aesthetics or as a byproduct of less intensive exploitation of resources such as forests and mines. While ecological modernization remains an anthropocentric doctrine, these possibilities suggest that even in Australia there does not have to be a zero-sum clash between economic imperatives and the interests of nonhuman nature. The ESD process was the closest Australia has come to embracing ecological modernization; the outcome illustrates the distance yet to be travelled.

Engagement with the state of the kind that reached a high point in ESD certainly absorbed a great deal of environmentalist energy, though it did not completely empty the green public sphere. This public sphere in the 1990s was alive if not especially healthy, as the high-energy campaigns of the 1970s and 1980s had no real counterpart. Actions against uranium mining at Jabiluka in Kakadu National Park, and woodchipping of native forests continued, although these were direct descendants of earlier unresolved issues. Green radicals of various stripes continued to organize (in some cases disorganize), associate, and debate.

Turning now to the other place to look for nature's inclusion – the development of institutions with the capacity to receive and act upon signals from the nonhuman world – there were in fact some interesting innovations in the 1990s, occasioned by the severity of agricultural land degradation, especially as a result of rising salinity levels caused by clearance of vegetation. On the face of it, bioregional authorities defined by ecological rather than arbitrary political boundaries have a greater potential to embody ecocentric values than (say) state or city governments, though a great deal depends on the thinking of those who operate such authorities. Australia's best-known bioregional authority is the Murray–Darling River Basin Commission, established in 1985. At a smaller scale, the Landcare initiative, jointly proposed by the National Farmers' Federation and ACF in 1983, led to the establishment of numerous local Landcare groups receiving government funding to combat salinity problems. Such groups proved to be composed only of farmers rather than representatives of the broader community, let alone environmentalists. As such, their orientation was mostly to the productive value of agricultural land, rather than any ecocentric concerns, and only anthropogenic agro-ecosystems were really at issue. Still, Landcare groups, and associated Total Catchment Management Programs, were in many ways better placed to respond to signals about local ecological degradation than were state bureaucracies. Given the positive-sum approach to the reconciliation of economic and environmental concerns (symbolized by the co-operation of the National Farmers' Federation and the ACF), such initiatives are also consistent with the idea of ecological modernization. Indeed, it is exactly this positive-sum character that establishes the connection to economic imperatives that enables such institutional innovations to occur.

As with the women's movement of the same era, in the late twentieth century Australian environmentalists had some interests that could be assimilated to state imperatives (especially economic imperatives). Some could find a home in the periphery of the state, explaining the degree to which government could take on the role of wilderness protector. Some clashed with core imperatives. As such, it is entirely appropriate that some segments of the movement ought to seek inclusion in the state, and that others – the more ecocentric, emphasizing the intrinsic value of non-human nature – should resist such inclusion. This theoretical division of effort does not however correspond to what we observe in the real world, where some ecocentrists have perhaps been incorporated too easily.

## Conclusion

To greater or lesser degree, all the groups surveyed in this essay have managed to attach their defining interest to core state imperatives. This attachment has been complete for the bourgeoisie, working-class, and NESB people. It is in important ways incomplete for women, Indigenous peoples and environmentalists, all three of which feature a conflict between some aspect of their defining interest and at least one state imperative. Thus for the latter three groups, maintenance of an active oppositional public sphere remains crucial.

Australian history has witnessed three great waves of inclusion in the state. The first was in the middle of the nineteenth century, with the arrival of self-government for the colonies and incorporation of the bourgeoisie. The second was at the turn of the nineteenth and twentieth centuries, with the entry of the working class into the state and the achievement of female suffrage. The third began in the late 1960s and continued into the 1980s, featuring (sometimes partial, for reasons I have explained) inclusion of Indigenous peoples, women, people of NESB background, and environmentalists. The second acted a bit like a vacuum cleaner on the public sphere, emptying it for over half a century. The third has not been quite so thoroughgoing in this respect.

The latter part of the third wave of inclusions coincides with the arrival of economic rationalism. Pusey (1991) blames economic rationalism for the decline of the public sphere in Australian political life, but I do not think he is quite right in the way he makes this claim. To begin with, the 'lifeworld' in which he is interested is very much that of senior public servants. He may well be right that economic rationalism with its emphasis on efficiency and competition has destroyed the ethic of public service among senior executives in the public sector, who now have more of an eye on personal advancement and the revolving door into private business. Pusey (1991: 185) calls this the 'privatization of motivation'.

I would argue that if economic rationalism undermines the public sphere, it is through a 'privatization of motivation' in social and political life more generally. That is, individuals motivated exclusively by material self-interest do not make good citizens. Inclusion of group leadership in the state along with this widespread 'privatization of motivation' is a deadly combination when it comes to the vitality of the public sphere.

If Australia has a persistent democratic deficit, it is to be found in its public sphere, not its state. This is not to say that Australia is worse than any other country in this respect. My own systematic empirical inquiries have been confined to the United States, the United Kingdom, Germany, Norway and New Zealand (Dryzek et al., 2001). On a rough accounting, at the end of the twentieth century Australia has a less vital public sphere than Germany, a stronger one than Norway and New Zealand, about the same as the United States and United Kingdom. Australia's deficit is a result of the relative ease with which group leadership has been included. Most of the inclusions I have analysed have been genuine rather than co-optive – that is, the group in question could attach at least some aspect of its defining interest to a core state imperative. This begs the question of why exactly inclusion in the state has generally been so early, easy, quick, and thorough in Australia relative to elsewhere. While some factors are unique to particular inclusions, the overall answer may have much to do with the fact that in Australia society (excluding indigenous society) has been from the very beginning a creation of the state. Thus even when unanticipated challenges arise from the public sphere, there is little resistance to the idea that legitimate social formations merit inclusion (though Australia has never gone to the Scandinavian extreme of actively organizing incipient movements into the state). While I have not analysed the question explicitly, the consequence of comparatively early and easy inclusion in the state may be that political reform has generally taken comparatively moderate form.

If I am right about the sources of Australia's democratic deficit, then there are ways in which democracy and democratization in Australia would benefit from a *more* exclusive state – a conclusion that surely flies in the face of all the well-meaning people who have ever contemplated this question.[10] One qualification is important here: we need to look at the democratic vitality of the polity as a whole. Most analysts make the mistake of looking only at the state. It is equally important not to make the mistake of looking only at the public sphere. And more important still is not to mistake a snapshot for an enduring reality. Coming to grips with the historical dynamics of democratization, the dialectical interplay of state and public sphere, is crucial.

In the late 1990s the Australian state did become more exclusive, as environmentalists and women's groups found their funding cut and access to government reduced, and labour unions found themselves shut out of the corridors of power. However, the results have not been especially salutary. The groups finding themselves out in the cold have not reacted by helping to constitute lively oppositional public spheres. Instead, they have devoted their energies to figuring out ways to re-enter the state. So perhaps there is little hope for these movements in the terms I have established. However, there may be greater hope for future movements, whose membership, content and character are not easy to predict.

So my final word of advice when it comes to Reshaping Australian Institutions is this: if you are interested in making Australia a more democratic country, design your institutions bearing in mind that benign exclusion can have positive effects, and that inclusion can sometimes have negative effects.[11]

But there is a catch. In the section on non-English-speaking immigrants I pointed out that a state agency motivated primarily by a desire to foster the political organization of oppositional groups is not plausible in a liberal capitalist political economy. No more plausible is a state agency charged with arranging exclusions so as to foster a lively public sphere. The state might indeed pursue exclusion for other reasons (for example, economic rationalism's requirement that interest groups need to be broken). Might the solution therefore be democratic institutional design by subterfuge? The difficulty with this solution is that subterfuge is itself intrinsically undemocratic. With that observation, my supply of happy endings has run out.

### Notes

For comments and criticisms, I thank Geoffrey Brennan, Francis Castles, Margaret Clark, Robyn Eckersley, and Marian Sawer.

1 'Near' because of the continued disenfranchisement of Indigenous adults.
2 Co-option occurs when a decision-making structure absorbs individuals or groups while denying them real influence (Saward, 1992).
3 Conservative paternalism also had a hand in welfare state development, beginning in Bismarck's Germany. But this paternalism alone did not produce *comprehensive* welfare states.
4 Made harder still by recent government de-funding of organizations such as National Shelter and the Australian Federation of Pensioners and Superannuants.
5 There may be some misperception on the part of these interests, given that it might prove easier for them to bargain with a group possessing clear property rights.
6 The other three are civic duty, cultural respect and social equity.
7 Governmental cultivation of peak bodies is an established co-optive practice, but its success is greater in ethnic politics than in any other realm in Australia.

8  Without having studied the matter myself, my conjecture is that in Australia ethnic clientelism advances the franchise dimension of democratization at the expense of the authenticity dimension.
9  Davidson's prescription is that Australia should try to emulate the multicultural democratic politics of the European Union. This prescription is unconvincing in light of the widespread agonizing in Europe about the European Union's 'democratic deficit'.
10  The best example of a 'passively exclusive' state conducive to a lively oppositional public sphere is Germany from the late 1940s to the 1990s; see Dryzek, Hunold and Schlosberg (2001).
11  Elsewhere I distinguish between passive (benign) and active (malign) exclusion. The former leaves civil society alone. The latter attacks and undermines the conditions for association in civil society. See Dryzek (1996a; 1996b).

**References**

Blainey, G. *A Land Half Won* (rev. edn, Sydney: Sun, 1995).
Bonyhady, T. *Colonial Earth* (Melbourne: Melbourne University Press, 2000).
Brown, D. 'The Politics of Reconstructing National Identity: A Corporatist Approach', *Australian Journal of Political Science*, vol. 32 (1997) pp. 255–70.
Bulbeck, C. 'Issues for Australian Feminism: The End of the "Universal Woman"?', in Paul Boreham, Geoffrey Stokes and Richard Hall (eds), *The Politics of Australian Society: Political Issues for the New Century* (Frenchs Forest, NSW: Longman, 2000) pp. 80–91.
Burgmann, M., and Burgmann, V. *Green Bans, Red Union: Environmental Activism in the New South Wales Builders Labourers' Federation* (Sydney: Allen & Unwin, 1998).
Burgmann, V. *Power and Protest: Movements for Change in Australian Society* (Sydney: Allen & Unwin, 1993).
Castles, F. G. *The Working Class and Welfare* (Sydney: Allen & Unwin, 1985).
——. *Australian Public Policy and Economic Vulnerability* (Sydney: Allen & Unwin, 1988).
——. 'A Farewell to the Australian Welfare State', *Eureka Street*, vol. 11(1) (2000) pp. 29–31.
Castles, S., Cope, B., Kalantzis, M., and Morrissey, M. *Mistaken Identity: Multiculturalism and the Demise of Nationalism in Australia* (Sydney: Pluto Press, 1988).
Christoff, P. 'Whatever Happened to Ecologically Sustainable Development?', *Capuchino Papers* (Australian Conservation Foundation), vol. 1 (1995) pp. 69–74.
——. 'Ecological Modernisation, Ecological Modernities', *Environmental Politics*, vol. 5 (1996) pp. 476–500.
——. 'Ecological Citizenship', in Wayne Hudson and John Kane (eds), *Rethinking Australian Citizenship* (Cambridge: Cambridge University Press, 2000) pp. 200–13.
Clark, M. *A Short History of Australia* (rev. edn, London: Heinemann, 1969).
Cohen, J., and Rogers, J. 'Secondary Associations and Democratic Governance', *Politics and Society*, vol. 20 (1992) pp. 393–472.

Davidson, A. 'Democracy and Citizenship', in Wayne Hudson and John Kane (eds), *Rethinking Australian Citizenship* (Cambridge: Cambridge University Press, 2000) pp. 45–55.

Department of Family and Community Services. *Participation Support for a More Equitable Society* (Canberra: Ausinfo, 2000).

Dryzek, J. S. 'Political and Ecological Communication', *Environmental Politics*, vol. 4 (1995) pp. 13–30.

——. *Democracy in Capitalist Times: Ideals, Limits, and Struggles* (New York: Oxford University Press, 1996a).

——. 'Political Inclusion and the Dynamics of Democratization', *American Political Science Review*, vol. 90 (1996b) pp. 475–87.

——. *Deliberative Democracy and Beyond: Liberals, Critics, Contestations* (Oxford: Oxford University Press, 2000).

Dryzek, J. S., Hunold, C., and Schlosberg, D., with D. Downes and H.-K. Hernes. 'States and Social Movements: Environmentalism in Four Countries', paper presented at the Annual Meeting of the American Political Science Association, San Francisco (2001).

Eckersley, R. 'The Discourse Ethic and the Problem of Representing Nature', *Environmental Politics*, vol. 8 (1999) pp. 24–49.

Fraad, H., Resnick, S., and Wolff, R. *Bringing It All Back Home: Class, Gender and Power in the Modern Household* (London: Pluto, 1994).

Galbally, F., et al. *Review of Post-Arrival Programs and Services to Migrants* (Canberra: Australian Government Publishing Service, 1978).

Goodin, R. E. 'Enfranchising the Earth, and its Alternatives', *Political Studies*, vol. 44 (1996) pp. 835–49.

Grimshaw, P. 'Only the Chains Have Changed', in Verity Burgmann and Jenny Lee (eds), *Staining the Wattle: A People's History of Australia* (Ringwood, Vic.: Penguin, 1988) pp. 66–86.

Habermas, J. *Legitimation Crisis* (Boston: Beacon Press, 1975).

——. *Structural Transformation of the Public Sphere: An Inquiry into a Category of Bourgeois Society* (Cambridge, Mass.: MIT Press, 1989).

Hajer, M. A. *The Politics of Environmental Discourse: Ecological Modernization and the Policy Process* (Oxford: Oxford University Press, 1995).

Hancock, W. K. *Australia* (London: Ernest Benn, 1930).

Hutton, D., and Connors, L. *A History of the Australian Environmental Movement* (Cambridge: Cambridge University Press, 1999).

Jakubowicz, A. 'State and Ethnicity: Multiculturalism as Ideology', in James Jupp (ed.), *Ethnic Politics in Australia* (Sydney: Allen & Unwin, 1984) pp. 14–28.

Jayasuriya, L. 'Rethinking Australian Multiculturalism: Towards a New Paradigm', *Australian Quarterly*, vol. 62 (1990) pp. 50–63.

Jupp, J. 'Managing Ethnic Diversity: How Does Australia Compare?', in Francis G. Castles (ed.), *Australia Compared: People, Policies and Politics* (Sydney: Allen & Unwin, 1991) pp. 38–54.

Kalantzis, M. 'Multicultural Citizenship', in Wayne Hudson and John Kane (eds), *Rethinking Australian Citizenship* (Cambridge: Cambridge University Press, 2000) pp. 99–110.

Kaplan, G. *The Meagre Harvest: The Australian Women's Movement, 1950s–1990s* (Sydney: Allen & Unwin, 1996).

Lake, M. *Getting Equal: The History of Australian Feminism* (Sydney: Allen & Unwin, 1999).

Lindblom, C. *Politics and Markets: The World's Political-Economic Systems* (New York: Basic Books, 1977).
Lindblom, C. E. 'The Market as Prison', *Journal of Politics*, vol. 44 (1982) pp. 324–36.
Macintyre, S. *Winners and Losers: The Pursuit of Social Justice in Australian History* (Sydney: Allen & Unwin, 1985).
——. *A Concise History of Australia* (Cambridge: Cambridge University Press, 1999).
National Multicultural Advisory Council. *Australian Multiculturalism for a New Century: Towards Inclusiveness* (Canberra: Ausinfo, 1999).
O'Connor, J. *The Fiscal Crisis of the State* (New York: St. Martin's Press, 1973).
Office of Multicultural Affairs, Department of Prime Minister and Cabinet. *National Agenda for a Multicultural Australia* (Canberra: Australian Government Publishing Service, 1989).
Papadakis, E. *Environmental Politics and Institutional Change* (Cambridge: Cambridge University Press, 1996).
Plumwood, V. 'Has Democracy Failed Ecology?', *Environmental Politics*, vol. 4 (1995) pp. 134–68.
Pusey, M. *Economic Rationalism in Canberra: A Nation-Building State Changes its Mind* (Cambridge: Cambridge University Press, 1991).
Putnam, R. D. *Making Democracy Work: Civic Traditions in Modern Italy* (Princeton: Princeton University Press, 1993).
Reeves, W. P. *State Experiments in Australia and New Zealand* (London: Grant Ritchards, 1902).
Routley, R., and Routley, V. *The Fight for the Forests: The Takeover of Australian Forests for Pines, Wood Chips, and Intensive Forestry* (Canberra: Research School of Social Sciences, Australian National University, 1973).
Rowse, T. 'Indigenous Citizenship', in Wayne Hudson and John Kane (eds), *Rethinking Australian Citizenship* (Cambridge: Cambridge University Press, 2000) pp. 86–98.
——. 'Democratic Systems Are an Alien Thing to Aboriginal Culture', in Marian Sawer and Gianni Zappalà (eds), *Speaking for the People: Representation in Australian Politics* (Melbourne: Melbourne University Press, 2001) pp. 103–33.
Saward, M. *Co-optive Politics and State Legitimacy* (Aldershot: Dartmouth, 1992).
Sawer, M. 'A Matter of Simple Justice? Women and Representation', in Marian Sawer and Gianni Zappalà (eds), *Speaking for the People: Representation in Australian Politics* (Melbourne: Melbourne University Press, 2001) pp. 162–88.
Skocpol, T. *States and Social Revolutions* (Cambridge: Cambridge University Press, 1979).
Wainwright, H. *Arguments for a New Left: Answering the Free-Market Right* (Oxford: Basil Blackwell, 1994).
Zappalà, G. 'Clientelism, Political Culture and Ethnic Politics in Australia', *Australian Journal of Political Science*, vol. 33 (1998) pp. 381–98.
——. 'The Political Representation of Ethnic Minorities: Moving beyond the mirror', in Marian Sawer and Gianni Zappalà (eds), *Speaking for the People: Representation in Australian Politics* (Melbourne: Melbourne University Press, 2001) pp. 134–61.

# 6  Waltzing Matilda: Gender and Australian Political Institutions

*Marian Sawer*

This chapter reflects on the relationship between feminism and social liberalism in Australian political history. It argues that social liberalism, as an ideology shared by Labor and Liberal leaders in Australia's nation-building period, played a crucial role in the shaping of Australian political institutions. Social liberalism made the provision of equal opportunity – the fair go – central to political obligation and the first responsibility of the ethical state. While social liberalism began by focusing on the inequalities of class, its themes of equal opportunity and the ethical state created discursive possibilities for feminism. If we are to understand the extraordinary flowering of state feminism in Australia in the 1970s and 1980s, the femocrat phenomenon regarded with astonishment internationally, we need to understand the discursive and institutional legacy that made it possible.

The founding fathers, while advocating and institutionalizing equal opportunity in institutions such as conciliation and arbitration, were insensitive to broader social and economic preconditions of equal opportunity for women. For the most part they assumed a gendered division of labour whereby women would perform unremunerated work in the home and be supported out of their husband's wages. Such assumptions meant a lack of attention to the restrictions imposed by financial dependence and by the narrow range of occupations deemed suitable for women. Laborist ideals of social equality, in particular, tended to stop short at the doorway to the family home behind which wives and mothers were to be protected rather than encouraged in active citizenship.

This chapter begins by setting out the relationship between social liberalism and the creation of Australia's national institutions, with particular attention to the institutions of conciliation and arbitration, old-age pensions and income tax. The second part considers another strand of institution-building – that engaged in by feminists over the century. This separate space, as epitomized by women's non-party organizations, enabled feminists to articulate their own versions of social liberalism and to bring pressure for more inclusive forms of equal opportunity. In the 1970s and 1980s feminists were responsible for renewed institutional experimentation both inside and outside the state, including community-based feminist collectives on the one hand and the creation of space for feminist discourse within political parties, parliament and bureaucracy on the other. The engagement and disengagement of feminism and social liberalism is not, however, the only story to be told about gender and Australian political institutions. The last part of the chapter introduces the counterpoint of the relationship between feminism and federalism. It notes that if there is a tension between federalism and substantive notions of the public good, then we might expect federalism, and the recurrent proposals for 'new federalism' to have significant gender implications which have so far been largely unexplored.

## Social Liberalism in Australia

Progressive liberal ideas, particularly those of John Stuart Mill and the philosophic radicals, found fertile ground in nineteenth-century Australasia. Along with Chartism, they fed into the political and administrative experimentation of the period. Manhood suffrage, the secret ballot, women's suffrage and proportional representation were all part of this experimentation. Traditional authority structures were less well entrenched in the New World and there was weaker resistance to such ideas than in their country of origin. By the time of the nation-building nineties, another strong influence had arrived in Australia, the new liberalism of T. H. Green, referred to henceforth as 'social liberalism', and its conception of the 'ethical state'.

Under the influence of T. H. Green, British liberalism in the 1880s and 1890s was rejecting many of the assumptions of classical liberalism, including the equation of liberty with freedom of contract and freedom from state interference. Green's concept of 'positive liberty' was accompanied by a profound moral critique of the existing social and economic constrictions on human development and choice. The state had the capacity and the duty to remove such barriers to human potential and this had priority over rights of property or sanctity of contract. According to Green, it was the business of government not only to uphold contracts but also to prevent contracts being made when, because of the inequality of the parties, they were an instrument of oppression.

In asserting the moral necessity of 'state interference' to prevent the making of contracts harmful to the development of human capacity, Green was moving liberalism into a new era where state interference could be seen as increasing rather than limiting the liberty of the individual. The social liberals regarded state interference as justifiable, and indeed desirable, as long as it was increasing the capacity of citizens to make what Green called 'the most and best of themselves'. Full development of potential could only occur through active citizenship, which would also ensure that the state remained the instrument of the common good. These precepts applied both to men and women, and the social liberals were at the forefront of the movement to increase women's educational opportunities as well as to ensure their civil and political rights. They also believed in the need for state interference in the family to secure the rights of women, particularly around the issue of domestic violence – and it is notable that, for example, under the NSW Electoral Act of 1893 an elector could be disqualified by a conviction for aggravated assault on his wife.

After Green's early death in 1882, his friends and colleagues took up the cause of propagating his ideas and putting them into practice. They were responsible for the settlement movement, which trained a generation of social reformers, including those who formed the heart of the Asquith government. This generation of liberals was convinced of the possibility of the ethical state where political obligation was grounded in the provision of equal opportunity rather than in the fictions of contract and consent. I have described elsewhere (Sawer, 2000b) the way in which these ideas were transplanted to Australia at a time of nation-building and were built into Australia's distinctive political institutions. In the 1880s and 1890s those who had absorbed Green's ideas at Oxford or Glasgow became opinion-leaders and social reformers in the colonies and staffed the new colonial universities. They were critical not only of the natural rights doctrines of early liberalism but also of Benthamite utilitarianism with its atomistic views of society and its materialism. Their vision of equal opportunity was of a substantive good, the unlocking of potential for personal and social development whereby the one contributed to the other and liberty increased in tandem.

Like their counterparts in Britain, Australian social liberals initiated anti-sweating leagues, the settlement movement, the Workers' Educational Association, kindergartens and creches. Liberal politicians in the colonies were well in advance of their British counterparts in legislating for free, compulsory and secular primary education and also in regard to political rights for women. The latter was related in complex ways to the changing nature of the state as it took on new functions of social regulation, redistribution and the public organization of caring – the secular shift from the nightwatchman state of classical liberalism (which had already become the developmental state in Australia) to the welfare state of social liberalism (Sawer, 2000a).

Lecture halls and journals gave currency to social liberal discourse. An author in the first issue of *The Australian Economist*, the journal of the Australian Economic Association, proclaimed confidently that 'the voice of Mr. Herbert Spencer, crying in the wilderness, only serves to remind us that, as far as state action is concerned, laissez-faire has had its day' (Scott, 1885: 5). The journal later reprinted the famous public lecture given by Francis Anderson when he was appointed professor of philosophy at the University of Sydney in 1890. In his lecture Anderson propounded Green's ideas on citizenship and equal opportunity and argued that 'the free development of citizens' must take precedence over freedom of contract or laws of competition (1891: 140–1).[1] Anderson took these ideas into his many spheres of activity, not only university teaching, but also the Workers' Educational Association, the Kindergarten Union, the teachers' college, the Council of Social Service and the Australasian Association for the Advancement of Science.

In particular, social liberalism inspired two important initiatives – the institutionalizing of third-party intervention in wage-setting and the introduction of old-age pensions. It also influenced attitudes to public finance and helped shape the nature of the income tax system. Here I analyse the ways in which feminism and social liberalism inflected these important institutional developments.

*Conciliation and Arbitration*

Green's critique of contract and justification of state interference in contract ([1881] 1984: 194–212), provided the discourse central to the creation of systems of conciliation and arbitration in the Australasian colonies. As Green's followers explained, it was the duty of the ethical state to provide equal opportunity to its citizens for self-development. Citizens must have the means, education and access to culture to participate fully in community life. This not only meant free, secular education and museums, galleries and libraries. It also meant 'state interference' in labour market contracts to ensure fairness in the context of unequal bargaining power. State interference was the hedge against oppressive contracts. As L. T. Hobhouse put it, the state owed each citizen the means of maintaining a civilized standard of life, a debt 'not adequately discharged by leaving him to secure such wages as he can in the higgling of the market'.

As translated by Henry Bournes Higgins in the Conciliation and Arbitration Court (*CAR*, 1909: 32), this social liberal precept came out as the need for the living wage to be a 'a thing sacrosanct, beyond the reach of bargaining'. Such a wage must be sufficient to meet 'the normal needs of the average employee regarded as a human being living in a civilised community' – including the need to buy books and newspapers so as to engage in active citizenship. Only third-party intervention to determine and enforce such wages could make Australia a land of equal opportunities for the coming generations (Callaghan, 1983: 62). Bernhard Wise, the author of the NSW arbitration system and a former student of T. H. Green's, justified his own pioneering legislation by reference to the unacceptable wages, conditions and hours obtaining under 'so-called freedom of contract' and the need to intervene to ensure justice and equality. For the young H. V. Evatt, future Labor leader, the Australian conciliation and arbitration system was a significant example of 'the spirit of Liberalism taking its time to reveal itself, and teaching its adherents in the rest of the world its new possibilities in practice' (1918: 77).[2]

While the social liberal project encompassed equal opportunity for white women, at least at the formal level, there was a blind spot with regard to the wage system. The 'family wage' enshrined by Higgins in the Harvester judgement included the entitlement to provide for dependants in the male basic wage but not within female wages, which were set for most purposes at 54 per cent of the male rate. The assumption was that family welfare was maximized if a male breadwinner could afford to keep his wife at home. This reasoning was never accepted by feminists, who remained unconvinced that women could enjoy equal citizenship while remaining economically dependent on male breadwinners.

More recently, Carole Pateman (1998: 138) has described the Harvester judgement as an example of the fraternal contract of liberalism, made by brothers at the expense of women. I suggest, by contrast, that Harvester did not epitomize the idea of contract lying at the heart of classical liberalism, but rather the later social liberal critique of contract. Harvester interposed a substantive vision of fairness into traditional freedoms of contract – even though it was not the vision of fairness that we now entertain. It strongly reinforced the preceding labour legislation for which social liberalism had been responsible – some eighty Acts relating to working conditions and wages in New South Wales and New Zealand alone (Hampden, 1913: 253).

The fact that Harvester institutionalized interference in contract in the name of fairness made possible quite rapid progress towards equal pay, once that principle was accepted in the latter years of the twentieth century as part of the 'fair go'. In other words, although women remained second-class citizens in the industrial sphere for most of the twentieth century, the existence of a system of enforceable awards based on principles of wage justice made possible a rapid jump in female wages in the 1970s. In the five years from the equal pay for work of equal value decision, the wages of women full-time workers rose from 70 to 82 per cent of male wages (Gregory et al., 1986: 2, fig. 2). Such equity-based improvement in wage outcomes was impossible in countries with decentralized wage-fixing systems, where contract and market principles took priority in wage-fixing. In North America, progress towards pay equity relied on the painfully slow process of litigation, rather than the adoption of equal pay principles by a wage-fixing tribunal.

## Old-Age Pensions

State interference in contract was not the only social liberal idea institutionalized in the new Australian state at the turn of the century. Another important innovation was old-age pensions – for which social liberalism contributed both the philosophical arguments and the social research. At the normative level, advocates drew on the social liberal conception of citizenship as service to the community and the reciprocal obligations owed by the state to its citizens. At the empirical level, advocates drew upon Booth's *Life and Labour of the People of London* for evidence of the causes of poverty and the inadequacy of charitable solutions. Keith Hancock (1933: 85) has described the adoption of old-age pensions as a good example of the interplay of influences between Australasia and England: 'for the democracies of the Pacific, with very little fuss and trouble, carried into effect the reform for which Booth had long been struggling, and Booth at once made use of their practical example in a redoubled effort to secure the adoption of his idea at home'.

The rationale for old-age pensions given in the debates on the subject both before and after Federation (for example, the NSW Select Committee Report of 1896 and the Royal Commission on Old-Age Pensions of 1905–06) was that the past services performed by citizens, whether in war or peace, entitled them to help from the state during their declining years. There was great emphasis on all sides that old-age pensions were not a matter of charity but of right, and that they would be a statutory rather than a discretionary payment. The fact that in practice extreme economy characterized both levels of payment and criteria of eligibility, particularly in Victoria, does not negate the generosity of the original conception.

Liberal governments were responsible for the first old-age pension legislation in Victoria, New South Wales, Queensland and then the Commonwealth. During the debates of the constitutional convention South Australian Liberal, J. H. Howe, used the social liberal argument that citizens in their declining years had a right to share in the social wealth they had helped create. During the 1898 debate, such arguments were reinforced by reference to the practical benefits of a national (rather than State-based) pension system in a country characterized by a highly mobile population.

There was also an electoral argument that was persuasive for some. The sole labour representative at the convention, William Trenwith, described himself as converted to the inclusion of pensions among the powers of the new federal government by the realization that it would increase the vote for Federation. The Australian process of Federation was remarkable for its period in that delegates to the constitutional convention were popularly elected and, in addition to this, the draft constitution was voted on in referendums. It has been suggested that

Australia was the first nation created through the ballot box. The electorate was generally characterized by manhood suffrage, but in two of the colonies women also voted and may have been particularly interested in the idea of the new Commonwealth as a welfare state.

Right from the beginning women were the majority of old-age pensioners. And unlike the situation with paid work, or with any earnings-related pension scheme, women received the same amount as men. If they survived to old age, they received equal treatment for the first time, rather than, for example, the 'two-thirds' formula often used by arbitration courts. When the old-age pension was first paid in New South Wales in 1901 women were the majority of the applicants, and during the rush when the bank doors were opened the men had to be reminded to be 'gallant', according to the *Daily Telegraph* (cited in Reeves, [1902] 1969: 290–1). Women also formed the majority of those granted the Commonwealth old-age pension in 1909. They were further favoured when the age of eligibility for the pension was reduced to sixty for women in 1910.[3] Men still had to wait until sixty-five except in special circumstances. Nor was there a reduction in the rate where a husband and wife were living together, unlike the situation after 1963 when the (lesser) 'married rate' was introduced. Originally both husbands and wives were treated as citizens in their own right, with independent entitlements and no reduction for marital status.[4]

Interestingly, women's citizenship entitlement to the pension was also unaffected by marriage to an alien or an Asiatic or 'aboriginal native', even though the husband was ineligible.[5] The clauses excluding Asiatics from the pension, whether naturalised or not, were common to colonial pension acts in Australia and New Zealand.

Old-age pensions are a good example of the discursive opportunities as well as limitations of social liberal citizenship discourse. The degree to which women became direct beneficiaries of the social liberal welfare state has tended to be obscured both by the original terms of debate within all-male parliaments and by the subsequent image of Australia as the 'wage-earners' welfare state'. The latter image has proved persuasive since being introduced by Frank Castles in the 1980s and implied that women were only beneficiaries at one remove of the Australian version of the welfare state. However, they were primary beneficiaries of social liberal initiatives in education, maternity allowances and old-age pensions.

The social liberal concept of citizenship was in principle gender-inclusive, with citizenship revolving around community service rather than military service or property-owning. Indeed, suffragists believed that the role played by women as good citizens was a major argument for the vote. The NSW Womanhood Suffrage League pointed out in a petition to the Federal Convention of 1897 that women should have the vote because, *inter alia*, they did more than half of the educational, charitable and philanthropic work of society. Nonetheless, the type of service to the community specified in the parliamentary debates on the old-age pension made it clear it was a male audience being addressed. Citizens had earned their pension through their labours in opening up the country, through the taxes they had paid and the sacrifices they had made to maintain dependants. The nation had benefited from the labour of civilians in the same way it benefited from the service of soldiers or sailors – a popular precedent – and so incurred the same obligations towards them. The preamble to the NSW Act was quoted approvingly in the federal parliament: 'It is equitable that deserving persons who during the prime of life have helped to bear the public burdens of the Colony by payment of taxes and to open up its resources by their labour and skill should receive a pension in their old age' (*Parliamentary Debates* [H of R], 1908: 12010).

Even when women were mentioned, they were rarely positioned as citizens who had earned the pension through their contribution to the state. There were sporadic exceptions. John Cash Neild, who as Member for Paddington in the NSW parliament was responsible for putting old-age pensions on the parliamentary agenda, made gender issues central to his (successful) argument for a non-contributory pension. Shortly after the establishment of a parliamentary select committee on old-age pensions, Neild was given a commission to report on old-age pensions in Europe. Both in his report to the NSW government in 1898 and in his evidence to the Commonwealth Royal Commission on the same subject after he had become a Senator, Neild ruled out contributory pensions on the grounds they were a mockery for married women. He believed a contributory scheme was 'impossible for nine out of ten married women of the wage-earning classes, and being therefore impossible of universal application, cannot be accepted as the basis of any truly national scheme, such as the civilised world asks for today'. He also objected to witnesses who linked poverty to intemperance, pointing out that the majority of paupers in Britain were women, who were 'seldom intemperate'. Rather, they had spent their lives 'in attending to the wants of the breadwinner of the family', and so had no opportunity of providing for themselves (Neild, 1898; 1906).

Neild played a major role in the introduction of the NSW old-age pension and avoidance of the contributory model. Although his maverick political and military career and bad poetry made him a contemporary figure of fun, Neild's work on old-age pensions was consistent and gender-inclusive. In St James' Church in Sydney a plaque installed after Neild's death in 1911 is inscribed 'A tribute of loving gratitude for his great work on their behalf. From a number of old age pensioners.'

E. W. O'Sullivan, Member for Queanbeyan in the NSW parliament, was another who was mindful that old-age pensions were of particular relevance to women. In 1896 he had successfully amended a motion of Neild's on pensions in order to achieve the immediate objective of a select committee of inquiry. In the debate on the adoption of its report, O'Sullivan stressed the nature of old-age pensions as a right earned by men and women, not a hand-out to the poverty-stricken: 'We are dealing with men and women outside who walk with the elastic tread of free people, and have a right to come to the State they have so well served and claim this pension just the same as a soldier or sailor would' (*Parliamentary Debates*, 4 May 1897: 197–8; see also Kewley, 1965).

Another exception to the general tendency to pass over in silence the services performed by women citizens was an article by prominent Sydney wool-broker, W. H. Chard, on old-age pensions, written for *The Australian Economist* in 1898. Chard made explicit the analogy between the services provided by soldiers and sailors, 'whose claims for pensions have always been allowed cheerfully in war times', and the services provided by mothers:

The State depends for its very existence on those women who annually undertake the risks and labour of maternity, and who train generation after generation of new citizens during the long period from infancy to adult life. What more appropriate reward could the State give to women than to recognise their claim to a pension for old age? (1898: 89)

Feminist discourse during this period, by contrast with the public discourse of parliament, placed much emphasis on the service performed for the state by mothers in giving birth to and raising children. Feminists welcomed the introduction of maternity allowances in 1912 (a non-means-tested payment of £5) as the first instalment of 'the mother's maternal rights' (Lake, 1999: 75). The feminist argument at the time was that motherhood should be endowed by the state so that women would no more be made economically dependent through childbearing than men were through military service. While the maternity allowance was mainly intended to pay for medical assistance with childbirth, there was a faint echo of the maternal citizenship discourse in federal parliament. W. M. Hughes described the maternity allowance as a recognition both of the value of children to the state and of the services provided by women in rearing them (*Parliamentary Debates* [H of R], 1912: 3338). The feminist point that more lives were lost in childbirth than on the battlefield was also picked up in the Commonwealth debate. However, while the maternity allowance was the equivalent to three or four weeks' wages at the time of its introduction, payable to the mother through the post office, the mother citizen did not receive further Commonwealth support for her role in raising children for many years.

*Income Tax*

World War I saw the introduction of the first federal income tax. It followed on from the federal land tax introduced by Fisher in 1910 to pay for old-age pensions. The federal land tax was characterized by its progressive structure, aimed at breaking up large estates and taxing unearned increment as well as raising revenue. The new federal income tax was even more remarkable for the degree to which it incorporated British social liberal thinking of Hobson and Hobhouse about repossessing the social component of wealth for social purposes. It had continuously rising marginal rates, above an exemption level linked to the living wage, as well as taxing property income at a higher rate. The ingenuity of the continuously rising marginal rates were described as distinctively Australian as the stump-jump plough (Smith, 1993: 45).

The federal income tax was notable not only for its highly progressive structure but for adopting the individual (rather than the family) as the unit of taxation. This was the case in only two other countries at the time – New Zealand and the United States (and the latter subsequently switched to family-unit taxation). The importance for women of having the individual as the unit of account can be seen by looking at the obverse – family-unit taxation. Family-unit taxation provides disincentives to women's workforce participation, particularly where there is a progressive tax system. There is no tax-free threshold for the second earner, and the second earner is taxed at the higher rate within progressive systems.[6] This is a major equal opportunity issue, as the tax threshold provides recognition of the costs of earning an income, including transport and childcare, while the second earner under a family-unit tax system is usually the woman, whose earnings will incur the higher rate. Australian exceptionalism in this regard began in the colonial period, starting with South Australia in 1884.

It was hardly a coincidence that it was the social liberal Charles Cameron Kingston who introduced the South Australian Taxation Act. The other colonies followed suit in terms of treating married women the same as unmarried women, with only Tasmania briefly experimenting with joint taxation of husband and wife. Louisa Macdonald, first Principal of Women's College at the University of Sydney, explained to the Australian Economic Association in 1893 why economists needed to see the basic unit of society 'not as two, viz., a man and his wife, but as one, the adult human being whether man or woman, married or single' (1893, 1894; compare Hamilton, 1909). This was an almost direct quote from John Stuart Mill, who in his *Principles of Political Economy* had written of the unit of society as being no longer the family or the clan, but the individual. The claims of the individual, as against the family, were the litmus test of social liberalism and distinguished it on the one hand from social conservatism and on the other hand from labourism (discussed further below).

During the Economic Association's debate over her paper, Macdonald was particularly scathing in response to Professor Walter Scott, who had asserted that equal opportunity for women would result in nobody being available to do household work. This has been a consistent theme of conservative opposition to equal opportunity for women for more than a hundred years. 'Who will mind the babies and who will cook the dinner?' was the standard rhetorical question asked by opponents of women's rights, raising the spectre of men being expected to engage in such tasks. It was often assumed, and sometimes stated, that the interests of marriage and the family required the economic dependence of women and that women would abandon household work if they had alternatives.

The damage to the social fabric caused by equal opportunity for women has also been a theme of the neo-liberal revival of the last thirty years. For example, Patrick Jenkin, one of Margaret Thatcher's frontbenchers, spoke of there now being 'an elaborate machinery to ensure [women] equal opportunity, equal pay and equal rights; but I think we ought to stop and ask: where does this leave the family?' (quoted in Sawer, 1990a: 58). There has been a similar emphasis on the damage done to the family by equal opportunity in the publications of Australian neo-liberal think tanks such as the Centre for Independent Studies; 'equal opportunity' has been blamed for problems ranging from juvenile crime to drug-taking to the 'overloaded state' and excessive expenditure on community services.

Back in the late nineteenth century, social liberalism was sufficiently strong to ensure the embedding of the principle of treating the individual as the unit of account in the new income tax systems. The principle was not, however, fully incorporated. For example, in the federal system the tax deduction for children was only available to married men, with married women being treated the same as single women and it being assumed that neither single women nor single men were supporting children (Smith, 1994). Despite some practical achievements, social liberal discourse had a number of blind spots in relation to the economic role of women. Direct payments by the state to female citizens, as through old-age pensions, or the economic autonomy of women implicit in the adoption of the individual as the unit of taxation, were not highlighted as this was discordant with the prevalent ideal of the family headed by a male breadwinner and serviced by a woman working for the family rather than for the state.

Despite these blind spots, the strength of social liberalism at the time of Federation created windows of opportunity for women's political advancement. South Australian social liberals ensured that Federation did not result in loss of political rights already won for citizens of that colony; the constitutional provision they insisted on led to levelling up elsewhere. Most women were granted both the right to vote and the right to stand for the national parliament under the Commonwealth Franchise Act of 1902. Despite efforts in the Senate the Act did not, however, extend uniform voting rights to Aboriginal people. The latter were excluded unless they were already entitled to vote under State law, which was not generally the case in Queensland or Western Australia. The federal franchise did not become uniform until 1962. And while there was almost universal franchise in relation to both the upper and the lower house at the national level, at the State level there were some very long delays in removing the property franchise for the upper house. Ironically the worst case was South Australia, where this barrier was only finally removed in 1973.

Despite the early achievement of political rights, there was considerable ambivalence within the suffrage movement about women actually standing for parliament. The vote itself was seen by many as a sufficiently powerful instrument for the achievement of social reforms – without becoming entangled in the cynical world of party politics. The vote, however, was never seen in isolation from an institutional context that would enable women to exercise their vote effectively and assist them in taking up both the rights and responsibilities of citizenship. The next part of this chapter looks at two waves of such institution-building, that stemming from the 1880s and encompassing both suffrage and post-suffrage organizations, and that triggered by the arrival of women's liberation in the 1970s.

### Feminist Institution-Building

Estelle Freedman, in her classic work (1979) on female institution-building in the United States in the period after 1870, described how the creation of a separate female sphere helped women gain a political identity for themselves and political leverage in the wider society. Separate space helped sustain women's social and political activism during this period – as in the settlement house movement and the suffrage movement. At the founding meeting of the Karrakatta Club in Perth in 1893 the creation of public space for women was clearly linked to social liberal ideas of self-development through doing things worth doing in common with others. Separate institution-building would give women the confidence to become active citizens, and in doing so help push the nation in the direction of idealism and away from the rule of material interests. Separate institutions meant public space in which women were central and where women-centred perspectives could be crystallized. As we shall see, such perspectives eventually crossed over into 'mainstream' political institutions, reshaping social liberal discourses, challenging laborist discourses and creating new domains of public policy. I now examine separate institution-building both 'inside' and 'outside' mainstream political institutions, including non-party organizations, feminist collectives, political parties, parliament and bureaucracy.

### Non-Party Organizations

In 1909, shortly after women had won the right to participate on an equal basis in mainstream political institutions, Laura Bogue Luffman set out the rationale for the continuation of separate institutions. She spoke of the need to give the political world the full benefit of women's distinctive contribution through associations acting with, rather than under, men. Such associations would be, in her words, 'free to make their own laws, think their own thoughts and work out their own political salvation' ([1909] 1980: 282). As Nancy Fraser has put it more recently, if members of subordinate groups have no space in which to deliberate free from the supervision of dominant groups, they will be less likely to find the right voice or words to express their thoughts and less able to develop counter-discourses (Fraser, 1992).

The 'non-party idea' took on organizational forms in all States in the post-suffrage era and at the national level through the creation of what became the Australian Federation of Women Voters (AFWV) in 1924. The idea of a non-party women's political organization has had a continuing presence in Australia up to the present day. The non-party idea was to meet the need for 'education for citizenship' so that women could fulfil the obligations of citizenship and realize their potential for political good. It proclaimed the need for women to stand together, regardless of class or party, to achieve equal citizenship and to protect the interests of women, children and the home.

The platform of the women's non-party organizations generally included equal rights issues such as equal divorce laws and guardianship rights, the right of married women to retain their nationality, equal pay and equal opportunity. The platforms also included welfare-oriented demands relating to juvenile justice and child protection, the appointment of women as police, as prison officers, as jurors, Justices of the Peace and magistrates, and advocacy on behalf of Aboriginal women (Paisley, 1998).

The pull of the non-party idea in the post-suffrage era derived both from women's experience of creating their own public sphere and from women's ambivalence over the form taken by man-made politics, the perceived dominance of power-broking and deal-making over virtue and principle. It was not unrelated to the idealism of social liberalism. Some women who had been active in the suffrage movement ran for parliament as independents – hoping, like Vida Goldstein, that sex loyalty would prevail over party loyalty. Even women with party endorsement often displayed considerable independence, relying on a political base in the women's movement. For example, Edith Cowan, Australia's first woman parliamentarian, declared in her maiden speech that her election showed 'women can and do stand by women, and will stand by women in the future if only to help get rid of some of that painful party spirit'.[7] Many of the first women MPs had an extensive background in community advocacy. Their campaigns for state intervention to ensure pure food and clean milk were an extension of the work of housewives' associations and foreshadowed the leadership roles taken by women in today's consumer movement.

In 1943 the wartime mobilization of women led to a renewed attempt to mobilize women politically and both the Women for Canberra Movement and the Australian Women's Party stood candidates. Women's parties were an extension of the non-party idea and were forerunners of later 'non-party' parties such as the Australian Democrats and the Greens which also protested against the dominance of traditional party politics by vested interests. Women's parties reappeared in Victoria in 1977 and in 1995 in Queensland. While women's parties have not been electorally successful in Australia or elsewhere in the world, except for a brief period in Iceland, they have helped bring pressure on the major parties to pay more attention to women and their concerns.

*The Second Wave*

The arrival of women's liberation in late 1969 brought with it another wave of institution-building, this time a self-conscious attempt to create institutions which would pose an alternative to masculine hierarchies of function, expertise and power. The feminist collectives of the 1970s pioneered the democratic delivery of a whole new range of women's services. There was a much more explicit commitment than previously to incorporating feminist principles of empowerment into organizational design. There was at first little recognition of continuity in feminist institution-building. There was a generation gap between the elderly women who had been undertaking polite and patient lobbying for decades and the young women with their new demands for action.

Once the initial impact of US women's liberation theory had subsided, and with it the anti-state attitudes more characteristic of the United States than of Australasian liberalism, there was a rapprochement with the kind of feminist advocacy conducted since the 1880s. The return to a more positive engagement with state institutions was vastly encouraged, as we shall see, by the election of reforming Labor governments, particularly in South Australia and at the federal level.

The collectivism and distributed leadership characteristic of the more recent feminist organizations has, however, limited their scale and influence on public policy at the national level. In the 1980s ad hoc coalitions were the most characteristic forms taken by attempts to influence the broader policy framework, and these were usually defensive in character. In the 1990s renewed efforts were made to create ongoing structures which, in an era of increasingly professionalized policy advocacy, would give women a more effective voice in public policy while retaining feminist organizational principles.

The continuing emphasis on process led to extensive use of networking principles in the creation of structures such as the Coalition of Australian Participating Organisations of Women (CAPOW!) launched in 1992 and the electronic network, Pamelas-List, created in 1999. Over sixty national women's organizations representing diverse communities of women are now in regular communication with each other.

Governments were uncomfortable dealing with such non-hierarchical structures. In the 1990s the federal Labor government commissioned a feasibility study for a peak body, to enable 'single channel' communications with women's organizations. The succeeding Howard government placed increasing controls over round-table meetings with women's organizations and then commissioned 'capacity-building' workshops, to teach feminist organizations how to develop more hierarchical structures. It has been argued that separate institution-building inevitably leads to marginalization and knocking on doors rather than occupying the seats of power. The next sections examine the role of separate institution-building in influencing 'mainstream' party, parliamentary and bureaucratic institutions.

### Political Parties

Separate institution-building does not preclude participation in the broader political system and indeed is often instigated by political parties as they try to capture new constituencies. Historically, the Australian Women's National League (AWNL) in Victoria and Tasmania, the Women's Liberal League in New South Wales, and the Women's Electoral Leagues in Queensland and Western Australia were, on the one hand, a means for conservative parties to win women to their cause but, on the other hand, gave women an independent base and influence over preselections. The AWNL had the largest membership of any conservative political organization between the world wars, with some 50,000 members at its peak. It operated within conservative discourse concerning the primacy of familial roles for women, at first opposing the right of women to run for parliament. When the modern Liberal Party was formed in 1944, the AWNL leaders, however, struck a hard bargain in return for merging their resources into the new organization – half of all executive positions in the Victorian Liberal Party up to the position of State President were to be (and still are) reserved for women. Social liberalism remained strongest within the Victorian and South Australian branches of the new Liberal Party, although many of the social liberals departed in the 1970s to join the Australian Democrats, a new 'postmaterialist' party where social liberalism was less hemmed around by business interests.

Women's organizations were also created within the Labor Party to encourage women to canvass over the back fence. They were important in the post-suffrage era in promoting feminist policy initiatives such as maternal and child endowment. The women's Labor Leagues created in the 1900s did not, however, have equal entitlements to send delegates to State Conference, being limited to one delegate regardless of size of membership. In general during this period, as Edna Ryan notes (1984: 50), women in the labour movement found it necessary to form separate organizations outside the labour movement, such as the Women's Progressive Association, in order to lobby for equal rights. The labourist version of equal opportunity was firmly anchored in class. Women were not seen as part of the true Labor heartland, made up of workers and their families. Working-class welfare required a wage to support a wife at home, not female competition for male workers. The feminist idea of the relationship between economic independence and equal citizenship, whether coming from paid work or from motherhood endowment, fitted uneasily into this picture.

The labourist view of women's employment can be illustrated by reference to John Curtin, one of the most revered Labor leaders. In 1913 Curtin believed that modern society was paying the price for the expansion of women's economic sphere and deplored the fact that women were being 'dragged or lured from the fireside'. He was confident that it was the excessive employment of women in Victoria that was responsible for relatively low wages in that State, as well as for the fall in the birthrate and the 'admitted tendency to race deterioration' (1913: 4). When he was a commissioner on the Royal Commission on Family Allowances in the 1920s he rejected the calls for motherhood endowment, while supporting child endowment. He argued that working men must have an additional component in their pay either for the support of a wife or, in the case of a bachelor, to pay for services which would otherwise be provided by a wife. The citizenship entitlements of women did not similarly provide for support services.

In the 1930s Labor stalwart Muriel Heagney did run a concerted campaign for equal pay from within the labour movement, but it made little progress against the sanctity of the family wage. Despite the renewed mobilization of women during World War II and some progress with regard to wages where women were working in male occupations, the party remained suspicious of feminism as a middle-class project. When Prime Minister Curtin made 400-odd appointments to government boards and committees in his first year of office, only one of these was a woman, and she was confined to the Women's Employment Board.

In the 1970s the arrival of the second wave of the women's movement re-energized women's organization within the party. Not all the older bodies had survived – increasingly in the 1960s they were seen as sidelining women and as little more than the catering division of the party. Now they played an important role in the campaign for affirmative action and for a systematic approach to women's policy. In the 1980s this bore fruit, but never without contestation; there were always critics standing ready to accuse feminists of coming between the party and its heartland. Moreover, a countervailing trend was the consolidation of the factional system in the 1980s, which cut across sisterhood. In the 1990s the campaign for an enforceable quota of winnable party seats and the creation of EMILY's List, a fund-raising trust modelled on the American organization of the same name, represented renewed efforts at female institution-building within the party. The surge in numbers of Labor women in parliament after 1996 owes much to this catalyst, as well as to the change in the electoral tide which was bringing in Labor governments.

*Reshaping Parliaments and Parliamentary Discourse*

As Carole Pateman has pointed out (1988: 222), women have been differentially incorporated as citizens, meaning that their primary obligations as citizens have historically been construed as being in the private rather than the public realm. It is only in the last twenty-five years that there has been real discussion, let alone action, on how public life might be changed to accommodate family responsibilities. Prior to this, women's family responsibilities were construed as insuperable barriers to equal participation in public life.

Parliamentary arrangements have assumed that parliamentary representatives are not at the same time primary carers for family members.

Indeed political careers have been regarded in the past as typically a two-person career, where the 'incorporated wife' not only takes over full responsibility for the care of the family but also stands in for the representative, particularly in constituency roles. Today, recommendations for childcare centres, family-friendly sitting hours, parliamentary sessions aligned with school terms and increased travel for family members have become standard in proposals to reduce the pressure on parliamentarians with family responsibilities. In Tasmania the premier recently limited parliamentary sitting times to 6 pm, stating that later sitting hours were discriminating against women with young families (*Canberra Times*, 16 March 1999: 5).

Another aspect of masculine institutional bias is the kind of confrontational politics encouraged by Westminster two-party systems, exacerbated by the physical configuration of the chamber so that the rival teams line up against each other. Few women perceive themselves as doing well in such adversarial chamber politics where they have to contend with both psychological and physical intimidation, such as the hostile wall of sound from the benches on the other side. Women parliamentarians tend to feel more 'at home' in more intimate forums such as those provided by parliamentary committees, in which members from different parties sit next to each other rather than shouting at each other from opposite sides of the chamber. One recent inquiry in South Australia into the effects of parliamentary procedure and practice on women's parliamentary participation suggested that a way to both facilitate women's participation and improve the quality of legislative debate was to enhance the role of parliamentary committees in the legislative process, as has happened most markedly in the Australian Senate (Parliament of South Australia, 1996). Certainly, the persistence of adversarialism, and its privileging by the electronic media, not only disadvantages women but also fuels popular distrust in parliamentary institutions

As we have seen, female institution-building has provided the possibility for woman-centred political discourses and for pushing social liberalism towards a more inclusive version of equal opportunity. The discourses of the women's movement have been counter-discourses in terms of prioritizing women's experience, but they occupied space created by public discourses of equal opportunity and the ethical state. They drew attention to the need to accommodate the different lived experience of women into public policy if equal opportunity was to be achieved. This often meant eroding the public/private boundaries that underlay political abstractions.

For example, the maiden speech of Edith Cowan, Australia's first woman parliamentarian, included a telling example of the way in which legislation and policy neglected impact on women and thus undermined equal opportunity. She suggested that were the Minister for Railways made to parade the streets of Perth for the whole of one afternoon with a heavy infant on one arm and a bag of groceries on the other, it might make him more sensitive to the plight of mothers unable to bring prams to town because of the shilling charge for them on the train (Sawer, 1996: xiii).

Some women MPs have disassociated themselves from female institution-building and seen it as limiting and constraining women's political contribution. One explanation of the disinclination to be identified with women is based on the effect of proportions on group life (Kanter, 1997). As a small minority, women politicians are highly visible and more likely to be subject to loyalty tests than members of the dominant group. They have to work harder to earn trust, because of the distrust generated by their 'difference'. Distancing themselves from other women may be one way of demonstrating reliability and support for dominant group values.

Despite their minority status and the extra pressures imposed on them, analysis of the content of parliamentary debate shows that women politicians have been important vectors for social movement discourse. They have been responsible, for example, for focusing attention on central issues of citizenship and equal opportunity, such as the prevalence of violence against women. Similarly, it was women with the help of women MPs who made sexual harassment into a key equal opportunity issue, put it on the public policy agenda and made it a subject for legislation. Not all women politicians have played this role; networking with women's organizations is an important predictor of propensity to raise gender issues in parliament.

While women MPs have had some success in importing feminist discourse into parliamentary debate, they have been less successful in changing the dominant adversarial culture. As Janine Haines, former leader of the Australian Democrats, once said, it is very difficult to run onto the field playing soccer when everyone else is playing Aussie Rules.[8]

*Bureaucratic Feminism and Femocrats*

The conjuncture of social liberal and feminist discourses made possible an internationally remarkable development of state feminism in the 1970s and 1980s. Reforming Labor governments operating within social liberal equal opportunity frameworks were pressured by the new wave of feminist organizations into establishing feminist structures within the state. The Australian invention of the 'femocrat', that is a feminist appointed to government with a mandate to improve policy outcomes for women, was an important example of the discursive possibilities created by social liberalism. The idea of creating structures within government to monitor the gender impact of policy, and hence advance equal opportunity, assumed the social liberal idea of the ethical state.

Sara Dowse, one of the earliest femocrats and one of the ten thinkers recently selected by Ian Cook to exemplify Australian liberalism, has argued that the women's movement came into the political arena with the same expectations as previous claimants on the Australian state. As in earlier political history, the state was seen as representing 'collective power at the service of individualistic rights' (Dowse, quoted in Cook, 1999: 143). Like other femocrats, Dowse made a clear distinction between equal opportunity in public employment and ensuring more equitable policy outcomes for women in the community. The latter did not follow naturally and inevitably from the former. It required structures and processes to evaluate the differential impact of public policy on men and women. Such different impacts arose from the differing location of men and women in the social division of labour, differing patterns of workforce participation and different levels of responsibility for non-market caring work. Social justice for women, like that for working men, required the development of innovative institutional responses on the part of the state.

The origins of the femocrat phenomenon go back to 1972, the year a reform wing developed out of the women's liberation movement, focusing on getting women's demands onto the political agenda. This new organization, the Women's Electoral Lobby, was firmly located within the Australian non-party tradition and looked to the state as the vehicle for social justice. This pro-state position of WEL was, however, strongly contested at first.

Women's liberation had arrived in Australia in late 1969. It brought with it the anti-state orientation of US liberalism, reinforced by the women's liberation critique of the state as an irredeemably patriarchal institution. Feminists involved in the new feminist enterprises within government were accused of co-option, of becoming 'painted birds'. It was suggested that taking the Queen's shilling inevitably meant becoming the instrument of state imperatives, whether these were the reinforcement of patriarchy or the creation of the conditions for continued capital accumulation. Such arguments did not go unanswered by those attempting to reform the state to serve the needs of women. American-born Sara Dowse, for example, saw women in Australia as having an advantage over those in the United States, because of the existence of a political culture which legitimized looking to the state to obtain rights and to further rights claims.

On a more theoretical level, some queried whether the state was a coherent unity with imperatives to which social movements could be co-opted, or that co-option was a meaningful description of the interrelationship between social movements and the state. The idea of unified state imperatives under-rated, reformers said, the degree of policy contestation within the state, which might be more appropriately seen in terms of arenas of discursive conflict and multiple agendas within which feminists might engage (see Watson, 1990). Policy outcomes were not preordained and many feminists were attracted by the idea of using state power, seeing it as the only counterbalance to the inequalities produced by markets, whether local or global. In terms of global imperatives, Carol Johnson (2000) has nicely shown that domestic policy outcomes remain politically determined. Even when successive governments such as those of Paul Keating and John Howard have very similar neo-liberal economic agendas, this agenda may be accompanied by the socially inclusive approach of the Keating government or the more repressive approach of 'governing for the mainstream', introduced by John Howard.

Others questioned the concept of co-option, which assumed, they said, that the claims of social movements were fixed and given, rather than evolving within dynamic processes of policy negotiation wherein claims became more diversified and complex and new issues were thrown up by constantly shifting boundaries of policy domains. Feminist influence within the state had to be brokered through electoral imperatives, like all other claims, but also assisted in the mobilization of new identities and the creation of new constituencies. For example, federal funding assisted women from non-English speaking backgrounds, women with disabilities, lesbian women and farm women to become organized at a national level, to undertake policy research and to be represented in policy forums. This meant that the women's movement could speak with more diverse voices within policy processes, and proposals could be tested against a broader range of lived experience.

Regardless of more theoretical debates over state imperatives or co-option, many took the pragmatic stand that although compromises were entailed by engagement with the state, they were also entailed by every other form of social action. Anne Summers, a founder of Australia's first women's refuge and later head of the federal Office of the Status of Women, described the unacceptable conditions in the months before federal funding was achieved for the refuge, when she was reduced to selling marijuana to raise funds (1999: 327–33). It seemed self-evident that gains such as the wide range of funded women's services, the national childcare program or financial transfers to primary carers were preferable to the absence of such services, and the presence of punitive sole-parent regimes in countries such as the United States where the women's movement was 'purer'.

WEL was assisted by a favourable opportunity structure in 1972, the election of the reformist Whitlam government, with an agenda shaped by social liberal discourse. Feminists designed a model for women's policy machinery which they presented to the Royal Commission on Australian Government Administration (the Coombs Commission). It was a centre–periphery model, with its hub in the major policy co-ordinating agency of government and spokes in line departments and agencies. The goal was to analyse all policy for its impact on women and contribution to equal opportunity objectives. The central location with access to Cabinet and Budget submissions from all areas of government was to be an essential element in the effectiveness of this model.[9]

The emphasis on monitoring, co-ordinating and auditing policy, rather than on separate women's programs, was a distinctive institutional design by world standards, although twenty years later its 'mainstreaming' principles became the benchmark adopted by the United Nations for machinery of government to enhance gender equality. The Australian model was based on the feminist insight that, given the different location of men and women in the social division of labour, no government activity was likely to be gender-neutral in its effects, however neutral on its face. This focus was strengthened from 1984 with the development of cross-portfolio Budget documents providing gender disaggregated breakdowns of Budget outlays. Under the federal Labor governments of the 1980s and 1990s femocrats were able to influence policy over a range of sectors – such as the national childcare program, women's services, shifting of family support to primary carers, national programs on violence against women, programs to promote equal opportunity for workers with family responsibilities, and the development of sex discrimination and affirmative action legislation.

By the 1990s the social liberal concern for gender equity brought femocrats into an uneasy relationship with neo-liberals, who believed that interventions in the market of any kind were counter-productive. The regulatory regime which had made possible the implementation of equal pay principles in the 1970s was being wound back, while democratically run women's services which combined service delivery with political action were being threatened by the compulsory tendering processes associated with competition policy. Despite this, the feminist project remains part of the bureaucratic landscape within Australia at one level of government or another, and the creativity of femocrats has often resulted in 'least worst outcomes'.

Over time, the women's movement has manifested both engagement and disengagement with mainstream public institutions. The disengagement has been important in fostering alternative perspectives and institutional forms; the engagement has been necessary to claim women's share of public benefits. Separate institution-building has helped ensure that women do not disappear in the mainstream, or within the ever-diversifying rivulets, but retain capacity for collective agency. The final part of this chapter examines the intersection of federalism with this pattern of discursive and institutional engagement.

## Feminism and Federalism

So far, I have focused on the relationship between feminism and social liberalism in the shaping of Australian political institutions. The engagement and disengagement of feminism and social liberalism is not, however, the only story to be told about gender and Australian political history. This section introduces the counterpoint of the relationship between feminism and federalism. It deals not only with the nature of the division of powers between different levels of government, but also with the nature of the decision-making between these levels of government.

Theorists of federalism have often argued that federalism is an important means of limiting the power of government through dividing it between competing units. The fragmenting of government in this way is believed to safeguard individual rights.[10] In an Australian version of this argument, the purpose of federalism, as a form of liberal constitutionalism, is to enshrine institutional processes that 'guarantee citizens and groups the right to pursue their own happiness, and to restrict governments from legislating happiness schemes. No public good is presupposed, but rather a multiplicity of private goods' (Galligan and Walsh, 2000: 197; see also Sharman, 1990 and Galligan, 1995). On this interpretation, federalism would be quite at odds with the social liberal concept of the ethical state, a state dedicated to the substantive goal of equal opportunity for its citizens.

If there is a tension between federalism and the substantive goal of equal opportunity, we might expect that federalism would have significant gender implications. However, with very few exceptions,[11] we would not discover what these implications were from reading Australian books on federalism. The gendered nature of the theory and practice of federalism has received more attention from political scientists in Canada than in Australia. Canadian political scientist Jill Vickers (1994) has commented on how little attraction the idea of federalism as a means of limiting government has had for feminists. Feminists have located the main threat to enjoyment of rights as coming from sources other than government and have sought to enlist government to protect the rights of women and children. As social reformers and equality seekers, women have generally tried to get governments to take on *more* responsibility. Within federal systems they are to be found seeking uniform rights protection and uniform standards of social provision across jurisdictions. They have generally had relatively little stake in the autonomy of sub-national levels of government except where feminism and nationalism coincide, as in cases such as Quebec or Scotland. In Australia 'States' rights' arguments have generally been raised in opposition to the equality rights being sought by women's organizations.

Australian women's organizations have had a long-standing interest in framework issues and the nature of the federal compact. Some leading suffragists, such as Rose Scott, were opposed to Federation on the grounds it removed government too far from women's lives. State governments were seen as more accessible to women's concerns and offering more opportunities for women's citizenship. In the years since federation, however, organizations such as the Australian Federation of Women Voters (AFWV) have usually been found campaigning for the federal government to take on more responsibilities. For example, the AFWV and its State affiliates made a number of submissions to the 1927 Royal Commission on the Constitution, asking for the Commonwealth to be given powers in relation to widows' pensions, child endowment, public education and nature conservation, but particularly focusing on family law and Aboriginal affairs. Evidence was given concerning the injustice to women and families made possible by the disparities in family law between the States and the ability of husbands and fathers to avoid their responsibilities by moving to another State. In the 1920s feminists advocated that the Commonwealth use its existing powers in relation to family law and be given additional ones in relation to custody and guardianship of children, including ex-nuptial children.

Another issue on which women's groups campaigned from the 1920s onwards was the need to amend the constitution to give the Commonwealth power in relation to Aboriginal affairs. The affiliates of the AFWV appearing before the Royal Commission argued that this was the only way to achieve more effective care and protection for Aborigines generally and for women and girls in particular. In the 1950s the AFWV was still campaigning for this in its submission to the Constitutional Review set up by the Menzies government. Women such as Jessie Street, Ada Bromham, Faith Bandler and Kath Walker were to take leading roles in the ten-year campaign that led to the Aboriginal affairs referendum in 1967 and to the Commonwealth finally acquiring this concurrent power.

From World War II, women's organizations added to their agenda a demand for an equality guarantee in the Constitution, to give the Commonwealth powers to deal with sex discrimination. This demand was included in the Australian Women's Charter of 1943 as well as in regular submissions to constitutional reviews such as that initiated by Menzies. The final report of the Hawke government's Constitutional Commission recommended such a guarantee, although it was never acted upon. Other demands made by women's organizations since the 1980s, such as a general human rights power for the Commonwealth, have also fallen by the wayside. The Commonwealth remains dependent on the external affairs power for its human rights legislation, which means it can implement international conventions to which it is party, but cannot go beyond them.

The expansive interpretation of the Commonwealth's external affairs power by the High Court (particularly the Koowarta decision of 1981) has, however, enabled the Commonwealth to go some way towards meeting the demand for national equality guarantees. Although lacking a constitutional human rights power, federal governments have been able to pass anti-discrimination legislation as part of their implementation of international conventions. The longstanding feminist demand for a federal Aboriginal affairs power was met through the successful 1967 referendum. And the demand for national standards of social provision was met in part by the Commonwealth's use of its financial power and ability under s 96 of the Constitution to attach conditions to its grants to the States.

Women's organizations have had a strong interest in the building up of a Commonwealth role in community services through tied grants. Beginning with the Whitlam government in the 1970s, innovative services such as women's refuges, women's health centres, childcare centres, working women's centres and women's legal services as well as domiciliary and respite services have been funded in this way. The growth in Commonwealth responsibility for social programs has always been met, however, by some 'new federalism' proposal to return these responsibilities to the States. These recurrent proposals for devolution provide the rhythm of the 'federalism foxtrot'. For example, under the 'new federalism' of the Fraser government, responsibility for a number of the innovative Whitlam programs was progressively transferred to the States (Summers, 1979). During the first year of the Fraser government refuge funding was devolved in the form of block grants. The Queensland premier promptly refused to pass on money to two refuges that he believed were run by Marxist lesbians. Further 'untying' of refuge money took place in 1981, after which it was simply left to the States to fund (or not) refuges out of their health budgets. Refuge workers and residents camped outside Parliament House in Canberra and angry scenes took place in the corridors (McFerren, 1990). In 1983 the newly elected federal Labor government restored tied grants in the form of the newly created Women's Emergency Services Program.

A review of Commonwealth functions had been established in 1981 (the 'razor gang'), and it became widely rumoured that the Commonwealth's involvement in children's services might also be substantially reduced and that the Commonwealth might even turn these functions completely over to the States. In response childcare activists mounted a highly effective campaign, organizing demonstrations in the major cities and gaining considerable media attention. According to journalist Anne Summers, 'for weeks afterwards ministers spoke, almost in awe, of the extraordinarily well-organised campaign' (quoted in Brennan, 1994: 108). Behind the scenes Dame Beryl Beaurepaire, convenor of the National Women's Advisory Council, also played an important role in convincing the prime minister not to transfer responsibility for childcare to the States. The intention of devolving responsibility was quietly dropped.

Under the federal Labor government of the 1980s a renewed emphasis on gender accountability in government extended to the intergovernmental arena. A number of Ministerial Councils (bringing together relevant ministers from Commonwealth, State and Territory jurisdictions) established specialized bodies for this purpose. Examples included the National Women's Housing Issues Working Party established by the Housing Ministers' Conference; the Subcommittee on Women and Health established by the Australian Health Ministers' Advisory Council; and the Working Party on Women and the Labour Force which developed the Australian Women's Employment Strategy. The Australian Education Council endorsed the National Policy for the Education of Girls in Australian Schools. Other Commonwealth–State bodies were the Task Force on Domestic Violence and the Council on Non-English Speaking Background Women's Issues.

However the 1990s began with another round of 'new federalism' proposals. This was part of an ambitious plan under the Hawke government to renegotiate Commonwealth–State financial relations and to replace much tied funding with unrestricted general-purpose funding. Women's groups expressed strong concerns over the effects of such a change on community services in general, including those which had been shaped by women, such as the Home and Community Care Program. There was a particular concern for impact on women's services, including those funded under the Supported Accommodation Assistance Program and the National Women's Health Program. Because Commonwealth payments to States were to remain at their existing low levels, the untying of grants would be a means of alleviating the financial problems of the States through the ability of the latter to abolish services (Gray, 1991: 9). Similar developments were occurring in Canada, with the limitation and then abolition of the Canada Assistance Plan, which provided federal funding for women's shelters and childcare.

The untying of grants always means the possibility of State governments alleviating their financial problems through abolishing services of particular benefit to women. A paper that encapsulated many of the traditional feminist concerns over devolution was adopted by the Commonwealth/State Ministers' Conference on the Status of Women at its first meeting in 1991. It pointed out that a high proportion of specific purpose payments made to the States were made to human service areas and that attachment of conditions was a significant means of enhancing the status of women. Such conditions might include provision of specific kinds of statistical information and forms of monitoring and review, as well as directing how Commonwealth payments were to be used. The paper adopted by the Women's Ministers was critical of the argument that devolution was required to give scope to diversity in approach by the States. It suggested that social policy must respond to diversity, but that diversity in the lives of women, including the special needs relating to culture and ethnicity, did not correspond to State boundaries (Australia, Commonwealth/State Ministers' Conference on the Status of Women, 1991).

Neither this initiative nor the women's policy bodies created to advise intergovernmental ministerial councils, part of feminist institution-building within government, have had much effect on the federalism foxtrot. Under the Howard government there has been a renewed thrust towards devolution, at the expense, for example, of the national women's health policy. Another salient issue since the 1980s concerns the source of State revenue. The progressive reduction in Commonwealth/State transfers led the States to rely increasingly on revenue sources that were at best socially undesirable. State governments became dependent on revenue from gambling, and acquired an interest in promoting this industry and competing for the gambling dollar (Smith, 2000). Taxes on gambling were regressive, as heavy gamblers disproportionately come from low-income households. The effects of gambling on low-income families was a prominent concern of first-wave feminism and increased reliance by governments on gambling revenue has been an issue viewed with great concern by feminist social policy activists.

Apart from the gender impact of changes in Commonwealth/State financial relations and devolution of responsibilities, another ongoing concern has been over democratic accountability. As Martin Painter has observed, 'Intergovernmental relations are notoriously opaque and hard to access for the public, with conventions of secrecy and bureaucratic habits of confidentiality dominant most of the time' (1998: 71). Executive federalism leads not only to a general problem of democratic accountability but also to specific problems in relation to gender accountability. Negotiation over key policies has increasingly been undertaken behind the closed doors of intergovernmental forums with no preceding analysis of differential gender impact. The paper adopted by the Women's Ministers Conference recommended that client groups of services, including women, be consulted in the review process, that government and non-government bodies concerned with the status of women be involved in the review and its outcomes and that there be impact statements on client groups including women. This attempt to push open the door was unsuccessful, as were the attempts by the New Federalism Steering Committee established by non-government women's groups in 1991. Calls for the protection of services and preservation of national standards appeared to fall on deaf ears. The difficulty in responding to the perceived threat of the new federalism played a significant role in the creation towards the end of the year of a stronger networking structure for national women's organizations. In the meantime the 'new federalism' proposals of the Hawke government were to fall victim of the change of prime minister at the end of 1991.

The Hawke government's 'new federalism' proposals and subsequent initiatives by the Keating government, particularly the competition policy agreements of 1995, raised new questions about the effectiveness of women's input into intergovernmental arrangements. Framework agreements such as these have been largely driven by Premier's Departments and Treasury with little community input or accountability for gender impact. This direction in Commonwealth–State relations was exacerbated from 1996 under the Howard government. The women's committees which advised intergovernmental bodies on gender impact were allowed to wither and there was a new push to devolve Commonwealth responsibilities in areas such as health and to untie funding for specific programs such as the National Women's Health Program.

The positions adopted by Australian women's organizations on jurisdictional issues reinforce the truism that in federations those interested in equality will tend to seek more power for the centre, while those interested in cultural recognition will tend to seek more power for sub-national levels of government. This has also been expressed as the contrast between 'movements promoting centralization for social reasons and those advocating decentralization for political reasons' (Vickers, 1994).

On the division of powers within the federal compact, Australian women's organizations have generally sought more power for the centre, in the interests of uniform social provision and gender equality. But while this has been the general pattern, there has been some interesting debate over the advantages or disadvantages of a federal system in terms of policy gains by women. One argument is that having to win battles over and over again, where there are different levels of government with concurrent powers, is demanding too much of chronically under-resourced women's groups (Gray, 2002).

Contrariwise, it has been argued that this multiplicity enables some momentum to be maintained through intergovernmental relations, despite the election of conservative governments at one level or another

(Chappell, 2001; Sawer, 1990b). One mechanism through which sharing of best practice occurs has been the Standing Committee of Commonwealth/State Women's Advisers created in 1978. Like other Australian officials meetings, this regularly brings together not just the women's advisers to the Prime Minister, State Premiers and Territory Chief Ministers, but also the head of the Ministry of Women's Affairs in New Zealand. Intergovernmental relations can have this positive aspect, of sharing or competing over 'best practice' – indeed an argument often made in favour of federalism is that it provides scope both for policy experiment and for policy learning. The negative aspects of intergovernmental agreements made behind closed doors and without adequate scrutiny of social impact have, however, become increasingly apparent.

## Conclusion

We have seen that Australasian social liberalism, with its themes of equal opportunity and the ethical state, provided discursive space and institutional possibilities for the advancement of women. Ideas of state intervention and state provision in the interests of equal opportunity infused the nation-building period and inspired the creation of the system of compulsory conciliation and arbitration. The latter institutionalized the idea of 'state interference' with contracts being necessary for equality of opportunity. Regulation was required to introduce fairness into labour and other contracts and to mitigate the inequalities generated by the market.

The social liberal idea of the state as vehicle for social justice did, however, have basic flaws in relation to race and gender. Assumptions were too easily made that equal opportunity for women could be achieved while women remained financially dependent on men, while the issue of equal opportunity for Indigenous Australians or those from non-Anglo backgrounds was not seriously addressed until two things had happened: first, political mobilization around disadvantage linked to race and ethnicity; and second, the election of reformist governments in the 1970s. The governments of Don Dunstan and Gough Whitlam were committed, at least by their leaders, to addressing these basic contradictions within dominant equal opportunity discourse. Even then, there was continuous contestation over what forms of cultural recognition were required for equal opportunity to become a reality. The extension of equal opportunity discourse to encompass the needs of gays came first with Dunstan in South Australia, while action to ensure that those with disabilities had a voice in the policies that determined their opportunities did not come until the 1980s.

Today the discursive space opened up to accommodate difference within social liberal discourse has again been closing. 'Governing for the mainstream' has meant the discouragement of counter-discourses and their representation within the policy process. The term 'social justice' is no longer part of the lexicon of the state, and there has been a general cessation of policy monitoring to ensure equal benefit from government policies and programs. This has been accompanied by sloganeering about the need to treat all Australians equally, with equal treatment meaning same treatment despite the disparate impact of such treatment. Social liberal discourse, with its prioritizing of equal opportunity for citizens, has itself been displaced by the revival of older forms of liberal discourse with their presumption of natural laws of economic competition and the dangers of state 'interference'. The institutions of arbitration and old-age pensions have been sidelined by decentralized wage-bargaining and occupationally based superannuation, both of which enhance, rather than moderate, market-based inequalities. It is too early to announce the strange death of Australasian social liberalism, with the 'fair go' still being a central political reference, but the prognosis is poor. The centennial dream of the ethical state has definitely faded.

### Notes

My thanks to Julie Smith and Marian Quartly for their contributions to this essay, to Gillian Evans for assistance with historical material, and to Frank Castles, Frank Jones and Peter McCarthy for valuable editorial suggestions.

1 Another major influence in the pages of *The Australian Economist* was Henry George.
2 This essay won the Beauchamp Prize at Sydney University in 1916.
3 It was generally agreed by witnesses appearing before the Royal Commission on Old-Age Pensions in 1906 that women of 60 had more difficulty in earning a living than did men and, for example, that domestic employers did not want to look at them.
4 There was, however, means testing on marital assets.
5 At least one Senator, E. Needham, disagreed with this, arguing that a woman who married an Asiatic should be disqualified from the pension because the aim of the White Australia policy was to keep the white race inviolate: Commonwealth of Australia, *Parliamentary Debates* (Senate) vol. XLVI, 4 June 1908, p. 12010.
6 The same kind of effect can be achieved where the individual is the unit of account through reducing tax rates for higher-income earners but not for low-income earners, on the assumption that the latter are 'secondary earners' – i.e. women. This was done during the 1980s tax reforms in New Zealand, but a similar move in Australia was defeated through an alliance of feminists working from within and outside government. The initial proposal, endorsed by the Australian Council of Trade Unions, was for tax cuts for those on wages above the level of average female earnings.
7 In the event Cowan lost both party endorsement and the support of a number of women's organisations (because of her support for compulsory notification of venereal disease) by the time she stood unsuccessfully for a second term.

8 This issue has been explored at length by Sharon Broughton (2000).
9 Described more fully in Sawer (1990b); Sawer and Groves (1994).
10 For a classic statement of federalism as a means of securing liberty see Elazar (1987).
11 Works which looks at issues of gender and federalism include: Gray (2002); Chappell (2001); Rubenstein (1998); and Irving (1996: 98–107).

## References

Anderson, F. 'J. R. Green (sic) of Balliol: His Ethical and Political Teaching', *The Australian Economist*, vol. 2(16) (23 July 1891) pp. 140–1. Also in Butlin et al. (1986), vol. 1.

Australia. Commonwealth–State Ministers' Conference on the Status of Women. 'Women's Interests Paper: Commonwealth/State Relations Review', February 1991.

Brennan, D. *The Politics of Australian Child Care: From Philanthropy to Feminism* (Cambridge: Cambridge University Press, 1994).

Broughton, S. 'Leadership is a Feminist Issue: Do Women in the Australian Parliament Make a Difference?' PhD Thesis (Department of Government, University of Queensland, 2000).

Butlin, N. G., Fitzgerald, V. W., and Scott, R. H. (eds), *The Australian Economist 1888–1898*, facsimile edn, 2 vols (Sydney: Australian National University Press, 1986).

Callaghan, P. S. 'Idealism and Arbitration in H. B. Higgins' New Province for Law and Order', *Journal of Australian Studies*, vol. 13 (1983) pp. 56–66.

Chappell, L. 'Federalism and Social Policy: The Case of Domestic Violence', *Australian Journal of Public Administration*, vol. 60(1) (2001) pp. 59–69.

Chard, W. H. 'Old Age Pensions', *The Australian Economist*, vol. 6(1) (22 December 1898), pp. 89–91. Also in Butlin et al. (1986), vol. 2.

Commonwealth Court of Conciliation and Arbitration. *Commonwealth Arbitration Reports* III (Melbourne: Commonwealth of Australia, 1909).

Commonwealth of Australia. *Parliamentary Debates* (House of Representatives and Senate), vol. XLVI (1908).

——. *Parliamentary Debates* (House of Representatives), vol. LXVI (1912).

Cook, I. *Liberalism in Australia* (Melbourne: Oxford University Press, 1999).

Curtin, J. 'Women at Work', *The Timber Worker* (9 August 1913) p. 4.

Elazar, D. J. *Exploring Federalism* (Tuscaloosa: University of Alabama Press, 1987).

Evatt, H. V. *Liberalism In Australia* (Sydney: Law Book Company, 1918).

Fraser, N. 'Rethinking the Public Sphere: A Contribution to the Critique of Actually Existing Democracy', in C. Calhoun (ed.), *Habermas and the Public Sphere* (Cambridge, Mass.: MIT Press, 1992) pp. 109–42.

Freedman, E. 'Separatism as Strategy: Female Institution Building and American Feminism, 1870–1930', *Feminist Studies*, vol. 5(3) (1979) pp. 512–29.

Galligan, B. *A Federal Republic: Australia's Constitutional System of Government* (Cambridge: Cambridge University Press, 1995).

Galligan, B., and C. Walsh. 'Australian Federalism – Yes or No?', in G. Craven (ed.), *Australian Federation: Towards the Second Century* (Melbourne: Melbourne University Press, 1992) pp. 193–208.

Gray, G. 'New Federalism Spells Doom for Society's Poor', *Canberra Times* (18 October 1991) p. 9.

———. 'The Impact of Federalism and the Elusive Search for Theory', paper to Department of Political Science, University of British Columbia, 19 February 2002.

Green, T. H. 'Liberal legislation and freedom of contract' [1881], in Paul Harris and John Morrow (eds), *T. H. Green: Lectures on the Principles of Political Obligation, and Other Writings* (Cambridge: Cambridge University Press, 1984) pp. 194–212.

Gregory, R. G. et al. *A Tale of Two Countries: Equal Pay for Women in Australia and Britain*, Centre for Economic Policy Research Discussion Papers no. 147, Canberra, Australian National University, 1986.

Hamilton, C. *Marriage as a Trade*, 2nd edn (London: Chapman & Hall, 1909).

'Hampden'. 'The Advancement of the Masses Achieved through Liberalism: Part 1', *Liberty and Progress* (25 November 1913) pp. 252–5.

Hancock, W. K. 'England and Australia: A Study in Democratic Development', in his *Politics in Pitcairn and Other Essays* (1933; reprint, London: Macmillan, 1947) pp. 65–93.

Irving, H. 'A Gendered Constitution? Women, Federation and Heads of Power', in her (ed.), *A Woman's Constitution? Gender and History in the Australian Commonwealth* (Sydney: Hale & Iremonger, 1996) pp. 98–107.

Johnson, C. *Governing Change: From Keating to Howard* (St Lucia: University of Queensland Press, 2000).

Kanter, R. M. *Men and Women of the Corporation* (New York: Basic Books, 1977).

Kewley, T. H. *Social Security in Australia: The Development of Social Security and Health Benefits from 1900 to the present* (Sydney: Sydney University Press, 1965).

Lake, M. *Getting Equal: The History of Australian Feminism* (St Leonards, NSW: Allen & Unwin, 1999).

Luffman, L. B. 'The Principle of Women's Associations for Women Alone', paper to the Commonwealth Conference in Brisbane [1909], in K. Daniels and M. Murnane (eds), *Uphill all the Way: A Documentary History of Women in Australia* (St Lucia: University of Queensland Press, 1980) p. 282.

Macdonald, L. 'The Economic Position of Women', *The Australian Economist*, vol. 3(11) (30 December 1893) pp. 367–72. Also in Butlin et al. (1986), vol. 2.

———. 'Reply by Miss Macdonald', *The Australian Economist*, vol. 4(3) (23 April 1894) pp. 396–8. Also in Butlin et al. (1986), vol. 2.

McFerren, L. 'Interpretations of a Frontline State: Australian Women's Refuges and the State', in Sophie Watson (ed.), *Playing the State: Australian Feminist Interventions* (Sydney: Allen & Unwin, 1990) pp. 191–205.

Neild, Lieut.-Colonel J. C., MP, *Report on Old Age Pensions, Charitable Relief and State Insurance in England and on the Continent of Europe* (Sydney: Government Printer, 1898).

Neild, J. C. (Senator) 'Evidence' in *Report of the Royal Commission on Old-Age Pensions; Together with Proceedings, Minutes of Evidence, Appendices and a Synopsis of the Evidence* (Parliamentary Papers: Session 1906, vol. 3, Victoria, 1906) pp. 252–8.

New South Wales. *Parliamentary Debates*, 4 May 1897, pp. 197–8.

Painter, M. *Collaborative Federalism: Economic Reform in Australia in the 1990s* (Cambridge: Cambridge University Press, 1998).

Paisley, F. 'Federalising the Aborigines? Constitutional Reform in the late 1920s', *Australian Historical Studies*, vol. 29(111) (October 1998) pp. 248–66.

Pateman, C. *The Sexual Contract* (Cambridge: Polity, 1988).

Reeves, W. P. *State Experiments in Australia and New Zealand*, 2 vols (South Melbourne: Macmillan, [1902] 1969).

Rubenstein, K. 'Feminism and federalism', paper to conference on Constitutional Law, Administrative Law and Institutional Ethics: The Role of Feminist Values, 1998.

Ryan, E. *Two-Thirds of a Man: Women and Arbitration in New South Wales, 1902–08* (Sydney: Hale & Iremonger, 1984).

Sawer, M. 'The Battle for the Family: Family Policy in Australian Electoral Politics in the 1980s', *Politics*, vol. 25(1) (May 1990a) pp. 48–61.

——. *Sisters in Suits: Women and Public Policy in Australia* (Sydney: Allen & Unwin, 1990b).

——. 'Guest Editorial: Challenging Politics? Seventy–Five Years of Women's Parliamentary Representation in Australia', *International Review of Women and Leadership*, vol. 2(1) (1996) pp. i–xvi.

——. 'Gender, Metaphor and the State', in Joni Lovenduski (ed.), *Feminism and Politics*, vol. 1 (Ashgate: International Library of Politics and Comparative Government, 2000a) pp. 519–35.

——. 'The Ethical State? Social Liberalism and the Critique of Contract', *Australian Historical Studies*, vol. 114 (April 2000b), pp. 67–90.

Sawer, M., and Groves, A. *Working From the Inside: Twenty Years of the Office of the Status of Women* (Canberra: Australian Government Publishing Service, 1994).

Sawer, M., and J. Vickers. 'Women's Constitutional Activism in Australia and Canada', *Canadian Journal of Women and the Law*, vol. 13(1) (2001) pp. 1–36.

Scott, W. 'The Cash Nexus', *The Australian Economist*, vol. 1(1) (3 March 1888) pp. 2–6. Also in Butlin et al. (1986), vol. 1.

Sharman, C. 'Australia as a Compound Republic', *Politics*, vol. 25(1) (1990) pp. 1–5.

Smith, J. *Taxing Popularity: The Story of Taxation in Australia* (Canberra: Federalism Research Centre, Australian National University, 1993).

——. 'Families and Taxation in Australia: An Historical Perspective', paper to Economic History Seminar, Australian National University, Canberra, 28 October 1994.

——. 'Gambling Taxation: Public Equity in the Gambling Business', *Australian Economic Review*, vol. 33(2) (June 2000) pp. 120–44.

South Australia. Parliament. *Final Report of the Joint Committee on Women in Parliament*, Parliamentary Paper no. 209 (1996).

Summers, A. 'Women', in Allan Patience and Brian Head (eds), *From Whitlam to Fraser: Reform and Reaction in Australian Politics* (Melbourne: Oxford University Press, 1979) pp. 189–200.

——. *Ducks on the Pond: An Autobiography, 1945–1976* (Ringwood, Vic.: Viking, 1999).

'Tas Houses to clock off at 6 pm', *Canberra Times*, 16 March 1999, p. 5.

Vickers, J. 'Why *Should* Women Care about Federalism?', in D. Brown and J. Hiebert (eds), *Canada: The State of the Federation 1994* (Kingston, Ontario: Institute of Intergovernmental Relations, 1994) pp. 135–51.

Watson, S. (ed.). *Playing the State: Australian Feminist Interventions* (Sydney: Allen & Unwin, 1990).

# 7 Australian Democracy and Indigenous Self-Determination, 1901–2001

*Geoffrey Stokes*

> Australian democracy is genuinely benevolent, but is preoccupied with its own affairs. From time to time it remembers the primitive people whom it has dispossessed, and sheds over their predestined passing an economical tear.
>
> W. K. Hancock, *Australia* (1930: 21).

Beneath the relatively peaceful growth of liberal democracy in the 'settler' democracies of Australia, Canada and New Zealand lies their turbulent, and often violent, political relationship with indigenous peoples. Such difficulties stand out in sharp relief in a Commonwealth of Australia which is often represented as the epitome of peaceful democratic evolution. Although the federal government – building upon previous colonial reforms – pioneered the universal franchise at the national level in 1902, the vote was denied to many Aborigines and Torres Strait Islanders at both state and federal levels until the 1960s. The early Commonwealth laws also denied indigenous peoples[1] access to those systems of social welfare and arbitration that were a mark of a distinctive, albeit limited, Australian social democracy. A primary outcome was their exclusion from the political process and their relegation to the periphery of the capitalist economy and white society. This did not entail an exclusion from institutions. On this 'periphery', particular state institutions and forms of institutionalization had an overwhelming influence over the lives of generations of Aborigines and Torres Strait Islanders. The consequent struggle for equitable and non-discriminatory institutional inclusion marks a distinctive dimension of indigenous politics over the century. Nonetheless, that is not the whole story. In many areas, indigenous people have sought alternative forms of autonomy within, alongside and outside liberal democratic institutions. They have also confronted regular opposition from those who would reverse these gains and introduce new programs of assimilation.

This chapter offers a way of understanding the problematic relationship between Aborigines and Torres Strait Islanders and the institutions of Australian democracy from 1901 to 2001. While many of the facts about indigenous people and their difficult relations with the Australian state are widely known, it is the interpretation and organization of this information into a plausible conceptual or theoretical schema that is often absent. This chapter reflects upon that dilemma, devises a model for comparative inquiry, and applies it to two periods of Australian history, 1901–11 and 1991–2001. The proposed model deploys the concept of a 'domain' to demonstrate the significant political patterns, tendencies or propensities in the evolution of relations between indigenous people and Australian democracy. The chapter identifies three relevant and often overlapping political domains, the domain of *liberal democracy*, the *indigenous* domain and the domain of *protection and segregation*. Each domain delineates a political order and context in which indigenous people have encountered the institutions of the Australian state. I argue that, within each domain, a dominant political tendency or 'political logic' may be discerned that organizes the choices available to indigenous people and that effectively establishes the opportunities for, and constraints upon, them. These three competing and often overlapping tendencies or 'political logics' may be called *liberal inclusion, indigenous self-determination* and *paternalist exclusion*. A key focus will be upon the unfolding of the various citizenship regimes imposed upon indigenous people and their struggles to resist, transform and reshape them. The result is a broad account of indigenous people and the institutions of Australian democracy that may be used as a future research program.

## Theoretical and Conceptual Background

One of the inherent difficulties for an Australian social and political science that wants to contribute to our knowledge of indigenous peoples and democracy is that the problem appears to defy easy understanding and explanation. Because the political relationships between indigenous people and the state did not unfold evenly over the country, or proceed in a linear fashion, it is difficult to make straightforward generalizations about the process. Nor is there any consensus over the kinds of concepts and theories that would be most useful to portray the present situation.[2] Whatever the conceptual or theoretical insight, there always seem to be empirical facts and situations that do not fit. For some, this conclusion is cause for celebration because it is considered that such generalizations can only distort history and even contribute to the oppression of indigenous people. Nonetheless, if it is conceded that accounts that reach beyond particular situations are essential to any worthwhile social analysis and effective collective political action, then the key issues are simply their intellectual plausibility and political utility. That is, do the conclusions bear up under the evidence and does the analysis fulfil its promise of shedding new light on the problem or open up a new research program? In addition, it must be asked whether they enhance or inhibit political projects, such as indigenous political agency or liberal democracy? It is in this regard that generalizations about indigenous people and the institutions of Australian democracy are often found wanting.

Within traditional political science (Bennett, 1989; 1999), for example, it would be tempting to see Aborigines and Torres Strait Islanders simply as one interest group among many, competing for power in a liberal pluralist democracy. Such an approach misses the historical point that for most of the twentieth century, indigenous people were excluded from democratic institutions, and that this may have some bearing upon whether and how they came to assert their interests. For Colin Tatz (1982a: 207), more was to be gained from pursuing rights through the courts than conventional party politics. A Marxist approach based upon political economy allows for a powerful critique of colonialism and the exploitation of indigenous people. Certainly, the concepts of 'internal colonialism' (e.g. Rowley, 1972a: 1–26; Hartwig, 1978; Beckett, 1982; Jennett, 1987: 85) and 'welfare colonialism' (Beckett, 1988; Sackett, 1990) cast some light upon the condition of indigenous people. Nonetheless, these concepts have not escaped criticism for their limitations in explaining key characteristics of indigenous relations with the state (e.g. Peterson, 1998).

With its focus upon the processes of political inclusion, the concept of democratization (Dryzek, 1996) would appear to allow a multi-faceted understanding of indigenous political struggles in a democratic state.[3] Here, conceivably, the theories of social movements (e.g. Touraine, 1985; Offe, 1985) would be relevant to Australia (see Burgmann, 1993), as would related questions about the incorporation of indigenous people into liberal democratic institutions. Yet, much indigenous politics is concerned with escaping the instrumental rationalities of the liberal democratic state, or at least transforming or subverting them. While, for the most part, the imperatives of Australian democracy are widely understood, the complexities of Aboriginal interests are misunderstood or neglected. Where anthropologists have contributed the most detailed and theoretically sophisticated analyses of indigenous culture and politics, these are often focused on discrete groups and regions and, understandably, make few broader claims.

Most of the concepts and theories referred to above *do* provide illuminating insights into indigenous–state relations. Indigenous people are indeed an interest group of sorts, and governments would certainly like them to behave more predictably as one. Various national institutions, such as the National Aboriginal Consultative Committee (1973–77), National Aboriginal Conference (1977–85) and the Aboriginal and

Torres Strait Islander Commission (1989– ), have been established to channel and unify indigenous interests, but the radical differences among indigenous interests have constantly undermined actual and possible political unities. Indigenous people have been exploited industrially (Stevens, 1974; Rowley, 1978: 84–109), and also resisted exploitation,[4] but in many cases, the seasonal conditions of work often fitted in with their social order and cultural inclinations (Rowley, 1978: 89). In some respects, the political struggles of Aborigines and Torres Strait Islanders resemble those of a social movement which has also been incorporated into the Australian state. Yet, various studies have also shown how indigenous people have often adopted key liberal democratic practices and made the institutions work for their own purposes.[5] The question arises of whether there is any plausible way of integrating these insights into a larger story that takes due account of politics, history, culture and economy, and without rendering the account simplistic or inaccurate.

A vital criterion, however, is that any story must also take some account of indigenous views of their situation. When indigenous people claim to be the 'Original Australians' (Patten and Ferguson, 1938: 3), an 'Aboriginal nation' (see Jennett, 1987: 88, fn10) or a 'first nation', and make demands for self-determination, autonomy and territory, this puts Aboriginal and Torres Strait Islander politics into a different category. These identity claims and policies based upon them put indigenous politics outside the usual confines of interest groups, class and social movements, because the political claims are of a higher moral order and they seem to assert a higher priority for settlement. At one level, indigenous politics becomes an exercise in ethno-nationalism and this characteristic also puts a premium on successfully engaging in symbolic politics. For example, indigenous people must necessarily establish their claims on the basis of radical reassessments of history and these revisions are not always palatable to those who have benefited from that history. The so-called 'black armband' view of history threatens dominant perceptions of national status and achievement, and is hotly contested. Part of the intense conflict around indigenous politics therefore arises from attempts to reject the more radical agendas and reduce the claims to more mundane ones. The model proposed below is intended go part of the way towards an analysis that meets the criteria of conceptual plausibility, factual accuracy and regard for indigenous perspectives.

## Theory: Domains, Political Logic and Identities

The term 'domain' allows for a multi-dimensional understanding of the evolution of Aborigines and Torres Strait Islanders and liberal democratic institutions, which also incorporates indigenous political standpoints. Currently, the word domain is widely used in a non-technical way in social theory to denote a place or site of action, or a sphere of influence or activity. In its older meaning, however, the term referred specifically to the 'complete and absolute' ownership of land or territory (Webster, 1977). One's domain was literally an area over which one could exercise dominion. The link between influence and land is implied in the use of the word in a select Australian literature on Aboriginal relations with white Australians (von Sturmer, 1984; Trigger, 1986; Rowse, 1992). While acknowledging my debt to the anthropological literature, I would like to use the term in the broader sense, as a sphere of influence or activity, but allowing for the possibility of this including land or territory.

My main concern here, however, is with *political* domains. These comprise institutional, geographical and even temporal sites and spaces in which power, authority and language are exercised in ways that shape political options and decisions. Each political domain comprises a set of values, institutions and practices, as well as various assumptions about its constituent political actors, and 'policies' – actual or implied – that guide the conduct of social and political life. In this regard, I am most concerned with assumptions about the capacities of political actors. For example, within each domain there is a predominant view of Aboriginal identity that shapes particular normative goals and prescribes means for achieving them. These different conceptions and definitions of Aboriginal identity are crucial to both the official institutional practices and 'unofficial' Aboriginal politics. As others and I have discussed before (Stokes, 1997: 5), depending upon the nature of the identity, individuals and groups can legitimate claims to certain rights and require the performance of obligations.[6]

Another way of representing a political domain is to say that it comprises a field of political forces or propensities that may or may not be realised.[7] Within each domain, it is conjectured that there is a dominant political tendency or 'logic', based upon certain conceptions of identity and oriented towards a particular set of values or objectives. That is, in a particular domain, the dominant political logic works towards certain political outcomes and in so doing it tends to influence the nature of political identity and the structure of choices available. Nonetheless, there is no inevitability about achieving a political result because of the influence of countervailing tendencies within a domain or those emanating from other domains.[8] Indeed, this model hopes to show how particular political propensities are deflected and changed.

In some respects, this account of a domain and its political logic depicts the 'situational logic',[9] regarded as central to explanation in social science, but one that has a more dynamic character. Although the domain and its primary political logic enable description and explanation, it also indicates the sources of certain kinds of prescription. In one sense, these political logics provide rudimentary theories that can be used to guide inquiries into institutional evolution and the politics surrounding it. Here we can discern relatively coherent political agendas, as well as policies and institutional programs, and also why some were attained and others were not. It is proposed that, through establishing the character of these domains, their associated political logics, and the interaction between them, we may understand a little more about the reshaping of those Australian institutions that bear upon the lives and politics of indigenous people.

For the purposes of this chapter, I identify three political domains of acute significance for indigenous people and the institutions of Australian democracy. It is contended that the problems of indigenous politics in Australia may be better understood with reference to the interaction between the domain of *liberal democracy*, the *indigenous* domain, and the domain of *protection and segregation*. The various projects for indigenous self-determination are inherently influenced and shaped by the logics of inclusion, and paternalist exclusion, for example, which are characteristic of the other domains.

In the anthropological literature on domains, generally there is reference only to two somewhat independent domains, those pertaining to Aborigines and the white settlers. If we apply the concept to indigenous politics, however, it is evident that there exists a third political domain which indigenous people occupy, but which was originally constructed by white settler democracy as a means of dealing with the special characteristics of indigenous social and economic life. Rowse (1992: 35), for example, writes of balances being struck between the Aboriginal domain and 'welfare colonialism'.[10] On my account, it may perhaps be more useful to portray it as a balance being struck at the intersection of the indigenous domain, the liberal democratic domain, *and* that of protection and segregation. Where welfare colonialism is part of the political logic of liberal (and social) democracy, it is implemented in a domain previously dominated by protectionist institutions, and in which indigenous people adapt the programs to their own cultural needs.

Similarly, contributors to public debates often assume that there are only two main contending domains and interests, those of indigenous people and self-determination and those of liberal democracy and inclusion. This lack of differentiation serves distinct political purposes. A major objective for certain elites, for example, is to reject the very existence, influence, or legitimacy of any domain other than that of liberal democracy. Great effort is put into trying to render invisible or illegitimate the continuing effects of other domains in which Aborigines and

Torres Strait Islanders have lived. One effect of this is to re-establish the political conditions of paternalism and exclusion that provoked earlier indigenous quests for self-determination.

Such conceptual schemes necessarily oversimplify the intricacies of history and politics. Nonetheless, these categories may contribute to a better understanding of the shifting contours and layers of Aboriginal politics within Australian political institutions.[11]

*The Domain of Liberal Democracy*

The formation of the Commonwealth of Australia in 1901 constituted the creation of a new federal, political domain, comprising formal constitution, liberal democratic institutions, values and practices. Building upon colonial democratic precedents, this national *domain of liberal democracy* put a premium on political equality among citizens. Ideally, it consisted of instruments for (a) protecting the legal and political rights of individuals, such as the common law, the constitution, and legal statute, and (b) selecting governments that have authority over citizens, which is then exercised through the instruments of the state. In Australia, the federal system also ensured that sovereignty was divided between the Commonwealth and the states.

Through Section 51 (xxvi), the original constitution prohibited the Commonwealth from making special laws for 'aboriginal natives' and effectively left power over indigenous people with the states. In addition, the states, through their 'residual powers', were awarded constitutional jurisdiction over land. This fact and the condition of divided sovereignty had a significant influence upon the evolution of relations between indigenous people and the state, largely to the detriment of the former.

Traditionally, clear boundaries are drawn between the political domain and other domains, such as the economy, civil society, family and religion, where different, sometimes more authoritarian, values may rule. In one version of its ideal form, liberal democracy prescribes no great content to social or religious life; it is simply a neutral process or political method. For example, because the founders valued religious pluralism and toleration, the Commonwealth constitution maintains a clear separation between church and state (Section 116). Yet, through a combination of social liberal and social democratic initiatives considered necessary to protect and advance democracy, Australian governments also implemented extensive social, economic and cultural policies that extended the rights of individuals beyond those of basic civil, legal and political rights. This trend has allowed the development of public policies that give general support to life in the private sphere of family and community, but also to the formation of large, hierarchical bureaucracies, such as in the fields of health and social security.[12]

The instruments of government (bureaucracy) and law (courts) are also supposed to operate impartially and impersonally according to strict, formal rules of procedure. That is, the dominant imperative is that of instrumental rationality. The objective is to ensure that political decisions are made fairly, on the basis of their contribution to the wider public good, and not on the basis of friendships, family ties, or any arbitrary personal inclinations. If members of governments were to bestow favours upon close family or kin or friends, this would usually be regarded as a form of political corruption, open to prosecution and punishment.

Ultimately, Australian governments are supposed to be publicly accountable through parliament and elections, to the people, understood as individual citizens. The primary political identity is a civic one concerned with the public good and whose loyalty to Australia (or Australia and Great Britain) is supposed to over-ride any religious, ethnic or racial commitments.[13] Citizens are encouraged to participate actively in politics, primarily by voting in national or state elections. Given that elections only occur every three or four years, participation by ordinary citizens is minimal. Intense political participation occurs primarily among the leaders of parties, factions, movements or interest groups who compete over the resources of the state and its capacity to regulate economic and social activity. This feature puts a premium upon dealing with those who can speak for their groups or constituencies.

Following colonial precedents, early in the history of the Commonwealth, only certain kinds of people, usually whites, were deemed to have the capacities for democratic citizenship. As a consequence of later political struggles, however, this liberal democratic political domain gradually expanded the types of people who could be officially designated as citizens (Chinese, Aborigines). Such a process may be categorized as one of *liberal inclusion*, in which previously excluded groups are given entry into liberal democratic institutions, and then begin to participate in them. This process of inclusion involved not only the granting of votes, but often also legal rights and other institutional and material resources.

This political logic of inclusion works primarily towards the protection and reproduction of liberal democracy. While the peaceful expression of criticism is regarded as legitimate, the system functions to manage and absorb dissent through the application of common liberal democratic procedures. The outcome is generally the incorporation or assimilation of deep political differences into democratic and bureaucratic practices, guided by established principles of procedural justice and instrumental rationality. In the main, liberal democratic politics is conducted by political leaders with the power and authority to negotiate issues. The main features of this domain are represented diagrammatically in Figure 7.1 below.

**DOMAIN of LIBERAL DEMOCRACY**

*identity* – active civic identities, individual and group

*policies* – political reproduction = incorporation, integration, assimilation

*institutions* – liberal democratic, federal, hybrids

*political logic* – inclusion, participation, representation, public accountability, instrumental rationality

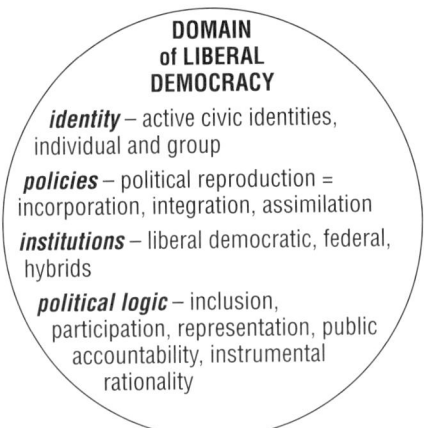

**Figure 7.1**

For indigenous people, the logic of inclusion tends to produce particular political and social outcomes. The general citizenship regime for Aborigines and Torres Strait Islanders remains a liberal democratic one that is little different from that of the rest of the society. This process of liberal inclusion tends to require the political assimilation of indigenous people into the prevailing values and practices of Australian citizenship. Indeed, one tendency, associated with the interests of the liberal democratic state, is to incorporate the newly included groups and remould them into compliant civic actors. The political disposition here is still to reshape the indigenous domain and make it conform better to established forms of political and administrative rationality. Regimes of consultation and indigenous self-management are characteristic of this political logic.

*The Indigenous Domain*

Before the arrival of the white settlers, Aborigines and Torres Strait Islanders lived in politically autonomous and self-determining communities. Although they would not have used such labels, there is no overwhelming reason why these terms cannot be applied to describe their original situation. Certainly, the indigenous peoples lived within their own distinctive institutions of culture, religion and politics, oriented towards the reproduction of their material life and society. These institutions provided continuity and the means for maintaining order, but were rarely recognized as such by early Europeans. Central to their way of life were kinship relations, attachment to – ownership and guardianship – of land, and a philosophy where the interests of the group took precedence over those of the individuals comprising it. Aboriginal people lived in societies that required each member to take seriously their responsibilities to kin and clan as well as religious obligations to the land. Aboriginal identities were largely determined by systems of kinship and attachments to land that were local and regional.

Although we can have no direct knowledge of Aboriginal politics before the invasions, there is sufficient evidence from later observers and studies of Aboriginal life in areas where the older values remained strong, to construct a broad framework of tendencies. There seems to be a convergence of opinion among anthropologists that in traditional Aboriginal communities there were no 'enduring hierarchies of authority for the administration of public affairs' (Hiatt, 1986: 10). That is, there was no political leadership of the kind evident in liberal democracies, where, by virtue of one's place, role, status and authority in a hierarchy, one could give orders and expect obedience. If significant decisions affecting the community had to be made, they were generally discussed and determined by the whole group. For many observers there was a strong egalitarianism in indigenous political life (Ibid: 11).

Although no exclusively political instutitions existed, social control or authority was exercised through the institutions of religion and kinship. In some areas, the competition for scarce resources and efforts to enhance reputations, usually among senior males, led to the emergence of 'big men' or 'bosses' who could speak on behalf of the group. Furthermore, there was a tendency towards gerontocracy where 'senior males exercise a degree of domination over junior males and females, especially in the sphere of religion' (Hiatt, 1986: 11). Generally, however, the practice of speaking on behalf of others was not encouraged. Although there was evidence of hierarchy based upon religious status, this did not usually translate into an *enduring* secular authority. There was, for example, no equivalent to the state – an institution that has a monopoly of force – in traditional Aboriginal society (Maddock, 1973: 182).

For Hiatt (1986: 12–13) it is more accurate to note that there are strong tendencies towards both egalitarianism and authoritarianism, and that the stress upon equal moral worth tends to inhibit the tendency towards selfishness, self-importance and ambition. He also suggests that in relations with whites the egalitarian tendency works against the 'emergence of black political leaders', while the religious authoritarianism may tend to encourage 'a ready acceptance of paternalism emanating from an external source', such as a white 'boss'. Where state institutions have intervened to formalize certain land ownership rights, a new type of 'big man' has come to prominence, who is not as responsive to the egalitarian tendencies (Ibid: 12, 15).

Further content may be given to the concept of an indigenous domain based upon its use in anthropological studies that seek to depict and explain relations between black and white Australians. Von Sturmer (1984: 219), for example, distinguishes between the Aboriginal and European domains. He has used the term to describe remote areas,

> in which the dominant social life and culture are Aboriginal, where the major language or languages are Aboriginal, where the dominant religion and world views are Aboriginal, where the system of knowledge is Aboriginal; in short where the resident Aboriginal population constitutes the public.

Nonetheless, the concept can include further dimensions beyond place, such as the often diminished physical spaces and times in which Aboriginal people maintained their autonomy while under white control. Drawing upon ethnographic studies, Rowse (1992: 100) describes this domain as 'a structure of political relations, of honour and indebtedness, of the relatively unfettered use of time'. The concept was devised to describe the features of Aboriginal life in isolated regions populated predominantly by Aboriginal people, which he calls 'Aboriginal enclaves' (Ibid: 21). Nevertheless, the concept may be extended to describe the traditions and practices that were retained and developed by indigenous people of mixed descent, who formed historical associations to land outside those regions, and especially in urban areas.

As Rowse (1992: 19) points out, the term can also incorporate a normative dimension that prescribes a political agenda for Aboriginal people. From this perspective, a central political objective has been that of protecting the indigenous domain. Engaging in resistance to white incursions into their way of life has been central and the goals have ranged from seeking to exclude whites from the indigenous domain to the regulation of their entry into it. The political agenda also included efforts to extend Aboriginal traditions, values and ways of communicating into other, primarily white, domains. This is not to claim that there is absolute continuity or unanimity among indigenous people about what constitutes their domain and the political agendas appropriate to it. It is simply to say that this domain provides the principal context in which indigenous people pursue autonomy and determine their political objectives. Where this occurs we may apply the term 'indigenous self-determination'. An outline of the indigenous domain may be found in Figure 7.2 below.

In the face of white invasion and settlement, a crucial political task for indigenous people has been to retain and protect their older values, institutions and lands, or at least their historical memory and adaptation of them. Where indigenous traditions and practices are dominant, we

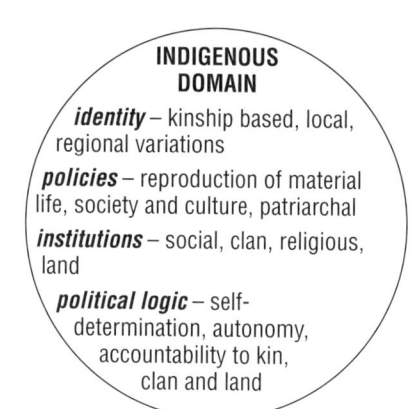

```
        INDIGENOUS
         DOMAIN
  identity – kinship based, local,
  regional variations
  policies – reproduction of material
  life, society and culture, patriarchal
  institutions – social, clan, religious,
  land
  political logic – self-
    determination, autonomy,
    accountability to kin,
      clan and land
```

**Figure 7.2**

may still apply the term *indigenous domain* and identify an associated political logic of self-determination oriented towards the reproduction of material life, society and culture. Further, the indigenous domains are not static but dynamic. Indigenous people have adjusted imaginatively to new conditions, and in so doing they have created new layers of meaning that have given even richer significance to the lands on which they lived (Goodall, 1996: 103).

In normative terms, criteria for indigenous self-determination may be found by assessing the extent to which the policies, institutions and practices enlarge the indigenous political domain or not. That is, indigenous self-determination may be evaluated against its potential to expand the places, spaces and times in which indigenous people can exercise their collective autonomy. It has to be said that there would be many different ways in which indigenous people would interpret autonomy and what it would require. This account does not make any moral judgement on indigenous practices. It simply acknowledges that the indigenous domain, which, depending upon the period, may be actually very small, is one in which indigenous perspectives and values prevail.

*The Domain of Protection and Segregation*

Again building upon colonial practices, all levels of Australian governments either sanctioned or created a second domain specifically for Aboriginal people, which we shall call the *domain of protection and segregation*.[14] Whereas this domain appeared to be one existing inside liberal democracy, for all intents and purposes, it had an autonomy untouched by liberal democratic values and practices. In many respects, it comprised a set of 'total institutions' (Goffman 1968), distinguished by the autocratic rule of officials or mission employees. Once the domain was created, the policies and the officials carrying them out became virtually impervious to criticism or reform, either from below and/or from above. For decades, the institutional regimes governing Aboriginal people were largely unaccountable to liberal democratic governments or parliaments (see Kidd, 1997). The State Protection Boards and their officials, for example, played a disproportionate, authoritarian and often brutal role in radically restricting Aboriginal social and political choices. Unlike in the domain of liberal democracy, there was also no accountability to those who were being governed and administered.

From the perspective of the Australian state, the political logic that best describes the values and practices oriented towards indigenous people during the first part of the twentieth century is the logic of *paternalist exclusion*.[15] The state policies and institutions were predominantly *exclusionist* because they functioned to prevent indigenous people from participating in the institutions of liberal democratic government or having access to social security benefits. Through official policies such as protection and segregation, indigenous people were denied citizenship rights and institutionally confined to state reserves under the power and surveillance of local managers and police.

This political logic was directed at the two major categories of Aborigines, the so-called 'full-bloods' or tribal Aborigines, and those of mixed race. Two different policies, either segregation or assimilation, were applied, based on the putative condition or capacities of these two categories of indigenous people. Underpinning these policies were racialist theories and mistaken beliefs that Aboriginal people did not have the capacities for citizenship. At worst, Aborigines were widely viewed as objects, largely devoid of humanity, and deserving elimination. At best, they were regarded as childlike creatures largely incapable of rational, autonomous thought and action. For tribal Aborigines, segregation was intended to protect them during the time it took the race to die out.

Those of mixed race were thought minimally capable of participating in white society and many of them were subjected to a policy of forced assimilation. The main strategy was to remove such children from indigenous families and place them in state institutions and white families so that they could learn to participate in the larger white society and economy. Over time, however, it was also thought and hoped that all trace of 'colour' would be bred out. For both the 'full-blood' Aborigines and those of mixed race, the policy was one of hastening the inevitable demise of race and culture. On such grounds, some would argue, these programs were attempts to bring about the ultimate exclusion of indigenous people, namely, their genocide (see Gaita, 1997; Reynolds, 2001).

The policies and the institutions were *paternalist* in the sense of treating Aborigines as people whose views ought to be ignored, and who needed to be guided by officials and others who claimed superior knowledge and judgement.[16] It is arguable that the strategy of incarceration, both as a general and specific strategy, was central to the preservation of this domain. To maintain order, the state laws established new categories of offences only applicable to indigenous people. According to Tatz (1979: 50), these included: 'drinking, leaving a reserve, entering one when barred, intermarrying, refusing to work, being cheeky, writing salacious letters to a boy/girl-friend, committing adultery, playing cards'. Those found 'guilty' of such offences were subject to a range of penalties such as fines, forced manual labour, confinement, or expulsion from the community.

Under these circumstances, citizenship for Aboriginal and Torres Strait Islanders was primarily a minimal legal and administrative category that enabled state governments to implement policies that were almost universally authoritarian, discriminatory and oppressive. Often, within this domain, Aborigines were forbidden to speak their native languages and their previous cultural practices were prohibited. In effect, the state aimed to draw more sharply the boundaries of the indigenous domain, reduce indigenous 'sovereignty' over important areas of life, constrain the autonomy of those living within it, and thus severely limit the scope of the choices that could be made. The concept of 'internal colonialism' (Beckett, 1982; Jennett, 1987: 85) has been widely deployed to describe the combination of governmental and economic tendencies within this domain. The definition by Beckett (1982: 132) of the 'internal colony' as 'a region or enclave, which is exploited and controlled from without through a set of distinctive institutions' indicates the general characteristics of this domain. For a summary representation see Figure 7.3 below.

**DOMAIN of PROTECTION and SEGREGATION**

*identity* – passive, narrow legal and administrative category

*policies* – hastening the inevitable demise of the race and culture

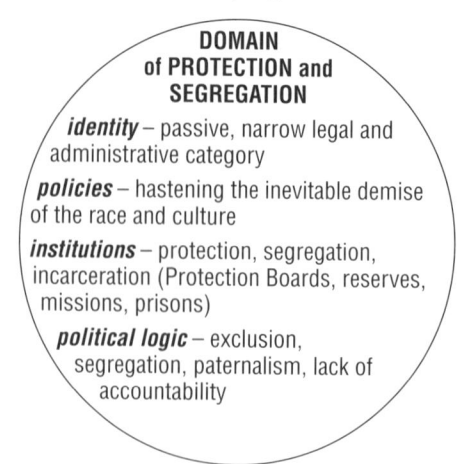

*institutions* – protection, segregation, incarceration (Protection Boards, reserves, missions, prisons)

*political logic* – exclusion, segregation, paternalism, lack of accountability

**Figure 7.3**

Few political options were available to Aborigines under this regime, apart from escape, withdrawal or resistance. (By maintaining their languages and practices in secret, they often retained a residual cultural autonomy.) For those removed from the protection of family and community, the only options were the dangerous ones of individual defiance and escape, both of which risked physical retribution. Given this context, the dominant objectives of early Aboriginal political struggles were to establish the conditions in which Aborigines could regain political autonomy with the aim of recovering and expanding the indigenous domain. Generally, this required trying to enter and reform the liberal democratic domain of the Australian polity. A key means to this end was to attain the civil, legal and political status of full citizenship in Australian democracy, and to secure equal opportunities to exercise their social and economic rights.

For indigenous peoples, inclusion could be pursued by engaging in acts of resistance to exclusionist policies, developing a political voice in the liberal democratic public sphere, campaigning against discrimination and seeking to gain representation in or alongside liberal democratic institutions. The primary task was to persuade government authorities that they were capable of responsible citizenship and to acquire all those rights that are held by other citizens. Where official forms of indigenous representation are granted, the logic of liberal inclusion entails a politics oriented towards, and influenced by, liberal democratic institutions. To the extent that indigenous citizenship is no longer simply a legal and administrative category, and allows for citizenship as a practice, it would amount to a significant advance upon the situation under paternalist exclusion.

On this account, indigenous politics emanating from this domain is marked by two major features. First, the orientation towards inclusion tends to produce political features, such as authoritative political leadership and means of political communication, which are valued and rewarded by liberal democracy. In this domain, the quest for indigenous self-determination is resolutely liberal democratic in character and always runs the risk of incorporation. Yet, in addition to gaining citizenship rights, the tendency towards self-determination also has the potential to become an instrument for recovering an indigenous way of life and culture, and a politics that is not necessarily liberal democratic.

A second more negative tendency arises, however, from the extension of other citizens' rights, which tend to reinforce the political logic of paternalism and exclusion. The award of rights to social security has often had uneven and deleterious effects for indigenous people in remote regions, in that it established a welfare economy that encouraged strong patterns of economic dependence. When applied to communities previously under the sway of protection, this 'welfare colonialism' (Beckett, 1988: 4), which originated with policies of liberal democratic inclusion, also shifted the dynamics of the indigenous domain. Further, the psychological and social damage inflicted on Aboriginal people by 'protective' institutions encouraged self-destructive behaviour, such as alcohol abuse. When combined with government neglect of basic service provision, these factors contributed to a self-perpetuating cycle of poverty and despair that has often limited the capacity to engage effectively in liberal democratic political struggles.

*Political Implications*

One of the aims of this conceptualization is to demonstrate more clearly the complex interactions between diverse political tendencies. For example, all three tendencies or logics may be evident at the same time, in tension or struggle with each other, but at any particular time, one tendency is likely to be stronger than the others.[17] Depending upon the time of day, their physical or institutional location, or interests, indigenous people may also regularly move from one domain to another and literally live in three different worlds. Some individuals and groups may feel more comfortable or resigned to life primarily in just one domain, only participating in the others when absolutely necessary. For a representation of this complexity, see Figure 7.4, which indicates areas of overlap between the domains.

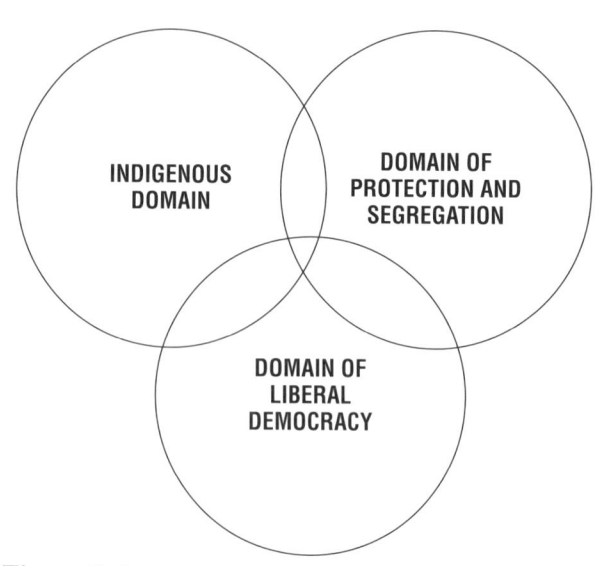

**Figure 7.4**

Although this conceptual scheme may not capture all the dimensions of democratization, as it relates to indigenous people in Australia, we may usefully apply it to demonstrate historically the conflicting imperatives evident in the process. I will now explore these issues with reference to policies and institutions of both the Commonwealth and the states in the first and last decades of the twentieth century. This comparative case study is not based on original research but relies heavily on the previous empirical work done by Colin Tatz, Bain Attwood, Andrew Markus, Heather Goodall, Ros Kidd, John Chesterman and Brian Galligan, among others. Nonetheless, certain preliminary conclusions may be reached about democratization. Perhaps predictably, there is no uniform or linear progression of policies and institutions. They vary marginally among the states and in the Commonwealth, and Aboriginal responses also differ according to their citizenship status and whether they lived in closer, settled areas or in the more distant outback areas. More important, certain patterns are discernible in the relations between the three domains and the relative strengths of their respective political logics.

## 1901–1911

By Federation, official estimates put the number of indigenous people at about 77,000 (Chesterman and Galligan, 1997: 63), and they constituted a very small minority in the larger population of 3,765,300. By far the largest numbers were in Queensland, the Northern Territory, and in Western Australia, if one uses consistent criteria of both 'full-blood' and mixed race. Furthermore, the dominant legal assumption that Australia was *terra nullius*, land belonging to no-one, had been reaffirmed a number of times in the colonial period (Reynolds, 1989: 66–8), leaving no apparent grounds for indigenous peoples to claim ownership rights to their land, unless through individual purchase. The original assumption was that the indigenous people would die out and public policies and institutions were devised to accommodate that inevitability. Over this period we can see the formal demarcation and consolidation of the domains of liberal democracy and protection, with a corresponding tendency to narrow the scope of the indigenous domain. The intention in establishing these boundaries was to ensure that they were not easily crossed.

### *Domain of Liberal Democracy*

In the domain of liberal democracy, white perceptions of Aboriginal identity, backed by a bowdlerized evolutionism, were crucial in influencing the policies adopted, as well as the design and administration of institutions. For example, Aborigines were widely regarded as a dying race, Stone Age remnants unable to survive in the modern world. Accordingly, the policy was to protect them through segregation and thus 'smooth the dying pillow' (Bolton, 1982: 59), although 'hastening the inevitable' might be a more accurate description. During the period of protection and segregation, Aborigines were widely considered to be less than human or with, at best, limited ability to learn. It was thought that Aborigines could not assume the civic identity and competence needed for democratic political participation. Nor were they considered to have the abilities necessary for regular employment. Furthermore, the classification of Aborigines by blood provided a basis for policy and administration. Their official identity was widely categorized in crude racial terms with reference to 'Aboriginal natives' who were 'full-blood' and 'half-castes', 'quadroons' and 'octoroons'. According to Gardener-Garden (2000: 1), 'till the late 1950s States regularly legislated all forms of inclusion and exclusion (to and from benefits, rights, places, etc.) by reference to degrees of Aboriginal blood'. Such assumptions provided the rationale both for exclusion from liberal democracy and paternalism within the state institutions charged with regulating Aborigines.

Within the liberal democratic domain, Aborigines were expressly prohibited from voting in Queensland and Western Australia, and other impediments made it difficult to claim the vote in most other colonies (Chesterman and Galligan, 1997: 66). These restrictions were carried over into the new federal system of government. Where two sections of the Commonwealth constitution appeared to complete their political exclusion from the nation, another offered to some the promise of inclusion. Section 51 (xxvi) empowered the federal parliament to make laws with respect to the 'people of any race, other than the aboriginal race in any state' and section 127 excluded Aboriginal natives from being counted in the census. Nonetheless, Section 41 of the constitution left open the possibility of Aborigines retaining the vote, where they had held it under state laws. Designed to protect the rights of women who had the vote in South Australia and Western Australia, it read:

No adult person who has or acquires a right to vote at elections for the more numerous House of the Parliament of a State shall, while the right continues, be prevented by any law of the Commonwealth from voting at elections for either House of the Parliament of the Commonwealth. [cited in Saunders, 1997: 43]

Even where Aborigines had been entitled to vote by state laws, many were later disenfranchised by administrative decisions and by narrow interpretations of this section (Stretton and Finnemore, 1993). The passing of the *Commonwealth Franchise Act 1902* also excluded Aborigines from voting and thus confirmed the 'worst practice' of the states (Chesterman and Galligan, 1997: 7). Consequently, although Aboriginal people were

British subjects, they could only have a very restricted Australian civic identity and certainly, they had few of the citizens' rights accorded to whites, either at the state or federal level.

Commonwealth policies largely followed previous state precedents and confirmed the exclusion of Aboriginal people in the areas and territories under its control (Chesterman and Galligan, 1997: 6–7). For example, political discrimination was complemented by social and economic discrimination. At first through specific Commonwealth laws (Ibid: 85–6), and later through a complex system of administrative rules based upon judgements of race and colour, social security payments, such as invalid and old-age pensions and maternity allowances, were denied to Aborigines. Elsewhere, the unregulated Aboriginal labour on outback stations resulted in economic exploitation. On outback cattle stations, Aboriginal men often worked as stockmen, but were remunerated largely with rations. When wages began to be paid, in the 1930s, these were well below award rates.[18]

In this period, the political logic of inclusion proceeded only up to certain limits set by laws based on erroneous assumptions about indigenous capacities for citizenship. As a result, indigenous people were deprived not only of political rights, but also rights to social security. We may portray the first decade after Federation as one in which Stanner's (1968: 18) phrase 'the great Australian silence' can be given a crucial political dimension. For it is during these years that Australian governments practically completed the disenfranchisement of indigenous people and made them virtually irrelevant to the liberal democratic domain. Such a context created the impetus towards the indigenous peoples' quest for inclusion.

*Indigenous Domain*

Only in the most outlying and isolated regions, such as Central Australia, Arnhem Land, the Pilbara, the Kimberley, Cape York and Torres Strait, could indigenous people have avoided regular interaction with white settlers and officials. Nonetheless, as we have seen above, there is sufficient evidence to indicate that indigenous ways of life, values and practices remained strong in many remote areas and to a lesser extent in more settled regions. Even where indigenous people were in regular interaction with, or even direct supervision by whites, key elements of their polity and society survived and flourished.

Aborigines working in the outback pastoral economy still continued their own ways of life. Certainly, in the more closely settled regions, where dispossession had been largely completed, a generation of indigenous people would have grown up in close contact with whites and taken on many of the skills, values and attitudes needed to survive in a modern economy. There is abundant evidence of indigenous communities successfully working farms on reserved lands and outside them (Goodall, 1996: 98–103). Many older Aborigines, however, would have lived a great part of their lives within indigenous social institutions that were marginally touched by the white liberal democratic domain. To this extent, their identities, social relations and politics remained determined by kinship, and followed the lines indicated in the general discussion of the indigenous domain above.

In the remote areas, one strategy was to try to incorporate whites into their culture and so bring them within the sphere of indigenous kin relations. By including whites within their networks of status and obligation there was a possibility of exerting some control over them. Indigenous politics in such regions included acts of resistance to incursions into their territory, society and economy. That whites in remote regions still resorted to violence, 'punitive expeditions' and massacre well into the twentieth century (Rowley, 1972b: 237) is partial testimony to the resilient presence of Aboriginal society and culture in the indigenous domain. In this struggle for control, however, the superior physical resources of the official institutions of the state tended to prevail.

For the more settled regions, we may draw on Goodall's account of Aboriginal engagement with liberal democracy in the late nineteenth century and extrapolate it into the early years of the twentieth. Goodall (1996: 76–7) explains how Aborigines in colonial New South Wales after about 1850 adapted three types of political strategy to secure land.[19] They made direct representation to government and newspapers; they recruited white allies or advocates from local police, priests or missionaries; and by simply reoccupying their lands they resorted to direct action. Furthermore, Goodall (1996: 101) stresses that such campaigns were not just to gain security of land for economic self-sufficiency, but were directly intended to regain traditional areas. Nor did these activists abandon their indigenous identity, but retained key elements of traditional ceremony and ritual for decades into the twentieth century. Although they had to survive in a capitalist economy, their priorities were also determined by indigenous values.

### Domain of Protection and Segregation

By 1901, most Aborigines had come under some greater or lesser form of protection initiated by the colonial governments (Chesterman and Galligan, 1997: 64). All states, by 1911, except Tasmania where it was presumed that Aborigines had died out, had enacted laws to impose protection. Aborigines lived under the guardianship of official 'protectors' and in most states 'Protection Boards'. State institutions generally based their policies, laws and programs upon the judgements of Aboriginal capacity referred to above, as well as arbitrary conferrals of identity. Within these institutions, Aborigines were forced to live under highly oppressive social and economic conditions.

The protection laws imposed severe restrictions upon the movement of Aborigines, their choice of employment, their remuneration rates, as well as access to and use of their money and property. The sale of alcohol (and opium) to Aborigines was also prohibited. As the literature in life under 'protection' shows, Aborigines were subject to harsh institutional regimes in which arbitrary decisions were the rule, and in which there was no means of appeal against such decisions (Tatz, 1982b: 29). This ensured that generations of Aborigines came to live under conditions amounting to incarceration and imprisonment for life. Charles Rowley (1980: 236), for example, has described life under protection as similar to that of a 'refugee camp'. Nonetheless, the Christian missions often served to shield indigenous people from the worst excesses of white society.

The institutional regime of protection was intended to protect full-blood or tribal Aborigines from the predations of Europeans and Chinese and to restrict miscegenation. Those of mixed descent, who could be expected to survive in white society, were to be removed from their families in full-blood or tribal society and encouraged to integrate into the mainstream. One of the assumptions was that all trace of colour would disappear after a certain number of generations of interbreeding with whites. Those of mixed descent were therefore removed from their parents and placed in the homes of white families or orphanages, where the females were 'trained' to be domestic workers and the males apprenticed into a trade. One of the aims was to ensure that such children did not learn any of their original language and culture, so enabling them to assimilate better into white society. For those living under protection, their choice of marriage partner was also strictly controlled to maintain racial purity.

Such acts were sanctioned by legislation and carried out by individuals working for the institutions of 'protection'. The history of Aboriginal politics in New South Wales by Goodall (1996) is again instructive. In 1911, the Aborigines Protection Board began to lease out reserve land in order to finance its programs for removing children of mixed descent from Aboriginal reserves (Ibid: 120–1). So began a further erosion of security for Aboriginal occupation of land, stimulated also by growing demands for land from white farmers. This pressure intensified with the return of soldiers from World War I and the state government's creation of a Returned Servicemen's Settlement Scheme in 1917.[20] These pressures contributed to a 'second dispossession', as Goodall (1996: 125) terms it, which also coincided with an expansion of segregationist policies and actions.

Because Aborigines had so few legal and political rights and resources, they could only deploy relatively limited political strategies. As outlined above, Aborigines pressed their claims on government by recruiting allies, writing letters, submitting petitions and making direct representations. They argued for more land and resources, and against their removal from the land they currently occupied, and they also requested the return of their children.[21] Aborigines campaigned on their own and sometimes with assistance of white sympathizers. All their appeals had to be put in the language and discourse of white liberal democracy, but none of their representations required official response or action, and very little was given.

In some circumstances direct action was the only option. Aborigines engaged in passive resistance (Lippman, 1991: 17–19) by refusing to co-operate with white management. In many places, Aborigines refused to move off their land and, when forcibly removed, they often returned and re-established their communities. Although these actions represented a struggle for autonomy, neither active nor passive resistance held much prospect of changing the institutional conditions under which Aborigines lived.

From the 1920s, Aboriginal people increasingly sought to change government policy by deploying more conventional liberal democratic tactics. These included challenging Protection Board orders through the courts, agitating to enrol their children in local schools, publicizing their case in local newspapers, writing letters and organizing petitions calling for governments to recognize both their rights to citizenship and to land. Such activities were part of an Aboriginal political movement to gain more autonomy and control over their lives. It also indicates an intensified process of liberal inclusion, but often in terms that set out a claim for difference. That is, implicit and explicit in their claims was an understanding of Aborigines as prior owners of the land.

From this brief account it is clear that the dominant political logic during this period was the exclusion and segregation of indigenous people from mainstream Australian politics and society. This imperative entailed the complementary practice of paternalism. Aborigines' views on what they wanted were routinely ignored or dismissed. Accordingly, most Aborigines held the status of captive subjects rather than free citizens. Even where Aborigines held the legal status of citizen, other laws commonly curtailed those citizens' rights and reduced them to an inferior civic category, similar to that of children or the mentally ill. There were few options available to indigenous people and their sympathizers to win legal or political reform.

Over the period 1901–11 we can observe the nation-wide formation of a closed, political domain of protection and segregation that was intended to encompass most Aborigines in Australia. The political logic of this domain operated relentlessly to restrict the autonomy of the indigenous domain. The most powerful political pressures emanated from the domain of protection and segregation in which the dynamics of paternalist exclusion were being confirmed and extended. The policies of segregation were state initiated and administered through institutions designed either to segregate blacks from whites, or for preparing suitable children of mixed descent for entry into white society. This state of affairs withstood most attempts at reform and accountability until the 1950s when new policies were implemented, albeit slowly and unevenly, that encouraged assimilation.

Although Aborigines had the vote in a few states at Federation, their franchise was gradually eroded by administrative means. Citizenship for the 'Aboriginal native' was primarily a legal category that allowed their segregation and control. Although many indigenous people lived according to their traditional ways, few escaped the administrative hand of government. There is little evidence of sustained political activism by indigenous people in the domain of liberal democracy until the 1920s. Over the later period of the 1950s and 1960s, the propensity towards liberal inclusion came to prominence and indigenous people came increasingly to operate effectively in the liberal democratic domain. In 1962, the Commonwealth finally repealed the discriminatory provisions of the Commonwealth Electoral Act and enfranchised all indigenous people. Nonetheless, until 1983 enrolment was made voluntary instead of compulsory, as it was for other citizens (Chesterman and Galligan, 1997: 162).[22] At the same time that the political logic of liberal inclusion seemed to be sweeping all before it, many indigenous people were looking beyond reforms in the domain of liberal democracy to envisage a recovery of the indigenous domain and more radical forms of self-determination.

## 1991–2001

According to official census figures, by 1991, the numbers of indigenous people increased to 265,458, though they still remained a small 1.6 per cent of the total population of Australia (Gaminiratne, 1994: 889). By the 1996 census, 352,970 people (2.1 per cent of the total population) identified as indigenous, which was a 33 per cent increase on the previous census, due both to an increase in self-identification and an increased birthrate (HREOC, 2001: 1). By the time of the 1967 referendum, which awarded the Commonwealth constitutional primacy over Aboriginal affairs, most official regimes of discrimination against indigenous people had been dismantled and, as individuals, they had been granted full political equality.

One vital instrument in overcoming discriminatory practices was the *Racial Discrimination Act 1975*, which, according to Hocking and Hocking (1998: 122), was 'the first political acknowledgement and formal legal guarantee of equal treatment for non-white Australians' and 'crucial to the possibility of recognition of Aboriginal rights in Australia'. Over the last quarter-century, governments at state and Commonwealth level also granted statutory group rights to land.[23] Further, in 1982, a landmark case had begun in the High Court of Australia in which Eddie Mabo and four others sought to have confirmed their ownership of land on the Murray Islands in Torres Strait. Reforms to voting and other laws, as well as creative acts of political protest, such as the Aboriginal Tent Embassy outside Parliament House in Canberra, had given indigenous people a significant presence in public life.

### Domain of Liberal Democracy

By 1991, on most of the formal political criteria, indigenous people had achieved 'inclusion' in Australian democracy. They held the vote on the same conditions as other citizens and they had gained parliamentary and even ministerial representation through major political parties in state, territory and Commonwealth parliaments.[24] For a short period in 1976, Pastor Doug Nicholls was Governor of South Australia and a number of noted Aborigines have been appointed as senior public servants.[25] Many indigenous activists, publicists and writers have gained high public profiles through their work in public sector institutions or as critics of them.[26] Given the expanding space for public expression of, and engagement with, indigenous views, it can be said that indigenous people have achieved a relatively high degree of participation within the liberal democratic public sphere.

Australian public policy also shifted more to reflect indigenous concerns and interests. Despite uneasiness with the term, governments generally maintained 'self-determination' as the dominant policy practice throughout the 1990s. Official support for self-determination did not legitimate the secessionist pursuit of a separate sovereignty sanctioned in the United Nations Charter of Human Rights or the International Convention on Civil and Political Rights. Self-determination largely meant varying degrees of indigenous self-management of their affairs, with institutional functions and funds delegated from more powerful bodies, and often accompanied by the indigenization of related bureaucracies.[27] In the domain of liberal democracy, self-determination signified a radical rejection of assimilation and an acceptance of integration. That is, equality of rights, the recognition of difference, and the right of indigenous people to make decisions affecting them, were the values behind public policy.

Regarding their official identity, indigenous people now bear the same legal civic identity as other Australian citizens. By virtue of the growth of indigenous representative institutions, however, they can also exercise an indigenous citizenship based upon individual and group statutory rights (see Rowse, 1998; 2000). Indigenous identity may be claimed on the basis of Aboriginal or Torres Strait Islander descent, self-identification, and acceptance by the indigenous community in which they live (Gardener-Garden, 2000: 1). Far from the situation in the early part of the century, indigenous identity allowed for the claiming of several layers of official rights from different branches of the state.

The recognition of Aboriginality and policies of self-management and empowerment provided the rationale for the Commonwealth to establish the Aboriginal and Torres Strait Islander Commission in 1989. ATSIC is a unique, representative and administrative institution that exemplifies a radical extension of the process of liberal inclusion. As a statutory authority, ATSIC performs three main official functions: the democratic representation of indigenous people; the formulation of policy on indigenous affairs; and the implementation and administration of policy. Although it is not the only such body to give policy advice to national government or administer programs for indigenous people, it is by far the largest and most important, with a budget for 2000/01 of $1.033 billion (HREOC, 2001: 7).[28]

The High Court of Australia's *Mabo* judgement in 1992 recognized actual and potential common law indigenous rights to land, or native title, where it had not specifically been extinguished by government legislation. This judgement served to extend the process of liberal inclusion and allowed potentially greater indigenous control over land and marine resources. Accordingly, the decision also opened up the possibilities for greater self-determination in particular regions. Like the 1967 referendum, the *Mabo* judgement was, in addition to its substantive content, immensely symbolic for the recognition it gave to indigenous people, whether they had the possibility of claiming land or not. One year later, the passing of the *Native Title Act 1993* signified what Frank Brennan (2000: 3) has called 'the high water mark of Aboriginal participation in the mainstream political processes'. Whereas one group of indigenous leaders played a crucial role in negotiating with Prime Minister Paul Keating, another group negotiated with the minority parties and the independent Senator Brian Harradine who held the balance of power in the Senate. ATSIC's participation in negotiations over the Native Title Act also demonstrated its potential to operate as an indigenous non-government organization or lobby group, and not just as an arm of the state.

Nonetheless, the passage of the Native Title Act, which established the Native Title Tribunal to regularize the claiming of land, resulted in a number of outcomes that closed off certain legal options. By validating all land grants made before 31 December 1993, it confirmed extinguishment of native title over much of Australia and made the process of claiming native title difficult and complex. While the High Court acknowledged previously existing indigenous rights, the parliament radically curtailed them, on the grounds of judicial efficiency and uniformity. The later *Wik* judgement (1996) allowed that native title could coexist with certain kinds of pastoral leases, but where conflict exists pastoral use had primacy. This decision too became the subject of fierce campaigns to eliminate the indigenous right.

Although the policies and institutions of racial and cultural assimilation had been rejected, we can see the political logic of inclusion working persistently towards political assimilation. That is, there is a constant imperative for indigenous political cultures and the new 'self-determining' institutions to adapt to the values and procedures of liberal democracy. In such a process, we may also observe regular attempts to reduce the status of indigenous people to that of one minority interest group among many. Such a political logic sets part of the agenda of indigenous politics, which is to consolidate hard-won rights and to extend the parameters of self-determination. This activism now occurs over four levels of government – local, regional, state and Commonwealth – as well as internationally, through the committees of the United Nations. The ways in which these goals are pursued will be discussed in the next section.

*Indigenous Domain*

Throughout the last decade of the century, the indigenous domain became increasingly interconnected with that of liberal democracy, but it also remained deeply affected by the legacies of the domain of protection and segregation. For example, in a number of places there has been an erosion of male authority and an increase in that of females (Davis, 1992). The indigenous domain has included a wider mix of old and new values and encompassed a greater variety of indigenous communities, cultures and practices. It also comprised a number of levels or sites of political action, and a greater diversity of forms of political expression.

There was now the possibility of assuming multiple indigenous identities, official and unofficial, as well as local, national and international. For many, a kin-based identity associated with local region remained dominant, but indigenous people could hardly avoid being associated with a national public identity of indigeneity. Aboriginality was a means for transcending local differences and facilitating collective political action at a national level. It enabled indigenous people to make claims for rights upon the institutions – governments, parliaments and courts – of liberal democracy.

The element of self-identification in claiming Aboriginality and the selection of cultural content to suit the context of public engagement brought a mutability to indigenous identity. For both official and unofficial purposes, one's indigenous identity had become more a matter of choice, depending, up to a point, upon personal inclination, group acceptance and political intent. A declared membership of the 'fourth world', for example, enabled indigenous people to assume a shared international identity suitable for global campaigns to exert international pressure on Australian governments. The important issue is that indigenous identity was no longer defined by the state, although the state or courts could be called upon to arbitrate disputed claims to indigeneity.[29]

The passing of the *Aboriginal Councils and Associations Act 1976* contributed to the formation of a new indigenous constituency (Rowse, 2000: 92). Indigenous people could now work in and through a variety of hybrid, public and private institutions, established for various legal, political and economic purposes. The first land councils in the Northern Territory, established under separate Commonwealth legislation, were also a way of consolidating indigenous interests into legal corporate entities that could manage the land returned to them, deal with any mining royalties due, and with which the state could negotiate. As representative and administrative bodies, they provided instruments for the *outward* expression of indigenous interests and sites for the articulation of *internal* indigenous politics. Although a number of such organizations were created and partially funded through Commonwealth and state agencies, their daily operations were immersed in indigenous values and politics.

The term 'indigenous sector' has been coined to describe the plethora of institutions established under the policy of self-determination. These institutions fulfil a diverse range of functions including political representation, service delivery, policy-making and owning land. Rowse (2000: 1) points out their political importance:

Without the Indigenous Sector, Indigenous Australians would lack public policy recognition of their needs and aspirations; they would be invisible, as Indigenous Australians, within Australian society and they would be unable to make any demands, as Indigenous Australians, on Australian institutions. … The 'Indigenous Sector' is what puts into practical effect the 'self' in self-determination.

Where these organizations were involved in the exercise of political power, service delivery and distribution of material resources, the fulfilment of kin obligations was an inescapable, if much criticized, component of indigenous politics.

Another remarkable feature of indigenous politics is the emergence of an indigenous public sphere. The creation of ATSIC as a national representative body and the growing use of modern communication technologies have all enabled indigenous people to convey their political concerns to virtually all other indigenous communities in Australia. Newspapers, radio and television broadcasting and the internet sites owned or controlled by indigenous people and dedicated to indigenous issues have all played a catalytic role.[30] This extension of the indigenous sector has meant that internal indigenous political interests are more readily pursued over wider areas and are also more easily inserted into the liberal democratic public sphere. Furthermore, the publicizing of internal indigenous conflicts can also be particularly effective in embarrassing or undermining the legitimacy or credibility of indigenous political leaders operating in both the indigenous and liberal democratic domains.[31]

The policy of self-determination is no longer one just promoted by government, but one self-consciously chosen and practised by indigenous people. For many indigenous people, the general principle is taken from Article 1 (1) of the *International Convention on Civil and Political Rights*, which states: 'All peoples have the right of self-determination. By virtue of that right they freely determine their political status and freely pursue their economic, social and cultural development.' Even where a more radical interpretation of this right is maintained, the diversity among indigenous peoples ensures that there is little agreement on how best to pursue or implement self-determination. The Aboriginal Provisional Government and the National Aboriginal and Islander Legal Service, for example, have kept issues of sovereignty and self-government to the forefront of their indigenous advocacy (Roberts, 1998: 263). Other groups seek lesser forms of political autonomy.[32]

With the institutions of the indigenous sector supplying a political and financial base, the resources for self-determination have become more powerful. This political logic has also been a central force in reshaping both state and indigenous institutions. For example, Aboriginal people have participated as voters in a variety of electoral constituencies including ATSIC, where the voting is not compulsory and the turnout averaged 20–25 per cent over the years 1990–99 (Sanders, Taylor and Ross 2000: 502). Sanders, Taylor and Ross conclude that the levels of voter participation 'compare reasonably with other voluntary elections in which political parties are not greatly involved' (2000: 512). All these indigenous bodies have provided political leadership in a liberal democratic sense, and are critical for transactions and negotiations with the domain of liberal democracy. Yet, they could not be effective without including elements of older indigenous traditions, such as the use of consensus decision-making and the practice of publicly acknowledging respect for elders.

Central to maintaining the political legitimacy of this domain is a symbolic politics that promotes wider public recognition of indigenous identities and cultures. This type of politics enables indigenous people to seek greater control over policies, places, names and practices that they regard as relevant to them. It is also essential for building political unity among diverse indigenous groups and between them and white supporters. The reconciliation movement, for example, was not just a way of gaining wider acknowledgement of indigenous people but also for broadening the understanding of their history of exclusion and oppression. Joint white and indigenous campaigns for a treaty were important as much for their political symbolism as the immediate practical outcomes that could accrue. Such activism was essential to inoculate public debate against the return of the 'great Australian silence' on indigenous affairs.

*Domain of Protection and Segregation*

By the official political criteria, the domain of protection and segregation with its policies and institutions no longer exists. Yet, there remains a residual, but powerful, logic of social exclusion that ensures the continuing degradation of indigenous communities. Indigenous Australians, as a group, have higher rates of ill-health and lower life expectancies than other Australians (e.g. Burdon, 1998: 198–9; Megalogenis, 2000: 1, 4). Although they have the vote for both the usual parliamentary institutions and dedicated indigenous institutions, on average, indigenous people do not have a comparable quality of life or equal access to health and educational resources.

For reasons slightly different to those of the past, regimes of incarceration also continue to figure prominently and disproportionately in the lives of indigenous people. The problem of Aboriginal deaths in police custody resulted in the massive Royal Commission into Aboriginal Deaths in Custody (1991). Bennett (1999: 3) sets out the comparative significance of this problem: 'In 1992, ... Aboriginal people were in custody at 26 times the rate for the remainder of the population; approximately one prisoner in seven was an indigenous Australian.' The recent Northern Territory laws that required magistrates to impose mandatory custodial sentences on repeat offenders had a disproportionate impact upon indigenous people and represent a further example of the working out of a political logic of exclusion and segregation.

Within a number of more remote indigenous communities, the quality of social and economic life has ensured the continuation of citizenship as a passive legal and administrative category, under conditions aptly described as 'welfare colonialism'. With reference to communities in Cape York, Noel Pearson (2000: 4) writes: 'During the last three decades, we have won victories politically and legally, but socially, in our communities, the last three decades have been a time of disintegration and regression.' On most of the social and economic criteria that accompany liberal inclusion, a great proportion of indigenous people remain excluded. As a social and economic project, liberal inclusion remains radically incomplete.

Politics in the worst areas takes on a number of distinctive forms. For example, where previously, the drinking of alcohol was illegal, Aboriginal drinking represented a mode of resistance to white laws. This activity often expressed (and still does express) the assertion of a civil right for indigenous people. This 'politics of defiance' based upon alcohol functions to resist incorporation and 'maintain a degree of autonomy' (Sackett, 1988: 67). Such activities, however, have severely damaged indigenous communities. Noel Pearson (2000) attributes the wider social problems both to 'passive welfare' and substance abuse. Not only the capacities for citizenship, but also many other social roles are impaired by alcohol abuse, illicit drugs and petrol sniffing. As one of the younger generation of indigenous leaders, Pearson (2000) has argued for a new direction in indigenous policy that includes zero tolerance of substance abuse, the abolition of 'passive welfare', and the introduction of innovative programs to strengthen families *and* community. Such policies address problems that had their origins in the earlier domain of protection and segregation, but which were given new form by the abolition of discrimination in social security. Pearson's policies aim to overcome a political logic of exclusion, segregation and lack of accountability that has had consequences of social harm similar to those earlier in the century.

Among many urban Aborigines, the legacies of policies of the previous domain of protection remained a powerful force in their present lives. The practices of removing children of mixed descent from their indigenous parents and communities and sending them to orphanages, white families or foster homes left many with permanent emotional scars. These adult children of mixed descent, now popularly known as the Stolen Generations, endured great suffering, and were often subjected to various forms of abuse that adversely affected their capacity to live fulfilling lives.[33] Many indigenous people still live daily under the psychological influence of the domain of protection and remain under the sway of a political logic of exclusion.

Paternalist attitudes have also remained strong among members of a conservative elite, comprising former government ministers, such as Peter Howson, John Herron and Gary Johns.[34] A strident ideology of paternalism has reappeared in public debate that constantly seeks to deny both the relevance of previous protectionist policies and any merit to self-determination (e.g. Johns and Brunton, 2000).[35] In noting the serious problems in remote communities, the conservative critics invariably attribute the causes to the policies of self-determination and the award of land rights (Johns, 2001: 11). Their broad remedy is to abandon all the former 'separatist' policies and replace them with those enabling 'integration' (e.g. Howson, 2000; 2002). The ruling assumption is that indigenous people ought to be free to make their own choices, but as individuals, not groups. Further such choices must inevitably be to abandon indigenous cultural traditions and join 'the mainstream'. When these policies are inspected for content, it is difficult to see how they differ from assimilation.

For all these reasons, it would not be too strong to say that the protectionist and segregationist past 'weighs like a nightmare on the brain of the living' (Marx, [1852] 1968: 97).

The period 1991–2001 saw the rise of indigenous people to prominence in the liberal democratic public sphere, the emergence of an indigenous public sphere and the abolition of assimilation and formal discriminations. On the surface, indigenous relations with Australian democracy would appear to be in good shape. At nearly every level of formal politics there seems to be a degree of openness to indigenous participation that would have been unimaginable a century earlier. There is official recognition of multiple indigenous identities and dedicated institutions and resources to support their political expression. Indigenous people have the option of whether to exercise their civic identity or not in various political fields. The award of citizenship to indigenous people has provided a liberal democratic footing for programs to recover and radically extend indigenous rights. In this context, the project of self-determination has taken many forms and changed from an unreflective practice to become more politically self-conscious, if diverse in doctrine.

Unlike earlier in the century, in the 1990s there was a large degree of overlap between the political domains. This meant also that the boundaries between the three domains were less distinct and more permeable, as indigenous people could more easily traverse them. ATSIC, for example, is both an extension of the institutions of Australian political democracy, with all its bureaucratic apparatus, *and* an exercise of indigenous self-determination. These two dimensions of ATSIC, however, bring serious strains that impair its capacity either to fulfil its liberal democratic objectives or to pursue satisfactorily indigenous self-determination.

Although designed partly on the advice of Aboriginal people, ATSIC bears many of the characteristics of a Commonwealth bureaucracy, but with extra systems of accountability. As well as accountability to the Minister for Aboriginal and Torres Strait Islander Affairs, parliamentary committees and the Auditor-General, there is a unique, internal Office of Evaluation and Audit, which reports both to the Minister and ATSIC board.[36] In many respects, ATSIC bears the marks of a liberal institution designed to check the exercise of arbitrary authority and the power of untrustworthy office-holders.[37]

Nor has the political imperative of liberal inclusion, on average, brought social and economic inclusion to indigenous people. It is evident that the domain of protection and segregation has not disappeared and large numbers of indigenous people exist within its boundaries. The reasons for this are the subject of intense political and ideological debate, which reflect struggles between the different domains for power and authority over the agenda for indigenous affairs policy. The success of the process of democratization has created new tensions between the political logics of liberal inclusion, indigenous self-determination and paternalism. With the growing indigenous activism within international bodies such as the World Council of Indigenous Peoples and the United Nations, another political domain can be seen emerging, whose imperatives will place constant pressure on the other domains.

## Conclusion

This chapter has offered a critical perspective on the reshaping of Australian political institutions as they apply to indigenous people. A focus on their struggles for citizenship and democratic inclusion demonstrates how the Australian state has dealt progressively with the question of racial and cultural differences. The diversity of responses from the state and indigenous people over the century indicate high levels of flexibility, adaptability and political creativity. Yet, this study also keeps us aware of the determined opposition that arises in response to the state's recognition of indigenous difference.

A further aim has been to propose a conceptual approach that draws out the complex patterns and recurring tendencies apparent over the twentieth century. The concept of domain, for example, may enable us to sharpen our perceptions of the contexts – assumptions about identity, policies and institutions – in which indigenous–state relations have been conducted. Conceivably, the account of the three domains allows us to see the structural continuities, understood as propensities or 'political logics', operating in this field. Further, this study attempts to portray the recursive and multi-dimensional character of relations between the three domains. The concepts of domain and political logic may demonstrate how certain problems have arisen and persisted into the present. Just as important, they require us to recognize and deploy indigenous perspectives.

This conceptual framework may assist in explaining the complexity of indigenous relations with the state and why the conflicts are so entrenched. For example, it is evident that at the heart of liberal democracy is an inherent tendency towards political assimilation. In recognizing group differences it must also seek to limit their political consequences and it does so by drawing indigenous people and others more tightly into liberal democratic procedures. Similarly, indigenous peoples cannot give up on self-determination. To do so would be to discard a key element of their identity and risk forgetting their history. It would also entail abandoning the prospect of living more enriched lives as *indigenous* people within Australian society, and not simply as workers and consumers in a capitalist economy. Just as unyielding are the constant pressures for social and economic assimilation. The imperative to withdraw state recognition of difference and to press for uniformity of culture seems ever present, whether the uniformity is that of 'British civilization', the 'Australian way of life' or global capitalism.

It may be ventured that past relations between indigenous people and state institutions are best understood as a product of the three competing political logics of liberal inclusion, indigenous self-determination and paternalist exclusion. This observation also has a relatively weak, but important, prescriptive value for policy. Any future state programs that did not take proper account of these three tendencies would be destined to failure. For indigenous people, the political challenge of self-determination is to formulate plausible representations of the Aboriginal domain that allow them to make best use of liberal democratic institutions, while at the same time resisting incorporation and cultural assimilation.

**Notes**

I am grateful to the Reshaping Australian Institutions program at ANU for the award of a fellowship that gave me time to work on this chapter. Thanks are also due to the many people who have commented on various drafts and provided helpful advice and direction. Although I could not incorporate all their suggestions, I am most indebted to Geoffrey Brennan, Frank Castles, Marian Sawer, John Dryzek, Tim Rowse, Will Sanders, Peter Jull, Julie Connolly and Karen Gillen. Any errors or misinterpretations, however, remain mine.

1 I use 'indigenous people' as the generic term for Aborigines and Torres Strait Islanders, though much of what follows mostly applies to Aborigines.
2 See the discussion of different approaches in Jennett (1987).
3 See Chapter 5.
4 See for example the accounts of exploitation and resistance in the Pilbara (Mandle 1977) and in the Northern Territory (Rowley 1972a: 337–43).
5 See for example Loveday and Sanders (1984), Fletcher (1992: xv) and Rowse (2001).
6 Identity is used here as a generic concept to cover the variety of ways that individuals and groups distinguish themselves from others and determine relations with those like them and those deemed to be different. On this reading, the substantive content of identity claims may, for example, derive

from social, political or cultural contexts, and may include kinship categories. Nonetheless, it must also be said that identities are often mutable and negotiated categories, and it is possible, if not essential, for individuals to have multiple identities.
7 See the discussion of Popper's propensity theory as it applies to the physical world in Stokes (1998: 109–12).
8 The institutional phenomenon of modern bureaucracy supplies examples of this process. Bureaucracies are generally oriented towards particular objectives and are supposed to be devoted to intrumentally rational principles, which in turn require certain types of organization, ethics, and even personalities. Yet, ministers and CEOs, historical events and other factors may assist, transform or impede this process.
9 See for example the discussions of situational logic in Popper (1985), which is a variation of Weber's 'ideal type', and the critique in Stokes (1998: 84–6).
10 See also Rowse (1992: 100)
11 This is not to say that a similar scheme may not apply to other groups in Australian society.
12 During the last quarter of the twentieth century, however, the delivery of social services was increasingly carried out by hybrid public and private institutions, which were essentially non-governmental organizations, supported by a combination of public and private funds.
13 Formally, Australians were 'subjects' of the British crown and did not become 'citizens' until 1948 (Chesterman and Galligan 1997: 157).
14 Such regimes of incarceration may be typical of Australian policies towards those it cannot yet regard as citizens. It is evident in the recent treatment of asylum-seekers and refugees who arrive illegally in Australia by boat.
15 The main principles of the logic of paternalist exclusion were inherited from the colonial period.
16 As there are various kinds of exclusion, the term 'paternalist exclusion' is not necessarily oxymoronic. The imprisonment of criminals is a form of exclusion from society that is authoritarian but hardly paternalist.
17 It may even be possible to assess the relative strengths by quantifying selected indicators, such as the extent of independence of institutions from government in the indigenous domain, the levels of active indigenous participation and representation in the domain of liberal democracy, or the rates of incarceration or deaths in custody in the domain of protection and incarceration. But this is not my objective here.
18 See Rowley (1972a: Part III) and Burgmann (1993: 32).
19 See also the documentary records of Aboriginal activism and protest in Attwood and Markus (1999).
20 Due to administrative discrimination, only 2 of the 154 returned Aboriginal servicemen from New South Wales were awarded land from the scheme (Goodall 1996: 123–4).
21 See the documents in Attwood and Markus (1999).
22 Western Australia soon followed by granting full voting rights in 1962, but Queensland held out until 1965.
23 Land rights laws of varying quality were passed in South Australia (1966, 1981, 1984), New South Wales (1983), Victoria (1984) and Queensland (1990) and Commonwealth level (Northern Territory 1977).

24 Ernie Bridge was a Labor MLA 1980–88 and Minister for Aboriginal Affairs 1986–88 in WA. Neville Bonner was a National Party Senator for Queensland 1971–1983 and Aden Ridgeway has been an Australian Democrat Senator for NSW since 1999. In August 2001, four indigenous candidates were elected to seats in the NT Legislative Assembly (Paul Toohey, 'Making up lost ground', *Australian* 22 August 2001: 4), and one, John Ah Kit, became a minister.
25 During 1984–89 Charles Perkins was Secretary of the Commonwealth Department of Aboriginal Affairs. From 1981, Pat O'Shane was Secretary of the NSW Ministry of Aboriginal Affairs and, since 1986, she has been a NSW magistrate. Eric Wilmot has held numerous senior positions in state and Commonwealth public service and education bureaucracies.
26 Among the more well known are Oodgeroo Noonuccal, Lowitja (Lois) O'Donoghue, Marcia Langton, Charles Perkins, Michael Mansell and Noel Pearson, Mick Dodson and Pat Dodson.
27 See the discussion in Jull (1991).
28 ATSIC is not without indigenous and non-indigenous critics. See Sullivan (1996).
29 This became a particular issue for ATSIC elections in Tasmania.
30 Given the nature of the medium, access to the internet allows for both the renovation and loss of indigenous culture (Nathan 2000 and McConaghy 2000). See also McKee and Hartley (2000).
31 The controversies arising out of allegations against Geoff Clark, the Chair of ATSIC, that were raised in the mass media were a pertinent example.
32 See the diversity of approaches in Fletcher (1994).
33 See National Inquiry (1997) and Bird (1998).
34 These figures are also central in the formation of the Bennelong Society in 2001, which has as its objective the review and reform of indigenous affairs policy.
35 Other critics (e.g. Windschuttle 2000) have worked assiduously to try to refute certain historical facts and judgements, such as those about the numbers of Aboriginal deaths resulting from invasion.
36 On multiple accountability, see the argument by former chair of ATSIC, Lowitja O'Donoghue (1996).
37 Charles Perkins (Saunders 2000) estimated that 'one-quarter of the commission's time and money has been spent answering to various auditing bodies and parliamentary committees'.

## References

Attwood, B., and Markus, A. *The Struggle for Aboriginal Rights: A Documentary History* (Sydney: Allen & Unwin, 1999).
Beckett, J. 'The Torres Strait Islanders and the Pearling Industry: A Case of Internal Colonialism', in M. C. Howard (ed.), *Aboriginal Power in Australian Society* (St Lucia: University of Queensland Press, 1982) pp. 131–58.
Beckett, J. R. 'Aboriginality, Citizenship and the Nation State', in 'Aborigines and the State in Australia', *Social Analysis*, vol. 24(4) (1988) pp. 3–18.
Bennett, S. *Aborigines and Political Power* (Sydney: Allen & Unwin, 1989).
——. *White Politics and Black Australians* (Sydney: Allen & Unwin, 1999).

Bird, C. (ed.). *The Stolen Children: Their Stories* (Sydney: Random House, 1998).
Bolton, G. 'Aborigines in Social History: An Overview', in R. M. Berndt (ed.), *Aboriginal Sites, Rights and Resource Development* (Perth: University of Western Australia Press, 1982) pp. 59–68.
Bourke, C., Bourke, E., and Edwards, B. (eds). *Aboriginal Australia* (St Lucia: University of Queensland Press, 1998).
Brennan, F. 'Delivering Equity and Reconciliation through Inclusive Institutions', paper to Reshaping Australian Institutions Seminar, Parliament House, Canberra, 1 November 2000.
Burdon, J. 'Health: An Holistic Approach', in C. Bourke, E. Bourke and B. Edwards (eds), *Aboriginal Australia* (St Lucia: University of Queensland Press, 1998) pp. 189–218.
Burgmann, V. *Power and Protest: Movements for Change in Australian Society* (Sydney: Allen & Unwin, 1993).
Chesterman, J., and Galligan, B. *Citizens Without Rights: Aborigines and Australian Citizenship* (Cambridge: Cambridge University Press, 1997).
Davis, E. R. 'The Dominant Female: Politics in the local Aboriginal Community', *Australian Aboriginal Studies*, vol. 2 (1992) pp. 34–41.
Dryzek, J. 'Political Inclusion and the Dynamics of Democratization', *American Political Science Review*, vol. 90 (1996) pp. 475–87.
Fletcher, C. *Aboriginal Politics: Intergovernmental Relations* (Melbourne: Melbourne University Press, 1992).
—— (ed.). *Aboriginal Self-Determination in Australia* (Canberra: Aboriginal Studies Press, 1994).
Gaita, R. 'Genocide and Pedantry', *Quadrant*, vol. XLI(7–8) (1997) pp. 41–5.
Gaminiratne, K. H. W. 'Population (Growth)', in D. Horton (ed.), *The Encyclopedia of Aboriginal Australia*, vol. 2 (Canberra: Aboriginal Studies Press, 1994), p. 889.
Gardener-Garden, J. 'The Definition of Aboriginality', *Research Note*. Department of Parliamentary Library, Number 18 (2000) pp. 1–2.
Goffman, E. *Asylums* (Harmondsworth: Penguin, 1968).
Goodall, H. 'Land in our Own Country: The Aboriginal Land Rights Movement in South-eastern Australia, 1860 to 1914', *Aboriginal History*, vol. 14(1) (1990) pp. 1–24.
——. *Invasion to Embassy: Land in Aboriginal Politics in New South Wales, 1770–1972* (Sydney: Allen & Unwin, 1996).
Hancock, W. K. *Australia* (Brisbane: Jacaranda, [1930] 1961).
Hartwig, M. 'Capitalism and Aborigines: The theory of internal colonialism and its rivals', in E. L. Wheelwright and K. Buckley (eds), *Essays in the Political Economy of Australian Capitalism*, vol. 3 (Sydney: ANZ Book Co., 1978) pp. 119–41.
Hiatt, L. R. *Aboriginal Political Life. The Wentworth Lecture 1984* (Canberra: Australian Institute of Aboriginal Studies, 1986).
Hocking, B. J., and Hocking, B. A. 'A Comparative View of Indigenous Citizenship Issues', *Citizenship Studies*, vol. 2(1) (1998) pp. 121–31.
Howson, P. 'Assimilation [sic] the Only Way Forward', *Australian* (24 May 2000) p. 15.
——. 'Black Politics have Bred Failure', *Australian* (21 January 2002) p. 11.

Human Rights and Equal Opportunity Commission (HREOC). *Face the Facts: Section 3 Aboriginal and Torres Strait Islanders*, 2001, <www.hreoc.gov.au/racial_discrimination/face_facts/sec3.html>

Jennett, C. 'Incorporation or independence? The struggle for Aboriginal equality', in C. Jennett and R. G. Stewart (eds), *Three Worlds of Inequality: Race, Class and Gender* (Melbourne: Macmillan, 1987) pp. 57–93.

Johns, G. 'Look for Strength in the Mainstream', *Australian* (22 November 2001) p. 11.

Johns, G., and Brunton R. 'Separate Path to Division', *Australian* (12 April 2000) p. 15.

Jull, P. *The Politics of Northern Frontiers in Australia, Canada and Other 'First World' Countries: A Discussion Paper* (Darwin and Canberra: North Australia Research Unit, 1991).

Kidd, R. *The Way We Civilise* (St Lucia: University of Queensland Press, 1997).

Lippman, L. *Generations of Resistance: Aborigines Demand Justice* (Melbourne: Longman Cheshire, 1991).

Loveday, P., and Sanders, W. 'Aboriginal Votes and Aboriginal Candidates', in P. Loveday and D. Jaensch (eds), *A Landslide Election: The Northern Territory, 1983* (Darwin: North Australia Research Unit, 1984).

Maddock, K. *The Australian Aborigines* (London: Allen Lane, 1973).

Mandle, W. 'Donald McLeod and Australia's Aboriginal Problem', in his *Going it Alone: Australia's National Identity in the 20th Century* (Ringwood, Vic.: Penguin, 1977) pp. 172–200.

Marx, K. 'The Eighteenth Brumaire of Louis Bonaparte', in K. Marx and F. Engels, *Selected Works in One Volume* (New York: International Publishers, [1852] 1968) pp. 97–180.

McConaghy, C. 'The Web and Today's Colonialism', *Australian Aboriginal Studies*, vols 1–2 (2000) pp. 48–55.

McKee, A. and Hartley, J. *The Indigenous Public Sphere: The Reporting and Reception of Aboriginal Issues in the Australian Media* (Oxford: Oxford University Press, 2000).

Megalogenis, G. 'Sorry States – blacks dying younger', *Australian* (26 December 2000) pp. 1, 4.

Nathan, D. 'Plugging in Indigenous Knowledge: Connections and innovations', *Australian Aboriginal Studies*, vols 1–2 (2000) pp. 39–47.

National Inquiry into the Separation of Aboriginal and Torres Strait Islander Children from their Families. *Bringing Them Home*. Report (Sydney: Human Rights and Equal Opportunity Commission, 1997).

O'Donoghue, L. 'Who's accountable to whom?' *Weekend Australian* (15–16 June 1996) pp. 26.

Offe, C. 'New Social Movements: Challenging the Boundaries of Institutional Politics', *Social Research* 52(4) (1985) pp. 817–68.

Patten, J., and Ferguson, W. *Aborigines Claim Citizen Rights!* (Sydney: The Publicist, 1938).

Pearson, N. 'Strong Families then Strong Communities. Address to the Indigenous Families and Communities Roundtable, Canberra', 24 October 2000 <www.brisinst.org.au/papers/noel_pearson_Strong/print-index.html>.

Peterson, N. 'Welfare Colonialism and Citizenship: Politics, Economics and Agency', in N. Peterson and W. Sanders (eds), *Citizenship and Indigenous Australians* (Cambridge: Cambridge University Press, 1998) pp. 101–17.

Peterson, N., and Sanders W. (eds). *Citizenship and Indigenous Australians* (Cambridge: Cambridge University Press, 1998).

Popper, K. R. 'The Rationality Principle', in D. Miller (ed.), *Popper Selections* (Princeton: Princeton University Press, 1985) pp. 357–65.

Reynolds, H. *Dispossession: Black Australians and White Invaders* (Sydney: Allen & Unwin, 1989).

——. *An Indelible Stain? The Question of Genocide in Australia's History* (Ringwood, Vic.: Penguin, 2001).

Roberts, D. 'Self-determination and the Aboriginal Struggle for Equality', in C. Bourke, E. Bourke and B. Edwards *Aboriginal Australia* (St Lucia: University of Queensland Press, 1998) pp. 259–88.

Rowley, C. D. *The Remote Aborigines: Aboriginal Policy and Practice* (Ringwood, Vic.: Penguin, 1972a).

——. *The Destruction of Aboriginal Society* (Ringwood, Vic.: Penguin, 1972b).

——. *A Matter of Justice* (Canberra: Australian National University Press, 1978).

——. 'Aboriginals and the Australian Political System', *Politics*, vol. 14(2) (1980) pp. 232–48.

Rowse, T. *Remote Possibilities: The Aboriginal Domain and the Administrative Imagination* (Darwin: North Australia Research Unit, 1992).

——. 'Indigenous Citizenship and Self-determination: The Problem of Shared Responsibilities', in N. Peterson and W. Sanders (eds), *Citizenship and Indigenous Australians*, (1998) pp. 79–100.

——. 'Indigenous Citizenship', in W. Hudson and J. Kane (eds), *Rethinking Australian Citizenship* (Cambridge: Cambridge University Press, 2000) pp. 86–98.

——. 'Democratic Systems are an Alien Thing to Aboriginal Culture …', in M. Sawer and G. Zappalà (eds), *Speaking for the People: Representation in Australian Politics* (Melbourne: Melbourne University Press, 2001) pp. 103–33.

Royal Commission into Aboriginal Deaths in Custody. *National Report* (Canberra: Australian Government Publishing Service, 1991).

Sackett, L. 'Resisting Arrests: Drinking, Development and Discipline in a Desert Context', *Social Analysis*, vol. 24 (1988) pp. 66–77.

——. 'Welfare Colonialism: Developing Divisions at Wiluna', in R. E. Tonkinson and M. Howard (eds), *Going it Alone? Prospects for Aboriginal Autonomy* (Canberra: Aboriginal Studies Press, 1990) pp. 201–17.

Saunders, C. (ed.). *The Australian Constitution* (Melbourne: Constitutional Centenary Foundation, 1997).

Saunders, M. 'Body Blows', *Weekend Australian* (4–5 March 2000) p. 26.

Stanner, W. E. H. *After the Dreaming: The 1968 Boyer Lectures* (Sydney: Australian Broadcasting Commission, 1968).

Stevens, F. *Aborigines in the Northern Territory Cattle Industry* (Canberra: Australian National University Press, 1974).

Stokes, G. 'Introduction', in G. Stokes (ed.), *The Politics of Identity in Australia* (Melbourne: Cambridge University Press, 1997) pp. 1–20.

——. *Popper: Philosophy, Politics and Scientific Method* (Cambridge: Polity, 1998).

Stretton, P., and Finnemore, C. 'Black Fellow Citizens: Aborigines and the Commonwealth Franchise', *Australian Historical Studies*, vol. 25(101) (1993) pp. 521–35.

Sullivan, P. (ed.). *Shooting the Banker: Essays on ATSIC and Self-determination* (Darwin: North Australia Research Unit, 1996).

Tatz, C. *Race Politics in Australia: Aborigines, Politics and the Law* (Armidale, NSW: University of New England Publishing Unit, 1979).

——. 'The Recovery and Discovery of Rights: An Overview of Aborigines, Politics and Law', in R. M. Berndt (ed.), *Aboriginal Sites, Rights and Resource Development* (Nedlands: University of Western Australia Press, 1982a) pp. 201–26.

——. *Aborigines and Uranium and Other Essays* (Melbourne: Heinemann, 1982b).

Touraine, A. 'An Introduction to the Study of Social Movements', *Social Research*, vol. 52(4) (1985) pp. 749–87.

Trigger, D. S. 'Blackfellas and Whitefellas: The Concepts of Domain and Social Closure in the Analysis of Race Relations', *Mankind*, vol. 16(2) (1986) pp. 99–117.

von Sturmer, J. 'The Different Domains', in *Aborigines and Uranium: Consolidated Report on the Social Impact of Uranium Mining on the Aborigines of the Northern Territory* (Canberra: Australian Government Publishing Service, 1984) pp. 218–37.

*Webster's New Collegiate Dictionary* (Springfield, Ma: Merriam, 1977).

Windschuttle, K. 'The Myths of Frontier Massacres in Australian History' Parts I–III, *Quadrant*, vol. XLIV (2000): (10), pp. 8–21; (11), pp. 17–24; (12), pp. 6–20.

# 8 The Grammar of Colonial Legality: Subjects, Objects, and the Australian Rule of Law

*Martin Krygier*

The concerns of this chapter are twofold. One is part of a general interest in the character, conditions and consequences of the rule of law. From that point of view, it just happens that this time Australia is where I look. If I had been asked to write for a project on the reshaping of Alaskan institutions, I would have looked elsewhere (though perhaps come to the same conclusions). Second, however, like many Australians today, I am also concerned to understand and come to terms with some aspects of our history. That concern is driven less by curiosity than disquiet. Australia was established as a certain sort of country with a certain range of institutions and practices. Like many others, I am attached to this country and to many of those institutions and practices. One of them is the rule of law. In recent years, also like many others, I have belatedly sought to come to terms with what happened to Australia's Aborigines while these remarkable achievements were under way.

This chapter attempts to connect these concerns. Its subject is the rule of law, how it made its way in Australia, and what that tells us about it and about us. One range of questions raised by this juxtaposition of concerns has to do with whether there were deep and not merely accidental connections between the ultimately happy white and the ultimately terrible black story. Were the things our forebears introduced, even ones we value most, even those we rightly value, in intrinsic ways connected with the damage that was caused? Of things we don't value, such as the terrible effects of disease, or of some we do, such as the pastoral foundations of our prosperity, the answer is plain. Law is more complicated, and yet the question is worth asking, in relation to both the interests which motivate this chapter.

Law first made its way here on the backs of convicts and Aborigines, with dramatically contrasting results. We have histories of both encounters, but specialists tend to focus on one group or the other and they are rarely closely juxtaposed. However, it is important to consider them in connection, for both analytical and historical reasons. Analytically, both have implications for our understanding and appreciation of the nature, conditions and consequences of the rule of law. Australia was a testing ground for many experiments in the late eighteenth and early nineteenth centuries. Transportation of the rule of law was one of them. Second, they are both equally parts of our history and of each other's history. Moreover, there was a specific link between them from the start. For, as Atkinson has observed:

> In Britain, with the end of the American Revolution, two great issues dominated the conversation of polite and ambitious men and women. These were, first, the status of Blacks throughout the empire and, secondly, penal discipline. Slaves and convicts both challenged the imagination of reformers. Both seemed to live within a restricted, oppressive and exotic culture of their own, beyond the sweetness and light of an improving civilisation. Both might be touched by the humanity of educated men and women and their lives enlarge. (Atkinson, 1997: 44)

A major institution through which both convicts and Aborigines were to be 'touched by the humanity of educated men and women' was law. I hope that from juxtaposing the markedly different ways in which law touched settlers and indigenes, we might gain a more complex appreciation of what the rule of law meant in Australia's early development and, more generally, of the character, virtues, limitations and presuppositions of the rule of law itself. Along the way we might also learn something about ourselves.

My discussion will proceed in five stages. In the first, I say something about the significance of our beginnings. In the second I develop a particular conception[1] of the rule of law, in terms of which my discussion proceeds. This conception is concerned particularly to focus on the *social*, rather than just the formal-legal, conditions of the rule of law, the rule of law 'in action', so to speak, rather than merely 'in the books'. I then survey some of the ways law and the rule of law affected the lives of convicts in the early colony. Then I turn to the impact of law on Aborigines in two formative moments: first, the early years of settlement, when such law as applied to them was supposedly the same as applied to anyone else; and, second, the late nineteenth and early twentieth centuries, when the newly self-governing colonies developed legal regimes specifically to deal with Aborigines. I conclude with some remarks on institutions and moral imagination.

### Transplants and Transitions

In his recent Boyer lectures, (Gleeson, 2000: 1) the Chief Justice of the Australian High Court, Murray Gleeson, draws on a passage from Robert Bolt's *A Man for All Seasons*, in which Sir Thomas More defends his devotion and submission to the positive law of the land. More wouldn't transgress its limits, even at the risk of giving 'the Devil the benefit of the law'. Against his interlocutor's angry retort that he would 'cut down every law in England' to get the Devil, More hotly replies:

> Oh? And when the last law was down, and the Devil turned round on you – where would you hide, ... the laws all being flat? ... This country's planted thick with laws from coast to coast ... and if you cut them down ... d'you really think you could stand upright in the winds that would blow then? ... Yes, I'd give the Devil benefit of law, for my own safety's sake. (Bolt, 1963: Act One)

Gleeson endorses these sentiments, and though it is an old Australian habit to do so, he is not just thinking of England. For he takes from More the title of his first chapter, 'A Country Planted Thick with Laws', and the country of which he writes is Australia.

Yet, like so many things gained and lost in translation, More's metaphor has a somewhat different resonance in its new home. The laws with which England was 'planted thick' had to be transplanted here, and this is a more specific, deliberate, activity than is suggested by More's passive participle. Those laws were, after all, products of processes that had gone on, if not 'from time out of mind', then for a very long while indeed. It would be a real task to discern what parts were deliberately planted by anyone in particular, and what just grew. That can be done, but it is not More's task. For he is not interested in the process but in the product, in the result not its origins or sources. He believes the English are, and it is good that they are, protected by what he calls 'the thickets of the law'. But he is not concerned with, nor would it be easy or brief to say, how those thickets came to be planted, nourished and tended, how they came to grow or what they displaced as they came to flourish.

In Australia we can be more precise. The laws which govern this country do so because of a specific event, the landing of Governor Phillip in Sydney in January 1788. With him came 9 officials, 212 marines, 759 convicts and, because the colony of New South Wales, where it all began, was regarded as 'settled' rather than 'conquered', all the laws of England that were 'applicable to their own situation and condition of any infant colony' (Blackstone, 1830: 111). Once planted in local soil, law grew in a range of distinctive, even peculiar, ways; but its roots, and those who planted them, are easy to identify.

And this points to another difference between the way in which England was 'planted thick with laws' and what it means to say those laws were planted here. More speaks of dense 'thickets' that provide security, apparently for everyone, 'from coast to coast'. Get rid of them, he says, and no-one could stand upright. But in Australia in 1788, none of *them* was here.

To be sure, there were the long-established laws of Aboriginal societies, but neither More nor Gleeson was speaking of them. In any event those laws were not developed to deal with conquest (the accurate, though not the legal, term in our context) by strange invaders from another country, who would not go away. These invaders, in turn, were ignorant of those laws, only sporadically interested in them, and never contemplated their applying to themselves.

So they brought their own. These were new to the place they came, as was everything else the British brought. And so, therefore, became everything touched by them from the time of their arrival.[2] To be sure, Aborigines had lived here for thousands of years – *their* societies and laws were as old as could be. And the settlers weren't newly minted either, for all that convicts came to be called 'currency lads'. What was new was their existence and juxtaposition in this place, and *that* novelty affected everyone – Aborigines, convicts, free settlers, and all of us who live in the society formed out of their encounters.

In the last decade or so, we have come to be familiar with a new family of terms: 'transitional' societies, 'transitional justice', the 'transition to democracy and the rule of law', indeed transitions galore. Not to mention transitologists. Post-communist Europe is full of them, so too Latin America, South Africa, and only a little earlier Spain and Portugal. Of course everyone knows these are not the first such 'transitions', for even in the twentieth century there were the post-war transformations of West Germany, Japan and Italy from dictatorship to democracy. However, many scholars consider the post-communist transformations in particular to be unprecedented, since they involve *simultaneous* political, economic and social transformation. But so did our own. One hundred years after Federation, and a little over two hundred after white settlement began, Australians might usefully recall their contribution to transitology.

Many scholars who consider these contemporary developments now demur at talk of transitions, notwithstanding the ubiquity of the term. They prefer less teleologically loaded terms such as 'transformations', since they are less confident than many were in 1989, about where things are going. Australian transitologists around, say, 1800, might have felt something similar. Yet, even as we admire the wisdom in Zhou En Lai's response to a request for assessment of the consequences of the French Revolution – 'it's too soon to tell' – there are some things we can say about the results of Australia's transition. One of them is that it has issued in 'democracy and the rule of law'.

This was not inevitable, nor was the transition simple or seamless. Nor still did it bring equal good fortune for all. But it occurred, and more quickly than is common. In many ways, indeed, it is an exemplary transition, one of the best of its kind.

But a paradox lies at its heart: that is, that while benefiting the settler population almost immediately, it had no such salutary consequences for indigenous Australians. Indeed if the criterion for the end of transition is success, theirs is still continuing. That paradox might be explained in short order – 'imperialism', 'racism', 'hypocrisy', the 'culture cult', and so on – but these epithets, while often appropriate, do not take things very far and since they explain everything they do not take us into the specificity of anything. I want to focus on one specific thing: the paradoxical sway and effects of law, and the ambiguous bearing of the rule of law, in our early history.

I use 'early' loosely, and in fact will range over some distance in our short history, but I am discussing genealogy rather than current developments. Some of our formative moments have left direct marks on our present; some have led to reactions, occasionally salutary, which have moved us in different directions. Either way, they are important for an understanding of what we were and what we have become.

**The Rule of Law**

Whether institutions are viewed as structures or as rules, the law is uncontroversially full of them. Indeed a legal system is an archetypal institutional order in both senses, full as it is of structures for the generation, interpretation, enforcement and application of rules. The rule of law, on the other hand, is better viewed as a cluster of values for legal institutions, which might be greatly or scarcely at all, more or less, better or worse, *institutionalized* in particular legal orders. Where these values are strongly institutionalized within a legal order, they are likely to be internalized by members of the order, professional and lay, and they will affect its practices, its procedures and the character of its structures. They themselves will be among the higher-order institutional rules of the game in a particular order, and the values and standards that infuse those rules,[3] affecting the purposes and character of more specific legal rules, standards and practices.

That sort of institutionalization, however, is not inevitable. Such higher-order values might be unknown in a particular order. Alternatively, they might be well known but not institutionalized, because they conflict with, maybe are alien to, the animating ideals or practices of existing institutions which *are* institutionalized, or because significant actors are hostile to them, or because no-one gives them any heed, or because they are difficult in particular circumstances to institutionalize, even where there is a will to do so. So while legal institutions are commonly central to the institutional architecture of states, the extent to which the rule of law is institutionalized varies greatly across space and time.

And so, when Chief Justice Gleeson observes that 'The imagery of law as a windbreak carries an important idea. The law restrains and civilises power', he speaks of what is certainly an important idea, but that idea needs to be unpacked. For clearly not every law or legal order 'restrains and civilises power'.

Many legal orders have no such ambition. In many states, law has been conceived of as an instrument for repression or at least top-down direction of subjects, and nothing more. Indeed the word 'subject' is ambiguous in regard to them. The ruled were subjected *to* the law, and in that sense more subjects than citizens. On the other hand, they did not relate to the law as active subjects, as a subject does to a verb, for example. They are better seen as the objects of power and the institutions through which it is exercised, including law. Its subjects were the rulers, who used laws, among other instruments, for their own purposes. Indeed law has often been a very useful vehicle (and at times equally useful camouflage) for the exercise of unrestrained and uncivilized power.

Consider this telling epitome of the long-lived Russian legal tradition: 'Count Benckendorff, the chief of police under Nicholas I, once said: "Laws are written for subordinates, not for the authorities." As a logical consequence, laws did not need to be made public in order to go into effect. Those who broke the law would find out anyway' (Hedlund, 2001: 50). Clearly when Benckendorff spoke of laws being written for subordinates, he did not mean 'for their sakes', or 'for their protection, guidance and use'. The Russian tradition is particularly striking in its starkly top-down, instrumental view of law, but it is far from unique. More rare, indeed, are regimes where laws, or a substantial proportion of them, are written for the protection, guidance and use of citizens, where this is widely assumed to be the case and thought properly to be so. In these regimes, the cluster of values known as the rule of law is strongly institutionalized.

Politically pliable, draconian, discriminatory laws; incompetent, venal, weak, suborned administrators of law; rulers who, to adapt Habermas' distinction, (Harbermas, 1986: 212) use law solely as a 'steering medium' for the effective exercise of power, leaving no room for it to serve as an 'institution' of the everyday life world itself, available to citizens as a resource and protection in their relations with the state and with each other; laws which, against other sources and forms of power, simply do not *count* either as restraints on power or as resources in everyday life. None of these sorts of law, and they are hardly rare, is likely either to restrain or to civilize power.

Alternatively a legal order might embody laws which do restrain some things, or in some spheres, or in relation to some people, yet in doing so contribute to a larger incivility. One example is what Ernst Fraenkel called a 'Dual State', dual for it includes both a 'normative' and a 'prerogative' component (Fraenkel, 1941: xiii). In the former 'an administrative body endowed with elaborate powers for safeguarding the legal order,' governs some classes, races or domains. The latter wields 'unlimited violence unchecked by any legal guarantees', over other classes, races, or everyone in other domains (such as politics). In such orders, the 'prerogative state' has the final word, though it might often find it useful to allow the normative state to operate routinely in particular areas of life. Nazi Germany was Fraenkel's example; South Africa under Apartheid a more recent one. Law in such states is not well characterized as a 'windbreak'.

The distinctions drawn here are not merely matters of the ends that law is asked to serve, for where values are not merely pious sentiments but operative ideals, their institutionalization will shape and favour particular legal assumptions and practices, and not others, particular ways of treating legal actors, particular views of the character of the actors themselves.

Law is often characterized in general terms – the command of a sovereign or a vehicle of ruling ideology – as though it were a kind of tool or implement whose character remained indifferent to whatever purpose it was directed to. Like a hammer or chisel: hit a wall or a head, the implement is unaffected. However with regard to law that is a deep mistake, which the Soviet jurist, Evgenii Pashukanis (1980: 89), was one of the first to note and which a number of more recent writers have sought to expose and avoid (Kamenk & Tay, 1975: Unger, 1976; Nonet & Selznick, 1978). Pashukanis pointed out that the form and character of law[4] differ systematically with what is asked of it, in ways whose significance is hidden by our common tendency to describe as law every form of governmental regulation.

Legal orders whose primary aim is repression, or managerial direction, or social transformation, for example, will embody – not simply serve but literally embody – different views of the nature and proper relationships between ruler and ruled, and between the ruled themselves, views different both from each other and all the more from one which has as a central purpose to guard individual interests and facilitate co-operative interactions among agents pursuing their own self-chosen projects. Moreover, not only are the ends very different, but the character of the legal means will also differ systematically. For particular forms of law are more congenial to some purposes than to others. Laws intended to achieve centrally determined repressive or bureaucratic or transformative objectives, for example, will follow different logics and embody systematically different characteristics from laws intended to aid individuals to choose, plan, co-operate, and stay out of gaol. The nature and identities of principals and agents will be differently understood and located, the degrees of official discretion allowed, publicity required, flexibility of thought warranted, formality insisted upon, all will be affected by the often unarticulated but presupposed point of the law.

Of course, no politico-legal order has just one aim. All are mixed and the balance between different aims varies between orders, within them, and over time. So too with the particular means developed to achieve them. However, distinctions can be made between the predominating aims that have institutional significance in particular orders, and they are revealing.

Since legal aims, assumptions and functions so infiltrate form, one has two options: on the one hand, knowing the former to infer the latter or, on the other, knowing the latter to work back to the former. The first route is the one commonly taken by theorists of the rule of law, such as Fuller (1969) and Selznick (Nonet & Selznick, 1978), who move from conceptions of what the law might be asked to do to characterizations of what is required to do that. The second route is the one Durkheim took, imaginatively if not completely successfully, in trying to test hypotheses about the sources of social solidarity by looking at the predominant character of law in different societies (Durkheim, 1984). It is also what Roberto Unger appears to have had in mind when he claimed that 'Each society reveals through its law the innermost secrets of the manner in which it holds men together. Moreover, the conflicts among kinds of law reflect different ways of ordering human groups' (Unger, 1976: 47).

Here I will take the first path, and begin by delineating a general ambition, and three reasons that support that ambition, for the rule of law. I will then move on to sketch in a general sense what that might require of the law and of its subjects. After that, I will reverse direction and take the second path. In neither case will I treat the point(s) of the enterprise separately from its (their) practices. For central to my argument is the claim that the rule of law is not a mere technical matter of the forms of legal rules, institutions and practices. Rather those forms are connected with, emanate from, and enable, particular aims, assumptions and functions. To strive for the rule of law, then, is to carry into the law and through it the burden of these underlying presuppositions. Its good functioning will depend upon them substantially approximating the character of the social relations with which the law deals. If rule-of-law forms are substantially absent, on the other hand, not rule-of-law ambitions, but others, might be presumed to lie behind the law.

Implicit in More's and Gleeson's encomiums, then, should not be sought a blanket endorsement of everything that can be called, in some bland and undiscriminating sense, 'law', but rather a particular normative conception of what law can and should do, one which will only be realized by certain *kinds* of law that serve certain sorts of ends in certain sorts of ways. That normative conception is conventionally summed up as 'the rule of law'.[5]

The rule of law is commonly understood by contrast with arbitrary exercise of power. That, above all, is the evil that it is supposed to curb. The *reasons* one might want power to be so restrained are various, but they include most prominently what might be called a *protective* and a *facilitative* element. The protective aspect has to do with diminishing the chances that subjects will be assailed by unrestrained exercise of power; the facilitative with contribution to interpersonal knowability and predictability, from which might come mutual confidence, co-ordination and co-operation. These are both good reasons, and it is hard to see a limit to their usefulness. Where would it be better to be unprotected against dangers from our fellows? Where would lonely solipsism be better than productive co-operation? The difficult questions, and the contingent limitations to the answers, have to do with how we can serve these goals. The answers are deeply influenced, even when their authors are unaware of it, by the nature, size, complexity, degree of differentiation and institutionalization, particular histories and traditions, of the societies in which they are conceived.

In the modern European tradition, Hobbes supplemented by Locke, and more recently Judith Shklar are theorists of the first reason; Hobbes emphasizes the importance of an effective state to protect us from others, Locke stresses the need for protection against the state itself. Adam Smith and more recently Lon Fuller and Friedrich Hayek are theorists of the second reason. All these writers presuppose a lot about the societies they are talking about: most obviously, for example, that they are not small or nomadic or what used to be called 'stateless' (Fortes & Evans-Pritchard, 1948; Krygier, 1980). There is plenty of evidence that small societies without our sorts of institutional apparatus can nevertheless contrive to protect their members from familiar dangers (unfamiliar dangers, particularly unprecedented ones such as alien invasions, are a different matter), and encourage certain sorts of necessary co-operation, without a war of all against all. If the societies endure, one has to assume that this has to some degree been achieved, though it is an empirical matter how and a normative one how well. It is also an empirical matter, on which social theory bears, how well such societies can cope with the introduction and intervention of societies of other sorts.

That said, modernity militates against the endurance of such societies on the basis of their internal social control mechanisms alone. It destroys many and renders others ineffective. Among other things that wreak such destruction, modern states and law do. The present chapter draws on abundant evidence of that, and such destruction and erosion have occurred in many parts of the world. So, for better or for worse, there are many places where the concerns and observations of Hobbes, Locke, Shklar and Smith are or have become indispensable, if only to restrain the power of the institutions they presuppose. In societies with large and concentrated centres of power (traditionally political power, but the point can be generalized), we do better if we can rely on institutions that are able to lessen the chances of that power being exercised arbitrarily, capriciously, without authority or redress. We do better, too, in large societies, where we are constantly interacting with non-intimates, if we can know important things about people we may not know well in other respects. Such things include their and our rights, responsibilities, risks and constraints. In small societies, as in families, we can know many of these things from personal everyday experience. In larger agglomerations such knowledge is often not available. Where the rule of law *matters* in a society, however, we can know these things even about strangers. That makes their and our activities more predictable to each other and might make us less fearful of and more co-operative with them, and, of course, them of and with us. This can lead to a productive spiral of virtuous circles (Krygier, 1997), where each gains by reasonable trust in others.

Some authors claim the rule of law offers a third benefit. Not merely valuable as a constraint on power, it is a way of *realizing* certain values, among them 'respect for the dignity, integrity, and moral equality of persons and groups. Thus understood, the rule of law enlarges horizons even as it conveys a message of restraint' (Selznick, 1999: 26; cf Dyzenhaus, 1998). These values, too, are not universally upheld, but in Western societies at the very least, they have strong constituencies. The view that the rule of law encompasses the realization of important values is contested, however, with many writers preferring a more austere, formal conception, and contending that links between the rule of law and the realization of those values are contingent at best. I think the connections are several and intimate. Again, I am presupposing an institutional fabric which is not known everywhere.

There is, at the very least, a practical, if not a logical, connection between the rule of law and important values. It is a negative connection, important for what it seeks to block. A government which seeks to treat its citizens as mere means or in a substantially discriminatory way, even more in despotic or terroristic ways, is very likely to violate the rule of law. The rule of law conspires to bring exercises of power into the light, and it gets in the way. Since many rulers prefer the dark and do not like anything to get in the way, doing so is a central part of the point of the rule of law. Such rulers might well contrive to uphold a façade of the rule of law, but not the rule of law itself, not 'the imposing of effective inhibitions upon power and the defence of the citizen from power's all-intrusive claims' (Thompson, 1977: 266).

Moreover, the connection between the rule of law and the morality of law is not merely practical and negative, but more immediate and positive as well. For, as a number of authors have remarked (Fuller, 1969: 162; Raz, 1979), the rule of law's assurance that citizens will be penalized only on the basis of laws knowable when they act, is a condition of the state's treating people with respect, as the subjects of laws rather than their objects, as responsible agents whose interests and projects the law should serve and facilitate, rather than things, beasts or children which the law can freely mould, direct and control. Observing the forms of the rule of law is not, of course, a sufficient condition for this. A clever manipulator might seek greater productivity from a despised workforce, say, by treating them as though they were subjects; they might even get to wear jeans to work. He might then unceremoniously sack them, if it suits him. It is not clear he has treated them with much respect. Nevertheless, a regime which systematically violates the rule of law, and deals with citizens on the basis of secret, surprising, retrospective, ad hoc, decrees and whims, is certainly not one which treats them with respect, so the rule of law might be considered a necessary condition for modern governments to do so.

These benefits are inherent in even the narrowest, most procedural, versions of the rule of law, but on another view, though formal regularity should be an important component, it should not be the limit of one's ambitions for the rule of law. Legal orders typically embody and generate certain values, both in their animating principles and in the complaints they provoke when their practices flout the values that give them legitimacy. These include values such as those of equality before the law, procedural fairness or due process, and in particular legal traditions much more. On this view, which I share, the rule of law is incomplete to the extent that those values are not honoured.

These, then, are reasons why the rule of law has been thought to matter deeply in certain sorts of societies: those with large populations and differentiated legal and political institutions. It seeks to protect citizens from arbitrary power, facilitate fruitful interaction among them and between them and the state, and secure that they are treated in accordance with important legal values.

Less easy to specify in the abstract is what in particular is necessary to achieve these ends. Different societies, with different traditions, have sought (and achieved) the rule of law in different ways, and arguably could not all have achieved them in the same ways. Achievement of the rule of law is, in any case, always a matter of degree, and similar degrees of achievement can be attained in various ways. Nevertheless, there are some general conditions which need substantially to be fulfilled. I will mention four, three of them having to do with the nature of legal institutions and official behaviour. These are staples of the jurisprudential literature. The fourth, which I consider more important, is rarely much explored.

First, the *scope* of the law is crucial. To the extent that powerful players are above or beyond the law, the rule of law must suffer. Law must reach everyone, including those at what Lenin called the 'commanding heights' (though he made sure it never reached there), and it must do so in the polity, the economy and the society.

There have been many polities where the ideal of subjecting governments or notables or relatives to law was unknown and would seem outlandish. Even where the idea exists, the extent to which it is realized by a legal order will vary markedly between polities and over time. To the extent that the idea and the practice are lacking, however, so is a crucial element of the rule of law.

Second, people will not be able to use the law to guide their own acts or their expectations of others unless they can know and understand it (either directly or through agents such as lawyers, accountants, associates). So the law must be of a *character* such that it can be known. Lawyers have developed lists of the particular characteristics necessary for that to be possible. The law, they say, must at least exist, of course, but it must also be public, comprehensible, relatively clear, stable, non-contradictory, prospective, and so on. These lists are well known, and however long they are their rationale is the same: the law must be of a character that people can guide their actions and expectations by it. These criteria are never fully complied with, and the rule of law is never perfectly attained. There can also be circumstances where, to correct deficiencies in the rule of law, such as secret laws, a government might have to contemplate breaching one or other of these standards, and, for example, consider retrospective, curative, laws. So mechanical ticking-off of check-lists for the rule of law is singularly inappropriate, though it is often done.

The necessary thing is that the law be knowable. How that is done is an essentially empirical, socio-legal question, to which lawyers can offer the fruits of legal experience, but rarely much empirical knowledge. For lawyers often stop at the place such investigation should start, the legal vehicle of transmission, or at a somewhat skewed sample of law-affected behaviour later, where legally relevant bruises and projects are brought to them. They do not regularly investigate those places where legal transmissions are most typically and crucially received and acted upon – in the myriad law-affected everyday interactions of individuals and groups, which go nowhere near lawyers or officials but where law in a rule-of-law society does its most important work.

For successful attainment of the rule of law is a *social* outcome, not a merely legal one. What matters, here as everywhere with the rule of law, is how the law affects subjects. The general truth is that no-one can guide their actions by laws that they do not know. The contingent propositions, often offered as though they were necessary, tell us what sorts of characteristics of law itself are thought by lawyers to serve that end. But since the distance between law in books and action is often long, and the space full of many other things, it is a matter of investigation and social theory what might best, in particular circumstances, in particular societies, further that goal.

A third condition of the rule of law takes us beyond the rules to the ways they are administered. The law must be administered and enforced by institutions and in ways that take its terms seriously, interpret it in non-arbitrary ways that can be known and understood publicly, and enforce it fairly. So there must be institutions to apply and enforce the law and the law must effectively nourish, guide and bind the thought and action of those who occupy the institutions. Again there is no single obvious way in which these conditions must be complied with, and again social effects are more important than 'mechanical jurisprudence', but it is often obvious when these conditions are not being met by officials. What under communism was called 'telephone law' (where Party officials ring judges and direct them in particular cases) is an example. There are many others.

Finally, to be of sociological and political, rather than purely legal, consequence, the rule of law depends on law that does, and is widely expected and assumed to, *matter*. Law *counts*, as a constituent and as a frame in the exercise of social power, both by those who exercise it (which, where citizens make *use* of the law, should be far more than just officials) and by those who are affected by its exercise. What is involved when the law counts is a complex sociological question on which the law bears. It is not in itself a legal question, for it depends as much on characteristics of the society as of the law, and on their interactions. But the rule of law depends upon it.

What does it mean for law to count in a society, in such a way that we feel confident saying that the rule of law exists there? All the questions asked here have a sociological dimension, this one above all. It asks about the social *reach* and *weight* of law, and the answers, whatever they are, will have to attend to questions of sociology and politics, as much as of law. Indeed, social and political questions are central ones to ask about the place of law in a society, and they will be answered differently in different societies, whatever the written laws say or have in common. This is not because the law has no significance, but because the nature and extent of that significance cannot be read off from the law itself.

Where the law really does count, we can foreshorten the question why, as lawyers commonly do, and answer it in terms of the provisions and institutions of the law. For when the law is socially and politically significant, the legal position will bear closely on the factual position and the hour of the lawyer is at hand. But that is only because what lawyers do not know, the conditions of legal effectiveness, gives significance to what they do, the law. When those conditions are lacking, lawyers' talk is not only often boring, as it can be at the best of times, but beside the point. For if no-one is listening it doesn't matter too much what the law is saying.

Legal philosophers usually mention that the law must be *effective*, but that merely hints at the complexity of what the rule of law depends on, far greater complexity than is needed for a merely effective legal order. Effectiveness begins with obedience in any legal order. For the rule of law to exist, that must be manifest to a considerable degree both by ordinary citizens and the powerful. But for the rule of law to thrive, beyond mere obedience, *use and manner of use* matter as well.

If the laws are there but governments by-pass them, it is not the law that rules. So exercises of governmental power must be predominantly channelled through laws that people can know. But governments, as we have seen, are not the only addressees of the rule of law. And for the rule of law to count in the life of its subjects, as important as mere *submission* to law, or even adequate *access* to and *supply* of laws and legal institutions, though far less remarked upon than either, is constraint by *demand* for, and (often unreflective) use of legal services and resources. Such demand and use extend beyond, and frequently will not involve, direct enlistment of legal officials or institutions. They are manifest in the extent to which legal institutions, concepts, options, resources frame, inform and support the choices of citizens.

This can occur, and vary, in two ways. The most obvious is in direct invocation of legal institutions. Possibility of access to them varies greatly between societies and within them. Willingness and ability to take advantage of possibilities of access vary greatly as well. In many times and places, people might even be willing to approach legal institutions but they are excluded from access to them. In others, including contemporary Russia, it appears that they are unwilling to make much use even of laws and institutions they could use (Hendley et al., 1999: 88–108; Holmes et al., 1998: 70–88). In yet others, like the United States, many citizens, perhaps too many, are both willing and able. Hyperlegality is perhaps a pathology of law, but so is hypolegality, its impotent mirror image.

More socially significant than citizens' (generally rare) direct invocations of official channels, however, is the extent to which they are able and willing to use and to rely upon legal resources as cues, standards, models, 'bargaining chips', 'regulatory endowments', authorizations, immunities, in relations with each other and with the state, as realistic (even if necessarily imperfect) indicators of what they and others can and are likely to do. For it is a socio-legal truism, which still escapes many lawyers, that the importance of legal institutions is poorly indicated by the numbers who make direct use of them. The primary impact of such institutions, as Marc Galanter has emphasized,[6] is not as magnets for social disputes, a very small proportion of which ever come to them, but as beacons, sending signals about law, rights, costs, delays, advantages, disadvantages, and other possibilities, into the community. Even when these signals are bright and visible, and people take them seriously, they are not the only ones that are sent out or received in a society.[7] In turn, the receivers are not a single entity or homogeneous group but plural, different, self-and-other-directed, within numerous, often distinct, sometimes and in some respects overlapping, 'semi-autonomous' groups which affect them, often deeply.

Preparedness to draw on, or assume the relevance of, legal resources and entitlements, then, is a contingent and variable sign of the extent to which the rule of law is a living presence in a society. For it is a presupposition particularly of the second goal of the rule of law: to facilitate planning and fruitful interaction among people. If people know nothing of the law, or knowing something think nothing of it, or think of it but don't take it seriously, or even, taking it seriously don't know what to do about it, then their lives will not be enriched by the rule of law (though if it applies to governments they might still be partly protected by it).

Another way of addressing this point is to say that, especially in its facilitative role, the rule of law presupposes a particular descriptive and normative view of the people it affects. They are supposed to understand themselves to possess rights and duties defined by law, shared with others, and usable as reliable underpinnings for interpersonal relations, particularly among non-intimates, or even among intimates when things go awry (Waldron, 1993: 370–91). And such interaction is supported, that is, actually helped and also considered worthy of support, by the values inherent in the rule of law.

Treating such people in such a way, as legal 'right-and-duty-bearing subjects', is, as we have seen, to treat them in just one of the ways among many in which power might treat them. It is a condition, to repeat, of the state treating them as subjects, not mere objects, of the law, or in another idiom, to treat them with respect. Refusing to treat such people in such a way is commonly to treat them as objects and without respect, though there are circumstances of youth, disability, weakness, or poverty where lack of respect is not the sole reason.

Even where the rule of law is thickly institutionalized (Selznick, 1992: 234–5), it is never the only guiding value of a legal order. Laws do many things. Not all laws are addressed to citizens. Some branches of law do not raise rule-of-law issues as directly or dramatically as others. We demand many things of government besides respect: and governments do many things for and to us besides respecting us. And in any event we're not perfect. And even where we believe the rule of law to be strong, the picture will be messy, overlain with partial achievements, and other achievements which cut across the rule of law. There may be respectable reasons for governments to act in ways other than required by the rule of law. But it is important always to recognize the difference between an order where the rule of law is strongly institutionalized and socially significant, and one where it is not.

Understood to refer to the rule of law, then, there are in many circumstances serious grounds for the conviction shared by the Chief Justice and the Archbishop, that law 'restrains and civilises power'. Does the planting and growth of law in Australia bear that conviction out? The answer is clear: yes and no. I begin with 'yes' and move on to 'no'.

**Yes**

> The end of the law is, not to abolish or restrain,
> but to preserve and enlarge freedom.
> 
> John Locke

My primary text in this matter is David Neal's excellent book, *The Rule of Law in a Penal Colony* (1991. See also, Atkinson, 1997; Braithwaite, 2001; Hirst, 1983), the thesis of which is simple and, though the word is unfortunate in this context, arresting.

Neal begins his book with an exemplary, extraordinary and now often told tale: that of Henry and Susannah Kable, separately sentenced to death for burglary in England, reprieved, and transported to Australia, after having met and had a child in Norwich Castle Jail. The captain of the hulk onto which Henry and Susannah were loaded initially refused to take their child on board. A sympathetic prison turnkey took pity on the distraught parents, rode (with the child) the several hundred mile return journey to see, and successfully plead with, the Home Secretary, Lord Sydney, in London, and returned the child to his parents in time for them to travel together to the other side of the earth. His mission attracted great public interest, and led to a public subscription of a substantial amount (£20) with which the couple bought goods for their new life and which they loaded onto a transport ship, the *Alexander*.

A month after they arrived in New South Wales, Henry and Susannah were married, but the newly-weds were without their parcel. So they began the first civil case ever held in Australia, against the captain of the ship which had charge of it. They won:

Thus, the first sitting of a civil court in Australia and the first civil case to be heard, occurred at the behest of two convicts under sentence. Moreover, it named an important figure in the colony, a ship's captain, as defendant, subjected him to the power of the court's jurisdiction and officers, and made an order against him. It vindicated the property rights of two convicts and publicly demonstrated the ability even of convicts to invoke the legal process in the new colony. Nor was it to be the last time that convicts used the legal system to assert their rights in the colony. (Neal, 1991: 6)

From that time on, Henry was unstoppable, becoming in 1789 a police constable, then chief constable of Sydney (from which position he was dismissed in 1802 for misbehaviour), a successful if somewhat shady businessman, father of eleven children, and ultimately a rich and fulfilled octogenarian. Still today his numerous descendants are scattered through the land. But the story is not really about him or them, but about what his treatment and his case symbolizes. And this is Neal's topic.

Neal's book seeks to answer an intriguing question: how was it that an often harsh and brutal penal colony came, within the space of fifty years, to be a free society? After all, the first white settlers in Australia did not come here for a holiday, nor did they get one when they arrived. Early New South Wales was not a pleasant or easy place to be. Apart from the harshness of everyday life there was 'one fact that everyone in the colony knew, both convict and free: convicts were sent there as a punishment' (Neal, 1991: 45–6). Against more sunny accounts of the early settlement, such as John Hirst's, Neal insists on the dark and stark significance of that for all those who first settled here. In accordance with that fundamental fact and purpose, the nascent penal colony had no representative political institutions, no jury trials, almost no lawyers (except for some convicts), a dominant military presence, and governors whose formal powers were great and whose practical autonomy, in this wilderness at the end of the world, was even greater. Fifty years later, while the majority of its population was still convict or ex-convict, it was a free society, with considerable legal protection against arbitrary power, and a representative legislature. There is no evidence that the British government planned it that way. Nor was the result inevitable. Nevertheless the transformation occurred, and most Australians are its beneficiaries. Why that happened is a matter of more than local or antiquarian interest.

Neal is well aware that there are many reasons for the changes to which he draws attention. However the major argument of his book is that one of the central reasons that New South Wales became a free society has to do with law, in a very special sense. His argument is that it was not just convicts who were transported, but particular ideas and ideals – ideas and ideals about law. What transformed Australia from penal colony to free society was what the convicts carried from Britain in their heads, 'as part of their cultural baggage'. Central to that cultural baggage was belief in the rule of law, belief that the law should and could matter, that it should be respected by their rulers and that it should and could form the basis of challenge to these rulers. 'A cluster of ideas known as the rule of law provided the major institutions, arguments, vocabulary and symbols with which the convicts forged the transformation.' (Neal, 1991: 62) Convicts fought, and often won, political and other crucial battles in the courts. When they won it was because their opponents' hands were tied. They too, after all, had the same baggage in their heads. And even where they didn't, the courts did, insisting on their independence under British law, and the subordination of the apparently autocratic governors to that same law.

There were many ways in which this could have been otherwise. What if the convicts had come from Russia? There would have been no tricky issues about the legal rights of free-born Russians. The penal colony would not have had – from the very beginning – courts in which convicts could sue their masters, and oftentimes win, and this for two reasons: courts would not have been provided, and had they been few people would have thought to use them. There would have been no fuss about trial by jury. Nor would the governors of the colony have constantly had to battle against prickly judges, conscious of their independence and attached to their traditions, or free settlers against far-too-smart emancipist lawyers, such as Wentworth and Wardell, who were often able to best them in court.

What if – more plausibly – the convicts had been cynically dismissive of the legal system? What if they had been imbued with then current ideas of universal rights or had chosen strategies of armed revolt? It is clear that many convicts were aware of these options, but in the main they were not chosen. Instead, as Neal demonstrates:

the terms of political debate in New South Wales proceeded on very traditional lines. The protagonists relied on their British birthrights and deployed the language of the rule of law to secure them and to forge new social and political order out of the penal colony at Botany Bay. (Neal, 1991: 25)

The reasons for this owed a great deal to British institutions, in one of the two senses mentioned earlier. Institutional *structures* were pretty rudimentary at the start, but institutions in the sense of rules, norms, common understandings, were thick on the ground, or at least in people's heads. Institutions of this kind were not rudimentary, and not new, in any sense. For the Britain from which the convicts came was an unusually law-suffused country, and more than that, a highly rule-of-law-suffused one. It had endured a century of struggle over the political centrality of law, a struggle full – as Neal observes – of 'powerful icons', among them Chief Justice Coke's rebukes to his sovereign James I: in particular his insistence that no-one, including the king, was above the law. As E. P. Thompson has argued eloquently, 'Turn where you will, the rhetoric of eighteenth-century England is saturated with the notion of law' (Thompson, 1977: 263; and see Atkinson, 1997: Ch. 1). That law was not merely something which rulers used, but a language in which people of all classes spoke, argued, claimed, and a source of rights for which they demanded respect. Not always successfully, certainly not with equal power, but insistently. To an extent unmatched anywhere in the world then, except perhaps the other British offshoot, America, law mattered in England; and, as Neal shows, it mattered consequently – and in some ways uniquely – in the unpropitious circumstances of New South Wales too.

This cultural inheritance was exported with our first white settlers, implausible avatars of the rule of law. What political historians of Australia – H. V. Evatt apart – have tended to regard simply as political struggles over civil liberties, Neal locates as far deeper arguments over the proper role of law in political and social life; more traditional arguments too, understandable only in the light of far older struggles and arguments over Magna Carta, the liberties of British subjects, and a 'government of laws and not of men'.

Indeed in some ways the inheritance was augmented by transportation. It is already notable that, unlike most prisons of that time, this Antipodean one was provided with courts from the start. That was not intended, until as late as November 1786, when Lord Sydney 'seems to have decided that too much was being left to chance' (Atkinson, 1997: 89). In the months before the departure of the First Fleet, it was decided both that convicts would be given the protection of a judicial system, and also be entitled to absolute rights in land. Both decisions were consequential. The first, in the absence of other available public institutions in which struggles over power and status could be transacted, made available institutions useful for political fights, in which talk of the rule of law was useful rhetoric. It was, however, far more than that. Convicts fought battles for status and recognition in terms of their entitlements under the law, believed in the rule of law, insisted that the authorities should respect it, demanded rights that they believed flowed from it. A great deal flowed from these beliefs. In the term used here, the scope of the law reached both high and low, to the governor and to the convicts; convicts knew and insisted upon that; they were rather liberally granted legal rights; and they made use of them, often to good effect.

Indeed, convicts had several legal rights that they would not have had in England. As John Hirst emphasizes, masters were not allowed to beat their servants themselves. That could only happen at the hands of authorized floggers under court order (Hirst, 1983: 58). John Braithwaite nicely captures the significance of this:

> Consider in historical context the procedural innovation involved here. Masters of convicts were being required to have their corporal punishment authorized by a court when British naval and military commanders were not so constrained, when masters under English common law could flog apprentices and indentured workers on the spot, schoolmasters could do so to students, and it was not long since husbands had a right/duty to do so to recalcitrant wives. (Braithwaite, 2001: 20; see Hirst, 1995: 270)

Convicts retained other important rights as well. They could petition the governor, could be witnesses in court against their masters, could bring actions against abusive masters, could not be punished except by due process of law, and 'While the adversity of floggings was terrible, mostly it could be avoided by sticking to the rules' (Braithwaite, 2001: 21). They could, as we have seen, own property and sue to protect it. Australia's British subjects believed they had rights under the law and insisted that the authorities should respect them. Apart from all that, convicts ate and dressed better than at home as well, and the sun shone.

Sunshine apart, none of this had to happen. As felons, convicts forfeited their civil rights in English law and the various rights allowed them here could quite legally have been withheld. Even the Kables' suit could have been prevented from the start. How such a policy might have been sustained in a society where convicts constituted the majority is not obvious, and this was clearly a major reason that they were treated better than the law might have allowed. Their labour and their co-operation in building the colony were necessary, and seen to be so, from the start. So interest conspired with ideals to fashion a strange bitter-sweet concoction – rather quickly more sweet than bitter – for the convicts of New South Wales.

A striking feature underpinning this story, for all its brutality, corruption, and harshness, is that convicts were conceived not only as 'British subjects', as they were in law, but 'subjects' in a much more robust sense of the word. There were things that could not be done to them, facilities that must be afforded to them, demands that they could make, and which were listened to. They could *use* the law, not merely suffer it. They would undoubtedly have preferred not to be convicts, and they were often treated harshly, but they could not complain that they were systematically treated in ways that denied their humanity or personhood.

A subject is the author of his acts. Not necessarily the author of the law that applies to him; that is the promise of democracy not the rule of law. Moreover convicts were subject to particular restrictions, for they were criminals sentenced to be punished; subjects under sentence, as it were. But like other British subjects, the law assumed convicts to be, in considerable measure, the real and proper authors *of their lives*, and many of them took advantage of this by proving that that is just what they were.

Unfortunately, I do not know of evidence that tells us how much convicts' sense of the law entered into their everyday affairs, as distinct from their demands on public institutions. What I have read about convicts and law has tended to focus on direct encounters or uses of such institutions. My guess is that a society whose inhabitants are self-conscious enough of their rights to use official institutions will be effectively aware of their rights in their interpersonal dealings, even though the reverse is not necessarily the case. But that is amateur speculation, and one could offer alternative speculations. Perhaps, for example, law was reserved for dealings with officials, and convicts were after all experienced in such dealings, but irrelevant to their everyday lives together. Evidence of how law entered everyday interaction would be important evidence to have, as an indicator of how much the rule of law entered into interpersonal, and subject–state relations in a way that might have facilitated the civil society that ultimately grew here. Were I a historian of this period, it would be where I would next seek to look. Perhaps historians have done so, and I would welcome word of that.

There is, however, one indirect indication which may bear on what went on 'in the shadow of the law'. It suggests that the treatment of convicts as subjects was not merely a morally attractive fact, but turned out to be salutary in its larger implications. John Braithwaite compares the fate of non-criminal slaves in the United States and criminal convicts in Australia, and demonstrates that 'during the nineteenth century, Australia was transformed from being a high crime frontier society to a low crime society, while the US was transformed from a low to a high crime society' (Braithwaite, 2001: 17). He explains the Australian transformation thus:

When one shares an identity as a citizen[8] of a just legal order, there is a willingness to comply with that order. To realign the identities of convicts to those of law abiding citizens, convicts need to be persuaded that they are now in reach of a society where the rule of law is something that offers practical protection to them and is therefore worthy of being honoured. Brutality is more bearable when its end can be imagined and seen and when its excesses can be challenged by fair procedure. Neither Australian Aborigines nor American slaves could imagine its end in the same way the white Australian convicts could. (Braithwaite, 2001: 21)

One should not over-romanticize this story. Much of the law was extremely harsh, and in any event the rule of law was not the only inheritance with which the convict settlement endowed us. For example, as it grew, as Braithwaite has shown, so too did a robust tradition of police corruption that stems from the first convicts-turned-policemen (including Kable again) who quickly came to participate in the government of this penal colony. And of course there are the legendary traditions, or myths, of Australian distaste and disregard for law and authority, which, though they might seem far-fetched to a visiting Romanian, or Indonesian or Fijian, are among our most resonant myths.

But they *are* myths. Compared to most contemporary societies, at any rate those I know and know of, our distaste and disregard for law is far less striking than our remarkable routine obedience and invocation of it. We are a strikingly law-filled society. Rather British, as a matter of fact. The law provides many of our symbols, highest office-holders, governors-general galore, investigators of all manner of contentious issues, whether or not they involve breaches of the law, and until recently a frame for industrial bargaining viewed, indeed, as 'a new province for law and order'. That frame, the industrial conciliation and arbitration system, was intended to answer the question put by its author and first President of the Conciliation and Arbitration Court, 'Is it possible for a civilized community so to regulate these relations as to make the bounds of the industrial chaos narrower, to add new territory to the domain of law and order?' (Higgins, 1922). That recent governments have decided it is impossible, or at least unprofitable, does not diminish the significance of law in our history, even if it cuts back the legal imperialism so prominent in Australia's development. Indeed one author complains that law has so dominated our polity that it has altogether squeezed out popular sovereignty in favour of sovereignty of the judiciary (Davidson, 1991). I find that argument over-heated and implausible, but the mere fact that it can be made seriously and at punishing length suggests something of the weight of law in our polity.

The moral of this story is that – notwithstanding initially autocratic institutional structures of frequently indifferent quality, subjects with an unhappy relationship with legal and political institutions, and harsh and difficult circumstances – the settlers of New South Wales laid the foundations of a free and law-governed society in a very brief span of time. One of the most important assets they had was the institutionalized cultural baggage that they brought to the colony; baggage which, unlike the Kables' parcel, could not easily be stolen. As Neal remarks:

Neither the imperatives of a penal colony nor those of a military outpost had displaced the principle that English people, even convicts, carried with them such of their rights as were not forfeited. Hence, New South Wales experienced the paradox of the rule of law in a penal colony. However, in the Antipodes, where strange creatures abounded, one having fur like an animal but a bill like a duck, paradox was plentiful.[9]

**No**

Do not shoot me. I'm a B-b-british object.
David Malouf, *Remembering Babylon*[10]

The Kables' victory did not mean, of course, that nothing could be stolen in the new colony. Indeed a whole continent was, under cover of law. Nor is the paradox Neal describes the only one to accompany the introduction of the rule of law to the colony. Another is a direct result of the same process that Neal describes, but it is a very different result, for it led to the dispossession and decimation of scores of thousands of people and hundreds of peoples.

The plight of Australia's indigenes was so overdetermined that it is difficult to estimate the role of law in it, but it has surely been considerable. Why it has is itself a question with many mutually reinforcing answers. Both evasion of the rule of law and commitment to it are among those answers. Where it might have helped, it was rarely achieved and often not sought. Where elements of it were insisted upon, they often couldn't help and instead had to harm. I deal with two formative moments here. In the first, the reach of the law was limited; in the second, while it reached far enough, its aim was askew.

When Governor Phillip landed, he brought with him instructions that required the colonists to

> endeavour by every possible means to open an intercourse with the natives, and to conciliate their affections, enjoining all our subjects to live in amity and kindness with them. And if any of our subjects shall wantonly destroy them, or give them unnecessary interruption in the exercise of their several occupations, it is our will and pleasure that you do cause such offenders to be brought into punishment according to the degree of the offence.

For the first part of his term, Phillip appeared genuinely in sympathy with these aims. Instructions to later governors were similar, but already by the later parts of Phillip's rule and increasingly thereafter, they had less and less to do with what was happening here. By 1835, when Lord Glenelg had taken over as Secretary of State with responsibility for the colonies, such instructions had taken on a disconcerting mix of piety with impotence. Writing to Governor Stirling of Western Australia, he directs:

> It will be your duty to impress upon the settlers that it is the determination of the Government to visit any act of injustice or violence on the natives with the utmost severity and that in no case will those convicted of them remain unpunished. Nor will it be sufficient simply to punish the guilty, but ample compensation must be made to the injured party for the wrong received … whenever it may be necessary to bring a native to justice every form should be observed which would be

considered necessary in the case of a white person and no infliction of punishment, however trivial, should be permitted except by the award of some competent authority.

Hasluck drily records that Stirling, who was at least in part the object of this lesson, printed extracts from the despatch in the *Government Gazette*, and also 'Without comment, but with obvious satiric intention, he republished above it [his] despatch of 1832 which told settlers to protect themselves' (Hasluck, 1970: 50).

Whether Glenelg believed he would be obeyed or was merely writing for the public[11] or history, his injunctions were of little effect. Of course, had they and the earlier instructions to governors been successfully enforced, or indeed enforceable – given the lack of financial and administrative commitment to support them and the mysterious complexity of the encounter – we might have been able to say that the first goal of the rule of law, protection from arbitrary exercise of power, had purchase in the colony. But, for two reasons, that was extremely unlikely from the start.

First was the contradiction, well expressed by Henry Reynolds, inherent in the imperial government's position in the early years of New South Wales (and Tasmania):

Governors were exhorted to treat the tribes with amity and kindness while according no recognition to Aboriginal ownership of land. They counselled peace but sanctioned the use of military force and declarations of martial law when the Aboriginal tribes resisted the incursions of the settlers and their flocks and herds. (Reynolds, 2001: 56)

If occupation of land is non-negotiable, resistance can be assumed to follow. Civil relations are inconsistent with the combination. To insist on the primary goal and affect surprise at its readily foreseeable (and very soon visible) consequences can seem disingenuous.

Second, as Hobbes understood, protection from arbitrariness requires a government with a monopoly over the imposition of force, and in the early years of settlement in New South Wales there was no such government much beyond the limits of Sydney. Thus on the relentlessly expanding frontier restrictions on the use of force by settlers (and natives) were not enforced, and given the nature of white settlement could not have been. This was what prompted the despair of James Stephen at a problem which would 'set all legislation at defiance': 'how to provide for the Government of persons hanging on the Frontiers of vast pastoral country to which there is no known or assignable limit … To coerce them by Statute of any kind would I should conceive prove in the result a vain undertaking.'[12]

Even when public officials arrived, in the form of police and magistrates, they were often too few and too weak to stop established practices and often had no interest in doing so, but collaborated with settlers who were, after all, their own people. Rowley points out, for example, that governments have only been able to check the depredations of settlers in colonies when the governments led and the settlers followed. The standard pattern in Australia was the reverse. Rowley identifies the logic of the situation thus:

> The problem of a cultural frontier in the colonial situation is basically the same everywhere. If the frontier is expanding, law and order depend on the government leading the way and taking charge of the processes of trade, settlement, recruitment of labour; and establishing by use of superior force the best approximation to a rule of law possible in these very difficult conditions. This has happened only rarely in colonial history ... In any case, more 'development' is necessary for more revenue. Development involves the taking of land: and in spite of legal theories about certain lands being 'waste and vacant', practically all land is the object of indigenous claims to ownership. There may be violent resistance, and reprisals by the settlers taking the law into their own hands. Efforts by police to keep the peace tend to come later. In practice, the police will go where there is 'trouble'; and the nature of the trouble will be described for them by the settler community. So the first contact of the Aboriginal with the police has been characteristically in the role of an avenging force. (Rowley, 1970: 123–4)

Settlers were often isolated, frightened[13] and, in the nature of things, on the make. And what they were intent on making, pastoral success, involved them in taking Aborigines' land and waterholes, killing their game as pests, killing them, too, for a variety of reasons. This is precisely the sort of situation Hobbes envisaged, and that stems from a truth often enough manifested and noted: *Homo homini lupus*. Often nothing more high-falutin' is necessary to explain it. In the nineteenth century, not always but often, it was as basic and shabby as that. Sometimes it was better, and not infrequently it was worse, helped along as it was by the weakness of restraints on the frontier, the superior power of the settlers, the fact that real interests were at stake, and beliefs that Aborigines were barbarian, not quite human, anyway nothing like us, and, by the late nineteenth century, doomed to die out.

What was the government to do? Rowley contrasts the policy of J. H. P. Murray in New Guinea with what typically occurred in Australia. Murray formulated 'Australia's only really humane frontier policy', that officers act only as civil police and only use force where necessary for the purpose of arrest. The policy was often 'in violent contrast with the facts', but Rowley observes:

There is a difference, nonetheless, between the practices that arise from a policy based on reprisals and those that arise from the breakdown of a principle based on the rights of the person ... No matter how inapplicable the law may be to the circumstances, once it may safely be assumed that the law does not bind the officer and settler on the frontier there can be no barrier against the worst tyranny and crime. (Rowley, 1970: 150)

The tyranny was not primarily state-imposed, though, and the crime not state crime. State protection was largely absent, and officers of state were often complicit, but settlers were the motors of the action. At least this was the observation of a visitor in the 1820s, who investigated the position of the Aborigines for the Methodist Missionary Society. Blacks, he wrote, were in

[a] state of exposure to caprices and wanton punishment ... exposed to the caprice, interests and whim of everybody, they are cast on the mercy of all and find protection from none. They are exposed without any fair means of redress to the ill treatment of all ... The White assumes within himself the power of punishment, and inflicts it upon the black just as the feeling of the moment impels. (Reynolds, 1996: 69)

Ultimately, however, from the perspective of the Aborigines and of the rule of law, it does not much matter whether it was the state directly, or the settlers on their own account, who acted 'just as the feeling of the moment impels'. Either way, where the reach or scope of the law ceases, so too must the rule of law.

Numerous authors mention the ambivalent way Aborigines were looked upon in the beginning, sometimes enemies with whom settlers were at war, sometimes British subjects entitled to the protection of the law.[14] The first interpretation might have justified lawlessness on the frontier, and, whatever the law, it was the most plausible gloss on the dispossession that was the basis of white history here. However, by the 1830s, it was unambiguously not the official interpretation: Aborigines were British subjects, in principle protected by and able to make use of British law. However if it is hard to see how they were or could have been protected by that law in the circumstances I have sketched, it is even less clear how they could make use of it.

In the first stages of contact, this was not primarily or even significantly a result of the character of the formal law. With a few exceptions, law had yet to be devised specifically for Aborigines. The 'law in the books' was generally that which applied to convicts. But contact brought out in the most dramatic and extreme forms the depth of those truisms of sociology of law that stress the distance between 'law in books' and 'law in action', or between official law and what Ehrlich and Petrażycki, respectively, call 'living' or 'intuitive' law (Ehrlich, 1936; Petrażycki, 1955). Those distances exist in every society, however familiar and obedient to law. But some societies are not at all familiar with it, and among those who are, not all are obedient. In this connection, I would repeat the following observation, born of reflection on Eastern Europe, which is even more dramatically applicable here:

> for the rule of law to *count*, rather than simply to be announced or decreed, people must *care* about what the law says – the rules themselves must be taken seriously, and the institutions must come to matter. They must enter into the psychological economy of everyday life – to bear both on calculations of likely official responses *and* on those many circumstances in which one's actions are very unlikely to come to any officials' attention at all. They must mesh with, rather than contradict or be irrelevant to the 'intutive law' of which Leon Petrażycki wrote, in terms of which people think about and organize their everyday lives. None of this can be simply decreed. (Krygier, 1999: 89–90)

Whatever the formal law was like, Aborigines did not and for a long time could not know it, or understand it. If Poles under Russian or Prussian or Austro-Hungarian rule throughout the nineteenth century, or under communism in the twentieth, took the law to be alien and imposed, were reluctant to enlist the legal system and not much used to doing so, then early-nineteenth-century Aborigines, assailed with the finest fruits of the common law tradition, were astronomically less well placed. And how could it have been otherwise? As Hasluck comments:

> These new British subjects did not know British law and they did not believe it was a good law, and even if they had known and believed, their situation and condition meant that the law was not accessible to them and that they were not amenable to it. They knew nothing of the process of sworn complaint, warrant, arrest, committal for trial, challenging the jury, pleading, legal defence, recovery of costs, suit for damages, summons for assault, evidence on oath, and so on. Those living in the bush did not know that it was wrong to resist arrest or hinder a policeman in the execution of his duty and they also frequently refused to stop when called upon to do so. (Hasluck, 1970: 123)

The notion in such circumstances of Aborigines *using* the law makes little sense. That is dramatically true of criminal law, where the process was in the hands of whites, and it was even more true of the sorts of action that led to Henry Kable's ascent. For, as Hasluck again notes, 'in any civil relation ... the move for redressing injury or maintaining a right rests with the wronged person' (Hasluck, 1970: 147–8). It takes a great deal to imagine crowds of avid Aboriginal litigants in the early years of settlement. Still less the far more important service that the rule of law is supposed to provide in informing and supporting the relations of citizens who never go to court but act on understandings of the law in countless routine individual acts, accidents and forms of co-operation in daily life. None of this 'tacit knowledge' was or could quickly be available to the Aborigines upon which the penal colony had been inflicted. In the long meantime, at so many levels in so many ways, British law contradicted exactly that 'living', 'intuitive' law that legal sociology has shown to be fundamental to people's ordinary lives, and to the structures, roles, culture and expectations that underpin them.

The rule of law, then, presupposes a lot to be effective and a lot to be good. In early contact with Aboriginal society its presuppositions did not exist even where the will to adhere to it did. And as we have seen that often did not exist either.

What of the values of the rule of law? If we accept these to extend to 'respect for the dignity, integrity, and moral equality of persons and groups', then they were denied from the beginning in ways already mentioned, and most momentously, by the denial of indigenous rights to land. This was not merely one legal choice which happened unfortunately to underlie the destruction of whole ways of life. After all that could just be an unfortunate accident: 'The operation was successful. The patient died.' However, at least after it was realized that Australia had been long inhabited 'from coast to coast' by people who depended upon, and had deep spiritual attachments to the lands they were losing, the denial of any prior rights to land presupposed a deeper, if not always conscious, commitment, sustained till 1992: denial of the full humanity of the landholders. It was the extreme example of a point that Raimond Gaita has made in his appreciation of the High Court's recognition of native title in *Mabo* as:

a belated recognition of their [Aborigines'] true humanity, because it is the recognition that they are beings with inner lives of the same depth and complexity as 'ours' and that therefore they can be wronged as seriously as we can be.

... For many of the settlers, the Aborigines were not the kind of limit to our will, to our interests and desires, that we mark when we speak of respecting someone's rights, or treating them as ends rather than as means, or of according them unconditional respect, and so on.[15]

Henry Reynolds, who in less philosophical fashion has made this the point of his life, makes a poignant observation in this connection:

The injustice was gross regardless of whether the Aboriginal circumstances were compared with those of the settlers or those of indigenous people in other Anglo-Saxon colonies of settlement ... whose native title was recognised ...

The contrast between the respect accorded Aboriginal property rights and those of everyone else in early colonial Australia was even greater (than the latter). ... Convicts – and marines as well – were hanged for theft while Sydney was still only a few months old. Hangmen and flagellators continued to enforce the sanctity of private property for the first two generations of settlement. A community with such priorities could not find a more decisive way to illustrate its fundamental disrespect for another society than to ignore its property rights. Even an enemy beaten in battle might receive more consideration. (Reynolds, 1996: 186–7; see also McCorquodale, 1986: 8)

Even if we limit the values inherent in the rule of law to such things as (formal) equality before the law, the right to a fair trial, and allied process values, early Aborigines were severely handicapped not only in fact but in principle. If in our own societies there are strong internal structural reasons why 'the haves come out ahead' (Galanter, 1974: 95–160) in court, this was a result massively augmented in the rare encounters between whites and blacks which came to court (Davies, 1987: 313–35). All the procedures and values were totally alien to the latter and quite literally out of their hands, and these practical difficulties were not eased by the facts that, for a long time, as heathens, blacks could not testify in court, and that long after emancipated convicts won their battle to serve on juries, Aborigines could not. But perhaps one should not harp on legal discriminations in this period. Apart from the quite fundamental problem of denial of rights to land, they were not systematic in the formal law, but occasional. That, however, was not where the action was. In another example of the difference between the law in books and the law in action, we have Rowley's reminder that 'there was very little legal discrimination against Aboriginal British subjects at the time when their annihilation was in full swing' (Rowley, 1973: 41).

This attempt to apply British law to Aborigines was, then, a remarkably sustained failure, if serving the interests of Aborigines was any part of its aim. By the 1860s, a new phase of our history began, however, that of self-government, which was established by then in every colony apart from Western Australia. By this time, governmental authority had spread much further within the individual colonies. And one could imagine that the situation might markedly improve: Aborigines could be protected, since the sway of government had grown; knowledge and understanding of British law might have penetrated deeply enough to facilitate Aboriginal interactions with each other and with whites, they would by now be better placed to make use of it, and the values of the rule of law would infuse the law that they dealt with. On the other hand, self-government had placed power in the hands of precisely those settlers whom the British had ineffectively tried to restrain. That proved fateful.

The Grammar of Colonial Legality

The bulk of the Aborigines who did not die of disease or dislocation or guns were reduced to dependency on Europeans, typically in degrading settlements and conditions, because of the eradication of their own bases of food and life, physical and spiritual. In these circumstances, the increase in the hold of governments might indeed have curbed the Hobbes problem – unrestrained encounters between individuals – but it did so by raising the issue that Locke raised: who will protect us from our protectors? And in this phase, that was quite literally the problem Aborigines faced, for in the new regimes established by legislation devoted to this purpose, authority over Aborigines was in the hands of so-called Protectors of Aboriginals. As Pat O'Malley remarks:

in general Aboriginal people through most of Australia have been subject to an extraordinary degree of regulation, perhaps being one of the most governed people on earth. Legislation such as the *Native Administration Act 1936* of Western Australia (for which parallels existed in other states) gave the Chief Protector of Aborigines direct control over Aboriginal peoples' sexual relations, social relations, marriage, geographical mobility, residence, employment, income, property ownership and management, education, custody of children – even over where they could camp and what the law referred to as their 'tribal practices.' (O'Malley, 1994: 48)

Victoria established the first comprehensive system of Aboriginal administration under the *Act to Provide for the Protection and Management of the Aboriginal Natives of Victoria, 1869*. It was amended in 1886 by what came to be known as the 'merging of half-castes Act' and they together formed a regime which lasted for ninety years. In 1897, Queensland passed the most influential such Act, the *Aboriginal Protection and Restriction of the Sale of Opium Act*, which was the model for the Western Australian *Aborigines Act 1905* (amended in 1936 to exclude, *inter alia*, 'quadroons' and 'persons of less than quadroon blood') and two South Australian Acts (one for the Northern Territory in 1910; one for South Australia in 1911). There were differences between these laws in matters of emphasis, policy and detail, but the similarities are striking and considerable. All depended on racial classifications, many of them inconsistently applicable to the same individuals[16] (McCorquodale, 1986: 15; Chesterman & Galligan, 1997: 113–14); all gave awesome power over individual lives in their most intimate details – residence, marriage, correspondence, movement, rearing of children – to Protectors and other officials; all gave great and largely unreviewable discretion to the Executive officials in charge. Of the Queensland Act, for example, Chesterman and Galligan observe: 'The most extraordinary aspect ... was the breadth of regulatory power it ascribed to the Governor in

Council ... and ... such was the breadth of discretion afforded to the superintendents over their reserves, and the protectors over their districts, that the Act provided very little restraint on their exercise of power' (Chesterman & Galligan, 1997: 41). From the time of Federation, and especially in the 1930s, these regimes became increasingly discriminatory (Chesterman & Galligan, 1997: 8). They were not dismantled until the 1960s.

At federal level, similar classifications were used to exclude 'aboriginal natives' from the vote (*Commonwealth Franchise Act 1902*) and from pensions (*Invalid and Old-Age Pensions Act 1908*)[17] and other social services (*Maternity Allowance Act 1912*).[18] In the Northern Territory under Commonwealth Ordinances beginning in 1911, the Chief Protector was given power of 'care, custody, or control of any aboriginal or half-caste if in his opinion it is necessary or desirable in the interest of the Aboriginal or half-caste for him to do so'. Under the 1918 Ordinance he was to be the legal guardian of every Aboriginal and half-caste child, notwithstanding that the child has a parent or other relative living. Aborigines could not go into towns or travel from one reserve to another or from one part of the territory to another without permission, and a female Aborigine could not marry a non-Aborigine without permission. The Chief Protector could depute these powers 'to any other official designated a Protector, which included all police officers, and from a contemporary perspective constitutes an extraordinary governmental intrusion into the everyday lives of a particular section of the population' (van Krieken, 2001b).

What, from the point of view of the rule of law, is wrong with any of this? One might object to its *content* on the basis of other values, though one might defend it too, as many have. However one feels about that, it is commonly agreed that the rule of law is not of itself the rule of *good* law (though, as we have seen, there is disagreement about the extent to which certain legal values are part of the rule of law). So, whether or not we consider the law to be bad, it is a separate question whether it is a denial of the rule of law.

If one tries to identify the rule of law with particular attributes of legal rules, as is commonly done, the problem might escape you. Thus, some accounts of the rule of law would automatically attack the race- and 'blood'-based classifications on which all this and other legislation is based, as necessarily in conflict with the rule of law. For on these accounts, among them Rousseau's, laws must always be general in scope, applying in the same way to everyone and in no distinctive way to anyone in particular. If that is what equality before the law requires, however, it is impossible to achieve since, as Barney the dinosaur tells our children, everyone is special in his and, of course, her own way. And law-makers have many purposes. In consequence, law continually classifies and must do so.[19]

So other writers distinguish between classifications which of their nature do not violate the principle of equality before the law and those which do. On the one hand, for example, those which admit candidates to higher education on the basis of 'relevant' considerations, such as test scores and, on the other, those which rely on characteristics which are irrelevant to the purpose in hand, such as race. The latter are said to be of their nature discriminatory. Were this so, then we could read the violations of the rule of law from the face of the hundreds of pieces of legislation which use classifications such as 'Aboriginal native' to bestow or, more usually, withhold benefits available to others. But this simple distinction also will not do. The notion and the grounds of a judgement of 'relevance' need to be unpacked and defended. Many people who oppose racial discrimination, for example, believe that some references to race, for example, are relevant to proper purposes of legislation, among them some rectificatory purposes. There are issues of justice here which will not reduce to simple mechanical invocations of the rule of law.

Another deceptively simple approach is to seize on the discretionary nature of Protectors' powers as the characteristic that distinguishes the laws granting them from the rule of law. However, many modern pieces of legislation grant large discretions to administrative officials. So, even though Justice O'Loughlin is right to observe that 'The powers of the Director under the 1918 (Northern Territory) Ordinance were exceptionally wide',[20] wide discretion would not categorically distinguish this legislation from many other modern effusions of administrative and regulatory states in which the rule of law can still be said to exist.

Yet there is still something deeply wrong, from the point of view of the rule of law, to say nothing of other points of view, with the classifications and powers which proliferated in state and Commonwealth legislation. What is wrong can be seen if we focus less on the details of particular rules severally and for their own sake. Rather we should consider what in combination they reveal about the extent to which the law applying exclusively to Aborigines embodied the underlying aims and assumptions of the rule of law; the extent to which, in other words, the rule of law was institutionalized in those legal regimes.

The failure or lack of institutionalization is betrayed less by lawyers' discriminations among forms of law, than in what they reveal about rulers' discriminations among subjects or, rather, between subjects and objects. Where classifications based on (arbitrarily drawn)[21] racial characteristics define particular groups of persons *comprehensively* in ways that form the basis for withholding a whole range of benefits available to others, where they allow a regime of deep and systematic and unreviewable authority over, intrusion into, and regulation of the lives of people on one side of the classification, which are applied to no groups (except in response to their acts) on the other side; where they are coupled with the grant to those who make such intrusions of extremely broad discretions in the exercise of their power and *subject* their objects to them without escape, then they deny comprehensively and profoundly the protections, facilities, and values that the rule of law is supposed to embody. For where power-holders are deliberately left free of legal restraint in relation to Aborigines, Aborigines themselves are in no position to avail themselves of many of the legal facilities that law provides the rest of the population, and inherent values of the rule of law are denied them. Thus we witness something closer to a Dual State, in Fraenkel's sense,[22] than a rule-of-law regime, as Dicey understood it.

In all these regimes, Aborigines were largely and legally disempowered objects of law and regulation, whether it be for their 'protection', 'management', 'merging', 'welfare', 'civilization' or merely control. They were not its subjects. They were manifestly not authors of the law, but neither were the original convicts. On the other hand, by this time white Australians had advanced to being that, as well as what they had always been regarded to be: authors of their lives. In regard to the most basic, central, aspects of their lives, however, Aborigines were not regarded as authors at all.

*Law*, of course, is compatible with all these and other terrible things, but the rule of law is not. For, to recall, the rule of law is a *particular* conception, to do with restraint on arbitrary exercise of power and based on an underlying conception of human interaction as it is and should be. Each of the characteristics of the legislation mentioned above militates against such restraint and such a conception. All the more since they deal, not merely with professions, trades, licences for business, and so on, but with people's whole lives. So they militate against the rule of law.[23]

This is not just a matter of moral evaluation of the purposes of these laws – whether humanitarian or genocidal, benign or malign, civilizing or barbarous. Clearly the intentions of some of these Acts and regulations were protective, or thought to be; others, in particular in the 1930s, arguably something else. Those purposes are important to understand and historians have begun to enlighten us about them. But I am not a historian and I have no privileged insights on those large matters. And there is a level worth capturing where they do not make a difference. Whether intended to be benign or malign, the purposes of this legislation lend characteristics incarnate in its form: it is that sort of legislation which, by the power it gives officials, the discretions it arms them with, the unreviewable breadth of those discretions, and above all – more important than these matters of legal form – in the profound power they give officials over the lives of Aborigines, renders those subjects no subjects at all.

Too often today, debates hinge solely on judgements or claims that the intentions of such legislation were well or ill-meant, as though the former would deliver a clean bill of health. But though that is an important debate, it is not one with which I am engaged here. For there is a deeper issue, identified in W. E. H. Stanner's laconic observation, as late as 1964: 'Our intentions are now so benevolent that we find it difficult to see that they are still fundamentally dictatorial.'[24]

Seen in this light the policy which has most spurred the modern popular interest in relations between whites and blacks in this country – child removal – is not out of character, and should hardly have caused the surprise (though it has appropriately caused the discomfort) that has been visible in the last several years. I have not discussed that policy in this chapter. Yet it might well stand as a fitting concluding example of my theme.

Robert van Krieken sums up the legal aspects of this policy thus:

The strategy adopted here was simply to remove Aboriginal parents' common-law rights over their children and to make the state the legal guardian of all children of Aboriginal descent, to be removed at will and sent to a mission, a child welfare institution or to be fostered with a white family if sufficiently light-skinned. The legislation enabling this was introduced in relatively weak form between 1905 and 1909 in all Australian states, strengthened around 1915, and further reinforced in the 1930s. (van Krieken, 1999: 306)

Legislation and regulations in several states allowed officials to deem 'any child born of an aboriginal or half-caste mother' (*Industrial and Reformatory Schools Act 1865* NSW) to be neglected, and so be sent to reformatories or boarding schools. Many other legal ways of removing 'half-caste' children from their mothers have been documented.[25] Parental consent was not required.[26] Such practices continued until the 1960s; thousands of children were removed, commonly without parental permission and without specific evidence of neglect, to foster homes and institutions of various sorts. The consequences were frequently devastating for the parents and children involved. And one might have thought that was predictable. Certainly it should have been predicted by readers of *The Norfolk Chronicle* of 11 November 1786, which noted, when the Kables received permission to take their child to Sydney:

The laws of England, which are distinguished by the spirit of humanity which framed them, forbid so cruel an act as that of separating an infant from its mother's breast ... it cannot be but a pleasing circumstance to every Englishman to know, that, though from the very nature of the situation of public Ministers, they must, on most occasions, be difficult of access, ... when the object is humanity, and delay would materially affect the happiness of even the meanest subject in the kingdom, the Minister himself not only attends to complaints properly addressed, but promptly and effectually affords relief. (Neal, 1991: 4)

## Conclusion: Institutions and Moral Imagination

Ultimately, though law led me to, and lies at the heart of, the paradoxical development that I have sought to sketch, that paradox did not in the first instance depend upon the law but underlay it and conditioned the ways it worked in the world. The paradox derived from a deeper split in the moral imagination of early Australian law-makers, enforcers, and, more generally, of settlers. This then made its way – often, one imagines, unconsciously, as part of obvious taken-for-granted views of the world – to be reflected in the practices, character, forms and obligations embodied in the institutions of law, and in the entitlements, or lack of them, of its subjects. Better, subjects and objects.

This chapter, then, has only dealt with the middle of the story. It does not explore how it began or how it came to change. For the bifurcated imagination I have described was generated, as all collective, widely shared, imaginings are, by social institutions within which actors think. The law is unlikely to treat people as subjects unless those who make and wield the law see them as subjects already. When that happens on a large scale, or when it does not on an equal scale, this is not well viewed as the coincidence of random individual decisions, a happy or unhappy accident, but rather as in large part the result of social institutions, many of them outside the law, which generate the categories within which social actors think and which they bring to bear in the law itself. For, as Mary Douglas has argued, 'the entrenching of an idea is a social process' (Douglas, 1987: 45), one in which social institutions generate shared ideas, or in Durkheim's phrase, 'collective representations', and we come to adopt them, indeed to think them without thought, as it were. This chapter has been concerned with some of the ways in which particular institutionalized imaginings, particular representations, worked themselves out through the institutions of law.

In the case of convicts, what elevated their condition was the thick institutionalization of rule-of-law values within the legal institutions that bore (often hard) upon them. In the case of Aborigines, either the forces that bore on them were not primarily legal, or the conditions of the rule of law, which had been officially promised them, were unrealizable, or, by the end of the nineteenth century, the legal institutions that applied to them were imbued with values other than, indeed contrary to, those of the rule of law. Many of the ultimate causes of these contrasting histories lie beyond the law, but then since they were associated with values that were embodied in law, within it as well. Whatever the causes, the consequences were similar: the singular benefits that the rule of law promises and often secures, were comprehensively denied them.

That our ideas are different today does not mean that we are better people. They might, though, be better ideas. For however one characterizes the motives of those who so degraded Aborigines, and they were doubtless various, there appears to have been all along a failure of moral imagination, that imagination which sees *all* persons as 'the kind of limit to our will, to our interests and desires, that we mark when we speak of respecting someone's rights, or treating them as ends rather than as means, or of according them unconditional respect' (Gaita, 1999: 79). For reasons that historians can explore, social theorists understand and moralists evaluate, this otherwise most humane of societies failed to register Aborigines in this way for a very long time.

I began with Chief Justice Gleeson's endorsement of Sir Thomas' horticultural world-view, so I will end with it: 'The imagery of the law as a windbreak carries an important idea. The law restrains and civilises power.' There is little doubt that the institutions of law can contribute to doing that, but not simply by being law. The values institutionalized in the law must conspire to that end. In the case of convicts they did. They need not, however, and with regard to Aborigines they did not. Law, as we have seen, might just amplify or undergird unrestrained and uncivilized power. Or it might aid power in a mission to 'civilize' not power, but *people* thought of as barbarous, or in some other deep way uncivilized.[27]

Once that mission is embarked upon, there is no simple way to go back to the beginning or abandon the undertaking, nor, for that matter, is it easy for disruptive and destructive invaders to act well, even were they to wish to. A comprehensive moral assessment of that enterprise is beyond me, though it nags away, for it is at the same time pressing and daunting. Tragedy was almost certainly written into our national history, as soon as whites decided to come here, and whatever we did. Nevertheless we did come here and we did some things and not others. There are, and have been, different ways of proceeding. I have tried to sketch some of our ways.

### Notes

I am grateful to Geoffrey Brennan, Frank Castles, Arthur Glass and Avishai Margalit for comments on earlier drafts of this essay, and to Robert van Krieken for both his comments and patience as I stumbled through territory unfamiliar to me but not to him. I also benefited from useful discussion at the seminar on this book held by the Reshaping Australian Institutions Project in August 2001.

1  For the distinction between concepts, such as justice or democracy or the rule of law, on which there is often widespread agreement, and particular *conceptions* of that concept, see Rawls, 1972, and Dworkin, 1977: 134–6.

2 Cf. Atkinson, 1997: 38: 'It is difficult to draw a picture big enough to show the significance of Phillip's arrival in Australia, embodying as he did new principles of life and death in Europe's Antipodes.'
3 On the importance within legal orders of such layers of rules, values and standards, see Krygier 1986: 237–62, Krygier 1988: 20–39.
4 To be precise, Pashukanis believed 'law' properly so-called was a form of regulation that developed only with capitalism and was quite different from other forms of governmental orders, which regulated affairs in other ways. But the point can be made without this idiosyncratic redefinition.
5 What follows draws upon Krygier 2001a & b.
6 See Galanter 1981: 1–47. As Galanter observes, 'The mainstream of legal scholarship has tended to look out from within the official legal order, abetting the pretensions of the official law to stand in a relationship of hierarchic control to other normative orderings in society. Social research on law has been characterized by a repeated rediscovery of the other hemisphere of the legal world. This has entailed recurrent rediscovery that law in modern society is plural rather than monolithic, that it is private as well as public in character and that the national (public, official) legal system is often a secondary rather than a primary locus of regulation' (p. 20).
7 For a classic statement of these points, see Moore, 1978: 54–81.
8 Not quite so. Australians were still British subjects.
9 (Neal, 1991: 91.) Compare Hirst (1995: 294): 'The convict colony invites judgment by the standards of a civil society because that is how it presents itself. This is its most surprising characteristic – that a society peopled so largely by convicts nevertheless mainained the rule of law for all, imposed no disability on ex-convicts, and gave them the opportunity for economic success through employment of convict labor. It is a society without parallel, a strange late flowering of the ancien regime in crime and punishment.'
10 In fact the character who speaks these words is himself white, but has been brought up for some years by Aborigines and is initially taken to be one by some children on whom he chances. As one child points a stick at him, in imitation of a gun, he blurts out this insight.
11 Cf. the comment of Backhouse, a Quaker traveller quoted by Hasluck (Hasluck, 1970: 125): 'I cannot but regard the professed recognition of the blacks as British subjects (however well intended in England) as practically a sort of blind to the British public, as to the real state of these injured people; their evidence being refused, because they do not understand the nature of an oath; and their violent deaths (many of which, there is reason to believe, take place by the white inhabitants of this colony) not being properly made the subjects of inquests, nor the perpetrators of them brought to trial.'
12 J. Stephen, memo to Glenelg, quoted in Reynolds 2001: 88.
13 The significance of fear in the frontier setting is emphasised in Reynolds 1996: 9–31, 44–50.
14 See Neal, 1991: 17, 151: 'some hybrid of outlaw, foreign enemy and protected race'; Reynolds 1996: 3–4, 154.
15 (Gaita 1999: 78, 79). As Robert van Krieken has pointed out to me, the legal position is more complicated than this. It is arguable that in the earlier Federal Court decision, *Milirrpum* v. *Nabalco* (1971), 17 FLR 267, Justice Blackburn already recognized Aborigines' 'true humanity', and that what is distinctive of *Mabo* is what van Krieken describes as a 'preparedness to

*buttress* that recognition with legal imagination' (personal communication). On the law van Krieken is clearly right, but the philosophical point that Gaita is making is unaffected.

16 In the 700 pieces of Australian legislation using such classifications, John McCorquodale has identified 67 different sorts. See McCorquodale 1986: 7–24; and McCorquodale 1997: 24–34.

17 The disqualification was lifted for 'exempt Aboriginal natives' in 1942, though another provision provided that the Commissioner may determine that the rate of pension payable to an Aboriginal native of Australia is less than the maximum rate and can be paid to an authority for his benefit.

18 In 1942 it was provided that exempted Aborigines could receive allowances. The *Social Services Consolidation Act 1947*, provided that age or invalid pensions, widows' pensions, maternity allowances could be paid to an 'Aboriginal native' if: a) an exempt native under the law of his domicile, or b) he resides in a State or Territory the law of which does not make provision for such exemptions, and the Director-General is satisfied that, by reason of the character and the standard of intelligence and social development of the native, it is desirable that a pension should be granted to him, but shall not otherwise be granted to such a native.

19 On this, and more generally on the host of issues raised by the notions of equality before and in the law, see Sadurski, 1998: 63–104.

20 *Cubillo & Anor v. Commonwealth* No. 2 (2000) 103FCR1 at 52–3. See van Krieken 2001a.

21 Though from this point of view it would not be better if they were not arbitrarily drawn.

22 Though not, I would stress, to the Nazi state which Fraenkel had in mind when devising the term.

23 It is one mark of progress made that our contemporary laws lack these characteristics. How adequately this ensures the rule of law to contemporary Aborigines is a complex matter that I won't touch on in this chapter, except to say that many of the most egregious aspects of the law that I describe have been removed. One related sign of progress is the extent to which Aborigines have come to be able to *use* the law, rather than merely be affected by it.

24 'Foreword' to Marie Reay (ed.), *Aborigines Now: New Perspectives in the Study of Aboriginal Communities* (1964) p. ix, quoted in van Krieken 2001a: 259.

25 Chesterman and Galligan, *Citizens without Rights* p. 49, cite a Victorian regulation of 1899 authorizing the Governor to order that 'any aboriginal child' be sent to 'the care of the Department for Neglected Children or the Department for Reformatory Schools', without having to establish that the child was neglected or in need of 'reform'; 'within a year the Board [for the Protection of Aborigines] had decided that all "half-caste" children on stations would be sent to industrial schools once they reached twelve years of age.' See Haebich, 2000; Manne, 2000.

26 '[T]he policy was silent on the subject of the mother's consent. A careful reading of the terms of the policy shows that, in the final analysis, a child could be removed against the express wishes of its mother.' O'Loughlin J., in *Cubillo & Anor v. Commonwealth No. 2* (2000) 103 FCR 1 at 88.

27 On the barbarisms often directly implicated and contained in this mission, see van Krieken, 1999: 297–315.

## References

Atkinson, A. *The Europeans in Australia: A History, the Beginning*, Vol. 1 (Melbourne: Melbourne University Press, 1997).
Blackstone, W. *Commentaries on the Laws of England*, Book 1 (18th edition, London: T. Tegg, 1830).
Bolt, R. *A Man for All Seasons* (London: Heinemann Educational, 1963).
Braithwaite, J. 'Crime in a Convict Republic', *The Modern Law Review*, 64 (2001) pp. 11–50.
Chesterman, J., and Galligan. B. *Citizens Without Rights: Aborigines and Australian Citizenship* (Cambridge: Cambridge University Press, 1997).
Davidson, A. *The Invisible State: The Formation of the Australian State, 1788–1901* (Cambridge: Cambridge University Press, 1991).
Davies. S. 'Aborigines, Murder and the Criminal Law in Early Port Philip, 1841–1851', *Australian Historical Studies*, 22(88) (1987) pp. 313–35.
Douglas, M. *How Institutions Think* (London: Routledge & Kegan Paul, 1987).
Durkheim, E. *The Division of Labor in Society*, trans W. D. Halls (New York: The Free Press, 1984).
Dworkin, R. *Taking Rights Seriously* (London: Duckworth, 1977).
Dyzenhaus, D. *Judging the Judges, Judging Ourselves: Truth, Reconciliation and the Apartheid Legal Order* (Oxford: Hart Publishing, 1998).
Ehrlich, E. *Fundamental Principle of the Sovereignty of Law* (Cambridge, Mass: Harvard University Press, 1936).
Fortes, M., and Evans-Pritchard, E. A. (eds). *African Political Systems* (London: Oxford University Press, 1948).
Fraenkel, E. *The Dual State*, trans. E. A. Shils et al., (New York: Oxford University Press, 1941).
Fuller L. L. *The Morality of Law* (New Haven: Yale University Press, 1969).
Gaita, R. *A Common Humanity: Thinking about Love and Truth and Justice* (Melbourne: Text Publishing, 1999).
Galanter, M. 'Why the Haves have come out Ahead: Speculations on the Limits of Legal Change', *Law and Society Review*, 9 (1974) 95–160.
———. 'Justice in Many Rooms: Courts, Private Ordering, and Indigenous Law', *Journal of Legal Pluralism* 19 (1981) pp. 1–47.
Gleeson, M. *The Rule of Law and the Constitution* (Sydney: ABC Books, 2000).
Habermas, J. 'Law as Medium and Law as Institution', in G. Teubner (ed.), *Dilemmas of the Welfare State* (Berlin: de Gruyter, 1986).
Haebich, A. *Broken Circles: Fragmenting Indigenous Families, 1800–2000* (Fremantle: Fremantle Arts Centre Press, 2000).
Hasluck, P. *Black Australians* (Melbourne: Melbourne University Press, 1970).
Hedlund, S. 'Can Property Rights be Protected by Law?', *East European Constitutional Review*, 10(1) (2001) pp. 48–52.
Hendley, K., Holmes, S., Åslund, A., and Sajó, 'A. 'Debate: Demand for Law', *East European Constitutional Review* 8(4) (1999) pp. 88–108.
Higgins, H. B. *A New Province for Law and Order* (London: Constable & Company, 1922).
Hirst, J. *Convict Society and its Enemies* (Sydney: Allen & Unwin, 1983).
———. 'The Australian Experience: The Convict Colony', in N. Morris and D. J. Rothman (eds), *The Oxford History of the Prison* (New York: Oxford University Press, 1995).

Holmes, S. et al. 'Citizen and Law after Communism', *East European Constitutional Review* 7(1) (1988) pp. 70–88.
Kamenka, E., and Tay, A. E-S. 'Beyond Bourgeois Individualism: The Contemporary Crisis in Law and Legal Ideology', in E. Kamenka and R. S. Neale (eds), *Federalism, Capitalism and Beyond* (London: Edward Arnold, 1975).
Krygier, M. 'Anthropological Approaches', in E. Kamenka and A. E-S Tay (eds), *Law and Social Control* (London: Edward Arnold, 1980).
——. 'Law as Tradition', *Law and Philosophy*, 5 (1986) pp. 237–62.
——. 'The Traditionality of Statutes', *Ratio Juris*, 1(1) (1988) pp. 20–39.
——. 'Virtuous Circles: Antipodean thoughts on power, institutions, and civil society', *East European Politics and Societies*, 11(1) (1997) pp. 36–88.
——. 'Institutional Optimism, Cultural Pessimism, and the Rule of Law', in M. Krygier and Adam Czarnota (eds), *The Rule of Law after Communism: Problems and Prospects in East-Central Europe* (Aldershot: Ashgate, 1999).
——. 'The Rule of Law', in N. J. Smelser and P. B. Yates (eds), *International Encyclopedia of the Social and Behavioural Sciences*, Vol. 20 (Oxford: Elsevier Science (2001a) pp. 13,403–13,408.
——. 'Transitional Questions about the Rule of Law', *East Central Europe/ L'Europe du Centre Est. Eine wissenscahftliche Zeitschrift* 28 (part 1) (2001b) pp. 1–34.
Manne, R. *In Denial: The Stolen Generations and the Right* (Melbourne: Schwartz Publishing, 2001).
McCorquodale, J. 'The Legal Classification of Race in Australia', *Aboriginal History*, 10(1) (1986) p. 8.
——. 'Aboriginal Identity: Legislative, Judicial and Administrative definitions', *Aboriginal Studies*, 2 (1997) pp. 24–34.
Moore, S. F. *Law as Process: An Anthropological Approach* (London: Routledge & Kegan Paul, 1978).
Neal, D. *The Rule of Law in a Penal Colony* (Cambridge: Cambridge University Press, 1991).
Nonet. P., and Selznick. P. *Law and Society in Transition: Towards Responsive Law* (New York: Harper and Row, 1978; reissued by Transaction Books, New York, 2001).
O'Malley. P. 'Gentle Genocide: The Government of Aboriginal Peoples in Central Australia', *Social Justice*, 21(4) (1994) pp. 46–65.
Pashukanis, E. B. 'The General Theory of Law and Marxism', in P. Beirne and R. Sharlet (eds), *Selected Writings on Marxism and Law* (New York: Sage, 1980).
Petrazycki, L. *Law and Morality* (Cambridge, Mass.: Harvard University Press, 1955).
Rawls, J. *A Theory of Justice* (Oxford: Oxford University Press, 1972).
Raz, J. 'The Rule of Law and its Virtue', in *The Authority of Law* (Oxford: Oxford University Press, 1979).
Reynolds, H. *Frontier* (Sydney: Allen & Unwin, 1996).
——. *An Indelible Stain?* (Ringwood, Vic.: Viking, 2001).
Rowley, C. D. *The Destruction of Aboriginal Society* (Harmondsworth: Penguin, 1970).
——. *Outcasts in White Australia* (Harmondsworth: Penguin, 1973).
Sadurski, W. 'The Concept of Legal Equality and an Underlying Theory of Discrimination', *Saint Louis-Warsaw Transatlantic Law Journal* (1998) pp. 63–104.

Selznick, P. *The Moral Commonwealth* (Berkeley: University of California Press, 1992).

——. 'Legal Cultures and the Rule of Law', in M. Krygier and A. Czarnota (eds), *The Rule of Law after Communism: Problems and Prospects in East-Central Europe* (Aldershot: Ashgate, 1999).

Stanner, W. E. H. 'Foreword', in M. Reay (ed.), *Aborigines Now: New Perspectives in the Study of Aboriginal Communities* (Sydney: Angus & Robertson, 1964).

Thompson, E. P. *Whigs and Hunters* (Harmondsworth: Penguin, 1977).

Unger, R. M. *Law in Modern Society* (New York: The Free Press, 1976).

van Krieken, R. 'The Barbarism of Civilization: cultural genocide and the "Stolen Generations"', *British Journal of Sociology*, 50(2) (1999) pp. 297–315.

——. 'Is Assimilation Justiciable? *Lorna Cubillo and Peter Gunner v. Commonwealth*', *Sydney Law Review*, 23(2) (2001a) pp. 239–60.

——. 'Rethinking Cultural Genocide: Settler-colonial State Formation and Indigenous Child Removal', paper prepared for the conference, The Genocide Effect: New Perspectives on Modern Cultures of Destruction, University of Sydney, 4–5 July, 2001.

Waldron, J. 'When Justice Replaces Affection: The Need for Rights', in *Liberal Rights: Collected Papers* (Cambridge: Cambridge University Press, 1993).

# 9 Political Leadership and Rhetoric

*John Uhr*

It is enough if ... [political leaders] can apply their experience to discern which of the many doctrines and projects that are seething up all around like bubbles in a boiling spring are most fit to be made the basis of wise legislation. Their function is to commend the best of these to the people, not waiting for demands, not seeming to be bent merely on pleasing the people, but appealing to reason and creating the sense that the nation is not a mere aggregate of classes, each seeking its own interests, but a great organized whole with a life rooted in the past and stretching on into the illimitable future. A democracy is tested by the leaders it chooses, and it prospers by the power of discernment which directs its choice (Bryce, 1921, vol. 2: 615).

This chapter explores the place of political rhetoric in establishing and transforming Australian institutions. Political rhetoric here refers to its simplest and most enduring form: exercises in public persuasion by leading politicians. Although all forms of politics contain many behind-the-scenes types of hidden persuasion, political rhetoric is one of the most prominent instruments of public persuasion used by democratic politicians. Analysts of Australian politics have paid little scholarly attention to the role of rhetoric in shaping Australian political relationships. This is surprising because political rhetoric itself has something of an institutional character, in that democratic politics demands it. Further, political rhetoric is an activity that has its own rules, norms and constraints.

The focus here is on the use of public rhetoric by Australian prime ministers. They demonstrate most clearly the general place of political rhetoric in Australian politics and, more specifically, the use of public rhetoric as an essential tool of national political leadership. Political leadership has many domains, such as leadership of faction, party, parliament, cabinet and government. For Australian prime ministers, one of the most challenging and ambitious domains is leadership of the nation where their most public skills are tested. Public rhetoric is one of the most basic of these skills. It is put to one of its most fundamental tests when leaders attempt to define their relationship with the citizenry they seek to lead. This latter activity is my focus here. As I will show by examples, leaders define this relationship in two ways: by reference to the responsibilities of leadership and to the obligations of citizenship. Thus public rhetoric helps institutionalize political leadership and, through their rhetoric, leaders cultivate and consolidate their public followers.

Two contrasting approaches mark out the conventional study of Australian political leadership. Both deal with institutional themes, but not explicitly with the institutional nature of political rhetoric. Both acknowledge political rhetoric, but neither sees it as an important institutional component of the political art. Both lead us to the world of leadership, but stop short of examining what a growing body of political research calls 'the language of leadership' (see, e.g., Handy, 1989: 235–41; see also Thurow and Wallin, 1984; Riker, 1986; Tulis, 1987; Riker, 1996; Hargrove, 1998; Miroff, 1998; Gaffney, 2001).

The dominant approach to the study of Australian political leadership deals with the institutional resources and external powers at the disposal of chief political executives, and the minority approach deals with the internal psychological power marshalled by leaders. Patrick Weller has done most to chart the external dimensions of the prime ministership and has compared Australian developments with those in other parliamentary systems (Weller, 1985; 1989; 1992; see generally Mughan and Patterson, 1992; Elgie, 1995). Graham Little has done most to map the internal curiosities of Australian prime ministers and demonstrate how leadership institutions depend on the personalities of leading individuals (Little, 1985; 1988; 1997; compare de Vries, 1993). This chapter adds a new dimension exploring leaders' rhetoric concerning their own role and their own understanding of the place of their public rhetoric in promoting that role.

The social science literature on leadership is now vast, covering business as well as political leadership. A surprisingly high proportion of this literature deals with the importance of language in the public exercise of leadership. Leaders exercise power over organizations in many ways, ranging from the secret and bluntly instrumental to the public and highly symbolic. Included in this range of powers is the power of language to shape organizational life. The use of language by business executives is directed in part externally to maintaining market confidence and, in part internally, to mobilizing the commitment of subordinates. The importance of executives performing as 'showmen' through the use of 'good stagecraft' is a prominent theme in leadership literature. We learn that leadership works in large measure by 'managing the meaning' of collective effort. Further, organizational studies note 'the theatrical elements of leadership' which only rarely get the attention they deserve among political analysts. The close attention to 'vision' and 'metaphor' in studies of business executives illustrates the related attention to 'the leaders' story', the 'leader as teacher' and to the more general management of 'the social architecture' of organizations evident in contemporary leadership literature (Gardner, 1997: 41–65; Bryman, 1996: 275–92; Hardy and Clegg, 1996: 630–1; and more generally van Maurik, 2001: 56–7, 100, 105, 117, 136, 198, 208, 210–12, 219–20). This chapter is in keeping with this growing interest in the language of leadership but it applies it explicitly to the political domain.

## The Choice of Case Studies

The centenary of Federation has thrown fresh light on the record of leadership exercised by Australian prime ministers. In this chapter, I draw on historical accounts of three prime ministers spanning the centenary since Federation: Deakin (1903–04, 1905–08, 1909–10), Menzies (1939–41, 1949–66) and Keating (1991–96, the last to complete a term as prime minister) – masters of the evolving rhetorics of print media, radio and television, in turn (Hargrove, 1967; Weller, 1992; Grattan, 2000). I examine each leader's public presentation of the two core topics of leadership and citizenship and their political rhetoric in promoting the public values of both.

Not all leaders, of course, display leadership. But those who do place high priority on what British statesman James Bryce, in the epigraph to this chapter, called 'the great organised whole' of citizenship. In Deakin's words, Bryce stands as 'an authority to whom our indebtedness is almost incalculable' (Quoted in La Nauze, 1972: 18–19, 85, 273). This was a reference to Bryce's pioneering interest in written federal constitutions, which later included a keen interest in the design and practical operation of the Australian constitution. In Bryce's view, leaders are political 'organisers', shaping the civic whole around concepts of citizenship. My selected cases suggest that prime ministers understand that they have a public duty to shape the civic outlook by clarifying the rights and responsibilities of citizenship. Prime ministers, of course, claim much more for their own charter of responsibilities, usually described in such grand terms as 'nation-building'. But the argument here is that political leaders appeal to citizen-building to justify many of their deepest claims to leadership.

I use my selected leaders to help us see the rhetorical dimension of leadership more clearly. These three prime ministers almost select themselves as case studies of the rhetorical aspects of Australian political leadership: they were attracted to leadership, reflected on it and, more particularly, spoke and wrote about it publicly. They might or might not have been great leaders in their own right, or even Australia's most effective national leaders; that is not my immediate concern here. I acknowledge their mastery of the adversarial system of party politics. But they saw their leadership contribution in terms that transcend party leadership. Each appreciated the democratic dilemma as Bryce formulates it: how to balance the complementary requirements of leadership and citizenship, all too frequently expressed in alternating displays of executive prerogative and populist protest. Ideally for Bryce, this dilemma is resolved by executive leaders who understand their responsibilities in terms that include the cultivation of democratic citizenship. The worst case, as Bryce feared for Australia, is that of leaders enlisting their rhetoric simply to pander to the people rather than calling on them to strive to adapt to evolving citizenship norms.

In their approaches to leadership, Deakin, Menzies and Keating share a perception of the role of public rhetoric in leadership. Each of them 'talked up' leadership, presumably in the belief that they individually had whatever it takes to display it. I accept that one or more of them might have been mistaken about their own abilities, or blind to the gap between their lofty rhetoric and their lowly performance. For my purposes, what matters more is that these three provide us with a base of important evidence about the place of political rhetoric – and specifically rhetoric about leadership – in Australian political and social life. The greatest value of this evidence is that it conveys leadership as articulated by three very influential leaders of Australian politics – leadership as seen from the inside, and as depicted to the outside.

Deakin is relevant as the exemplary founder, the shaper of Federation and the most constructive early prime minister who fought for what Paul Kelly has termed the Australian Settlement or what Deakin himself termed New Protection (Henderson, 1994: 34–7). Menzies refounded Deakin's Liberal Party in changed times, rediscovered 'the forgotten people', and taught Australians to think in terms of a new and different Commonwealth, the British Commonwealth of Nations, while emphasizing the liberal principles of anti-communism. Keating in turn reinterpreted the marriage of economy and identity of Australia (and the Australian Labor Party) in terms of economic restructuring, multiculturalism and the republic. Furthermore, during his pre-ministerial time as treasurer, close observers of the Hawke government noted that it was Keating 'who's the de facto prime minister' (Quoted in Campbell and Halligan, 1992: 24; see also 224–8, 231–7; and Campbell, 1988: 203–12). Keating wanted to be understood as replacing not only his Labor predecessor Bob Hawke but, more pointedly, prime minister Menzies and Menzies' influential promotion of the 'Britishness' of Australian citizenship.

All three prime ministers saw themselves as ambitious nation-builders. But more than this, all three reflected extensively on the role of political leadership, each in his own distinctive way. Deakin's contribution can be seen most dramatically in his anonymous weekly contributions to the British press (what Bryce, 1921 vol. 2: 608 called a leader's 'oratory of the pen') evaluating Australian politics, providing a fascinating public commentary on the value of Australia's leading politicians, including remarkably pointed criticisms of his own leadership record. My account refers to these journalistic contributions but draws primarily on Deakin's speeches during the first Commonwealth Parliament, when Deakin's prominence as a framer of Federation was at its height. Menzies' contribution emerges most obviously through his extensive speeches and written reflections on the art of politics, which provide readers with Menzies' own justifications of his use of prime ministerial power. These are surely in part rationalizations and we have to make up our own minds on their credibility. Keating's contribution comes through his unusually colourful public critiques of Australia's lack of political leadership (which in the eyes of many critics only served to prove his point). Of the three, Keating had most to say about leadership, and it is an open question whether his apparently loose language (for instance, the banana republic; the recession we had to have; Dr Mahathir's recalcitrance; a beautiful set of numbers) undercuts or actually underscores his claim to leadership – depending on whether the language is casual weakness or calculated daring (Day, 2000: 417–20, 429). Keating's rhetorical over-reach illustrates an important larger issue: I do not hide the fact that each of these prime ministers was also a master-politician, more than capable of deploying his political skills in the service of self-advancement and the destruction of political opponents.

My aim is to use these leading cases to help us better understand the place of political rhetoric in political leadership. My task here is to assess intentions rather than impacts: to try to understand the three prime ministers as they wanted us to understand their own leadership role. I acknowledge that this falls short of evaluating their rhetorical effectiveness, which would require an extensive examination of press and media treatments of their public speech and of community reception of leaders' intended messages. This chapter draws on a century of evidence to test Bryce's hypothesis that through their public rhetoric, national political leaders 'do much to create a pattern for the people of what statesmanship ought to be' (Bryce, 1921, vol. 2: 615). My essay is an exercise in exploration rather than explanation, opening up new leadership territory. The evidence suggests that the Australian 'pattern' of statesmanship comprises two dimensions dealing with the complementary roles of leaders and followers. I emphasize that this 'pattern' is a construct of leaders, reflecting their preferred view of these political relationships. The first dimension tracks the leaders' public articulation of their leadership role, and the second dimension tracks their public promotion of citizen-building as the basis for nation-building. But before proceeding to examine each dimension, I will draw a little further on Bryce's pioneering comparative political analysis to clarify my interpretative framework of political leadership and public rhetoric.

## Democracy and Political Leadership

Later in the chapter I will present evidence drawn from public speeches to illustrate Australian leadership rhetoric. Here, I want to locate the place of leadership more generally in the political life of parliamentary democracies, taking Bryce as my initial guide. Bryce's early-twentieth-century analysis of the institutional foundations of Australian and related democracies has retained its freshness, and still allows us to compare many aspects of Australian institutions with those of comparable nations (consider Burns, 1978; Pennock, 1979; Blondel, 1987; Hargrove, 2001).

I believe that Bryce is right to identify public persuasion as a core responsibility of democratic leadership and right to argue that this very public leadership responsibility is conditioned by institutional as well as individual qualities. The individual qualities are ones of character and political morality which aspiring leaders bring to the task of national political leadership. But these personal qualities are in turn affected by the institutional qualities of the political framework, as illustrated by the way that systems of responsible parliamentary government promote and reward a type of political morality associated with the norms of 'responsible parliamentary' conduct. The institutional expectations of political leadership under such parliamentary regimes allow and encourage, even if they do not strictly require, heads of governing parties to act 'responsibly' as heads of national governments. This orientation to national responsibility is reinforced by the institutionally appropriate conduct of opposition leaders with their countervailing norms of responsibility. These opposition norms support practical strategies of holding government leaders publicly accountable for their conduct, in part by ferreting out party interests exercising undue influence over government decision-making.

From Bryce's picture of this blending of individual and institutional qualities I derive this contention: that Australian politicians anchor their responsibilities of leadership in one policy task which is a prerequisite to all others – the promotion of a sense of national citizenship. I acknowledge that the substantive content of citizenship varies with successive political leaders, and I will document this variability with examples. But the main point here is my contention that Australian leaders seek to justify their claims to lasting leadership by reference to this one policy area of citizenship, regardless of their wider policy agenda of nation-building. Thus, citizen-building is a prerequisite for nation-building.

We can begin to explain this leadership convergence on the central importance of citizenship by noting Bryce's recognition of populism and demagoguery as the standing complaints against democracy. Populists and demagogues place democracy in jeopardy by their divisive schemes which effectively deny citizenship to groups not included in the leader's constructed category of 'the people' or 'the mainstream': ruling elites, foreigners, big business, greenies, indigenous peoples. Bryce's suggestion is that as a condition of democratic sustainability, responsible democratic leadership must construct a less divisive and more encompassing category as the focus of a shared and common political definition. Bryce appeals to such traditional concepts as social justice, the public interest and the common good, but my evidence suggests that citizenship is the appropriately inclusive Australian political category. Citizenship defines the people as one common class of political actors, just as leaders define themselves by their distinctive contributions to defining citizenship – as we shall see, some decidedly less inclusive than others.

Let me now deal in more detail with the merits of Bryce's perspective on Australian political leadership. Bryce was one of the most influential analysts of political leadership and he drew international attention to Australia as an experiment in constitutional democracy with few limitations on popular power and popularly endorsed leadership. In Bryce's view, the emerging Australian polity would test the capacity of political leaders to avoid populist leadership in favour of what might be termed civic leadership, promoting norms of democratic citizenship and building civic capacities appropriate to constitutional democracy. Leadership in modern democracies requires 'the power of persuasive speech' but it is an open question whether persuasive leaders have the courage recognized by Bryce as essential if they are to have 'the faculty of going before others instead of following after others' (Bryce, 1921, vol. 2: 606). In this view, populism takes root where political leaders cultivate popular legitimacy for their expansive or unbounded rule, exercised in the name of 'protecting the people'. This appeal to 'the people' is usually couched in terms of protecting a vulnerable segment of the population against privileged elites, class antagonists or foreign threats. Populism is a form of majoritarianism resting on popular fear of perceived threats, external or internal. Populism uses the authority of the people to invest political leaders with extensive executive power, justified as a security against these perceived threats.

Typical of the populist leader is the demagogue, a term which originally meant simply a popular leader. But in the constitutional perspective represented by Bryce, demagogue has come to mean a divisive leader capable of agitating a political following in the name of the people: 'one who tries to lure the people by captivating speech, playing upon their passions, or promising to secure for them some benefit' (Bryce, 1921, vol. 2: 607). A populist movement is reactionary in the sense that it defines itself by reaction to the threat or domination of competing interests: the many against the few, workers against business, the mainstream against privileged elites, and so on. Bryce's alternative leadership orientation seeks to encourage political leaders to limit their own ruling power, and indeed popular power, within a constitutional framework of citizens' rights and duties. Leaders with this commitment to a civic orientation would promote the rights and responsibilities of citizens as a common class. This focus on leadership anchored in citizenship reflects Bryce's own conviction that such an anchor can protect democratic politics 'against errors into which the people may be betrayed by ignorance, haste or passion' (Ibid: 509).

Put in this summary form, Bryce's model of political leadership resembles wishful thinking. What constitutional or institutional basis is there for expecting civic leadership of partisan politicians? Part of the answer is that Bryce had no easy expectation that Australian political leaders would comply with his understanding of the ideals of democratic citizenship. He appreciates that at the end of the day the quality of political leadership draws upon the political morality of individual leaders. This is in part a question of individual character and in part a question of institutional characteristics. Yet Bryce does not reduce the story of political leadership either to fine-grained portraits of individual character or to coarse-grained analysis of institutional characteristics. Australian political leadership emerges out of the constitutional framework of responsible parliamentary government, and Bryce understands the institutional design implicit in that framework. Although this design contains very few direct inducements for the political virtues associated with civic leadership, it does contain a range of relevant if indirect measures designed to suppress political vices of incompatible forms of political leadership. For instance, the two extremes of oligarchy and direct democracy get screened out, while the intermediate regime of representative democracy gets screened in. The constitution tolerates a wide range of leadership styles in representative democracy, but is intolerant of almost any leadership style associated with oligarchy or direct democracy.

The negative formulation of this situation would be that the Australian system works against both oligarchy and direct democracy, at least in their pure forms. The more positive formulation would be that the same system is open to the virtues of responsible civic leadership even when it is silent on the institutional support for these political virtues. To cite

Bryce's primary example, the Australian constitutional framework is silent about the role of political party. A tempting conclusion might be that party spirit is inimical to responsible parliamentary leadership – but this is not Bryce's position. Fearful of the capacity of a governing party to dominate the Australian parliament, Bryce was hopeful that party competition within parliament could promote leadership with national rather than simply party responsibilities. Party government is good to the extent that it rests on party competition between two alternating major parties as found in systems of 'responsible parliamentary government' (Bryce, 1921, vol. 2: 394, 511, 543–4; compare Brennan and Hamilton, 2000: 195–6, 201–3). Political parties can encourage responsible civic leadership in political executives in at least three important ways. First, by selecting as party leaders those individuals with capacity to use a civic focus to appeal to a wide and sustainable support base (as their parties expected of Deakin, Menzies and Keating). Second, by using the parliamentary system of checks and balances to hold governing executives publicly accountable for their leadership performance (as all three leaders faced when in government and attempted when in opposition). Third, by consolidating public support around a citizenship agenda which cements a lasting relationship between party leaders and supporters (as all three sought to do, with varying success).

As Bryce understands it, the Australian political order contains a variety of institutions (written constitution, federalism, bicameralism, separation of powers with an independent judiciary) with many checks and balances which act as obstacles to the ambition of populist leaders intent on mobilizing a popular faction. But as Bryce emphasizes, Australia is distinctive by virtue of its pronounced democracy, with a historically progressive franchise allowing voters to elect both federal chambers and to alter the constitution through referendum. Australia has many formal safeguards against populism but also unprecedented popular power. Thus the national political system is open to a range of leadership styles, including various forms of factional politics. One factional form is the conservative one of protecting minority interests behind the screen of formal checks and balances, and another is the progressive one of promoting majority interests by taking control over all or most of the countervailing institutions. Both forms require some sort of leaders, but neither measures up against Bryce's civic standard of democratic leadership.

Bryce's model of leadership consolidates executive power around the promotion of a set of common interests associated with the ideal of liberal democracy, derived from the formal political equality of all citizens found in classic liberal doctrine. Liberal democracy uses the institutions of representative government to transform this formal equality into operational reality by translating the high ideals of popular sovereignty into the shared rights and obligations of citizenship. In Bryce's view, citizenship is the underlying spirit of the constitution, which gives political life to the document's black letters. Democratic government is open to a wide variety of public policy ends, but all are ranked by their effect on the values and practices of citizenship. Donald Horne provides a contemporary version of this understanding of civic leadership with his analysis of the Australian 'state' as a civic rather than nationalist or ethnic category, comprising Australian citizens rather than Australian nationals or Australian ethnics (Horne, 2001, chapters 6, 11).

Bryce's anxiety over populism can be related to a longer tradition of concern over the tyranny of the majority and the vulnerability of minorities in democratic regimes. His hope was for a form of civic leadership that would thwart populist leadership by promoting capacity-building in citizenship. This is a subtle form of elite rule requiring leaders to win community support and then lead community opinion by instructing citizens in their obligations of citizenship (Bryce, 1921: vol. 1: 181–90; vol. 2: 605–17; Bryce, 1905: 270–342). The Australian system of parliamentary government is open to both the populist and civic leadership options, and indeed to many variations in between. As will be seen from the ensuing review of the leadership orientations of my three prime ministers, the Australian system of 'responsible government' leaves great latitude to heads of government to determine their own reach of responsibility. To anticipate my argument, the evidence here suggests that Australian prime ministers lean in the right direction: they are capable of and usually willing to exercise civic leadership. But they are also politicians equally capable of pandering to populism. Within this range of options, Australian prime ministers, or at least some of them some of the time, understand that among the most responsible of their public duties is the development of civics broadly understood. Australia is a good test case of Bryce's hypothesis that leadership in democratic regimes tends towards populism, and that the best precautions against populist leadership are a combination of legal and moral devices. Legal devices include the involuntary restraints on executive power found in written constitutions. Moral devices include the less reliable but no less valuable voluntary restraints found in the character and political morality of leaders, displayed to considerable extent in each leader's distinctive political rhetoric. Bryce's orientation reflects an elitism struggling against populism, but it is an early form of what later became known as democratic elitism, in Bryce's case distinguished by his promotion of not only the black letter of democratic constitutionalism but also the spirit of democratic citizenship (Bryce, 1909).

## The Language of Leadership

I will now look at examples of political rhetoric dealing with the topic of leadership, and then at examples dealing with the related topic of citizenship. I begin with leaders on leadership because this conveys their public presentation of the problems facing leadership. The discussion of citizenship rhetoric conveys their shared solution, as it were: their public persuasion in favour of a collective sense of citizenship rights and obligations. The substantive content of the three citizenship persuasions differs in quite fundamental ways, reflecting social developments in Australia since Federation. The three leadership orientations also differ, despite the shared appreciation of the importance of political leadership. I begin then with a brief comment on the three leadership orientations.

My selection of three prime ministers suggests a fascinating evolution in perspectives on political leadership. Deakin was the power behind the throne in the inaugural prime ministership of Barton and went on to hold office in his own right for nearly five of the first ten years of the Commonwealth (La Nauze, 1979: 270; Hughes, 1976: 24–5; Clark, 1985: 65–71; Marsh, 2001: 69–97). Yet despite Deakin's personal eminence, his orientation to leadership is primarily institutional, in marked contrast to the highly personal orientation of Paul Keating. Deakin locates leadership in the institutional arrangements of the system of government and not in the personal power of the head of government. Deakin's cultivation of constitutionalism reflects his federalist commitments, just as his promotion of such institutions as the High Court, the Commonwealth public service and later the conciliation and arbitration system reflects his commitment to a Commonwealth of dispersed powers and dispersed institutions of leadership.

Another pointer to Deakin's distinctiveness is the fact that his ministerial portfolio when head of government was usually that of external affairs, illustrating the comparatively modest reach of prime ministerial status in the early years of the Commonwealth. The first head of government to hold only the prime ministerial portfolio was his Labor successor Andrew Fisher, who also established the separate Department of Prime Minister. In marked contrast to Deakin, Keating located leadership not simply in the head of government but in the head of the governing party. For Keating, the Labor Party held greater national significance than the much younger Liberal Party, founded by Menzies who figures as the butt of so many of Keating's reflections on leadership. As Keating formulated it in a 1992 speech in honour of the Whitlam experience: 'We are the people who make the Australian history. We are the ones who nominate the heroes, we anoint the heroes of Australia, our Party sets the ethos of Australia, our Labor Party' (Keating, 1992: 128). Menzies' own orientation to leadership bridges these two evolving orientations, formally acknowledging the importance of constitutional norms while informally elevating the place of the prime minister from the *primus inter pares* formalities.

This development from the institutional focus of Deakin to the personalized perspective of Keating parallels what political scientists have called the growing 'presidentialism' of politics in Westminster-derived systems. Although Australian scholars have noted the limitations of this presidentialism thesis, it still serves a useful purpose in highlighting the enhanced public leadership role of recent prime ministers (Hart, 1992; see also Uhr, 1992). Even though Menzies has been identified as the likely starting point in the Australian chapter of this international story, it is important to note his frequent public disavowals of being anything other than 'first among equals' in a system of cabinet government (see, e.g., Menzies, 1972: 38ff; Horne, 2001: 59–72). Menzies stands at midpoint in the range of perspectives here under review. Before him, there is the record of Deakin's constant struggle for control over a parliamentary environment with limited party cohesion; and after him there is Keating's record of highly personalized rule with limited reliance on the collective capacity of cabinet for policy deliberation.

These three leadership regimes are reflected in the public accounts of political leadership presented by each of my leaders. Deakin is the first and in many ways most puzzling instance. Because Deakin wrote so extensively on contemporary politics, historians have tended to make extensive use of his word, thereby deflecting attention from many of the practical contributions to Australian governance of many of his opponents and indeed colleagues. This traditional reliance on Deakin's version of events has recently come under scholarly criticism, and Deakin's various accounts are being reviewed and treated with a new sense of caution. But I think that this understandable revisionism has its own limitations, one of which is our inattention to the distinctive theme of so many of Deakin's valuable 'insider' accounts of Australian politics. This theme is that institutions frame and confine the freedom of choice open to political actors, including leading actors like Deakin himself.

**Deakin's Model of Dispersed Leadership**

Two examples of Deakin's support for institutionally based leadership stand out. First, Deakin's *The Federal Story* written in 1900 (but not published until 1944) charts the development of what Deakin calls 'the federal cause' with remarkable attention to the evolving institutional settings of political debate and decision-making (Deakin, 1963). An important but neglected aspect of Deakin's accounts of Australian politics is his focus on the institutional in addition to the personal dynamics of political debate: Australian colonial politics, early intercolonial conventions, later elected conventions, popular referendums, British imperial strategy, Australian diplomacy, and the compromises struck for British passage of the Commonwealth constitution. One of Deakin's great themes is that institutional circumstances cannot be controlled simply by force of personality: political leadership takes a larger commitment to a lesser public role involving shared responsibility by many leading politicians, as 'the federal story' documents.

The second example is even more striking. This is the remarkable contribution made by Deakin as regular but anonymous writer on Australian politics for the London *Morning Post* during the first decade of Commonwealth politics. The standard edition of Deakin's most mature political journalism certainly makes for easy quotation against the pretences of many of Deakin's political opponents (Deakin, 1968). But the larger point is that this public material also makes for easy quotation against any pretensions Deakin (or more particularly his supporters) might have had about his pre-eminence as a practical statesman. Deakin's press articles complement rather than reinforce his political conduct, frequently highlighting his parliamentary isolation and limited scope for policy leadership. Their relevance here is that they tell a version of events that Deakin as political actor was unable to emphasize, often calling into question the institutional strength of Deakin's parliamentary situation and contrasting his parliamentary rhetoric with another, subtler rhetoric which lowered public expectations of Deakin and for that matter any other Australian parliamentary leader.

With considerable understatement, Deakin's biographer says that he 'had none of the traditional characteristics of the "strong" leader' (La Nauze, 1968: vii). This is true if 'strong' means 'singular'. Deakin's institutional model of political leadership assumes strong institutions rather than a single, strong central leader. The example that follows shows Deakin's ability to use political rhetoric to promote a range of institutional locations for leadership. To be sure, most political leaders can be relied on to pay public respect to the range of political institutions established under constitutional authority. But Deakin illustrates a rarer form of political leadership which actively constitutes those very public authorities and defends a system of dispersed leadership. My example deals with the establishment of the High Court during Deakin's contribution to the first Commonwealth Parliament, when Deakin frequently acted as prime minister as well as performing his substantive role as attorney-general. It is a fine example of Deakin's rhetorical gifts for promoting diversified rather than concentrated leadership.

The constitution protects the separate and independent basis of judicial power, leaving to Parliament the legislative responsibility for establishing judicial institutions. In early 1902 Deakin introduced the Judiciary Bill to establish the High Court of Australia, using all his rhetorical prowess to highlight the distinctiveness of this legislative proposal (CPD, 1902; see also Deakin, 1968: 92–3; 118–20). Deakin explained that this proposal dealt with 'matters wholly of principle', representing 'a fulfillment of the purposes of the Constitution'. Calling on Parliament to approach the legislation 'in a judicial spirit ... with an entire absence of party feeling', Deakin recommended unusually careful parliamentary deliberation, by which he meant a legislative process 'weighed without any considerations of personal antagonism'. Against the already established routines of adversary politics, Deakin hoped for more considered and considerate debate. He tried to model this standard of exceptional consideration in his second reading speech, from which the following account is derived.

To Deakin, the measure dealt with 'a structural creation which is the necessary and essential complement of a federal constitution'. The establishment of the new supreme court would affect all Commonwealth activities. To quote Deakin:

As such it affects the whole of the citizens of this community; as such it touches every class; as such it affects every calling. Indeed, although it relates to legal machinery, the purposes to be served by that machinery are but in a fractional sense legal, are in the main general, and in a very particular sense political – affecting directly not only the business and bosoms of our population, but also the representatives of the people in both Chambers of this Parliament; affecting directly the Executive of this country; affecting, in fact, every portion of that Constitution of which this court is created to be guardian.

In a memorable reference to the constitutional provision on judicial power, Deakin spoke of how the 'ten sections, numbered 71 to 80, like ten fingers, sustain in their grasp the judicial power, and in a sense, the legislative and executive power of the Commonwealth'. Deakin did not hide the probable alteration to traditional relationships between Parliament and the courts. The measure 'will complete so radical a reform of the legal relations of the people of these States to each other that it might fairly be termed a revolution'. In his view, this was a constructive revolution in the organization of fundamental judicial powers because it gave rise to 'a new centre from which they may be radiated to the greater advantage of the whole of this community'. Thus the bill promoted judicial powers as part of the federal compact of three inter-related powers of government, each with a role in securing good government.

Deakin described both Parliament and the new High Court as 'expressions of the union of the Australian people'. In his view, the constitution committed the 'political interests' to Parliament, and their 'judicial interests' to the new court. With this bill, Parliament was authorizing the establishment of formal institutions to implement the objectives of the constitution's provisions for an independent judiciary. But whereas Parliament was moving to *implement* the constitution, the future High Court would *interpret* the constitution. Judicial interpretation involves more than simply implementation: according to Deakin, the 'first and highest functions' of the High Court would be 'unfolding the Constitution itself'.

In words that might still invite suspicion among members of an elected representative assembly, Deakin stated: 'Our Constitution must depend largely for the exact form and shape which it will hereafter take upon the interpretations accorded to its various provisions. This court is created to undertake that interpretation.' Deakin did not hide his estimate of the high tasks falling to the High Court. Given that many constitutional provisions are 'as yet, vaguely defined', they are to be 'interpreted and safeguarded by this court'. Of the three fundamental conditions identified by Deakin as essential for federal government (a supreme constitution; a formal distribution of powers; and an independent judicial authority),

this is the one that is more essential than the others – the competent tribunal which is able to protect the Constitution, and to oversee its agencies. This body is the High Court. It is properly termed the 'keystone of the federal arch' ... What the legislature may make, and what the executive may do, the judiciary in the last resort declares.

Deakin understood that the court would contribute significantly to national leadership. As he stated:

So long as legislation is as it is today, the product of the clash of parties, and of the struggle between the two Houses, and involves the necessity of carrying public opinion with us by drafting devices, Bills must be placed on the statute book in confused and imperfect shape, and will require to be deciphered and construed by men especially trained to that work. They must be construed and harmonised before they are enforced, and it is to the enforcement of its laws that every Legislature looks in their preparation. We cannot separate ourselves, if we could, from the judiciary with which it is our lot to work. ... It is by its assistance alone that we can expect that highly artificial and complex creation – a federal system – to proceed with all its powers and institutions safely restrained in their respective orbits of action.

Deakin's political rhetoric gave the best case for judicial review of parliamentary conduct. One of the most important but least obvious objects of the measure was to arrange 'that the best brains that Australia possesses' interpret the constitution. In words that might still encourage judicial activism, Deakin counselled that:

the nation lives, grows and expands. Its circumstances change, its needs alter, and its problems present themselves with new faces. The organ of the national life which preserving the union is yet able from time to time to transfuse into it the fresh blood of the living present, is the Judiciary. ... It is as one of the organs of Government which enables the Constitution to grow and to be adapted to the changing necessities and circumstances of generation after generation that the High Court operates. Amendments achieve direct and sweeping changes, but the court moves by gradual, often indirect, cautious, well considered steps, that enable the past to join the future, without undue collision and strife in the present.

## Menzies' Model of Parliamentary Leadership

Menzies' practice was to deprecate the importance of his personal power during his record-breaking period of eighteen years as prime minister. But that very power was evident in his commitment to the many written justifications of his tenure at the top. One suspects that Menzies did 'protest too much' when denying his ambitions to control his colleagues. Claiming to be no more than 'first among equals', Menzies justified his cabinet style of management as consistent with his preference for the role of *expositor* over the alternative role of *chief executive*, which he associated with non-parliamentary presidential systems. Other aspects of the parliamentary system also attracted his interest for their leadership capacity, notably the role of the leader of the opposition, in which post Menzies himself served from 1943 to 1949 (see, e.g., Menzies, 1972: 38ff; see also Hughes, 1976: 156–7; Brett, 1997: 71–84; Martin, 2000: 182–3, 191–2).

Characteristic of Menzies' orientation to leadership are his radio broadcasts, later published as *The Forgotten People*, originally delivered when in opposition during the early years of World War II (Menzies, 1943; see also Brett, 1993: 1–27, 31–73 and Horne, 2001: 62–4, 102, 106). If Deakin looks to diversified institutional locations of leadership, Menzies looks in a more concentrated way to Parliament as the primary location of leadership. This is not to forget his many public appreciations of the civil service, or his promotion of universities, or his repeated praise of the rule of law. But political leadership is developed and tested in the parliamentary arena where law and policy are authorized under public gaze. It is not surprising then that Menzies' first and most extensive public discussion of political leadership occurs in his public radio talks when he began to cultivate the 'forgotten' middle class as the foundation stone of his revitalized Liberal Party (Menzies, 1958: 73; see also Starr, 2001: 177–95).

The book of the radio series identifies the theme of the public talks as 'the forgotten people and other studies in democracy'. That book identifies, as one of the most pressing problems of democracy, the lack of leadership caused by erroneous views of political representation. Defective views of representation hamper political leadership by modelling the function of parliamentary representation on 'mere phonograph records or sounding boards', which sit at the other extreme from genuine 'statesmanship'. Democratic statesmanship arises from a different view of parliamentary representation where the 'true function of a member of Parliament is to serve his electors not only with his vote but with his intelligence'. Leadership falls away when politicians sacrifice their duty to speak their minds by succumbing to the temptation to mouth mindless platitudes. Leadership involves more than simply speaking up for the people; it also involves speaking out against the people when the occasion requires.

Menzies concedes that the arts of public speaking are necessary but insufficient for the highest political leadership. He knows that 'To be a maker of good phrases is to travel half the journey towards popular power'; and that clever politicians with 'loose thinking and windy words' can capture popular power. Menzies' term for this public capture by wordy politicians is 'the sickness of democracy'. By contrast, the health of democracy is measured above all by the capacity for securing public approval for *un*popular measures, which is the challenge facing the would-be leader. Representative democracy requires a Parliament comprising 'the cream of the nation' and not the usual collection of 'loudmouthed careerists'. Parliament 'must provide the leaders of the people, not merely an average reflection of a fleeting popular will'. The 'candidate who plays up to them' is really undeserving of popular support. The widespread but defective picture of the elected representative is as 'a paid delegate to run our errands and obey our wishes', in contrast to Menzies' stated preference for the Burkean model, with representatives dedicated to contributing their judgement to public service. The 'first function of a member of Parliament' is to be an independent thinker 'and not a phonograph record, a guide and not a mere follower'. Consistent with this, Menzies also drew public attention to the dangers posed by speechwriters whose invisible scripts are part of 'the sickness of democracy' (Menzies, 1943: 16–17; see also Uhr, 1995).

Menzies' later treatments reinforce this orientation to leadership. Menzies defined the art of politics as 'above all, how to persuade a self-governing people to accept and loyally observe' the leader's policy prescriptions. The art of politics 'is in relation to public affairs, to provide exposition, persuasion, and inspiration' or 'to create a firm and understanding public opinion' (Menzies, 1943: 183, 186). Menzies acknowledges that the art of politics resembles the art of propaganda, but he argues that in democratic regimes it is really the art of public persuasion. Leaders are distinguished from typical politicians by their commitment to public persuasion of unfashionable alternatives. Thus two basic measures of democratic leadership are the extent to which the leader can turn around public beliefs and the extent to which the new policy directions generate sustained policy improvements.

Menzies' public models of democratic leaders are Churchill and Roosevelt, both of whom he describes as 'political artists'. Their art was 'the art of politics, which involves the persuasion and management of men'. In Menzies' own words: 'The art of politics is to convey ideas to others, if possible, to persuade a majority to agree, to create and encourage a public opinion so soundly based that it endures, and is not blown aside by chance winds.' Menzies' understanding of leadership rests on his appreciation that in politics, 'the art of speech or of written language becomes supreme'. But he builds on this foundation with his warnings against false prophets of leadership, especially 'the great actor, the showman' who features as a central carrier of 'the sickness of democracy' (Menzies, 1972: 14–15, 17).

## Keating's Model of Personal Leadership

The reach of Keating's ambition is reflected in the comment from his speechwriter Don Watson that Keating's public policies were 'designed to give the country a soul' (quoted in *Australian Financial Review Magazine*, March 2001: 39; see Watson, 2002). In his first Australia Day address, barely a month after his appointment as prime minister, Keating revealed his grand ambition in the words 'we must re-make Australia' (Keating, 1992: 4; compare Horne, 2001: 10–11 and Watson, 2002: 63–5). Critics have lost sight of the 'we' in Keating's bold declaration, and it is worth noting that most of Keating's public reflections on his leadership agenda convey the image of the leader as a conductor rather than a transformer. That is, Keating presented his role in terms of the public orchestration or facilitation of change and not in terms of the leader as sole change-agent. This distinction was not always adhered to, either in practice or in the public rhetoric.

Keating understood that his job as head of government was to promote 'the cultural shift, the shift in attitudes', or what he frequently called 'cultural reform, the reform of our outlook' (Keating, 1992: 32, 33, 44). He believed this would take Australia into a new realm as 'competitive, outward looking, phobia free' (Keating, 1995a: 32–3). The contrast was with earlier generations when 'the world passed us by'. Keating's favourite example is 'the doldrums' associated with what was then regarded as the so-called 'perfect peace' during Menzies' long reign from December 1949 to January 1966. Keating repeatedly identifies Menzies as the very model of 'Anglophilia and torpor', although privately he expressed his frustration with intrusive parliamentary demands on his prime ministerial attention by saying that 'For want of a better word, I should be Menziean' (Keating, 1992: 31, 38, 49, 125, 146; see also Edwards, 1996: 515).

But Keating's quest for a 'phobia free' future was not to be. To cite only the bleakest evidence, his 1996 defeat coincided with the rise of Pauline Hanson's One Nation Party, and with a conservative government apparently reviving Menzies' preference for exclusivist traditions. This conservative recovery owes something to Keating's rhetorical over-reach, fuelled by his quest for displaying leadership, with himself as a model of the remade Australian citizen. This apparent over-reach might also be a calculated effort to make the most of potentially adverse changes in electoral fortunes, by allowing a leader to lay down a range of policy markers for rediscovery by successors in better times. Whatever the motivation, Keating held firm to leadership conceived in his bold and dramatic terms of 'not so much in rethinking the state as in redefining the nation' (Keating, 1995a: 266).

The 1990 'Placido Domingo' address to the Canberra Press Gallery is a classic illustration of Keating's orientation to leadership (Keating, 1995: 3–8; compare Edwards, 1996: 338–9 and Watson, 2002: 20–3, 63–5). His starting point was that 'the nation is waiting to be led' and that 'politics is about leading people'. The importance of politics is that it is capable of changing the world: 'politics and politicians are about leadership', and the hardest test of leadership is its capacity to generate sustained policy change. According to Keating, one very grave challenge for Australia is that it lacks a tradition of leadership. Compared to the United States which has had a Washington, a Lincoln and a Roosevelt, Australia has only had that one 'trier' – wartime prime minister John Curtin.

To Keating, Curtin's exceptionalism only proves the point that by comparison Australia has never had 'that kind of leadership'. But without leadership, Australia will fail to secure economic and social reform. Public change requires public conversation, initiated by leaders gifted with public rhetoric. For Keating, 'leadership will always be about having a conversation with the public', although the public might wonder who ever listens to them. The 'conversational' task identified by Keating is to get public attention in order to prompt community reconsideration of current policies and practices. Conventional politics stops short, aiming simply to secure public approval for a party's quest for parliamentary power. But this traditional approach is the opposite of what is really required for Australia: 'leadership is not about being popular; it's about being right and about being strong. It's not whether you go through some shopping centres, tripping over TV crews' cords. It's about doing what you think the nation requires, making profound judgements about profound issues.'

The reference to opera singer Placido Domingo conveys Keating's belief that political leadership involves a public performance. As he puts it: 'I walk on that stage ... trying to stream the economics and the politics together. Out there on the stage, doing the Placido Domingo.' His performance role is that of 'spinning the tale, the great tale of Australian economic change, and wrapping it up in interesting ways, with interesting phrases and interesting words, which can communicate all these very complex ideas to our population'. Another classic exposition of Keating's leadership orientation is contained in a short speech at a sporting dinner (Keating, 1992: 33–4). In his pithy formulation: 'Leadership is about striking out, taking a position, being certain of a position and going for it.' Australian heroes are not like those US political heroes such as Washington, Jefferson and Lincoln but are Australian sporting greats. Here Keating confines his comparison to team leadership in sport and politics. The common leadership quality is 'to get the confidence back in the team'. National political leaders must restore confidence to the people, by helping them 'know who we are, what we are, where we are going'.

Keating's message is that 'politicians who believe in their cause are always conscious that they have a story to tell', and that leadership is in large part story-telling. Keating's special contribution is his rhetorical gifts for the memorable phrase and, for our purposes, his persistent explanation of the role of story-telling in political leadership. As he put the matter at the height of his power and authority: 'When a government cannot convey a story, a consistent story, the people lose faith in the government. It is one of the meanings of that expression of disaster – "losing the plot"' (Keating, 1995a: 53). Observers might wonder whether Keating's distinctive form of rhetorical over-reach was a tendency to allow the graphic phrase to distract attention (the leader's as well as the led) from 'the plot'. Leaders can 'lose the plot' through their own misplaced relish for rhetorical flourishes, especially in the form of personal reflections on political opponents, which can deflect public attention away from the larger story that needs to be told.

### The Language of Citizenship

Leaders are nothing without followers, and political rhetoric is valuable in rounding up followers. A common preoccupation of all three selected leaders is the development of citizenship. Leaders can be distinguished by their treatment of this subject: populist leaders tending to define citizenship in terms shared by their own support group, and civic leaders trying to shepherd all into a citizenship pen of their own making. My three examples fall between the two poles of populism and civic idealism, clustering nearer the civic end but illustrating the potential for movement in either direction. The content of their preferred citizenship varies considerably, which is not surprising when reviewing examples across a century of national political development.

My review of prime ministers' leadership rhetoric traced a development from Deakin's institutional orientation through to Keating's highly personal orientation. This pattern roughly parallels the rise of 'presidentialism' as the emerging model of political leadership. My companion review of prime ministers' citizenship rhetoric traces another pattern of development, with variations on degrees of social exclusion, beginning with Deakin's model of White Australia, moving through Menzies' model of anti-communism, and concluding with Keating's model of Australian republicanism. Each model illustrates a concept of Australian citizenship and national political identity, but in this case the most explicitly constitutional contribution comes from Keating as the most recent, rather than from the earliest of my selected prime ministers.

This reverse swing is also evident in the way that Deakin, as the earliest rather than the latest leader, carries the heaviest weight of personalized sentiment – with Deakin's personal beliefs about Australian racial purity dominating his political rhetoric. By contrast, Keating's republican model of citizenship rests on his promotion of multiculturalism, where loyalty to democratic norms replaces earlier insistence of racial homogeneity. The movement tracks an initial focus on race, through Menzies' focus on inherited political heritage, culminating in Keating's reconstruction of Australian distinctiveness. If my review of leadership rhetoric appeared biased in favour of Deakin, then my review of citizenship rhetoric might appear biased in favour of Keating. My aim is not to rank the selected leaders, but to use them to help us understand the institution of political rhetoric.

**Deakin's Model of New Protection**

Deakin's understanding of his civic duty can be seen in the establishment of the package of policy and legislation associated with New Protection. This legislative and policy package is something of an early form of what we now call 'mutual obligation'. The difference is that Deakin's original version extracted obligations from business in return for industry protection against foreign competition. The chief obligation extracted from business was that of compensating employees with 'fair and reasonable' terms and conditions of employment. Thus it dealt with individual and corporate citizenship. This package is still seen favourably by historians as 'a particular kind of nation-building social solidarity that would promote both equity and efficiency' (Macintyre, 2000: 49; see also Deakin, 1968: 209–11; 219–20; 236–7). Deakin's New Protection package was long understood as anchoring 'the distinctive ethics of Australian democracy', to use W. K. Hancock's description in his classic book *Australia* (Hancock, 1961: 66). This was so, at least, until it began to be dismantled under the fervour of micro-economic reform so celebrated by Prime Minister Keating, itself modelled on a new charter of citizenship dealing with the virtues of competing as Australians in a worldwide marketplace.

But my example here of Deakin's citizenship rhetoric is taken from his earlier contribution to the parliamentary debate over the 1901 Immigration Restriction Bill which instituted the White Australia policy (CPD, 1901; see also Deakin, 1968: 74–81). This example reveals much of the substructure of New Protection, particularly the protectionist fears of aliens and outsiders. My focus is on Deakin's unusual rhetoric rather than his commonplace racism. Deakin gave the best case available in promoting the exclusive immigration policy which can be seen as a foundation stone for the later edifice of New Protection. Deakin was attorney-general in the Barton government and used all his rhetorical powers to promote the protectionist immigration policy. What distinguishes Deakin's contribution to the parliamentary debate is his open acknowledgement that this measure by far exceeds all other Commonwealth legislation because 'so much anxiety' is associated with its passage. Where most parliamentary contributors debated the measure in terms of fear and security, Deakin organized his contribution around the more elusive theme of anxiety, balancing Australian anxieties against those of other nations, including Britain and Japan. Britain was urging Australia to respect the divergent races within the Empire. In Deakin's high-minded account, Japan represented the moral challenge of a non-white race of equal standing to white Australia. Deakin's artful contribution was to defend a racially discriminatory measure by reference to the virtues of democratic citizenship rather than the vices of xenophobia.

Deakin observed that this measure touched 'the profoundest instinct of individual or nation – the instinct of self-preservation – for it is nothing less than the national manhood, the national character, and the national future that are at stake'. What is notable is Deakin's subsequent efforts to try to elevate the debate from the level of self-preservation to the level of self-development, moving the focus from individual fears to collective hopes. This is no easy achievement, given Deakin's sympathy for the race sentiment driving Federation. He accepted that Federation came about because of a desire to be 'one people without the admixture of other races'. This racial quest transformed the pursuit of Federation from a preoccupation among political elites to a popular demand. Many

Australians who 'take little interest in contemporary politics' rallied round the idea that the new nation would be 'undiminished and uninvaded' after Federation. For Deakin, this 'aspiration nerved them to undertake the great labour of conquering the sectional differences that divide us'.

But Deakin has little public sympathy with active policies of race antagonism. For instance, he accepted that the Commonwealth constitution provides ample power for the basic self-protection of the Australian people, including the power of state governments to legislate in relation to indigenous Australians. But he counselled against state measures to penalize them. Although in Deakin's eyes they appeared to be 'a dying race', indigenous Australians deserved 'not simply the justice, but the generosity of the treatment which the white race, who are dispossessing them and entering into their heritage, are according them'. Wishful thinking perhaps, or maybe Deakin's too subtle attempt to promote racial tolerance.

Deakin's explicit defence of White Australia was also justified in terms of an openly declared policy commitment to the Australian people by the Barton administration at the first Commonwealth elections. But Deakin then contrasted the internal public legitimacy of White Australia with its potential external illegitimacy. Deakin warned that 'those who look at us with old world eyes' would be appalled at 'the arrogance of a handful of white men' intent on repelling 'an inflow that will seek every crevice in our statutory armour, and will require that we stop all possible leakages effectively one after another, as many of them and as rapidly as possible'. Deakin attempted to take this 'arrogance' out of the case for White Australia. He did this by changing the focus from the policy content of racial homogeneity to the policy process of democratic decision-making. He used his reply to Australia's external critics to try to turn parliamentary interest away from assertions of Australian 'arrogance' towards denials of external doubts about Australia's readiness for democratic self-government. This is the turn away from a negative posture of 'nativism' to a positive one of 'nationality'. His aim was to show that Australia as 'a democracy, in some respects impatient, is imposing on itself as a restraint in the interests of future generations, who are to enter into the country of which we at present only hold the border. This note of nationality is that which gives dignity and importance to this debate.'

Deakin's model of Australian citizenship rests on this concept of nationality as race. A 'united race' means that Parliament must do everything in its power to promote acceptance of 'the same ideas' and 'the same ideals' to cultivate 'a people possessing the same general cast of character, tone of thought – the same constitutional training and traditions'. Exclusionary immigration is the prerequisite of this very restrictive vision of a democratic political culture. Deakin accepted that 'unity of race is an absolute essential to the unity of Australia'. This pre-eminent public policy 'is no mere electioneering manifesto, but part of the first principles upon which the Commonwealth is to be administered and guided'.

Deakin read into the parliamentary record extensive extracts from Colonial Secretary Chamberlain's 'perfectly reasonable request' that the new nation avoid racial discrimination against Indian or Asian crown subjects. Deakin claimed that the measure respected that request because the real discrimination was vested in provisions for educational tests, adapted from the South African colonies which did not necessarily ban the entry of non-white immigrants – just as it did not necessarily permit the entry of each and every white applicant, as Deakin (1968: 69) emphasized. In relation to Japan, Deakin was at pains to emphasize 'how high a position that nation occupies in art and letters, and how worthy they are of the place, in our estimation, generally conceded to the highest and most civilised among the nations of the world'. Japan would be 'justified in resenting' any unnecessary reflection on its character by Australia when legislating to exclude 'the many uneducated races of Asia and the untutored savages who visit our shores'. Deakin's case against Japan was that 'the Japanese require to be excluded because of their high abilities' and 'their inexhaustible energy' that make them 'such competitors'. And protection against unfair competition, rather than racial purity as such, was one of the basic purposes of this aspect of Deakin's New Protection.

### Menzies' Model of Anti-communism

Menzies' promotion of Australian citizenship resembles Deakin's in being defined against a perceived threat. Menzies' anti-communism functions in much the same way as Deakin's racially defined defence of White Australia. The prominence of anti-communism in Menzies' underlying concept of citizenship can be traced back to the vulnerable place of 'freedom' in *The Forgotten People*. Communism represents the gravest threat to political freedom during Menzies' lengthy time as prime minister after 1949. What is striking is how quickly Menzies once in office spoke up about the threat of communism, internationally and nationally. Menzies' reign during the 1950s is often associated with his adroit management of the Petrov affair, particularly its damaging impact on the Labor Party which split over this Menzies-inspired issue of the place of communists in leadership positions in trade unions.

An alternative account of Menzies' understanding of Australian citizenship would involve examination of his sustained public rhetoric about the 'Britishness' of Australia (consider, e.g., Brett, 1993: 74–125 on the vice of communism, and 129–55 on the virtue of Britishness). That too can be traced back to *The Forgotten People*, where Australians are described as 'unhesitatingly British', 'utterly and soundly British', with Menzies describing himself as 'like you – dyed in the wool British' (Menzies, 1943: 41, 47, 78; see also Eggleston, 1953: 8–19; Uhr, 1995). But the most vigorous and dramatic exercises of Menzies' political rhetoric are those dealing with anti-communism, which illustrates the polemical edge of his Britishness. For Menzies, communism is the denial of all that he holds dear in Britishness. Australians 'are British through and through. We are for the Crown. We are the Queen's men and women' (Menzies, 1958: 201. See also Menzies, 1972: 207). Communists are 'the King's enemies in this country', engaged in 'treason and fifth-columnism' (CPD, 1950: 1955).

Menzies' attack on communism took the form of his quest to ban the Communist Party of Australia. Elected in 1949, he introduced legislation to ban the party in 1950. After two attempts in 1950 involving Senate obstruction, his legislation eventually passed Parliament, only to be declared unconstitutional by the High Court. Labor's shadow attorney-general, H. V. Evatt, argued the successful constitutional case before the High Court. Undeterred by this judicial rebuff, Menzies then initiated a referendum to alter the constitution to grant power to Parliament to legislate against communism. The referendum was only narrowly defeated. Nothing characterizes Menzies' political rhetoric on citizenship so much as his polemical attacks on the civic threats posed by communism. The fact that Menzies was unsuccessful in banning the Communist Party does not detract from its use in illustrating his mode of political rhetoric – any more than Keating's unsuccessful republicanism detracts from its use in illustrating the Keating style.

My example comes from Menzies' speech when first introducing his Communist Party Dissolution Bill in April 1950 (CPD, 1950: 1994–2007). The very wide measure proposed to ban the Communist Party as an organization prejudicial to national defence or to maintenance of the Australian constitutional order, and to prohibit other organizations engaged in similarly threatening activities. Menzies explained his measure as one primarily designed to secure 'the safety and defence of Australia'. Principles of free speech were now to be balanced against the strategic interests of the Cold War, involving Australia as with 'people all over the British world'. To those tempted to resist the measure on the basis that liberty demands tolerance, Menzies responded that the 'self-governing institutions' of a democracy must be protected: 'what liberty should there be for the enemies of liberty under the law?' Communism is 'an international conspiracy against the democracies, organized as a prelude to war'. Hence 'the communist is our enemy'. Menzies claimed that at the 1949 general election, the Communist Party won nearly ninety thousand votes; but their real threat was 'not numerical but positional', by virtue of communists' holding leadership positions – 'important union office in key industries'.

Menzies then named many alleged communists, posing 'the choice before us' as 'a grim but a simple one'. Australia could either do nothing to curb this 'traitorous minority' or 'fight him wherever we find him, leaving him no immunity and no sanctuary'. Menzies claimed that the ordinary Australian unionist was not 'a citizen indifferent to the march of communism' and that his good citizenship would want to be enlisted in the fight against communism. The many 'decent, honest, patriotic' unionists will not fall for the 'force, violence and fraud' of communism and its threat to law and order.

Citizenship is defined by reference to the constitutional order, and Menzies justified the legislation as a warranted defence of the constitutional order against 'a state of affairs both menacing and alarming'. The basis for the legislation was the defence power and what Menzies referred to as 'our right and duty to maintain the Constitution and the laws against any wrecking attack whatever'. His proof of the menace and the justification of his alarm was provided in the bill itself, which contained a preamble reciting indictments against the Communist Party. These recitals refer to communist doctrine, which Menzies elaborated with extracts from Australian editions of such texts as Stalin's *The Foundations of Leninism*, complete with Australian commentary from leading Australian communists. Menzies invited 'the attention of all good Australians who love their country and who value their own traditions' to examine these doctrines. Quoting Stalin on the need for destruction of the bourgeois order, Menzies recounted the origin of 'bourgeois' in terms of burgher and citizen, and claimed that 'we in this Parliament' belong to the bourgeoisie – as do so many 'other Australians dwelling peacefully in their homes and among their children'.

Menzies kept his *coup de grâce* until last: this was his use of Labor statements to indicate that the opposition was itself moving to clamp down on its association with communist organizations. The aim was to place Labor MPs in a dilemma: either they accept their own evidence about communist 'disloyalty' and support Menzies' measure, or they deny their own evidence and oppose the measure. The strategy was to convince the opposition to support the measure 'dealing with a conspiracy against the life of this country'. The strategy worked in the short run: Parliament approved the legislation but, with opposition support, the unions challenging the constitutionality of the law won their case and had the High Court overturn the law. But as mentioned above, this did not stop Menzies deploying his anti-communist rhetoric in other, more effective ways, dominating public life until his voluntary retirement from Parliament in early 1966.

### Keating's Model of Republicanism

Once chosen by his party as Hawke's successor as prime minister, Keating drove the Australian political debate over a republic, even when he appeared to have delegated the details to others. The establishment in 1993 of the Republic Advisory Committee, its report later that year and the subsequent proposal for a referendum before century's end are all illustrations of Keating's attempt to recast the constitution of political leadership in terms of a refashioned Australian national identity. The option for a minimalist republic was to prove unsuccessful, but this is not to deny Keating's leadership in making the republic issue an opportunity to rethink constitutional arrangements. Even the minimalist model rests on a substantial overhaul of the concepts of political sovereignty in the 1901 constitution – in effect, substituting the national sovereignty of Australian citizens in place of the foreign sovereign (Uhr, 1999: 1–8; 187–90).

Keating's understanding of the rhetoric of citizenship is explicitly related to his promotion of a new national identity, a multicultural orientation of an Australia that accepts its location in Asia, a new version of the Australian national story, a new interest in civics within schooling, and a revised charter of citizenship with fresh recognition of the rights of indigenous Australians. Observers have noted his enlistment of the historian Don Watson to help craft the right words to promote Keating's instinctive appreciation of Australian citizenship in terms of membership in a sovereign and independent nation.

Think of this strategy as involving three components. Part of this reshaped national story involved a rewriting of the British Commonwealth version left behind by Menzies; another part dealt with the significance of immigration and multiculturalism to 'retooling' Australia to compete on the world stage; and another part dealt with reconciliation with indigenous Australians, beginning with the famous Redfern Speech with its apologetic list of regrets. The 'productive diversity agenda' sought to justify multiculturalism to an increasingly suspicious public through 'a productivity dividend' of community prosperity. The merits of the policy were undercut by the weaknesses of the national economy and the invisibility to many voters of the proclaimed dividend (Keating, 1995a: 263–70; see also Watson, 2002: 288–91, 681–2, 690–2). While Keating may be right that 'in the end it's the big picture which changes nations', it is also true that big pictures hang heavy in the popular mind, and risk falling when that mind grows weary or suspicious of the merits of what it is being asked to support. Even sympathetic critics call this the 'crisis inflation' that Keating just had to have, eventually to his own political cost (compare Watson, 2002: 110–11 with Campbell and Halligan, 1992: 33, 222–3; Day, 2000: 422–5, 429, 434).

The example here of Keating's citizenship rhetoric is his 1995 parliamentary response to the report of his Republic Advisory Committee (Keating, 1995b; see also Edwards, 1996: 526–8, 536, 538 and Watson, 2002: 581–7). The speech is one of Keating's more grave and sombre performances, but is a fine expression of his ability to convey a story of abstruse legal complexity with words of memorable simplicity. The terms of reference given to the Republic Advisory Committee chaired by Malcolm Turnbull were explicitly confined to charting a path of minimalist change to the constitution. The committee's essential task was to substitute a new office of president for the existing office of governor-general. Keating's speech takes it as given that this 'one small step would make Australia a republic'. Subsequent public debate has challenged this minimalist proposition, less as a statement of fact than as an undesirably modest step in republican directions.

Keating rests his case on the plain and uncomplicated view stated in the opening sentence 'that Australia's Head of State should be an Australian'. The closing sentence ends with the words 'one of us' which was Keating's pithy refrain to enlist national sentiment in the cause of republicanism. Disclaiming radicalism, jingoism and 'the beat of drums – or chests', Keating justifies the proposed change as a requirement of 'our unique identity'. The republican option 'expresses nothing more than our desire to have a Head of State who is truly one of us'. The claimed importance of this one change is that it would signal Australia's revitalized nationality to the world. Keating identifies no greater need or demand for this change other than the looming centenary of Federation, which provided an appropriate opportunity to remove the 'anomalous' situation of a foreign head of state – now 'a remote and inadequate symbol' for Australians to take to heart.

Keating does not bother to explain that the constitution has no real definition of head of state, nor that the British monarch is now under Australian law the Queen of Australia. His simple message was that the proposed republic was an act of recognition rather than rejection: recognition of the place of an Australian citizen in the highest public office and not rejection of Britain or of its place in 'our heritage and its affections'. The proposed change would simply be 'the last step in a process which began one hundred years ago'. Australia is approaching its centenary of national political identity as 'a sovereign nation in all respects bar one'.

Keating explains the symbolism of the change to an Australian citizen as head of state in terms of 'our cultural diversity, our evolving partnerships with Asia and the Pacific, our quest for reconciliation with Aboriginal Australians, our ambition to create a society in which women have equal opportunity, equal representation and equal rights'. The aim then was to devise a procedure to select as head of state 'a citizen of high standing who has made an outstanding contribution to Australia and who, in making it, has enlarged our view of what it is to be Australian'. Keating spends considerable time weighing the merits of different appointment possibilities. His starting point is that the existing arrangement whereby the prime minister alone is responsible for the appointment of the governor-general is defective: prime ministers 'should not have such exclusive power'. But direct election is undesirable because it would concentrate too much power in the head of state, at the expense of the head of government. He fears that an elected head of state would claim a public mandate unavailable to any other political office. This poses difficult problems because the new office would attract 'an authority unheard of in our political system and discordant with some of the basic principles on which that system rests'. Furthermore, direct election would politicize the office which should be one 'above politics' to enable the president to 'represent the nation as a whole'.

The speech is impressive in its simplicity and its sweep. My comments here have been primarily about the former quality; but the sweep also deserves notice. Keating leads the audience through the careful dismantling of the direct-election option, the equally cautious critique of a constitutional convention and the almost silent rebuttal of the monarchist defence of the status quo. The fact that Keating lost office to John Howard who publicly favoured the constitutional convention takes little away from our historical interest in Keating's citizenship rhetoric.

## Conclusion

All Australian prime ministers aspire to be national leaders but few demonstrate sustained national leadership. The reasons for this leadership deficit are many: some prime ministers come to the job unprepared for its elevated national responsibilities, some find themselves out of their depth dealing with international issues, others have too little time or opportunity to make a lasting impact on political affairs. As Bryce feared, some leaders reduce statecraft to populism. Occupying an office as leader of government is no guarantee that the occupant will exercise political leadership. At the dawn of the second century of Federation, Australia is experiencing a searching public debate over political leadership, with persistent doubts raised about the leadership capacity of leading politicians. One of the main concerns is a suspicion that populism is on the rise, with politicians increasingly pandering to public fears and reinforcing prejudices relating to public insecurities. This environment makes it all the more relevant that we carefully review the degree to which these three exemplary prime ministers satisfy Bryce's anti-populist test of democratic statesmanship.

I do not want to be identified as claiming too much for the study of prime ministerial rhetoric. In this chapter, I have tried to interpret the three leaders' political rhetoric by reference to their own articulation of their leadership role. But there will be competing interpretations of political rhetoric. For instance, political scientists have long known that speechcraft is often little more than a clever form of stagecraft (consider Rustow, 1970: 25; Riker, 1986: ix–xi; Riker, 1996: 3–11, 253–63). In this view, political actors are scripted, speaking lines either given to them by others who are the real authors of, and authorities over, political conduct; or speaking lines that the leaders themselves make up, not because they necessarily believe them but because they will play well with the public. I have tried to select three examples of leaders who have been explicit about their craft of rhetoric and its place in their scheme of political leadership.

There are other objections that can be raised against my selective study of Australian political leadership. First, the personal speechcraft of chief political executives is only one part of their statecraft, a necessary but, on its own, insufficient to cope with the range of political decisions facing chief political executives. Furthermore, national statecraft is a collective activity involving the might of the state; heads of government have a role but they are not the only or even the most influential state actors. The focus on the official position of government leader should not blind us to the existence of many other leadership positions close to the political executive, from the largely invisible role of speechwriter to many other more visible roles in the executive and other branches of national government (Watson, 2002: 53–8; see generally Shapiro, 1981; 1984). Another limitation of my selection is that it is all-male. Although this is consistent with the historical practice of the Australian prime ministership, it would be very unwise to jump to hard-and-fast conclusions about the capacity of the office in the absence of evidence of how female political leaders might reshape the role. Australia has had valuable experience of female heads of government at state level, and a complete account of even so narrow a field as executive speechcraft would have to take account of that experience (Sawer, 1996; Sinclair, 1998).

But for all that, political rhetoric can still help us understand leadership. As stated earlier, part of my aim has been to explore Bryce's hypothesis that through their public rhetoric, national political leaders 'do much to create a pattern for the people of what statesmanship ought to be'. The leaders' rhetoric about citizenship is part of a larger project of political instruction, informing the people of what the leaders understand, or want the public to understand, to be the nature of democratic leadership. My review has highlighted just how open Australian prime ministers have been about their national leadership responsibilities and their view of the relationship between leadership and citizenship. I concede that the evidence tells us more about their public justifications than their private beliefs, but this is consistent with my interest in charting the contours of political rhetoric and the leaders' constructed public 'pattern' of Australian statesmanship.

Bryce's fascination with Australia grew out of his conviction that it provides an interesting test-case of the possibilities of democratic leadership. Bryce acknowledged that the Australian political framework 'represents the high-water mark of popular government. It is penetrated by the spirit of democracy'. In his view, Australia was more democratic than Britain because it did not entrench class rule; and it was more democratic than the United States because of its more flexible parliamentary system of governance. Both established regimes also gave more power to established wealth than did Australia. For Bryce, popular sovereignty had found a safe haven in Australia where the political institutions allow the people's elected representatives to 'give effect to their wishes with incomparable promptitude' (Bryce, 1905: 327–8). Contemplating a regime of a constitutional democracy that was very open to popular power, he wondered how elected political leaders would withstand the temptations of populism. He also wondered how the people themselves would withstand populism, including populist leaders.

Examining political rhetoric provides some but by no means all the answers. Indeed, the limitations of a focus on rhetoric were obvious to Bryce, whose own experience as a party politician made him somewhat suspicious of 'oratorical brilliance' and fearful of the sophistry often lurking behind political rhetoric (Bryce, 1921, vol. 2: 518). Bryce leans towards elitism; he tolerates but is never very enthusiastic about democratic rhetoric, which too often is a medium for populism and demagoguery. Why is it, he asks, that democratic leadership seems so often to fall to those with the power of 'captivating speech'? Is it inevitable that democracies will be ruled by clever talkers who 'can sway the minds and wills of the sovereign people'? (Ibid: 605). Bryce's keen interest in political rhetoric was near the centre of his interest in democratic government, in part because he thought that democracy would be tested by public suspicion that the rhetorical façade of democratic leadership disguised the hidden presence of oligarchy. A forerunner of what is now called 'democratic elitism', Bryce devoted a chapter of *Modern Democracy* to 'oligarchies within democracies' (Ibid: 594–604). This realistic appreciation of the limits of popular rule explains some of Bryce's interest in the dangers of populist leadership. It also serves as a reminder that, although indispensable, rhetoric is not the only element in a satisfactory account of political leadership.

## Note

My thanks for helpful comments from the editors and from Michael Pusey, Haig Patapan, Ian Marsh, Barry Hindess, Jane Kelsey, John Martin, and Tim Rowse.

## References

Blondel, J. *Political Leadership: Towards a General Theory* (London: Sage, 1987).
Brennan, H. G., and Hamlin, A. *Democratic Devices and Desires* (Cambridge: Cambridge University Press, 2000).
Brett, J. *Robert Menzies' Forgotten People* (Sydney: Sun Australia, 1993).
——. 'Robert Menzies in England', in J. Brett (ed.), *Political Lives* (Sydney: Allen & Unwin, 1997).
Bryce, J. *Constitutions* (Oxford: Oxford University Press, 1905).
——. *The Hindrances to Good Citizenship* (New Haven: Yale University Press, 1909).
——. *Modern Democracies*, 2 vols (London: Macmillan, 1921).
Bryman, A. 'Leadership in Organizations', in S. R. Clegg, C. Hardy and W. Norf (eds), *Handbook of Organization Studies* (London: Sage, 1996).
Burns, J. M. *Leadership* (New York: Harper Collins, 1978).
Campbell, C. *The US Presidency in Crisis: A Comparative Perspective* (Oxford: Oxford University Press, 1998).
Campbell, C.. and Halligan, J. *Political Leadership in an Age of Constraint* (Sydney: Allen & Unwin, 1992).
Clark, C. M. H. 'Heroes', in S. R. Graubard (ed.), *Australia: The Daedalus Symposium* (Sydney: Angus & Robertson, 1985).
(CPD) *Commonwealth Parliamentary Debates* Canberra: House of Representatives, vol. 4(12) (September 1901) pp. 4804–17).
(CPD) *Commonwealth Parliamentary Debates* Canberra: House of Representatives, vol. 8(18) (March 1902) pp. 10,962–89.
(CPD) *Commonwealth Parliamentary Debates* Canberra: House of Representatives, vol. 207(27) (April 1950) pp. 1994–7.
Day, D. 'Paul Keating', in M. Grattan (ed.), *Australian Prime Ministers* (Sydney: New Holland, 2000).
de Vries, M. K. *Leaders, Fools and Imposters: Essays on the Psychology of Leadership* (San Francisco: Jossey-Bass, 1993).
Deakin, A. *The Federal Story: The Inner History of the Federal Cause, 1880–1900* (edited by J. A. La Nauze) (Melbourne: Melbourne University Press, 1963).
Deakin. A. *Federated Australia: Selections from Letters to the Morning Post 1900–1910* (edited by J. A. La Nauze) (Melbourne: Melbourne University Press, 1968).
Edwards, J. *Keating: The Inside Story* (Ringwood, Vic.: Viking, 1996).
Eggleston, F. W. 'Political Leadership in Australia', in *Reflections of an Australian*

*Liberal* (Melbourne: Cheshire, 1953) pp. 8–19.
Elgie, R. *Political Leadership in Liberal Democracies* (New York: St Martin's Press, 1995).
Gaffney, J. 'Imagined Relationships: Political Leadership in Contemporary Democracies', in *Parliamentary Affairs*, 54 (2001) pp. 120–33.
Gardner, H. *Leading Minds: An Anatomy of Leadership* (London: Harper Collins, 1997).
Grattan. M. (ed.) *Australian Prime Ministers* (Sydney: New Holland, 2000).
Hancock, W. K. *Australia* (Brisbane: Jacaranda Press, 1961) p. 66.
Handy, C. 'The Language of Leadership', in W. E. Rosenbach and R. L. Taylor (eds), *Contemporary Issues in Leadership* (Boulder: Westview Press, 1989) pp. 235–41.
Handy, C., and Clegg, S. 'Some Dare call it Power', in S. R. Clegg, C. Hardy and W. Norf (eds), *Handbook of Organization Studies* (London: Sage, 1996).
Hargrove, E. C. 'Popular Leadership in the Anglo-American Democracies', in Edinger (ed.), *Political Leadership in Industrialized Societies* (New York: Wiley, 1967) pp. 182–219.
——. *The President as Leader* (Lawrence, Kans.: University of Kansas Press, 1998).
——. 'The Presidency and the Prime Ministership as Institutions', *British Journal of Politics and International Relations*, 3(1) (2001), April.
Hart, J. 'An Australian President? A Comparative Perspective', in P. Weller (ed.), *Menzies to Keating* (Melbourne: Melbourne University Press, 1992) pp. 183–201.
Henderson, G. *Menzies' Child: The Liberal Party of Australia, 1944–1994* (Sydney: Allen & Unwin, 1994).
Horne, D. *Looking for Leadership: Australia in the Howard Years* (Ringwood, Vic.: Viking, 2001).
Hughes, C. A. *Mr Prime Minister: Australian Prime Ministers, 1901–1972* (Melbourne: Oxford University Press, 1976).
Jones, B. D. (ed.) *Leadership and Politics: New Perspectives in Political Science* (Lawrence, Kans.: University of Kansas Press, 1989).
Keating, P. *Major Speeches of the First Year* (Canberra: Australian Labor Party, 1992).
Keating, P. *Advancing Australia: The Speeches of Paul Keating*, selected and edited by Mark Ryan (Big Picture Publications, 1995a).
——. *An Australian Republic: The Way Forward* (Canberra: Australian Government Publishing Service, 1995b).
La Nauze, J. A. *The Making of the Australian Constitution* (Melbourne: Melbourne University Press, 1972).
——. *Alfred Deakin: A Biography* (Sydney: Angus & Robertson, 1979).
——. 'Introduction' to A. Deakin, *Federated Australia* (Melbourne: Melbourne University Press, 1968) pp. v–xii.
Little, G. *Political Ensembles: A Psychosocial Approach to Politics and Leadership* (Melbourne: Oxford University Press, 1985).
——. *Strong Leadership* (Melbourne: Oxford University Press, 1988).
——. 'The two Narcissims: comparing Hawke and Keating' and 'Malcolm Fraser' in J. Brett (ed.), *Political Lives* (Sydney: Allen & Unwin, 1997).
Macintyre, S. 'Alfred Deakin', in M. Grattan (ed.), *Australian Prime Ministers* (Sydney: New Holland, 2000) pp. 37–53.

Marsh. I. 'The Federation Decade', in J. R. Nethercote (ed.), *Liberalism and the Australian Federation* (Sydney: The Federation Press, 2001) pp. 69–97.

Martin, A. 'Sir R. G. Menzies', in M. Grattan (ed.), *Australian Prime Ministers* (Sydney: New Holland, 2000) pp. 175–205.

Menzies, R. G. *The Forgotten People and Other Studies in Democracy* (Sydney: Angus & Robertson, 1943).

——. *Speech is of Time: Selected Writings and Speeches* (London: Cassell and Co., 1958).

——. *The Measure of the Years* (London: Coronet Books, 1972).

Miroff, B. 'The Presidency and the Public: Leadership as spectacle', in M. Nelson (ed.), *The Presidency and the Political System* (5th edition, Washington, DC: Congressional Quarterly Press, 1998) pp. 299–322.

Mughan, A., and Patterson, S. C. (eds). *Political Leadership in Democratic Societies* (Chicago: Nelson-Hall Publishers, 1992).

Pennock, J. R. *Democratic Political Theory* (Princeton: Princeton University Press, 1979).

Riker, W. H. *The Art of Political Manipulation* (New Haven: Yale University Press, 1986).

——. *The Strategy of Rhetoric* (New Haven: Yale University Press, 1996).

Rustow, D. A. 'The Study of Leadership', in D. A. Rustow (ed.), *Philosophers and Kings: Studies in Leadership* (New York: The Daedalus Library, 1970).

Sawer, M. 'Challenging Politics?', *International Review of Women and Leadership*, 2(1) (July 1996) pp. i–xvi.

Shapiro, M. J. *Language and Political Understanding: The Politics of Discursive Practices* (New Haven: Yale University Press, 1981).

—— (ed.) *Language and Politics* (Oxford: Basil Blackwell, 1984).

Sinclair, A. *Doing Leadership Differently* (Melbourne: Melbourne University Press, 1998).

Starr, G. 'Menzies and Post-war Prosperity', in J. Nethercote (ed.), *Liberalism and the Australian Federation* (Sydney: The Federation Press, 2001) pp. 177–95.

Thurow, G. and Wallin, J. D. (eds). *Rhetoric and American Statesmanship* (Durban, N.C.: Carolina Academic Press, 1984).

Tulis, J. K. *The Rhetorical Presidency* (Princeton: Princeton University Press, 1987).

Uhr, J. 'Prime Ministers and the Parliament', in P. Weller (ed.), *Menzies to Keating: The Development of Australian Prime Ministership* (Melbourne: Melbourne University Press, 1992) pp. 81–108.

——. 'The Rhetoric of Representation: Menzies' Reshaping of Parliament', *Legislative Studies*, 10(1) (Spring 1995) pp. 92–102.

——. (ed.) *The Australian Republic: The Case for Yes* (Sydney: The Federation Press, 1999).

van Maurik, J. (ed.) *Writers on Leadership* (Harmondsworh: Penguin, 2001).

Watson, D. *Recollections of a Bleeding Heart: A Portrait of Paul Keating PM* (Sydney: Knopf, 2002).

Weller, P. *First Among Equals: Prime Ministers in Westminster Systems* (Boston: Allen & Unwin, 1985).

——. *Malcolm Fraser PM* (Ringwood, Vic.: Viking, 1989).

——. (ed.) *Menzies to Keating: The Development of the Australian Prime Ministership* (Melbourne: Melbourne University Press. 1992).

# Index

Aboriginal affairs referendum, 171
Aboriginal and Torres Strait Islander peoples
 deaths in police custody, 209
 denial of civil and procedural rights, 247–8, 250
 exclusion from rule of law, 243–8, 250–4
 franchise, 159, 181, 198, 203, 204, 250
 genocide, 96–8
 identity and identity claims, 184, 190, 200, 205, 206–7
 Imperial Government's instructions, 243, 252–3
 importance of public sphere for, 130–2
 inclusion in the state, 129–31, 189, 204–6, 211–12
 native title to land, 205–6, 247
 paternalist protection of, 193–4, 202, 210–11, 248–52
 political exclusion, 129, 159, 193–4, 198–9
 political options and action, 130–2, 191, 195–6, 200, 202, 206–9, 210
 population numbers, 197, 203
 removal of children, 201, 210, 253–4
 role of law in dispossession and destruction, 242–53, 255
 self-determination, 129–30, 191–2, 195, 204–5, 207–9, 213
 social and economic exclusion, 96–8, 181, 199, 209–10, 212, 247, 250
 *See also* indigenous–state relations
Aboriginal Councils and Associations Act, 207
'Aboriginal enclaves', 191
Aboriginality. *See* identity: Indigenous Australians
Accord, 74, 125

adult male suffrage, 120, 122
adult suffrage, 114, 159
affirmative action, 104, 164
AIDS drugs, 87, 109–10
ALP. See Australian Labor Party
Anderson, Francis, 151
anti-communism, 284–7
anti-discrimination laws, 104
antitrust laws (US), 105–6
arbitration system. *See* conciliation and arbitration (of labour relations)
Asian immigrants, exclusion of, 64, 101, 132, 281–4
Asprey Committee, 79
assimilation policies, 129, 189, 193–4, 201–3, 211
associative democracy, 137
asylum-seekers, 101, 137
ATSIC (Aboriginal and Torres Strait Islander Commission), 129–30, 205, 208, 211–12
Australia
 as business laggard, 86–9, 105–7
 as colonial power, 98–9
 as democratic and governmental innovator, 26, 86–9, 99–100, 122, 149
 democratic deficit, 124, 143–4
 democratic inclusiveness, 115–16
 depleted public sector, 116, 125–6
 distinctive colonial experience, 90–1
 global political leadership, 86–7, 89, 109–10
 lack of leadership tradition, 279
 as law-filled polity, 241
 talent for good government, 86–8
 *See also* Australian egalitarianism; Australian exceptionalism
Australian Competition and Consumer Commission (ACCC), 69, 102
Australian Conservation Foundation (ACF), 138–41
Australian Council of Trade Unions (ACTU), 74, 124

295

Australian Economic Association, 150, 157
Australian egalitarianism
  demise, 102–4, 108, 124
  preconditions of, 45–6
  prospects for, 108–10
  racism as taint, 101
Australian exceptionalism, 10, 40–1, 47, 55, 78, 89–91, 269–70
  *See also* wage earners' welfare state
Australian Federation of Women Voters, 171
Australian Labor Party
  ethnic clientelism in, 135
  and financial deregulation, 71–2
  first governments, 26, 123
  loss of working class character, 124
  women in, 163, 164
Australian Settlement, 11, 264
  *See also* protectionist policy regime
Australian Women's National League, 162–3
authoritarian regimes, 28–30

basic wage, 43–4, 46
Bentham, Jeremy, 91
bioregional authorities, 141
boat people, 101, 137
Bond, Alan, 88
bourgeoisie, 119–21
Bryce, James, 263, 265–70, 289–92
Buchanan, James M., 54
Builders Labourers' Federation, 124
bureaucratic feminism, 166–70
Burns Philp, 98–9
business
  inclusion in state, 119–21
  poor leadership, 86, 88, 105–7
  regulation, 89

Cairns Group, 86–7, 97
Campbell Committee, 70–1, 79
capital punishment, 36
causal influences (on economic outcomes), 55–7
Chandler, Alfred D., 106
Chard, W.H., 165
citizenship
  coexistence with exclusion, 114
  Deakin's racial conception, 282–4
  ecological redefinition, 138
  Indigenous Australians, 130–1, 189, 194, 198, 199, 202, 209
  Keating on, 287–9
  liberal democratic concept, 188
  Menzies on, 284–7
  obligations, 269–70
  political leadership and, 266–70
  social liberal concept, 150, 153–7
  women, 159–60
clientelism, 135
co-option (by the state), 168
Coalition of Australian Participating Organizations of Women (CAPOW!), 162
Colonial Sugar Refining Company (CSR), 98–9
colonies. See corporate colonialism; penal colony (New South Wales)
committees of inquiry, 79–80
Commonwealth–State financial relations, 173–4
Communist Party of Australia, 124, 285
company tax. See corporate tax
competition, attitudes to, 65, 69–70
competition policy, 69, 72–3, 72–4, 102
competitive economic policy regime, 68–75, 72, 78–80
compulsory voting, 99
conciliation and arbitration (of labour relations), 43, 99–100, 123, 241
  institutional dismantling, 48–9
  as social liberal critique of contract, 151–2
  welfare effects, 43–7, 49
consensual democracies, 32–3
  impact on policy outcomes, 10, 34–7
Constitution (Australia)
  Aboriginal affairs powers, 171, 187
  character, 31, 33–4
  judicial interpretation, 274–5
  powers over women's issues, 170–2
'constitution' (of economic-political order), 54–5
contract, freedom of, 149, 151–2
convicts
  civil and property rights, 93–4, 235–41
  restorative justice for, 92–6
Coombs Commission, 169
corporate capitalism, 106–7
corporate colonialism, 89–91, 98–9
corporate management, 87–8, 105–7
corporate mergers, 106–7
corporate tax, 103–4
corporate welfare state, 104
corporatism, 41–2, 135
corporatization, 73–4, 90
Cowan, Edith, 161, 165–6
Crofton, Sir Walter, 93
Curtin, John, 163–4, 279

Deakin, Alfred, 43
  defence of White Australia policy, 281–4

# Index

institutional approach to leadership, 271–2
racial conception of citizenship, 281–4
demagogues, 267
democracy
  Australia as pioneer, 26, 99, 114
  Australia's democratic deficit, 143–4
  Australia's hybrid character, 33–4
  civic versus populist leadership, 266–70
  features and forms, 26, 32–4
  impact on economic performance, 9, 27–30, 35–6
  impact on welfare and well-being, 25–30, 34–5, 34–40
  as work-in-progress, 115
  *See also* associative democracy; democratization
democratic institutions. See democracy
'democratic pluralism', 134
democratization, 28, 115, 117–18
difference, denial versus recognition, 176–7, 213
domains. See political domains
Dowse, Sara, 167
drugs, 102
Du Cane, Edmund, 93, 95
Dual State, 225–6
Dunstan, Don, 176
Dutch East India Company, 90

'ecological modernization', 140–1
Ecologically Sustainable Development process, 140–1
'economic constitution', 54–6
economic imperative (of the state), 117
  and the bourgeoisie, 120–1
  and environmental concerns, 140–2
  and immigration and multiculturalism, 133
  and Indigenous Australians, 131
  and liberal feminism, 128
  *versus* native title to land, 131
  and women's temperance movement, 127
economic institutions
  Australia, 53–81 *passim*
  relationship to economic outcomes, 55–61
economic outcomes
  effect of economic institutions on, 55–61
  effect on policy regimes, 57, 59
economic performance
  Australia, 36
  effect of democracy, 9, 27–30, 35–6
  effect of federal institutions, 37–8
economic policy regimes, 55–6
  bipartisan support, 69, 79–80
  causal links with economic outcomes, 55–61
  explaining regime change, 58–9, 61–2, 75–81
  liberalisation in Western countries, 78
  protectionist regime, 61–8
  shift to competitive regime, 68–75, 78–81
economic rationalism. *See* competitive economic policy regime; neo-liberalism
economists
  as critics of tariff protection, 66–7, 77
  influence on policy regime change, 12, 58–9, 77–8, 79–81
  use of institutional analysis, 53–4
ecophilosophy, 137–8
education policy, 75
education spending, 37
egalitarianism. See Australian egalitarianism
electoral systems, 60–1, 99
  *See also* franchise
EMILY's List, 128, 164
Engineers' Case, 44
environmental organizations, 138–40
equal opportunity
  labourist view of, 163–4
  neo-liberal critique, 158
  as state's ethical responsibility, 148, 150, 151–2, 176–7
equal pay, 152, 164
equality
  impact of wages regulation, 44–6, 49
  *See also* Australian egalitarianism
ethical state, 149–50, 176–7
ethnic politics
  accommodation and quiescence, 134–5
  US-Australian differences, 134, 136
ethnicity
  and 'minority status', 134
  *See also* multiculturalism; Non-English-Speaking Backgrounds, people from
exchange rate deregulation, 70–1
exclusion
  of Asians, 64, 101, 132, 281–4
  of boat people, 101–2
  democratic benefits, 143–4
  of Indigenous Australians, 96–8, 129, 159, 181, 193–4, 198–9, 209–10, 212, 247–8, 250
  through funding cuts, 143

exclusion (*contd.*)
    trade unions, 144
    welfare-dependent underclass, 126
    of whites from indigenous domain, 191
    women, 152
export policy, 76–7

family wage, 152, 163–4
*Federal Story* (Deakin), 272
federalism, 32–3
    Australia, 31, 33–4
    gender implications, 170–6
    and indigenous affairs, 187
    policy impacts, 10, 37–40, 168, 175–6
    women's policy influence, 173–5
Federation
    bourgeoisie's support for, 121
    White Australia as motive, 132, 283
Federation of Ethnic Communities'
    Council of Australia, 135
Fels, Allan, 102
feminism, 127–8
    *See also* femocrats; women's
    organizations
femocrats, 127–9, 166–70
financial deregulation, 70–2
foreign direct investment, 108–9
foreign economic aid, 28, 30, 36–7
foreign policy, 136
*Forgotten People* (Menzies), 276, 284
Foucault, Michel, 105
franchise
    adult, 114, 159
    adult male, 120, 122
    Indigenous Australians, 159, 181,
    198, 203, 204, 250
    women, 26, 99, 154–5, 159
Fraser Government, 70–1, 72, 133, 172–3
Fraser Island, 139
Fuller, Lon, 228

GATT (General Agreement on Tariffs
    and Trade), 76–7, 86
gender equality and accountability, 37,
    102, 169, 171–2, 173–5
Gleeson, Justice Murray, 221, 255
global capital movements, 101–2
global population movements, 89, 91–5
globalization, 89
    and Australia's wages system, 48–9
    impact on Australian egalitarianism,
    102–4, 108
    of industry and safety standards,
    104–5
    of US-style mega-corporations, 106–7
Gordon-below-Franklin dam, 139
Grassby, Al, 133

Green, T.H., 149–50
green bans, 124
green parties, 139
Greenpeace, 139
Gruen, Fred, 78
GST (goods and services tax), 79

Hansonism, 104
Harvester Judgement, 43–4, 46, 152
Hawke and Keating Governments, 68,
    70–2, 133, 140, 173
Hayek, Friedrich, 228
Heagney, Muriel, 164
heroin, 102
Higgins, Justice H.B., 43–4, 99–100,
    127, 151, 241
High Court, 273–6, 286
Hilmer Report, 74, 79
Hobbes, Thomas, 228–9, 243–4
Howard Government, 68, 73, 125, 133
Howe, J.H., 153
H.R. Nicholls Society, 48
human capital provision, 75

ideas. *See* economists
identity
    Indigenous Australians, 184, 190,
    200, 205, 206–7
    Keating on Australia's, 287–9
    in liberal democracies, 188
immigrants. *See* Asian immigrants;
    Non-English-Speaking Backgrounds,
    people from
immigration restriction, 100–1
inclusion (in the state)
    the bourgeoisie, 119–21
    concept, 114, 188
    consequences for democratization,
    118
    convicts, 92–6
    Indigenous Australians, 130–1, 189,
    204, 211–12
    liberal democratic, 188
    nature, 138–42
    NESB communities, 132–7
    women, 126–9
    working class, 123–5
income tax, 157–8
Indigenous Australians. *See* Aboriginal
    and Torres Strait Islander peoples
'indigenous collectivism', 131
indigenous domain, 188–92, 199–200
indigenous politics, 195–6, 200
'indigenous sector', 207
indigenous–state relations
    contending theoretical approaches,
    182–3

# Index

in indigenous domain, 188–92, 199–200, 206–9
in liberal democracy domain, 197–9, 204–6
political domains of, 186–7
in protection and segregation domain, 192–6, 200–2, 209–11
industrial disputes
  corporatist self-regulation, 41–2
  *See also* conciliation and arbitration
Industries Assistance Commission, 98
industry policy, 75
inflation, 37–8
institution-building
  Deakin, 272–6
  feminist, 159–76 passim
institutional analysis, 3–7, 9, 53–7
institutional reshaping
  Australia's economic policy regime, 11–12, 41, 48–9
  effect on income inequality, 49
  of labour relations, 47–9, 99–100
  motives, 47–8
institution(s), 3, 5
  consequences and outcomes, 9, 25, 47, 55–7
  economists' usage, 53–4
intellectual property rights, 86–7, 109
intergovernmental policy making, 173–6
'internal colonialism', 183, 194
investment (corporate), 106–7
  *See also* R&D investment

Japan, 282, 284
  trade with, 76–7
Jayasuriya, L., 134

Kable, Henry and Susannah, 235–6
Kakadu mining, 139
Karpin Report, 88
Keating, Paul
  personalized view of leadership, 272, 278–80
  republican model of citizenship, 287–9
  rhetorical over-reach, 265, 279
  *See also* Hawke and Keating Governments

Labor Party. *See* Australian Labor Party
labour disputes. *See* conciliation and arbitration
labour market
  deregulation, 47–9, 74, 102
  indigenous exclusion, 96–8
labour shortage, 91–5, 100–1, 101
Lake Pedder, 139

land councils, 207
land tenure
  for Indigenous Australians, 131
Landcare groups, 141
law and legal institutions
  aims and form, 225–7
  and attainment of rule of law, 230–5
  as restraint on power, 221–2, 225–6, 235, 255
  role in Aboriginal dispossession, 242–53, 255
  social and political significance, 232–3
  transplantation to Australia, 222–3
leadership, and rhetoric, 262
legitimation imperative (of the state)
  and Indigenous Australians, 131
  and multiculturalism, 133–4
  and the working class, 122
'lesser eligibility', 93, 95
liberal democracy, domain of, 187–9
liberal inclusion. See inclusion (in the state)
Liberal Party, 163
liberalism. *See* social liberalism
Lijphart, Arend, 9–10, 32–6, 37–8
Little, Graham, 262
living wage, 43–4, 151

Mabo decision, 131, 204, 205
Macdonald, Louisa, 157–8
Maconochie, Alexander, 93
Macquarie, Governor Lachlan, 92
majoritarian democracy(ies), 10, 32–4
managerial capitalism, 105–7
Massachussetts Bay Company, 90
maternity allowances, 156–7, 250
Mathews Committee, 79
Menzies, Robert Gordon
  anti-communist concept of citizenship, 284–7
  on art of politics, 264–5, 277
  parliamentary conception of leadership, 276–8
micro-economic reform, 70–5
More, Sir Thomas, 221–2, 255
*Morning Post*, 273
Mortimer Inquiry, 75
multiculturalism, 132–3, 136, 287
Murray–Darling River Basin Commission, 141

National Farmers' Federation, 141
native title, 205–6
nature
  oppositional public sphere, 139, 141
  political inclusion, 138–42

Neal, David, 235–7, 241
Neild, J.C., 155
neo-liberalism, 41, 48–9, 102, 142–3, 169
NESB. *See* Non-English-Speaking Backgrounds, people from
networking, 162
'new federalism', 172–3, 175
New Guinea, 98–9, 244–5
'new institutionalism', 3
New Protection, 42–3, 47–8, 63, 281–4
'new regulatory state', 104–5
New Zealand, 43, 78, 99
Non-English-Speaking Backgrounds, people from
  inclusion of, 132–7
  involvement in ALP, 135
  lack of oppositional sphere, 134–7
North, Douglass, 27

old-age pensions, 153–6, 250
Olson, Mancur, 54, 63
One Nation Party, 136
oppositional public sphere
  nature, 139–41
  NESB lack of, 134–7
  women, 128–9
  working class, 122, 124
O'Sullivan, E.W., 156

Pamelas-List, 162
Papua New Guinea, 98
parliament
  masculine bias in, 165
  members' leadership responsibilities, 276–7
  women in, 159, 164–6
Pashukanis, Evgenii, 226
Pateman, Carole, 152, 164
patent monopolies, 110
paternalist protection, 195–6, 202, 210–11, 248–52
Pearson, Noel, 209–10
penal colony (New South Wales), 92–6, 236–41
penitentiaries, 93, 95
pharmaceutical patent rights, 87, 109
pharmaceutical standards, 105
Phillip, Governor Arthur, 242
policy outcomes
  causal links with policy regimes, 55–61
  forms of democracy and, 10, 34–7
policy regime
  concept, 55–6
  explaining regime change, 75–81
  impact on policy outcomes, 55–61
  *See also* economic policy regimes

political domains, 182, 184–7, 196–7
  *See also* indigenous domain; liberal democracy, domain of; protection and segregation domain
political leadership
  civic *versus* populist, 265–70
  Deakin on, 271–2
  in a democracy, 265–70
  Keating on, 278–80
  Menzies on, 276–8
  as national redefinition, 278–80
  scholarly approaches, 262
  as theatrical performance, 280
political logics, 182, 186–6
  indigenous domain, 190–2
  liberal democratic domain, 188–9
  protection and segregation domain, 193–6
political rhetoric
  Deakin, 273–6, 281–4
  Keating, 278–80, 287–9
  Menzies, 276–8, 284–7
  as tool of political leadership, 261, 263–5, 289–90
population movements, 91–5, 101
populism, 266–70, 267–8, 289
poverty, 46
preferential voting, 99
Prices Surveillance Authority, 69
private interests. See 'special interests'
privatization, 73, 87
  and regulatory growth, 104–5
protection and segregation domain (indigenous policy), 192–6, 200–2, 209–12, 248–53
protectionist policy regime, 11, 43, 63–8, 281–4
  dismantling, 68, 72–3, 102
Przeworski, Adam, 9, 27–30
public enterprises, 64, 73
public investment, 64–5
public sphere
  defined, 117
  depletion in Australia, 116, 125–6
  effect of economic rationalism on, 142–3
  Indigenous Australians, 130–2, 208, 211
  nature, 139, 141
  as oppositional site, 114–15, 117
  as site for democratic activity, 114
  women, 128–9
  working class, 122, 125–6
  *See also* oppositional public sphere
Pusey, Michael, 12, 58–9

Queensland rain forests, 139

# Index

Racial Discrimination Act, 204
racism, 101
  *See also* Aboriginal and Torres Strait Islander peoples; White Australia policy
R&D investment
  Australian corporate unwillingness, 89, 107
  by government, in Australia, 75, 91
reconciliation (with Indigenous Australians), 131, 287
Reeves, William Pember, 99–100
regulation, 41–3, 89
  *See also* 'new regulatory state'
republic, arguments for, 287–9
research and development. See R&D investment
reshaping. See institutional reshaping
restorative justice, 92–6, 96
rule of law
  benefits, 228–30
  conditions for successful attainment, 230–5, 243
  and ethical values, 229–30
  failure to protect Indigenous Australians, 242–55
  impact on convicts, 93–4, 235–41
  nature, 224–8
  transportation to Australia, 222–3, 235–41
rules, 54–5
Ryan, T.J., 99

safety standards, 105
secret ballot, 26, 99, 114
security imperative, 133
segregation policies, 192–3, 202
self-determination (indigenous), 129–30, 191–2, 195, 204–5, 207–9, 213
sex slavery, 102
Sherman Act, 105–6
social democratic parties, 121
social liberalism, 148–59
  conception of citizenship, 149–50, 153–7
  and intervention in employment contracts, 151–2
  and old-age pensions, 153–7
  and redistributive income tax, 157–8
'special interests'
  in Australia's protectionist regime, 63
  influence on policy outcomes, 59–61
squattocracy, 120
standards, global regulation, 105
state
  defined, 116–17
  feminist debates, 167–8
  feminist structures in, 128–9, 166–70
  inclusion in, 117–18
  as object of regulation, 105
  social movement co-option by, 168
  *See also* ethical state; 'new regulatory state'
state governments
  micro-economic reform, 73–4
  policy devolution to, 173–5
state imperatives
  defined, 116–17
  feminist debates about, 167–8
  and group inclusion in the state, 118
  *See also* economic imperative; legitimation imperative; security imperative
state interference
  social liberal justification of, 149–52
Stolen Generations, 210
subjects
  Aborigines as, 245
  convicts as, 239–40
suffrage. See franchise

Tariff Board, 65–7, 76
tariff protection, 63–5, 76
  dismantling, 68, 72–3
Tasmania, 95–6
Tasmanian Wilderness Society, 139
tax avoidance, 103
tax havens, 103
taxation, 37–8, 79, 103, 157–8
telecommunications
  international standards, 105
  privatization and deregulation, 73, 87
Telstra, 73, 87
temperance, 126–7
tertiary education sector, 75
think tanks, 119
Torrens system, 98
Total Catchment Management Programs, 141
trade, 76–7
trade practices legislation, 73
trade unions, 74, 121, 125, 136
transportation of convicts, 91–5
Trenwith, William, 153
TRIPs, 87

United Nations, 30
United States
  antitrust laws, 105–6
  as corporate colony, 90
  in Uruguay Round, 86–7
universities, 75
uranium mining, 139

Uruguay Round, 86–7

victim status, 136
Virginia Company, 90
voting behaviour, 80
voting rights. *See* franchise

wage-earners' welfare state, 43–7, 123, 127
　dismantling, 102, 124
　exclusions from, 97, 152
wage justice, 151–2
wages regulation, 43–7, 48–9, 63–4, 66
　deregulation, 47–9
　impact on gender equality, 44–6, 102
'Washminster mutation', 31
'welfare colonialism', 183, 186, 196, 209
welfare spending, 10, 35–9
welfare state
　advantages in global competition, 108–9
　Australia as, 39, 40–1, 43–7, 49, 101–2
　expansion in Western Europe, 42
　welfare spending as measure, 10, 44
　*See also* corporate welfare state; wage-earners' welfare state
Weller, Patrick, 262
Westminster democracies, 33–4
White Australia policy, 64, 101, 132, 281–4
Whitlam Government, 72, 79, 133, 137, 168–9, 169, 172, 176
Wik judgement, 206

wilderness defence campaigns, 139
The Wilderness Society, 139
Wise, Bernhard, 151–2
women
　affirmative action, 104, 164
　as beneficiaries of social liberalism, 154, 158–9
　in the bureaucracy, 127–8
　as citizens, 154, 159–60
　democratic inclusion, 126–9
　franchise, 26, 99, 154–5, 159
　oppositional public spheres, 128–9
　parliamentary representation, 127–8
　and political parties, 161, 163
　and state's economic imperatives, 128
　wages and employment, 45, 46, 127, 128, 152, 163–4
Women's Electoral Lobby, 127, 167–8
women's organizations
　demand for expanded Commonwealth powers, 170–2, 175
　feminist (post-1969), 161–2
　networking among, 162
　non-party, 160–1
women's policy coordination, 169
women's rights, 150
women's suffrage movement, 126, 154
women's temperance movement, 126–7
working class
　depleted public sphere, 122, 125–6
　inclusion in the state, 123–5
　as oppositional public sphere, 122, 124
World Wide Fund for Nature (WWF), 139–40